THE UNION IN CRISIS
1850–1877

SOURCES OF THE AMERICAN TRADITION

THE UNION IN CRISIS
1850–1877

EDITED BY
ROBERT W. JOHANNSEN
WENDY HAMAND VENET

Copley Publishing Group
Acton, Massachusetts 01720

ISBN 1-58390-027-6

Library of Congress Catalog Card Number: 2003103294

Cover: Rising of the people. "The drum-tap rattles through the
land."

Copley Publishing Group
138 Great Road
Acton, MA 01720
800.562.2147 • Fax: 978.263.9190
E-mail: textbook@copleypublishing.com
www.copleypublishiing.com

CONTENTS

INTRODUCTION

The Civil War was America's greatest tragedy. Its tragic proportions are not easy to comprehend, especially by a generation nearly a century and a half removed from the conflict, nor can they in all cases be easily measured. The romance of the antebellum South, the aura that has been cast about the "lost cause," the drama of battlefield maneuvers and shallow, uncritical hero worship have contributed to obscure the anguish of civil conflict. "The real war," wrote Walt Whitman, "will never get in the books." The suffering and pain of the four-year bloodbath have all too easily been forgotten. The shame of disunion and the failure of democracy have all too often been glossed over.

The physical damage inflicted on the nation by the war has been susceptible to measurement. Although figures frequently vary, the numbers of casualties, the destruction of property, the loss of capital, the burdens of widowhood and orphanage, the expenditure of money have all been subjected to scrutiny and investigation, and reasonably accurate estimations have been advanced. Not so easily determined is the amount of psychic damage which the nation suffered—the legacy of hate, the bitter feelings, the shattered illusions, and the loss of faith. The Civil War was truly a national traumatic experience, made more intense by its timing. The first half of the nineteenth century was a period of buoyant optimism when many Americans believed in progress, in the perfectibility of man, in the "manifest destiny" of the nation itself. Technological changes, the rise of industry, immigration, the westward movement gave a dynamic character to the American population. Human beings, either individually or collectively as the nation, recognized no limit to their potentialities. The institutions of democratic government, progressive and expansive, were deemed well-nigh perfect, for, as one orator said, they were adapted to the happiness of mankind. The United States had a solemn mission in the world—to demonstrate, through its example, the superiority of its democracy.

The rise of sectional hostilities and the ultimate destruction of the Union itself were crippling blows to this faith and confidence. The sudden realization that the enthusiasm of the Jacksonian years was not shared by all Americans dampened the ardor that had characterized the young republic. Some unexpected flaw in the social fabric seemed to have revealed itself, postponing and perhaps even eliminating the eventual achievement of perfection. Disunion destroyed the "mission of America"; American democracy was, it seemed, less than perfect after all. The war drove a deep wedge into the minds of Americans as it did into the nation. The resignation and even eagerness with which many people accepted the resort to arms seemed to indicate that something was awry in America's great experiment.

Like all national events of such large and tragic dimensions, the Civil War has challenged the thinking of generations of Americans. Even before the war had commenced, significant questions regarding the nature and origins of the conflict were being asked. With the opening of hostilities, the question of the causes of the war became paramount. What had gone wrong? Where had the nation taken its wrong turn? Was the war inevitable or could it have been averted? What were the issues that caused Americans to abandon democratic procedures in favor of violence? After a century and a half of discussion, Americans are no nearer to universal agreement on the answers to these questions than they were in the 1860s. The war has exerted a strong influence on the national culture in other ways. "After making all due allowance for the suffering and expense," wrote a Northerner in 1864, "it has so far been of great advantage to both sections. It will give them a history and local traditions, heroes, something to talk and sing about." Although Whitman's prophecy that a great national literature would arise out of the war has not been fulfilled, Americans have been talking and singing about it ever since the first shot was fired.

The roots of the civil conflict that convulsed the United States extended deep into the American past, but it was the decade of the 1850s that brought the crisis to its climax. The decade opened with the achievement of a compromise between the sections and ended with the failure of compromise. The persistent theme of these fateful years was the vain attempt to discover a workable solution to problems that seemed increasingly to be beyond solution.

The immediate issue of the sectional conflict during the 1850s was the issue of slavery and expansion. At the beginning of the decade, the question was of some practical importance but as discussion continued it became more and more abstract. As it grew abstract, as

Americans began to look upon it as a "matter of principle," the issue also grew more explosive. The question, however, was not debated in a vacuum. All the differences between North and South were brought to focus on the issue of slavery in the territories. Questions of tariffs, internal improvements, land policy—questions which had long divided the sections—became hopelessly entangled with this central issue. Not that the American people were so concerned with the Western territories in themselves; the discussions transcended the status of the distant, sparsely inhabited frontier regions, for implicit in the question was the fate of slavery itself. The abolitionist movement, which had received its impetus from the reform movements of the Jacksonian period, now concentrated on halting the expansion of slavery into the Western territories. A new channel of action was opened to the antislavery crusader. Serious constitutional questions had been raised by the opponents of abolition; it was not at all clear that the national government could constitutionally interfere with the institution of slavery in those states where it had been given legal existence. The power of the national government to restrict the spread of slavery into new lands, however, was one which could be constitutionally justified. Southern leaders, on the other hand, moved to increasing desperation by the attacks of the abolitionists, looked to the territories as the first line of defense for an institution that had become the keystone of their civilization. Their moral arguments as well as economic, constitutional, and political arguments were interjected into the debate. All the venom and bitterness of sectional disagreement came to be concentrated on the question of slavery's status in the West.

It was the Mexican War that touched off the great debate over slavery in the territories, igniting the spark that eventually exploded the powder keg. The issue had been "settled" almost three decades before when disagreement over the admission of Missouri to the Union as a slave state resulted in the establishment of a rigid line of demarcation between free and slave territory. But the Missouri Compromise of 1820 applied only to the unorganized territory then located within the boundaries of the United States, specifically the Louisiana Purchase area which lay on the western edge of the nation. The war with Mexico, fought for expansionist purposes, raised the prospect that vast additional tracts would come under the sway of the United

States. Thus the question of slavery in the West was fated to be discussed again. The annexation of Texas on the eve of the Mexican War had directed attention to the issue but open disagreement over the area had been averted by the obvious fact that Texas would be a slave state and by the extension of the Missouri Compromise line westward to encompass the new acquisition. No such agreement would prevail with respect to other lands of Mexico that might fall to the United States.

The Mexican War raised several problems for the American people—problems of Indian policy and transportation development, for example—but it was the problem of slavery that overshadowed all others. Slavery in Mexico had been abolished years before; any lands ceded to the United States as a result of the war, thought some Northerners, would automatically be free. Southern leaders, however, were determined to secure the opportunity to expand into the former Mexican territories with their institutions intact and protected. Excluded by the Missouri Compromise from the greater part of the Louisiana Purchase, the South looked to the lands of northern Mexico for the expansion of their economy and for their increase in political power. It is not enough to regard the Southern position as motivated principally by a desire to expand the plantation economy, nor is it pertinent to argue, as many have, that North and South were needlessly aroused because slavery had already reached its "natural limits of expansion" and could never flourish in the West.

Aside from the fact that evidence indicates the contrary, Southerners regarded the Western territories as essential to their section. Whether slaves could or could not be useful on the frontier, additional slave states were required if the South expected to keep pace with the growing North. Much had happened in the nearly thirty years since 1820 when both sections acquiesced in the Missouri Compromise; Southerners had become increasingly aware of their minority status in the Union.

The opening gun in the debate was fired by a young Democratic Congressman from Pennsylvania, David Wilmot, who, in 1846, introduced a resolution that would guarantee the exclusion of slavery or involuntary servitude in any lands secured from Mexico. The reaction of the nation to the Wilmot Proviso was immediate and pronounced. A constitutional discussion was launched that preoccupied Congress for the next four years and, in varying degrees of intensity, continued to dominate American politics for more than a decade. More than just the fate of the Mexican conquests was involved. The question more broadly concerned the power which Congress could legitimately and constitutionally exercise over the Western territories.

Three basic positions emerged, roughly approximating the three great sections of the nation, the North, South, and West. The North argued that Congress possessed sweeping and unlimited power over the territories and that a federal prohibition of slavery in the lands acquired from Mexico, as demanded by Wilmot, was clearly within Congress' sphere of action. The South, on the other hand, contended in a series of resolutions introduced in 1847 by John C. Calhoun that the Western territories were jointly owned by all the states and that Congress had no constitutional power to enact legislation that would deprive a Southerner of his equal rights in the West. No power existed that could prevent a citizen of a slave state from emigrating to a territory with his property; the question of slavery in a territory could be decided only when the territory moved into statehood. The third or Western position became known as popular sovereignty. Expressed early by Michigan's Lewis Cass and later developed by Stephen A. Douglas, the doctrine stipulated that slavery could exist in a territory only by virtue of action taken by the territorial settlers. Denying that Congress had power to establish or prohibit slavery in the territories, Cass and Douglas would leave the decision to the local population. These three positions, emerging in the late 1840s with reference to the Mexican cession, formed the basis for discussion during the following decade. Although the arguments were subjected to variation and refinement, they remained essentially consistent. In 1860, the parties divided along the lines of these three interpretations; the nation proved to be no nearer agreement on this fundamental question than it had been fourteen years before.

The problem of slavery in the lands acquired from Mexico also had a more ominous legacy than the initiation of a long and disruptive constitutional debate. The question of secession from the Union was widely and seriously discussed in the cotton states. The disagreement played into the hands of a group of Southern radicals who preferred withdrawal from the Union to submission to the North in the Territories. While most Southerners were unwilling to follow the lead of the "fire-eaters" at this time, it became clear that secession was a last alternative in the struggle to protect Southern institutions.

The fate of the Mexican cession was settled by the Compromise of 1850. A series of acts passed by Congress during the summer and early fall of 1850, the Compromise not only dealt with the territorial problem but attempted to meet some of the other issues that had disturbed North-South relations. California was admitted to the Union as a free state and the two new territories of Utah and New Mexico were organized on the basis of popular sovereignty (or "nonintervention" as some preferred to call it). In addition, the slave trade in the District of Columbia was prohibited and a new, more stringent fugitive slave law was enacted. The Texas–New Mexico boundary was adjusted and the national government assumed the Texas Republic debt. The Compromise, largely the work of Henry Clay and Stephen A. Douglas, was hailed by many Americans as the beginning of a new period of harmonious relations between the sections. Both the Whig and Democratic parties endorsed its "finality" in an effort to keep the issues of conflict out of national politics.

The effort was in vain and the hopes of those who thought that the Compromise had settled something basic and fundamental proved to be illusory. At best, the Compromise was merely a "truce" between the sections. To be sure, the status of the territory secured from Mexico had been agreed upon (although some disagreement persisted as to exactly what the nature of the agreement really was). But unsettled still was the fundamental constitutional question of Congress' power to determine the institutions of the territories. The power of Congress to legislate with respect to slavery in the territories was still very much a matter of dispute; none of the positions that had been argued was conceded. A more immediate threat to the success of the Compromise lay in the fact that the extremists, both North and South, repudiated it.

The radical Southern "fire-eaters" disavowed the Compromise and continued to promote secession as the only feasible solution to the South's problems. More moderate Southern opinion contended that the Compromise represented the last concessions the South would make. Any further victories for Northern antislavery sentiment would seriously endanger the existence of the Union. Upon the North's faithful execution of the new Fugitive Slave Act depended the continued acquiescence of the South in the Compromise as well as the future role of the cotton states in the Union [1].* Northern antislavery opinion was outraged at the terms of the Fugitive Slave Act. Resistance to the law was openly proposed and a series of slave "rescues" occurred in the North as citizens sought to frustrate efforts to apprehend runaway slaves. Men like Ralph Waldo Emerson publicly advised disobedience to the legislation [2]. In 1852 the North was further aroused by the publication of *Uncle Tom's Cabin*, in which Harriet Beecher Stowe attempted to portray the evils of slavery [3]. For a time, the fugitive slave problem became the dominant issue of the sectional conflict. Northerners were increasingly disturbed at the protection seemingly offered slavery by the 1850 act and sought through various means to render its enforcement ineffective. To the South, such actions demonstrated Northern infidelity to the Compromise of 1850 and emphasized the jeopardy in which slavery was placed. African Americans added their own voices to the national debate. Frederick Douglass used the occasion of a Fourth of July address to condemn America's political and religious institutions for upholding slavery [4]. The time was ripe for conflict.

The controversy over slavery had also taken its toll on the nation's political parties. The bonds of unity in both parties, Democratic and Whig, had been loosened. For Democrats, the years of expansion and conflict in the late 1840s had proved a time of trial. The annexation of Texas and the Mexican War resulted in the defection of significant numbers of Northern Democrats who viewed expansion as strengthening the Southern slave power. The debate over the Wilmot Proviso drove a further wedge into the Democratic ranks. Free-Soilers, strengthened by the reaction against the expansion of slavery, bolted the party and in 1848 supported Martin Van Buren, the heir of Jacksonian Democracy, as a Free-Soil candidate for the presidency. The split persisted in spite of the efforts of party leaders to apply the Compromise of 1850 as party cement. The leadership of the party became increasingly Southern in character and in purpose, continuing a trend that extended back to Polk's administration. The Whig party was hardly less affected by the sectional disturbances. Northern and

*Numbers in square brackets refer to chapters in this volume.

Southern Whigs drew apart over the issue of slavery in the Mexican cession; many Southern Whigs began a drift into the Democratic party, not only reducing the strength of the Whigs but enhancing the Southern power in the Democratic ranks. What seemed to be a successful strategy in 1848, when the Whigs ignored the dominant issue and elected Zachary Taylor as a hero of the Mexican War, backfired disastrously in 1852, when Winfield Scott was buried in a Democratic landslide.

The crippling blow to the parties was delivered by the emergence once again in national politics of the issue of slavery in the territories. Nothing illustrates more clearly the ineffectiveness of the 1850 Compromise than the storm that followed the introduction of the Kansas-Nebraska Act in early 1854. Written by Stephen A. Douglas, the act organized the territories of Kansas and Nebraska out of the Louisiana Purchase, an area that had been set aside earlier as an Indian reservation. Few people questioned the propriety of organizing the territories; it was long overdue. The manner in which the organization was carried out aroused the furor. The two territories were established on the basis of popular sovereignty, leaving the question of slavery to be decided by the local populations. In order to render this decision effective, Douglas' act repealed the Missouri Compromise, thus removing a long-standing barrier to the expansion of slavery in the Louisiana Purchase. Douglas explained that he merely based his act on a precedent established in the Compromise of 1850, where Utah and New Mexico were granted the same power of decision [5], but his explanations were rejected. Northern antislavery men were aroused to a white-hot fury by the repeal of the Missouri Compromise. Douglas was denounced for betraying a sacred pledge, for being a party to the conspiratorial designs of an "aggressive slavocracy," and for sacrificing the nation on the altar of his own ambition. His retort that slavery could not thrive in Kansas and Nebraska and that popular sovereignty, if given a fair trial, would eventuate in the expansion of freedom, not slavery, did not allay the Northern fear that slavery would now be swiftly extended throughout the Louisiana Purchase.

The passage of the Kansas-Nebraska Act not only aroused Northern opinion but it also shattered the national political organizations. A period of political confusion and chaos followed, resulting in a significant realignment of parties. The blow proved too severe for the rickety Whig organization, and the party of Henry Clay suffered its final decline. Southern Whigs moved into the Democratic ranks. The wedge in the Democratic party was driven deeper as the Northern Free-Soil wing objected vigorously to Douglas' act. Protest meetings were held throughout the North, uniting Whigs, Democrats, Free-Soilers and Know-Nothings (opponents of immigration) in a common opposition to the repeal of the Missouri Compromise. From out of these spontaneous protests emerged the Republican party.

The Republican party, like its predecessor the Whig party, had its origins in an opposition movement. Its unifying principle was a negative one—opposition to the extension of slavery into the territories of the West. The issue of slavery in its expansionistic aspects was vital to the party's existence but Republicans were concerned with more than the fate of the nation's frontier regions. The party was the "heir" of the earlier political antislavery movements; the Liberty and Free-Soil parties were important ancestors of the new organization. With its insistence on halting the spread of slavery and its disavowal of any immediate intention of interfering with slavery in the states, the party did much to soften the abolitionist crusade in the 1850s. At the same time, the party provided a strong and significant channel of political action to the radical abolitionist. Because of this, the party assumed a high moral tone and for the first time serious questions of morality were injected into political discussion. The Republican party was, in addition, a sectional party—the first major sectional political party in the nation's history. Unlike the Whig party, the Republican party was not national in scope; its membership and its appeal were confined to the North.

Like most opposition parties, the Republican party reflected a large variety of political positions and backgrounds. Old-line Whigs like Edward Bates were joined by staunch Jacksonian Democrats like Francis Preston Blair. Antislavery radicals like Salmon P. Chase and Charles Sumner rubbed shoulders with moderates and conservatives like Abraham Lincoln and William H. Seward. Nativistic Know-Nothings stood side by side with antislavery immigrant groups. Disagreement was rife on many questions of policy but on the question of the extension of slavery Republicans stood firm and united. The new party caught the Northern mood and mushroomed in size and strength. The attempts to enforce the Fugitive Slave Act in the North and the publication of Harriet Beecher Stowe's *Uncle Tom's Cabin* in

1852 had prepared the Northern mind for the antislavery crusade which the Republican party now represented. Party organizations appeared in most of the Northern states following the passage of the Kansas-Nebraska Act and in the presidential election year of 1856, the party was organized on the national level [7].

The growth of the Republican party was stimulated by events which transpired in Kansas during the years following the passage of the Kansas-Nebraska Act. The new Kansas territory was being settled for the most part by farmers from the older states of the Ohio and Mississippi valleys. There were, however, some who saw in the settlement of Kansas only an opportunity to extend or restrict slavery. There were enough abnormalities in the process of settlement to encourage these individuals to realize their goals. As a result, Kansas became an arena of conflict. Indeed, there are some who contend that the Civil War actually began in the 1850s on the Kansas prairies. When the territory was created by the 1854 legislation, no significant white population lived in Kansas. The area had been part of a vast Indian reservation; its population included soldiers, missionaries, traders, and Indians. Unlike other frontier areas, the territorial government was created before settlement appeared. The fact that the slavery question would be settled by the local population meant simply that the question would be determined by people who did not yet live there. To both the attackers and the defenders of slavery, the situation seemed ideal; whichever side could settle Kansas territory more quickly would carry the slavery referendum. In the North, the New England Emigrant Aid Company was organized to promote an artificial antislavery emigration to Kansas, while the residents of the western border counties of Missouri felt that desperate measures were in order to prevent Kansas from being "abolitionized." An additional element of strife and confusion existed in the land situation. No effort had been made before the passage of the Kansas-Nebraska Act to extinguish the Indian title to lands in eastern Kansas; consequently, when the act opened the area to white settlement, no land could be legally claimed. The first land office, where settlers could register and seek protection for their land claims, was not opened until 1856. Claims disputes were common and because there was no means by which a claim could be protected by law, violence was also common.

The first territorial government was controlled by pro-slavery Missourians. Being close at hand, they were first on the spot and, by using fraudulent means, they were able to determine the outcome of the first elections. A strict slave code was immediately extended over Kansas. Their actions, however, were not recognized by the remaining population. The legislature was dubbed a "bogus" legislature and its laws "bogus" laws. The opposition protested not so much over the extension of slavery over Kansas territory as over the violation of popular sovereignty by the proslavery element. To counteract the Missouri influence, an extralegal statehood government was established, the so-called "Topeka Statehood Movement," which served to rally free-state sentiment during the next few years. Two governments operating on different levels—one, the legal but fraudulently-elected territorial government; the other, the extralegal free state government—added to the confusion created by the uncertainty of land titles to make an almost hopeless situation. The appointed territorial officers, many of them little more than political hacks, proved inadequate to the problem and for a brief time the Federal government almost literally lost control over the territory.

To people in other parts of the country, however, and especially to members of the Republican party, it appeared that a great moral struggle over slavery was being waged on the Kansas prairies. Horace Greeley, the outspoken editor of the strongly antislavery *New York Tribune*, enhanced this impression by his use of the phrase "Bleeding Kansas" as a Republican campaign cry in the election of 1856. The events in Kansas seemed to demonstrate the true nature of popular sovereignty and to vindicate the arguments of Douglas' opponents. The question of slavery in the territories might very well be settled by violence in Kansas—or so many Americans thought. Kansas became a byword to both North and South; to each, the territory became a test case in the sectional conflict. The final showdown, however, was yet to come. The Kansas issue dominated Congressional debate, and the battle lines in the national legislature were more rigidly drawn than before.

The struggle over slavery was carried on not only in the political realm. Writers and literary figures, both North and South, used their pens to promote their respective causes. Harriet Beecher Stowe's runaway best seller *Uncle Tom's Cabin* demonstrated the power of the written word and revealed the existence of an antislavery mood in the North which other writers hastened to exploit. Southern writers produced a veritable flood of works defending their "peculiar institution." A score or so "anti-Tom" novels were published following the appearance of Mrs. Stowe's work, all of them correcting the Northern "distortion" by portraying the happy and secure lot enjoyed by the slave. William J. Grayson in 1854 elaborated a favorite Southern theme when he compared the idyllic life of the slave with the sordid existence of the Northern factory worker. College professors, clergymen, and scientists lent their talents to the proof that slavery was justified and desirable. The most significant of slavery's defenders in the 1850s was the Virginian George Fitzhugh who argued the superiority of the Southern slave system from economic and sociological grounds. In his books *Sociology for the South* (1854) and *Cannibals All!* (1857), Fitzhugh issued a scathing attack on the free society of the North [6]. Through such books, through the fiery speeches of Northern and Southern politicians, through the unrestrained utterances of radical newspaper editors, the issues of the sectional conflict became overdramatized and emotionalized. Little attempt was made to understand the problems faced by either side; misunderstanding led to distortion, as each section declared the other to be the aggressor and sought to defend itself against attack.

James Buchanan, the Democratic candidate, won the presidency in the election of 1856 and during the next four years the conflict rapidly moved toward its final showdown. The election itself was the harbinger of the difficulties ahead. Unlike the 1852 contest, there was no inclination to avoid disruptive sectional issues. The campaign was fought amid threats of disunion and emotional tirades against slavery's expansion on the part of the North. Buchanan finally realized his lifelong ambition to be president, but he could not have been elected at a worse time. The four years of his administration were dominated by the disintegration of the Union and of the Democratic party. Events moved swiftly to their climax.

Two days after Buchanan's inauguration, the Supreme Court of the United States entered the fray. The decision in the case *Dred Scott v. Sanford* placed the court in the Southern camp on the question of slavery in the territories, not only giving the South the support of judicial authority but also delivering a telling blow at both the Republican party and Douglas' popular sovereignty. The "august tribunal" immediately became the target of Republican scorn and hostility, while Douglas vainly and unpersuasively sought to reconcile the decision with his doctrine.

Not long afterward the Kansas struggle entered a new and more ominous stage. A statehood movement initiated by the pro-slave territorial administration resulted in the meeting of a constitutional convention in the territorial capital of Lecompton. Its members, chosen by means of an imperfect census and a boycotted election, were determined that Kansas should be a slave state. Their task was made the more urgent and desperate by the outcome of the territorial elections in the fall of 1857. Assured by President Buchanan's newly appointed governor, Robert J. Walker, that the election would be free from fraud, the free-state element for the first time since 1855 participated fully in a legislative election. The result was victory for the free-staters and defeat for the pro-slave group. To the former, the victory meant that their own abortive statehood effort, the "Topeka Movement," could be dropped; to the proslavery men, it meant that the Lecompton constitution was their last chance to fasten slavery on Kansas. With a demonstrated free- state majority in the territory, the members of the convention dared not submit the results of their deliberations to the people for ratification. Instead, they made a meaningless gesture toward submission which most everyone recognized as a subterfuge.

The controversy over the Lecompton constitution was perhaps the most significant episode of the sectional conflict in the late 1850s. The constitution obviously did not represent the wishes of the people of Kansas territory, yet it received the support of the Buchanan administration. The president's endorsement of the document drove Stephen A. Douglas into open revolt against his party leadership. The Democratic party, whose unity was at best nebulous, was split asunder, with Douglas and the Northwestern members of the party arrayed against the administration and Southern wing. The issue of the Lecompton constitution was bitterly fought in Congress during the winter of 1857–58, finally being settled by a compromise, the English bill, which seemed acceptable to both sides. Kansans, allowed to express themselves on the issue, preferred to remain a free territory. But the damage had been done. The days of the Democratic party as a united party were numbered—Douglas had rendered himself unacceptable to the South by his unforgivable defiance of the party leadership. He was denounced and attempts were made to read him out of the party. The issues between Douglas and the South were brought into sharper focus by Douglas' debates with Abraham Lincoln in 1858 when these two Illinoisans ran against each other for Douglas' Senate seat. Lincoln, sensing a political opportunity in the Democratic split, sought to force Douglas to restate clearly and unequivocally his opposition to the Southern designs. Douglas' "Freeport doctrine," widely referred to in the South as the "Freeport heresy," increased Southern hostility, especially as it seemed to rob the South of the effect of its victory in the Dred Scott decision. Douglas won his reelection to the Illinois Senate seat but when Congress reconvened in December, 1858, the Democratic caucus stripped him of his committee power.

The Lecompton controversy resulted in one of those curious shifts in party alignment that characterized the politics of the 1850s. The events in Kansas had demonstrated that popular sovereignty could result in the extension of freedom rather than slavery. Republicans, the bitter foes of Douglas in 1854, supported Douglas in 1858 in his attacks on the Buchanan administration. Lincoln was hampered in his own efforts to secure an election to the Senate by the fact that Douglas was leading the fight against the extension of slavery to Kansas. At the same time, Southern leaders recognized in popular sovereignty a threat against the expansion of their institution; Southerners who had supported Douglas earlier became his enemies in 1858.

The fears of the South increased as they saw arrayed against them not only the openly antislavery Republican power of the North but also a large proportion of the Northern wing of their own Democratic party. There were further signs in 1859 and 1860 that the crisis was at hand: John Brown's ill-fated raid at Harper's Ferry and the long, protracted contest for the Speakership of the House of Representatives that followed soon afterward. Southern institutions, it seemed, were more insecure than ever before; the rise of Republican power, the defeat in the Kansas struggle, the growing fear of slave revolt all pointed toward one uneasy alternative: victory and new guarantees of protection in the election of 1860, or withdrawal from the Union.

On the eve of the election year, the three positions on the troublesome question of slavery in the territories that had had their origins in the Wilmot Proviso struggle a decade before approached their final expression. The election would be fought on the basis of the issue that had convulsed American politics since the Mexican War and all agreed that it would be the final showdown. Douglas, in September, 1859, reiterated his commitment to popular sovereignty in a significant article in *Harper's Magazine*, seeking to ground his doctrine firmly in historical precedent and constitutional authority. Lincoln, rapidly emerging as the spokesman of the Republican party, answered Douglas' statement in his famous address at Cooper Institute (now Cooper Union). Although conservative in tone, the address emphasized anew the Republicans' conviction that slavery was wrong and hence ought not to be allowed to expand [8]. Shortly afterward, Jefferson Davis, senator from Mississippi and spokesman for the Southern interest, introduced a series of resolutions into the Senate which defined the Southern position on the question. He called for new guarantees for slavery in the territories in the form of a Federal slave code. Positive protection now replaced equal rights as the platform of the South.

The real struggle in 1860 took place in the Democratic national convention at Charleston. Douglas, the leading contender for the party's nomination, refused to retreat from the position he had held consistently through the fifties—the territories must be allowed to decide the question of slavery for themselves. The Southern leadership, supported by the Buchanan administration, would settle for nothing less than a platform based on Davis' resolutions. In addition, it was clear that Douglas was completely unacceptable as a candidate. Here, then, was the "irrepressible conflict." The convention was doomed to failure before it started. When the Alabaman William L. Yancey led the Southern walkout from the convention hall, the only remaining national party was destroyed. The sectionalization of parties was complete. With the destruction of the Democratic party, the Union itself was doomed.

The walkout in Charleston climaxed a trend in the Democratic party that could be traced at least as far back as 1844, when the heir-apparent of Jacksonian Democracy, Martin Van Buren, was displaced in the party convention by the young expansionist, James K. Polk. The struggle over the Wilmot Proviso and the arguments over the status of slavery in the territories of the West left an indelible mark on the Democratic party. In 1848 it was a quarrel between the popular sovereignty of Lewis Cass's "Nicholson Letter" and the slavery protection-ist Alabama Platform of William L. Yancey. Eight years later, in 1856, the same basic lines were drawn between the forces of Stephen A. Douglas and those of the Southern party leadership. The party platform drawn at Cincinnati in that year successfully glossed over the deep differences over slavery in the territories but it came to be recognized as a subterfuge. In 1860 the strain on the party fabric proved too great and the party of Andrew Jackson was reduced to a shambles.

The election that followed the disruption of the Democratic party was, in a large sense, an anticlimax to the bitter party battles that preceded it. The results were anticipated long before the ballots were counted. Lincoln's election surprised no one. To the South, Lincoln's triumph merely confirmed the fears that section had long felt. The government was now in the hands of a president who represented not the nation but only a section of the nation, a man whose candidacy was unrecognized in nearly one-third of the states of the Union. More important, Lincoln had spoken out in harsh tones against Southern institutions, he had taken a strong moral stand against slavery, and he had been emphatic in his declaration that slavery should be restricted and not expanded. All of his rather vague assurances that the South had nothing to fear from his election could not erase the conviction that he was an enemy and that with his victory Southern life and institutions were placed in grave jeopardy. It is still a moot question whether the Union could have been saved by compromise during the crucial months following the election; the fact remains that no compromise was even offered.

Were the issues that precipitated the conflict meaningless and of no substance? Someone once said that the war was fought over "an imaginary Negro in an impossible place." Some historians have argued that slavery had reached its natural limits of expansion in 1860 and that the war was fought over an issue that would have resolved itself in time. Aside from the evidence that slavery had not reached its natural limit (for example, there were several hundred slaves in Kansas in 1857, although the federal census three years later listed only two), those who argue this line greatly oversimplify the situation. The struggle over slavery in the territories was but the manifestation of deeper and more complex issues. At bottom, no matter how one approaches the problem, rests the institution of slavery—not in any restricted sense but broadly conceived as an economic, social, political, and moral issue. Southern society, culture, politics, economics—in short, Southern civilization—had become hopelessly intertwined with and dependent upon the institution of slavery, so much so that Southerners recognized the destruction of slavery as the destruction of their way of life. North and South had grown far apart during the prewar years, until a great gulf of misunderstanding yawned between them. The North had been swept along by a tide of change—"common man" democracy, humanitarian reform, and urban and industrial development. The South remained committed to its agricultural heritage, the institution of slavery, and a society based on hierarchy, not egalitarianism. In 1858, William H. Seward said, "They who think that it [the conflict] is accidental, unnecessary, the work of interested or fanatical agitators, and therefore ephemeral, mistake the case altogether. It is an irrepressible conflict between opposing and enduring forces, and it means that the United States must and will, sooner or later, become either entirely a slaveholding nation, or entirely a free-labor nation." Lincoln, earlier in the same year, had uttered similar sentiments. If the conflict was not of itself irrepressible it is undeniable that such statements as these soon made it so.

Other developments hastened the final showdown. When political parties became sectionalized, when parties no longer represented the nation but rather expressed only sectional positions, the American people were deprived of important meeting grounds for varying and differing points of view. The interjection of moral issues into political discussion brought closer the final reckoning. When moral questions became political questions and men became committed to the resolution of moral questions by political means, American politics lost all its flexibility, and compromise—an essential factor in the art of politics—became only a remote hope.

Students of the sectional conflict have been prone to employ hindsight in attempting to explain its causes; their judgment of the crucial events of mid-nineteenth-century America have too often been influenced by the standards of their own day. Shifting values during the past century, whether moral, economic, cultural, or political, have determined the changing pattern of interpretation of the causes of the Civil War. The tendency to search out single common denominators has evidenced itself in Civil War historiography as it has in other areas of study. It has proven easy to condemn past generations on moral grounds. However, those who insist upon viewing the conflict as one involving a moral question must bear in mind that it was not a struggle between good and evil but rather a struggle between two kinds of morality. Both Northerners and Southerners believed their causes to be morally right. The debate over the causes of the Civil War will probably never be resolved to the satisfaction of all but some appreciation for the extremely complex nature of the problem can be achieved. It was not as simple as Lincoln implied in his oft-quoted second inaugural address in 1865. "Both parties," he said, "deprecated war, but one of them would *make* war rather than let the nation survive, and the other would *accept* war rather than let it perish, and the war came." In seeking an understanding of the conflict, one must penetrate a great deal more deeply into the recesses of the past.

The guns of Charleston harbor converted the war of words into a shooting war. Each side placed the war guilt on the other; both sides found ample justification for the actions they took. In his message to the special session of Congress in July, 1861, President Lincoln placed the conflict on a higher level than that of simple national survival. The fate of democratic government itself was involved in the struggle. If the Union should fail, democracy would everywhere be cast into discredit. The outcome of the war would determine not only whether the nation would survive but would also decide for the world the larger question of whether democratic institutions would and could persist [10]. Months earlier, Lincoln's counterpart in the South, Jefferson Davis, stood before the Confederate Congress and reviewed the events and circumstances that had led to the outbreak of war. The Southern cause, he declared, was "just and holy;" the South was fighting for "freedom, independence, and self-government" [9]. Neither president could foresee the troubles and sacrifices that lay ahead.

The Confederate States of America was born out of the long sectional struggle. Up to the last stages of that struggle, the goal of the Southern leaders, except for a few hotheads, had not been independence but guarantees within the Union. Secession, long threatened, was accomplished in the spring of 1861 with great enthusiasm, but even then many regarded it as only a temporary action that would lead to a reunion of the states and to a "reconstruction" of the nation. It is doubtful if many Southerners who supported the secession movement were really aware of the consequences of their action. Many of them awoke rather unexpectedly to the difficult responsibilities of nation building. Their task, they discovered, was doubly difficult, for they not only had to create a new nation but they also had to fight for their right to do so.

In spite of the appeals of Southern leaders to revolutionary philosophy, the establishment of the Confederate States was to a large degree a conservative movement. The character of the new Confederate constitution and the choice of national officers at the Montgomery convention bear out this conclusion. Some felt that the South should simply readopt the United States Constitution since, in their minds at least, it had been the Northern states that had violated the tenets of the Founding Fathers. The document that was agreed upon followed the Constitution of the United States closely in many respects. The transition from United States to Confederate States was to be as smooth as possible; this was not a revolution, it was said, but merely a change of rulership. The choice of Jefferson Davis as president of the new nation further illustrates the conservative character of the movement. Although Davis had inherited the mantle of John C. Calhoun and was recognized as the spokesman for Southern interests, he was not numbered among the "fire-eaters." The vice-presidency of the Confederacy fell to an even more conservative individual, Georgia's Alexander H. Stephens. Setting the new government into motion would have been difficult under ideal circumstances but to set it into motion while fighting a war for survival proved to be an almost impossible task. All of the flaws and weaknesses of the Confederate organization were exaggerated by the problems which were forced upon the government.

From the vantage point of over a century's lapse of time, it is difficult to appreciate the optimism with which Southerners entered the war. The odds were stacked heavily against them. In population and manpower of military age, industrial output, and food production, the United States exceeded the Confederate States.

A Northern population of almost 21 million people faced a South of a little over 9 million, including over 3½ million slaves. In number of manufacturing establishments the North outnumbered the South by almost six to one. Over two-thirds of the railroad mileage in the United States was in the North. The financial strength of the nation was concentrated in the North, and even Southern banking was centered there.

But to the generation of Southern secessionists in 1861 the odds did not appear so uneven as they do now. These Southerners were fighting for freedom, independence, self-government—and what cause could be more ennobling or more favorable to divine intervention? For decades, they reasoned, they had labored under the yoke of Northern oppression, resisting Northern usurpation, defending the Constitution of the Fathers against the insidious movements and ideas which seemed to grip the North. They had been constantly schooled in the conviction that theirs was a superior civilization. The North was cast in the role of the subjugator; it was indeed to be a struggle between self-determination and empire.

But Southerners had other trump cards on which they thought they could rely. Their section was the world supplier of cotton, and cotton was king! The dependence of the textile industries of both New England and old England on Southern cotton had fostered an exaggerated sense of Southern importance to the world. No power would dare make war on Southern cotton, observed South Carolina's Senator James H. Hammond in 1858. All civilization, save that of the South, would topple. By carefully controlling the production and export of cotton, the Confederate government, it was thought, would be able to win the assistance of foreign nations. There was reason to believe, in addition, that the North would not unite in a war of conquest against the South. The Old Northwest, with its vocal Southern element and its link to the Gulf states by the Mississippi River lifeline, would not join with radical New England in coercing the South. The failure of the Southern cause is largely the story of the failure of these Southern expectations.

The war, however, opened ominously for the North. Initially, at least, the South seemed the better prepared to carry on the conflict. Secession had severed the economic ties between the two sections and the Northern states, still suffering the after effects of the Panic of 1857, experienced prolonged depression. The United States government, laboring under the illusion that the war would be a very short one, was unprepared to meet the emergency in a bold and imaginative manner. The defeat of Union arms at the First Battle of Bull Run in July, 1861, shattered Northern confidence and proved to be an important sobering experience. Although the army was reorganized under the skillful hand of General George B. McClellan, the new commander would prove to be more adept at regrouping his army than he was at sending it into battle. In a disastrous campaign designed to capture the Confederate capital of Richmond in the spring of 1862, McClellan halted his army a few miles from the city after an erroneous report exaggerated the Confederate army's strength. Not only did McClellan lose the opportunity to end the war quickly, but, following the wounding of Confederate General Joseph E. Johnston in fighting outside Richmond, President Davis elevated a new general to command the Confederate army in the East, Robert E. Lee. A whole new chapter in the war began.

Under Lee's command, the Confederate army became a formidable force. A bold and dynamic leader, he was not afraid to attack Union forces far larger than his. In a series of stunning victories in Virginia, Lee's men defeated Union armies at Second Bull Run in August and Fredericksburg in December. After the latter battle, Lincoln told an aide, "If there is a worse place than Hell, I am in it." As the president struggled to find a general who could match Lee's abilities as a strategist, Northern morale continued to sink lower and lower. The success of the Southern armies in the eastern theater, the military frustration of the Northern command, and the bloodshed that seemed without end—all worked a terrible impact on Northern morale. Even such a devoted soldier as Oliver Wendell Holmes, Jr., several times wounded in defense of the flag, often despaired that the South could ever be defeated by force of arms. The first two years of the war seemed to belong to the Confederacy.

Both sides recruited thousands of soldiers to fill their armies. By the time the war ended, nearly three million men had served in the Union and Confederate armies. Many enlisted out of loyalty to nation or in the case of the South, to state and region. Others were drafted, as both sides resorted to conscription beginning in 1862. Many soldiers wrote diaries and letters that provide historians with rich source material to study the conflict.

Among the many recorders of military life was Private John O. Casler, a member of the Army of Northern Virginia's 33rd Virginia Regiment. The 33rd became part of one of the South's most renowned military units, taking the nickname "Stonewall Brigade" from its first commander, Thomas J. Jackson. Casler spoke of army life in many of its facets, from the comical to the tragic [11]. More sobering than Casler's memoir is the account of a Union soldier, Sergeant-Major Robert H. Kellogg, a prisoner of war at the Confederacy's most notorious prison, Andersonville [12]. Of 359,000 men who served as prisoners of war on both sides of the conflict, 56,000 died in captivity, with Andersonville's mortality rate among the highest. Poet Walt Whitman wrote about the war from a different vantage point—one who served as a nurse with the Union army, revealing an awareness of the real importance of the struggle [13].

The war transformed the lives and attitudes of women in North and South, forcing them to become more independent and resilient. In the absence of menfolk, women operated family farms and businesses, cared for children, and still found time to serve as volunteers, rolling bandages and making food and clothing for soldiers in the field. Several thousand became salaried nurses, while many more worked informally in this capacity. In the North, the quasi-governmental United States Sanitary Commission cared for enlisted men's medical and nutritional needs. Mary A. Livermore of Chicago became co-manager of the Commission's Chicago branch office. Her description of a hospital inspection trip to Vicksburg, Mississippi, reveals both her concern for helping soldiers and her interest in the politics of war [14].

Although the exact date at which the fortunes of the North began to turn has been the subject of debate, it is clear that by 1863 the North had rounded the corner and had started down the road to eventual victory. In the western theater of the war, it began even earlier, when, in February 1862, forces commanded by General Ulysses S. Grant captured two strategically important Confederate forts in Tennessee, Fort Henry and Fort Donelson. In April of that year, Grant's forces suffered a temporary setback, when Confederates attacked them at Shiloh. Grant's forces ultimately repulsed the Confederates, but the battle produced the worst casualties of the war to date. Despite this setback, Grant's successes caught the president's attention, for he had the right combination of strategic skill and aggressiveness that had been lacking in McClellan and other Union commanders. In 1864 Lincoln would elevate Grant to command of the entire U.S. army.

There would continue to be Union military setbacks, of course, but fewer as time went on. There were still discouraging moments to come and Northern arms would yet experience severe setbacks, but through it all the nation was gaining the strength that did, in the final analysis, determine the outcome of the conflict. Late in 1862 the first Confederate invasion of the North had been blunted at the bloody battle of Antietam, European intervention on the side of the South was forestalled, and the war aims of the North were significantly altered. The nation made a rapid economic recovery from the nadir of two years before. Under the impetus of war demands, industry expanded. The superior resources of the North were marshaled and harnessed to the war effort. Economic strength was matched by growing military strength. Union armies under Grant's command in the West had virtually cut the Confederacy in two. In one July week the last link between the Trans-Mississippi and the rest of the South was destroyed when Confederates surrendered at Vicksburg, and Lee's army in the East suffered their greatest defeat of the war at Gettysburg. As Northern strength grew, the South weakened. The effectiveness of the blockade was felt, resulting in serious shortages of vital materials.

While Southern citizens began to feel the economic pinch, their government proved unequal to the challenges which had to be faced and surmounted. Southern morale plummeted. Desertion from the Southern armies, a sure yardstick of morale, increased.

Most shocking perhaps was the fact that the Southern people began to experience all the manifold horrors of war as Union armies moved south and east from the Mississippi valley. A new "total war" concept of Northern generals carried death and destruction into the heartland of the Confederacy. Sherman's march through Georgia and the movement of his army through South Carolina (the state his soldiers held responsible for the war) left behind the unequaled bitterness and hatred of the Southern people. Many women coped with deprivation and loss, including Dolly Burge of rural Covington, Georgia, a widow attempting to sustain a farm and support a young daughter [15], and Emma LaConte, an impressionable young woman of Columbia, South Carolina, who observed the devastation of her city [16]. By the end of the war, some Southern women, including Burge, had begun to question the South's decision to secede and the motives of those who promoted it. Increasing economic confusion and chaos, political disunity, suffering and destruction in the wake of the invading armies spelled the end of the Southern cause.

Political disunity must loom large in any explanation of the defeat of the Confederacy. While it is true that the superior resources and manpower of the North played the vital role in subduing the South, it is equally true that the Confederate states' government failed to command the full political support of its constituent parts. The administration of Jefferson Davis was assailed by critics from the very opening of the war. At first, Davis had to parry the thrusts of the "fire-eaters," who felt that he was not emphatic enough in asserting Southern nationalism. They accused him of timidity in the prosecution of the war and disagreed with Davis's policy of defense as the one most likely to win friends to the Southern cause. Of much more serious intent and purpose was the opposition Davis faced from the states'-rights element, the conservative opposition of the state governors. To these men, Davis was a tyrant, a dictator, grinding the rights of sovereign states under his heel. Having escaped one yoke of oppression, they were in no mood to submit to another, especially to one of their own making. Unaware that any war effort requires a vast centralization of power and authority, these states'-rights opponents objected to the creation of a national army, conscription, and to the suspension of civil liberties which Davis deemed necessary in some Southern areas. The national government of the Confederacy soon came to represent a conspiracy against the states. Among the leaders of this opposition was the nation's vice president himself, Alexander H. Stephens, who tirelessly assailed his own administration for overstepping the bounds of authority [17]. Some state governors even toyed with the notion of withdrawing from the Confederacy and of concluding a separate peace with the United States. Nothing revealed the inherent weakness of the Southern cause so much as this opposition. The contradiction between states' rights and nationalism was built into the Southern movement; the South was never able to resolve this contradiction. So important has this opposition seemed that some historians regard states' rights as the most important cause of Southern defeat.

The North likewise suffered from political disunity, but unlike President Davis, Abraham Lincoln was eventually able to surmount his opposition. Lincoln, like Davis, faced bitter opposition from both the radical and conservative sides. In the North, however, it was the radical opposition, opposition from his own political party, that gave the president his most serious concern. These were the antislavery extremists and abolitionists who argued that Southern slavery must be one of the casualties of the conflict, that to restore the Union with slavery intact (as Lincoln apparently intended) would solve none of the nation's difficulties. Lincoln insisted during the early stages of the war that he was concerned only with the restoration of the Union. In a classic letter to Horace Greeley in the summer of 1862, he made it clear that the government's policy toward slavery was clearly secondary to this primary purpose of the war. Yet at the very time he wrote to Greeley, Lincoln was preparing to compromise with his radical opponents. Following the battle of Antietam, as Lee's army beat a hasty retreat into Virginia, Lincoln issued the preliminary Emancipation Proclamation, declaring that all slaves in areas still in rebellion on January 1, 1863, would be free on and after that date. While the Emancipation Proclamation technically freed no slaves immediately and did not apply to slaves held in areas under the control of the United States, it was an executive recognition of emancipation as a Northern war aim. Lincoln expressed qualms concerning the constitutionality of the measure and justified it only as a measure of military necessity.

African Americans, who had been pressuring the Lincoln administration to make a move toward ending slavery, welcomed the Emancipation Proclamation as an important first step. Charlotte Forten, a free woman from a prominent Philadelphia family, volunteered her time as teacher to the freed slaves on Hilton Head Island. In her wartime diary, Forten described a celebration held on January 1, 1863 and expressed pride in black soldiers serving in the Union army {18}. By the end of the war 189,000 African American soldiers and sailors fought for the Union. Their frustration over the failure of the war to end slavery quickly is exemplified by the letters of Private Spotswood Rice of the 67th Colored Infantry in 1864. A loyal unionist in Missouri owned one of Rice's daughters and resisted efforts to free her {19}.

In the months following Lincoln's issuance of the Emancipation Proclamation, the conviction grew stronger among Northerners that one of the conditions of union victory must be the complete abolition of slavery in the United States. In the spring of 1864, the Thirteenth Amendment to the Constitution was proposed [20]. The amendment was finally ratified a year and a half later. In spite of this alteration of the war's aims, the radicals continued to snipe at Lincoln, annoyed not only with his conservatism on the slavery question but also with his moderate plans for reconstructing the South. Their opposition reached a peak in the presidential election year of 1864, when they proposed to unseat Lincoln with a more acceptable and radical member of the Republican party. The movement came to naught as Northern armies won some significant victories and Lincoln's popularity with the people increased.

The alteration of the war's principal aim, from the preservation of the Union to the abolition of slavery, aroused opposition to Lincoln from the conservative side. Centered in the Middle West and in the Democratic party, known loosely as "copperheads," these critics charged Lincoln with usurpation and dictatorship. Like the states'-rights opposition in the South, they opposed the centralization of power on the national level, hurling their epithets at the suspension of civil liberties, conscription, the economic policies of the government, and finally and most vociferously, at emancipation. The Emancipation Proclamation, they charged, violated Lincoln's pledge that he would never interfere with slavery in the states where it legally existed. They further stated that it was an unconstitutional act and could lead only to further subversions of constitutional guarantees. Many "copperheads" openly advocated a negotiated peace with the Confederacy, although they never seemed to realize that this could be accomplished only through a recognition of Confederate independence. The "copperhead" opposition, stimulated by the Emancipation Proclamation and general war-weariness in the North, made serious inroads into Republican strength during the Congressional and state elections of 1862, but never afterward posed a serious threat to Lincoln's leadership. The effort to defeat Lincoln in 1864 with a military candidate, George B. McClellan, who was pledged to the vigorous prosecution of the war while standing on a peace platform can only be regarded as ludicrous.

Why was the South's lost cause lost? The quality of leadership on each side provides one clue. Abraham Lincoln proved to be a shrewd manipulator of men, a bold and imaginative politician. He had a human quality which few of the nation's leaders have, before or since, possessed. Lincoln weathered the political storms that raged about his administration partly because of these essentially human traits. Davis, on the other hand, was miscast as president of the Confederacy. A stiff, unbending man, he did not work well with many of those who surrounded him. His bearing encouraged dissension rather than conciliation. He distrusted people and hence inspired little trust in himself. Personality differences can account for only a small part of any explanation of Southern failure and Northern success but they are, nonetheless, to be considered.

Lincoln's task was made easier by the growing strength of the North; Davis's the more difficult by Southern weakness. Resources and manpower, industrial and financial superiority, overwhelming odds on the field of battle—all added up to the difference between victory and defeat. The story of Southern failure is also the story of the failure of Southern hopes and expectations. Cotton proved considerably less majestic than the Southerners had thought. Foreign intervention did not materialize, as the North won on the diplomatic front. Northeast and Northwest made common cause, as the bonds of economic interest and antislavery sentiment proved stronger than the South had admitted. The North-South link of the Mississippi River had been supplanted by a new network of East-West railroads. Finally, there was the paradox of the Confederacy itself. A nation founded on states' rights and slavery proved to be no nation at all. To be successful, Confederate leaders learned to their dismay, states' rights must be subverted in favor of a national centralization. Proponents of states' rights arguments were just as uncomfortable in the Confederate states as they had been in the United States. Although the Confederacy was the agency through which Southerners sought to preserve their slave-based way of life, there is every likelihood that slavery could not have persisted even if the South had won. By withdrawing from the Union, the South had consigned to ultimate doom the two elements it sought so hard to defend—states' rights and slavery. What, one wonders, had Southerners hoped to achieve through secession and the establishment of their own nation?

The end of the Civil War in the spring of 1865 brought joy to African Americans as they learned during the spring and summer of 1865 that the institution had finally been abolished. Families separated by sale reunited, sometimes after walking great distances to locate loved ones. Couples flocked to Union army chaplains to make legal marriages that, during slavery times, planters had insisted must remain informally arranged unions. Although slavery had been abolished, what would now be the status of former slaves in the South?

The federal government created an agency known as the Freedmen's Bureau that helped former slaves by creating schools, setting up bank accounts, and negotiating working conditions. Yet the Bureau and the freedmen and women faced an uphill battle, as planters sought to maintain the *status quo*. Family letters from Roseland Plantation in Louisiana's St. Charles Parish reveal the difficulties that a black Union soldier's family faced while waiting for him to be mustered out in the summer of 1865 [21].

African Americans throughout the South celebrated their freedom and worked to create a better life by establishing a variety of institutions in their communities. They built churches and rejected the influence of white men in existing churches. In some instances, power struggles ensued, and the military held a delicate position as an army of occupation [22].

The atmosphere in both North and South was not conducive to a calm, rational attempt to resolve postwar problems. In the South were physical destruction, graphically described by Northern journalists [23], bitter memories of Northern invasions, and the inner conflict between an earlier faith in the superiority of Southern civilization and the present reality of humiliating defeat. The sight of Jefferson Davis in chains, prodded through Southern cities by Union bayonets, produced a rankling in the Southern breast that would not easily be overcome. The problem of dealing with the African American population, now suddenly freed and on the move, seemed staggering. A fear of violence, stemming from the earlier dread of slave revolt, gripped the South. In the North, the legacy of hate also lingered on. The tragedy of Lincoln's assassination superimposed upon the elation over Lee's surrender the week before, produced a vast national trauma. The smug, self-righteous belief in "might makes right" inspired feelings of vengeance toward the South and gave many Northerners a sense of moral righteousness. Republican concern that a speedy and smooth reconciliation of the sections would enable the South to rule the nation once again through the Democratic party gave to reconstruction policy a strong political motivation.

President Lincoln had begun to formulate a reconstruction policy before the war was over. His concern was primarily with the status of the seceded states and his plans were designed simply to restore those states to the Union as easily as possible. His program, however, was incomplete at the time of his death. It is erroneous to speak of Lincoln as having a well-formulated plan for the reconstruction of the Union since he had not come to grips with the problems of the postwar South before his untimely death. Lincoln's attitude was marked by moderation; his look was to the future and he was willing to forgive the past. Andrew Johnson sought to follow Lincoln's lead, with his own modifications of the terms Lincoln had proposed, but the fate of the presidential plans was finally determined by the legislative branch in the winter of 1865 when the newly-elected Senators and Representatives from the Southern states were refused seats in Congress. Both Lincoln and Johnson believed that reconstruction was the responsibility of the executive branch, that executive recognition was sufficient to bring the departed states back into the fold.

Opposition to Lincoln's attitude toward reconstruction was registered by radical members of his own party in Congress midway through the war. Not until after the conflict had ended, however, were the radicals able to marshal their strength successfully behind an opposing program. The radicals, led by such men as Pennsylvania's Congressman Thaddeus Stevens, acted from a variety of motives. Many of them were genuine, sincere humanitarians who sought to bring to Southern blacks the rights and privileges guaranteed them by the American tradition of freedom and liberty. To these, the war had been fought primarily to free the slaves from the bondage in which they had suffered. The humanitarian impulse was complicated, however, by other, less noble, desires—to reassert the leadership of Congress in a nation that had submitted for four years to almost unlimited executive control, to guarantee the political ascendancy of the North and the Republican party in the face of a reviving Southern power, and to humiliate the South through the imposition of a vindictive peace on the hapless Southern people [24]. As radical strength grew, the humanitarian impulse weakened and the political character of reconstruction became more pronounced. Radicals were aided in their plans by a heightening emotional atmosphere in the North and by the attitudes of President Johnson and white Southerners themselves, who never seemed to realize that the fate of the South was at the mercy of Northern public opinion. The passage of black codes by many Southern states, the elevation of former Confederate leaders to new positions of political power, and the reluctance to ratify the Thirteenth Amendment all gave to Northerners the impression that the South had learned nothing from its defeat. Harsher measures of reconstruction seemed in order.

President Johnson's weapon against radical policies was the presidential veto power, but this weapon proved of little effect against the increasing radical majorities. His position was made the more ineffective by his ineptitude and by his isolated status in the government. A Southerner and former resident of a slave state, he was distrusted by many Northerners. Although a Democrat, he had accepted a place on the Republican ticket in 1864 (labeled for certain reasons a Union ticket). As a result, he was repudiated by Democrats, yet never fully accepted by Republicans. Johnson registered vigorous protests against the radical measures [25], but these only enhanced radical strength. He could never quite escape his Southern and Democratic heritage, his concern for states' rights, and his rigorous constitutional scruples.

In 1866 Congress passed the Fourteenth Amendment that guaranteed citizenship rights to all men, including the former slaves. Section 2 threatened a reduction in the size of a state's congressional delegation if it refused to enfranchise all male citizens. Opposed by Johnson, the amendment passed both houses of Congress overwhelmingly and went to the states for ratification. After congressional elections that same year gave Republicans a veto-proof majority, radicals began to direct reconstruction policy with the president powerless to affect its outcome. The Reconstruction Acts of 1867 divided the South into military districts with the occupation army empowered to override state governments. States in the former Confederacy must now hold new constitutional conventions, grant black male suffrage, and ratify the Fourteenth Amendment.

In addition to resenting his efforts to thwart reconstruction, radicals in Congress grew to hate Andrew Johnson personally. Congressman George Julian of Indiana supported efforts to impeach the president, noting his subversion of congressional initiatives in the South and his "capacity for evil" [26]. Johnson's Senate trial, which lasted two months and captivated the nation, led to the president's acquittal in a close vote marked by the defection of several moderate Republicans from their party's hard line.

Although Johnson's unpopularity made his election to another presidential term improbable, the radicals' personal vendetta against the president lost them credibility in the public mind and the chance to select the party's presidential nominee in the next election. Instead the nomination went to General Ulysses S. Grant, whose victory over Robert E. Lee in the war elevated him to the status of national hero. A prewar Democrat, Grant had come to admire Abraham Lincoln and to embrace his party. As his inaugural address suggests, Grant began the first of two presidential terms with good intentions for bringing peace and stability to the nation [27]. However, his lack of a defined political philosophy and his failure to exert strong presidential leadership contributed to continuing instability in the South.

Scandal would also dog Grant's efforts. In addition to opening himself up to criticism because of his many patronage appointments, Grant was criticized when members of his administration were implicated in bribery and kickback schemes. Criticism of Grant encouraged political opposition including liberals in his own party who nominated Horace Greeley in 1872. As editor of the *New York Tribune* for thirty years, Greeley had championed a variety of causes including antislavery, so when the Democratic party also gave Greeley the nod, white Southern Democrats found it difficult to support him. Nevertheless, Greeley proved himself to be a surprisingly effective campaigner [28]. With the president's formidable strength among several voting groups, including veterans, Grant won the election.

To his credit, Grant did give his unqualified support to passage of the Fifteenth Amendment enfranchising black men. However, the amendment faced vocal opposition from a group previously supportive of rights for African Americans: woman's rights advocates. Already angered over the Fourteenth Amendment's definition of citizenship in male terms, Elizabeth Cady Stanton, Susan B. Anthony, and several other prominent activists opposed the Fifteenth Amendment for its proposed exclusion of women from constitutional enfranchisement. Their public debates with Frederick Douglass, Frances Ellen Watkins Harper, Lucy Stone, and others captured national headlines [29].

By the time the Fifteenth Amendment was ratified in 1870, a certain degree of stability had returned to the South. State and local elections, once the cause of violence, had become more orderly, with federal soldiers stationed in the region to keep the peace. Six hundred African American men won election to political office, including several con-

gressmen and two members of the United States Senate. But appearances could be deceiving. White Southerners who resented the new
racial order and federal interference in the region used a variety of
means to prevent black men from rising economically and politically.
Terrorist organizations, the most famous being the Ku Klux Klan, used
physical intimidation, even murder to keep blacks down. In 1871, Congress held hearings into the issue of Klan violence, publishing the testimony in 13 volumes the following year [30].

Even moderate white Southerners opposed political change in the
South. Henry William Ravenel, a South Carolina planter and amateur
botanist, kept a diary for many years which reveals his acceptance of
Southern defeat, but also his growing resentment of the army's presence in his state and the political clout of African Americans. He supported the efforts of white Democrats to "redeem" South Carolina
from Republican political control and expressed jubilation when former Confederate cavalry general Wade Hampton won election as
governor in 1876 [31].

The career of Blanche Kelso Bruce represents both the highs and
lows of Reconstruction. After the war, he rose rapidly in Republican
politics in Mississippi, and, in 1874, became the first black man to
serve a full term in the U.S. Senate. Bruce exposed "fraud and intimidation" in Mississippi's 1875 election, speaking with great eloquence
about the efforts of whites to prevent blacks from voting [32]. When
Redeemers recaptured control of the state, Bruce lost his Senate seat.

By 1876, many in the North had grown tired of Reconstruction.
With a series of labor disputes and strikes capturing national attention, Americans seemed anxious to move beyond the war and its
aftermath. Many supported the withdrawal of federal troops from
the South. The election of 1876 laid the groundwork for the end of
Reconstruction. The election pitted Republican Rutherford B. Hayes
of Ohio against Democrat Samuel Tilden of New York. When the
results came in, three southern states, Florida, South Carolina, and
Louisiana, had questionable returns. Because the southern states
tended to be Democratic strongholds, the party believed the victory
would be theirs. But a congressional committee designed to determine its outcome and dominated by Republicans found for Hayes on
a strict party line vote. Tilden did not contest the outcome, believing
that the nation needed stability and not continuing chaos. Nonethe-

less, his bitterness over his defeat is evident in his statement to the New York delegation in 1880 declining the Democratic nomination [33]. Hayes, as promised, withdrew the last remaining federal forces from the South. With the army's departure the federal government abandoned African Americans. Although the Fourteenth and Fifteenth Amendments had given them civil rights and voting rights in theory, in fact, many would be prevented from exercising these rights for the next century.

Although Reconstruction was a failure in many ways, the national government went far toward fulfilling the promise of the revolutionary philosophy which gave it birth. The South, long isolated from the nineteenth century, was brought back into the mainstream of national life. Reconstruction fell short in part because the Northern people who had proclaimed the crusade to integrate the South into the nation and to guarantee to all humans the rights which were naturally theirs became distracted and left the job unfinished.

The Civil War was a tragedy of mammoth proportions. The human loss was crippling to the youthful nation and the effects of this loss were felt for generations. Indeed, they are still in evidence. Six hundred and twenty thousand young Americans lost their lives in the conflict. About one out of every four soldiers in the war was a fatality. Additional thousands were wounded and maimed. Disease took a frightful toll and the suffering in the crude hospitals was immense. Staggering as was the human loss, it was but a part of the total cost of the conflict. David Donald has summarized some of the other factors: "[B]illions of treasure (Federal, Confederate, state, local, and unofficial), untold retardation of economic development, ruined homes, roads, buildings and fields, billions of dollar-value in slaves wiped out, a shattered merchant marine, and a wretched intangible heritage of hate, extravagance, corruption, truculence, partisan excess (lasting for decades), and intolerance." Futile efforts have been made to sentimentalize this shocking cost, to romanticize the horror of the conflict. Emphasis has been placed by those who would commemorate the contest on the waving banners, on the gallantry and the pageantry. But the Civil War was not a pageant; its story is incomplete without the filth, the plunder, the brutality and senseless killing. Some have argued that the war was necessary, that viewed from the perspective of time its results fully justified the sacrifices that were made and the losses that were suffered. Such speculation only increases the tragedy of the conflict. To concede that the emergence of the United States as a nation united and that the extension of freedom to all humans alike could only have been accomplished through such a holocaust is to admit a tragic weakness in the human makeup and to suggest a tragic flaw in the ideal of government by the people. The Civil War will always remain a subject for intensive and rewarding study. However, as Allan Nevins has written, "We should probe more deeply into its roots, a process that will expose some of the weaknesses of our social fabric and governmental system. . . . We should above all examine more closely the effects of the great and terrible war not on the nation's politics—we know that; not on its economy—we also know that; but on its character, the vital element of national life."

CHAPTER 1

A WARNING FROM THE SOUTH

An Anonymous Georgian: "Plain Words for the North"

Several years of bitter and acrimonious debate between the North and the South culminated in the passage by Congress of the Compromise of 1850, a series of acts approved during the summer and early fall months of that year. Although the debate had been triggered by the question of slavery in the new Western lands acquired from Mexico, the Compromise acts dealt with other aspects of the sectional conflict as well. California was admitted to the Union as a free state, Utah and New Mexico territories were organized on the basis of popular sovereignty (allowing the people in those territories to decide the slavery question for themselves), the slave trade in the District of Columbia was prohibited, the Texas boundary was adjusted, and a new, more stringent Fugitive Slave Act was approved. Although the backers of the Compromise, both North and South, were optimistic in their belief that agitation between the sections would now be silenced, the Compromise proved to be only a "sectional truce." Serious reservations were expressed by Northern and Southern extremist groups. A "Georgia Platform" was drawn up, warning that the South would make no further concessions, and declaring that the preservation of the Union would depend on the faithful execution of the new Fugitive Slave Act. The following selection, written by an anonymous Georgian, reflects this Southern position.

We have fallen upon times of profound and startling interest. In our day the crisis of trial to our free government has approached imminently near. . . . Effort after effort has been made to set aside the Constitution, because it was too stringent a bridle upon selfish prejudice and ambition. But its inherent strength, grounded upon the good sense and sound principle of our people, has so far repelled triumphantly such insidious assaults. In our time these assaults have been directed from a position peculiarly dangerous. The

35

fervor of religious zeal, the ardor of philanthropy, have been artfully enlisted in a most unholy crusade against the citadel of our confidence. To meet a band of enemies battling for wrong under the banner of right has been difficult. . . . Fanaticism and error, honest but dangerous, have existed on the subject of slavery ever since the foundation of our government,—error not confined to one section or one side of the question. Where these exist, the material is ready for the hand of the selfish and designing. In themselves aiming at the right, they are the ready tools of the most egregious wrong. . . . It is useless to disguise that the existence of our Union has been by recent events greatly endangered. It is folly to deny that a few more sessions of Congress like the last, and the Republic, freighted with earth's most glorious hopes, is for ever lost. The arena of public events has disclosed this state of danger. We have seen those bodies composed of the representatives of the Church, wherein discord and fear, we should think, could find no room, torn asunder by the operation of this cause. We have seen the two great parties, cemented by strong bonds, riven into fragments by the detonation of this bomb. We have seen the Congress of the United States spending month after month in the most vituperative and inflammatory debate upon this all-absorbing theme. We have witnessed public meetings composed of Northern men, of those who pride themselves upon adherence to law and order, advocating theft, arson, and murder. Omens grave and serious, these. But there are others, to Northern men almost unknown, which to Southern hearts are even more alarming. They are to be found in the condition of Southern feeling upon this subject. But a few years ago not a man in the South dared to avow himself in favor of Disunion. It was looked upon as the synonyme of treachery, and no man dared to avow it. Now, how different is the fact. South Carolina is not only ready, but anxious for the conflict. Her people almost unanimously look upon the Union as a tyranny, whose yoke they would gladly throw off. Her children turn with brow and word of defiance to those whom they consider their oppressors. Mississippi and Alabama partake of the same feeling. In others of the Southern States there prevails less bitterness and more calmness. But in all is the conviction fixed and fastened, that Disunion, aye, even war, is to be preferred to the horrible consequences of an interference with slavery among them. Georgia has called a Convention of her people. The action of that body was not difficult to foresee. They will not dissolve this Union, although many of her sons openly avow that thus only can her wrongs be redressed. She will remain in the confederacy, with the hope of obtaining thereunder her rights. But she well knows that but a step or two more taken, and she must defend those rights at all hazards. She will forgive, if possible, forget, the past. But she warns those who have attacked her privileges, that in defence of them we will band together to resist any encroachments. She presents to them the simple alternative, "We will have our rights in this Union, or out of it. You must elect which you prefer." But we, and we only, who have lived amongst her people, who were born and reared upon her soil, know how great has been the struggle in the minds of her sons between an almost superstitious veneration for this Union, and bitter sense of wrong and injury. None else can know how stern is the determination of her people that these wrongs and injuries must cease now and for ever;— cease, quietly and voluntarily if possible, but if not, then terminate in the night of violence and bloodshed. This is the feeling general, nay, unanimous in the South. . . .

In a government where sectional interests and feelings may come into conflict, the sole security for permanence and peace is to be found in a Constitution whose provisions are inviolable. . . . Every State, before entering into that compact, stood in a position of independence. Ere yielding that independence, it was only proper that provision should be made to protect the interests of those which would inevitably be the weaker in that confederacy. In a portion of those independent States a peculiar and most important institution had grown up. It had entwined its tendrils around every interest of the country where it existed,—had become essential to its prosperity. With the foundation of the institution the ancestors of those now warmest to denounce it were identified. Southrons saw that its abolition, nay, even its modification by other hands than their own, might plunge them into all the horrors of a new and more terrible "servile war." While cognizant of all this, they could see the vast interest which posterity might have in this matter; how the North would grow daily in numerical superiority over the South; how slaves would become in process of time the chief source of the wealth of their descendants, and how complex and important would be their relations to society. They also saw how the seeds of fanaticism would grow, how sectional jealousy would increase, how these germs would ripen into animosity. No wonder that they trembled at the prospect—that they demanded protection. Fortunately they had to do with statesmen of enlarged and salutary views. Those Northern men who at that day represented their States could not only perceive how reasonable it was that slavery at the South should be guaranteed in the new government, but also its immense advantages to their own constituency. Intent upon the formation of a great empire, which should embody the principles for which they had fought, they were not willing to yield so great a destiny to the demand of a false and baseless philanthropy. They well knew that those who lived under the institution were not responsible for its foundation; and they saw that its roots were so deeply imbedded, that to tear it away must bring the life-blood from the heart of the new confederacy. They acted wisely, and embodied in the Constitution all that the South could ask. But two Constitutional provisions are necessary to secure Southern rights upon this important question,—the recognition of slavery where the people choose it, and the remedy for fugitive slaves. By the first, foreign interference is prevented, and the whole control and direction of the subject left where it belongs, in the hands of those who only are qualified to understand and to direct it. By the other, is avoided a series of border intestine broils, with which the existence of a Union would have soon become incompatible. We hold that the Constitution of the Union does recognize slavery where it exists. But with the progress of time a spirit has arisen and grown strong, which refuses to make this recognition. True, no effort has as yet been made to attack this principle by abolishing slavery in our midst; but every nerve has been strained to exclude slavery from territories which are the common property of both North and South. Men have allowed the plain dictates of reason to be clouded and obscured by the flimsiest sophistry. A large portion of our States have adopted and allow slavery. The entire country becomes possessed of new territory, to the acquisition of which these slave States contribute mainly. The South admits the right of this new territory to choose for itself whether slavery shall or shall not exist there. But the North insists, that while the territory was partly acquired by Southern men, is partly owned by Southern men, that they shall be excluded from its soil,—that they shall not carry their property into their own land—

land which is theirs by the right of purchase. Thus it is rendered, if these views are carried out, simply impossible for any new State representing the Southern interest ever to come into the Union. The equilibrium which alone can preserve the Constitution is utterly destroyed. And to do this, flagrant violations of the plainest rules of right and wrong are committed. It is said, "You may become the inhabitant of this territory; nay, it is yours, we cannot forbid it; but your property must be left behind." Amounting in effect to the declaration, You may pay out your money to buy land, you may pour out your blood to conquer it, but it is ours; and over it shall be extended only our peculiar customs, our industry, our population: yours have no part nor lot in the matter. Men who would tamely submit to so palpable a usurpation, to so great a wrong, were unworthy to be freemen. Yet such was the famous "Wilmot Proviso." Nor was the course of the North in regard to the provision for the recapture of fugitive slaves less open to objection. Without this provision no Constitution could ever have been formed. Without it now every reasonable Southern man would acquiesce in the necessity of Disunion. We consented, for the sake of our great object, to accept a Constitutional guarantee. Of this Northern men have been well aware; yet the conduct of many of them has been a series of efforts to avoid fulfilling a plain, simple provision of the Constitution. Until the last session, Congress has allowed this provision to remain practically a dead letter. But even the few efforts which have been made to carry into effect its object have met resistance. Legislatures have passed laws with the avowed intention of preventing the execution of this clause of the Constitution, where every member had taken upon his conscience an oath to defend and carry out that Constitution. Judicial officers have forgotten the supreme law of the land, and been carried away by the rush of prejudices. Again in this important matter was the South outraged, her rights denied her.

During the last session of Congress it became evident that no further inroads upon the constitutional rights of the South could be permitted. Then, when the Union was endangered, statesmen of enlarged sentiments came forward to preserve it. The history of that struggle need not be written. It is fresh in the minds of all. Suffice it to say, that the Patriotism of the country rallied against its Radicalism. The conflict was severe; for against the Constitution were

leagued the enthusiasts of the North and the ultras of the South. But
there is sometimes a principle of strength in governments as in men,
which is only developed by circumstances of danger and trial. So in
our government has been found to exist a tenacity heretofore sufficient to resist all forces striving to draw it asunder. Our citizens are
thinking, reflecting men, and they have seen the disadvantages
which are inevitable upon a dissolution of the Union. A majority of
them have therefore always rallied to its support. So now, after every
effort to warp and pervert its principles, the Constitution prevailed.
The Congress acknowledged *both* the great sanctions which are
essential to cement together the Union. It admitted, in the Utah and
New-Mexico bills, that it had not the right to exclude slaves from territory common to the whole country, but that its adoption or prohibition depended solely upon the will of the people; and it provided a
stringent and effective law for the recapture of fugitive slaves. The
action of Congress in both these particulars was based on true principle—a determination to abide by the Constitution. The question
now simply is, Will this action be sustained? For the South we answer
unhesitatingly, Yes! There are doubtless many amongst us who
demand more than they have obtained. The misfortune is also that
they have asked more than they had any right to expect. Various
motives have urged on these men of ultra sentiments. Some have
been animated by a spirit of resentment against the North, which we
conceive to be unjust, unless that section of the Union sustains what
we hope is but a small and unthinking portion of their population.
Others have deemed that a separation would advance the interests of
the South; while others have but striven to produce a commotion, in
the hope that they would be thrown to the surface in the agitation
which must ensue. These men have claimed more than the South
obtained by the legislation of the last Congress. Having failed to
secure it, they now strive to make that legislation the signal for resistance. Such, we think, is not the sentiment of a majority of the Southern people. The most moderate indeed deem the admission of
California to have been irregular, and are pained at much that preceded that admission. But they look upon those irregularities as not
affecting the great question which arises upon her application, viz.,
the right of the people of a State to decide for themselves as to the
existence of slavery amongst them. A great majority of the Southern

people are satisfied that the people of California do not wish slavery. They contend that they have a right to the institution wherever the municipal law sanctions it. This they hold to be their right under the Constitution. The inference is irresistible that the same right of choice is preserved to others, and that slavery shall not go into territories where the inhabitants desire to exclude it. They therefore submit to the admission of California, notwithstanding the irregularities attending it, because they think that substantially the intent of the people was carried out. And this great test they are willing to abide by, whether it works woe or weal. But with other parts of the legislation of Congress we have better reason to be satisfied. Comprehending a surrender of the Wilmot Proviso, and an energetic law for the recovery of fugitive slaves, it includes all that is necessary to secure the rights of the South. But will the North abide by this just and equitable termination of the matter? Will she be content with the advantages which she will necessarily enjoy in the natural course of events; or will she open this wise and just settlement, and introduce again into the national councils the demons of distraction and terror?

Much of the evil that has threatened has arisen, not from actual assaults upon the vested privileges of the South, but from attacks upon the feelings of her people. As a whole, no people are more sensitive than those of the South, more quick to resent insult and injury. They are placed in a most peculiar position. Born long after slavery had become rooted in their country, they have no option but to sustain it. Even those most anxious to abolish it advance no feasible mode of accomplishing their end. The Southern man well knows it to be utterly impracticable. He sees its many advantages, and he only can feel its peculiar importance to himself. Yet he is doomed to see attack after attack made upon this institution by men who understand nothing whatever of its nature, and who are ignorant of, or indifferent to, the terrible consequences which may follow the intermeddling with its existence. He must be content to hear every term of reproach lavished upon him, as a human taskmaster, by those whose forefathers established the slave trade for gain, and who themselves gladly draw their wealth from the pockets of the much abused slave-owner. Nay, he sees publications filled with onslaughts the most ungenerous, and often untrue, upon his whole community. Southern men were fast becoming tired of vituperation, often obviously hypocritical, and always unjust and impertinent. This it was and is yet—this spirit of indignation which more than aught else endangers the Union. Men cannot and ought not to remain calmly indifferent while others seek to deprive them of their rights, and to awake in their midst a spirit which may prove fatal to all they hold most dear. The passage of the Compromise Bills acted like balm upon the wounded feelings of the South. The action of Northern men was essential to procure the success of those measures; and the purest and ablest amongst them came manfully forward to sustain Southern rights. By their assistance those rights were obtained. To a great extent the irritation in Southern minds had subsided. The Southern heart has warmed towards Webster, and Cass, and Dickinson, and Elliott. We have felt at length that those who seek to destroy us are but a faction, and that we believe neither numerous nor reputable, amongst our Northern brethren. Shall this state of feeling continue? The North must decide. It were idle to deny that the compromises of the last session will not remain unattacked in either section of the Union. But at the South, as we have indicated, they will be sustained. At the North the issue must mainly be fought. The vituperation and howling of enthusiasts we are prepared to expect, but we are beginning to learn how little must their ravings be considered as an exponent of true public feeling at the North.

The question is, Will the North remain content with the so-called Compromise Bills, or will her people persist in attempts to violate the Constitution? The issue must be fought north of the Potomac. And upon its result depends the existence of the Union. Already have the destroyers, defeated but not discouraged, raised the banner of revolt. The South regards them but little, confiding in the patriotism of the North to deprive these madmen of the power to do evil. But if this hope shall prove fallacious; if again a Northern party shall attempt to make the Government the arbiter of the existence of slavery, and to use their numerical power to exclude it, or shall endeavor to throw obstacles in the way of the slave-owner seeking to recover the fugitive, the knell of this Republic will have struck. It is time this matter should be comprehended. The people at the North have now a fair, clear field for the contest. It is not ours to interfere. Themselves must decide whether they prefer Disunion to a confederacy with slave States. They have before them every aid to arrive at a decision. But that decision must be made, and will in all probability be final. If a majority of the people of the North shall see fit to deny us the privileges with which we came into the Union, it will remain for us to seek our rights in independence. But ere we are forced to this alternative, it were well for Northern men to reflect on the path before them. The justice and propriety of slavery we do not intend to discuss. But it is, to one intimately acquainted with its workings, surprising to see the glaring misrepresentations which are common in regard to the slave. But we do not conceive the question which Northern men have to argue with themselves just now is as to the morality or propriety of slavery. If they do not wish it amongst themselves, we do not desire it should exist there. They are welcome to exclude it, and welcome to all the satisfaction to which its exclusion may entitle them. Most clearly if it exists not amongst them, they are not responsible for its grievous sin. The question is, whether it behooves them to sacrifice the Union in a crusade against what they are pleased to consider an abomination amongst their neighbors. The first view of the matter which strikes the mind of every sensible man who thinks at all upon the subject, is the utter hopelessness of the task. It matters not who is responsible for the introduction of slavery; practically its continuation is, as the entire South believe, inevitable. It is identified with the pecuniary, social, and personal interests of the South. But even were it not so, yet no feasible plan for its abolition has ever been offered. All suggestions for its present extinction terminate in anarchy and blood. With the terrible certainty that its abolition must terminate in the most fearful danger to themselves and all whom they love and cherish, can it be doubted that the men of the South will resist, even to the last extremity, any and all interference with this their peculiar institution? The same spirit which fought at King's Mountain, which struggled with Marion in the swamps of Santee, which conquered at San Jacinto and Chapultepec, will disdain submission. It is worse than idle then to persist in striving to accomplish an impossibility. The fearful risk which threatens our country, the dangers which are so apparent, are all to be incurred in the prosecution of a purpose utterly and hopelessly unfeasible. And for this is to be perilled the existence of the Constitution—the hopes of freemen. "Alas!" may we not exclaim, "what inexplicable madness!"

Our Union is but the symbol of Constitutional freedom. Like all symbols which are sanctified by time-hallowed memories, it is dear in itself. The South will be the last to forget the sacred recollections which are entwined alike around the hearts of the inhabitants of every portion of this wide country. Nor are her children insensible to the still more vast and general blessings which that Union dispenses to all mankind. Well do they love liberty, and well do they know that the hopes of its wisest votaries throughout the earth are centered on the success of our Republic. Deeply indeed would we mourn over the failure of the experiment which embodies the noblest principle. But it can never be presumed that the cause of freedom would be advanced by the yielding of one section of the Union to the tyranny of another. The eagle which at the head of the legions of Publicola was the banner of Roman liberty, floated before the army which crossed the Rubicon. The cross which Paul and Peter preached as the sign of meekness, humility and love, became the eidolon of Dominican persecution. It is not impossible that the stars and stripes may likewise be desecrated. The Union, without a living, vital Constitution, is but a vain and empty name. Nay, more, it is but a body powerless for good, strong for evil.

Its destruction is inevitable unless the original guarantees are respected and maintained. Of its consequences to the cause of human freedom, of the frightful intestine wars which must follow, of the hatred which will be sown between brethren, of the terrible effects of a people combating against enemies abroad and a race in bondage at home, it is not our purpose to speak. These thoughts must have occurred often to the mind of every man who is not blinded by the most narrow bigotry. But there are two views of the disasters attendant upon a dissolution, which it behooves Northern men well to think upon. In the first place, let them reflect, it will most seriously interfere with their pecuniary interests. Men of wisdom and experience at the South have sometimes doubted whether a dissolution of this Union would not be an advantage. But of its effect upon the pecuniary affairs of the North there can be no doubt. Let the South be stirred to a pitch of animosity sufficient to cause a dissolution; let Northern manufactures, Northern shipping, be put upon the same footing with those of France and England, and what would be the result? Can they sustain the burden? Those who are most interested well know not. But let not Northern men be deceived. Those amongst them familiar with the details of business, well know that we, the Southern States, with every power to become independent, have been content to share with the North our abundance, to contribute to her wealth and strength. But let us be driven to separate; let us be forced to withdraw our household gods from a Union no longer existing for our protection; let Northern men occupy the position of open, avowed enemies;—they will be looked upon with hatred and aversion. They will in vain look to us for support. We will be separated as widely, as effectively to all practical purposes, as though between us flowed a gulf of fire "measureless to man." No Northern man can fail to see the result of such a state of things; to be incurred, too, for the accomplishment of an object demonstrably Utopian. It seems impossible that the shrewd, sagacious men of the North, seeing and understanding the result, can be compelled to submit to what will prove ruinous to them through the violence of fanatic zeal. The struggle is for them. But again: The efforts of Northern men to interfere with slavery are unfortunate for their unhappy beneficiaries. If we are let alone, it will be our pride and our pleasure to increase the benefits and diminish the disadvantages of their situation; but if we are to be summoned, by those whose object and endeavor it is to poison the minds of those whose opportunities for evil are necessarily so fearful, to destroy our main dependence, nay, perchance to endanger our lives, most severely will these ill-judged efforts react upon the condition of the slave. He has been to us an object of attachment and sympathy. We have sustained and protected him, and in sickness and old age have extended to him every comfort. Nay, many of us have found amongst these humble beings friends whose devotion shames that of others far above them. Happy and contented, he has passed through life, throwing upon his master the entire load of life's cares and sorrows, desiring in his own condition no change. But if into these minds brooding and most dangerous thoughts are to be instilled; if a domestic traitor is to be implanted in every family; if we are to guard alike against the subtraction of this most valuable source of subsistence, and the dangers of their own passions, so savage when roused, we shall be compelled to introduce into our polity elements never before known,—to watch stringently, to restrict closely, to punish severely. The kind familiarity of the master will be gone, and in its place will be substituted the suspicious eye and stern hand of caution and severity. This is the change which is to be produced by the machinations of those who claim to be the peculiar friends of the slave,—men whom nothing will convince of the madness of their career, save a Union rent into fragments amidst the wild waves of a bloody convulsion. Alas! that in this age such fanaticism should not be met by the united execrations of every patriot—nay, of every philosopher.

With this matter we of the South have but little more to do. Some of us are, as has been already said, ready for the utmost. Others, we fondly believe a majority, are willing to forget the wrongs of the past and to hope for the future. But let the North refuse to abide by our rights, and the cry, which will go up from the hearts of the whole Southern people, will be, "Let us go out from among them." Meanwhile the battle rages at the North. The din of the conflict is borne to our ears. How it will end we may not know. We can but offer up heart-felt prayers for the success of those who battle for the Union and the Constitution.

CHAPTER 2

THERE IS INFAMY IN THE AIR

Ralph Waldo Emerson
on the Fugitive Slave Law

Ralph Waldo Emerson (1803–1882), philosopher, writer and lecturer, was the leading exponent of transcendentalism, America's most significant intellectual movement during the first half of the nineteenth century. Often called the "high priest" of democracy, Emerson preached a doctrine of individualism, self-reliance and the perfectibility of mankind. Trained at Harvard, he began his career as a Unitarian minister in his native Massachusetts, only to resign his post in the early 1830s in order that he might preach transcendentalism more freely. For the remainder of his life, he devoted himself to writing and lecturing. Emerson was an early supporter of the growing antislavery movement in New England; although he could be classified initially as a moderate, the events of the sectional conflict gradually forced him to adopt a more extreme position on the slavery question. The passage of the Fugitive Slave Act in 1850 profoundly disturbed Emerson. The full force of the law was brought home to Bostonians in February, 1851, when the slave Shadrach was arrested in that city. Although Shadrach was rescued shortly afterward, the incident created a strong reaction against the legislation. The knowledge that Massachusetts' Senator, Daniel Webster, supported the act as part of the Compromise of 1850 only intensified the opposition to the law. The selection that follows was delivered by Emerson before an audience in his own town of Concord, Massachusetts, on May 3, 1851, and reflects his attitude toward the law.

Fellow citizens: I accepted your invitation speak to you on the great question of these days, with very little consideration of what I might have to offer: for there seems to be no option. The last year has forced us all into politics, and made it a paramount duty to seek what it is often a duty to shun. We do not breathe well. There is infamy in the air. I have a new experience. I wake in the morning

with a painful sensation, which I carry about all day, and which, when
traced home, is the odious remembrance of that ignominy which has
fallen on Massachusetts, which robs the landscape of beauty, and
takes the sunshine out of every hour. I have lived all my life in this
state, and never had any experience of personal inconvenience from
the laws, until now. They never came near me to any discomfort
before. I find the like sensibility in my neighbors; and in that class who
take no interest in the ordinary questions of party politics. There are
men who are as sure indexes of the equity of legislation and of the
same state of public feeling, as the barometer is of the weight of the
air, and it is a bad sign when these are discontented, for though they
snuff oppression and dishonor at a distance, it is because they are
more impressionable: the whole population will in a short time be as
painfully affected.

  Every hour brings us from distant quarters of the Union the expression of mortification at the late events in Massachusetts, and at the
behavior of Boston. The tameness was indeed shocking. Boston, of
whose fame for spirit and character we have all been so proud; Boston,
whose citizens, intelligent people in England told me they could
always distinguish by their culture among Americans; the Boston of
the American Revolution, which figures so proudly in John Adams's
Diary, which the whole country has been reading; Boston, spoiled by
prosperity, must bow its ancient honor in the dust, and make us irre-
trievably ashamed. In Boston, we have said with such lofty confidence,
no fugitive slave can be arrested, and now, we must transfer our vaunt
to the country, and say, with a little less confidence, no fugitive man
can be arrested here; at least we can brag thus until to-morrow, when
the farmers also may be corrupted.

  The tameness is indeed complete. The only haste in Boston, after
the rescue of Shadrach, last February, was, who should first put his
name on the list of volunteers in aid of the marshal. I met the
smoothest of Episcopal Clergymen the other day, and allusion being
made to Mr. Webster's treachery, he blandly replied, "Why, do you
know I think that the great action of his life." It looked as if in the city
and the suburbs all were involved in one hot haste of terror,—presidents of colleges, and professors, saints, and brokers, insurers,
lawyers, importers, manufacturers: not an unpleasing sentiment, not
a liberal recollection, not so much as a snatch of an old song for freedom, dares intrude on their passive obedience.

The panic has paralyzed the journals, with the fewest exceptions, so that one cannot open a newspaper without being disgusted by new records of shame. I cannot read longer even the local good news. When I look down the columns at the titles of paragraphs, "Education in Massachusetts," "Board of Trade," "Art Union," "Revival of Religion," what bitter mockeries! The very convenience of property, the house and land we occupy, have lost their best value, and a man looks gloomily at his children, and thinks, "What have I done that you should begin life in dishonor?" Every liberal study is discredited,—literature and science appear effeminate, and the hiding of the head. The college, the churches, the schools, the very shops and factories are discredited; real estate, every kind of wealth, every branch of industry, every avenue to power, suffers injury, and the value of life is reduced. Just now a friend came into my house and said, "if this law shall be repealed I shall be glad that I have lived; if not I shall be sorry that I was born." What kind of law is that which extorts language like this from the heart of a free and civilized people?

One intellectual benefit we owe to the late disgraces. The crisis had the illuminating power of a sheet of lightning at midnight. It showed truth. It ended a good deal of nonsense we had been wont to hear and to repeat, on the 19th of April, the 17th of June, the 4th of July. It showed the slightness and unreliableness of our social fabric, it showed what stuff reputations are made of, what straws we dignify by office and title, and how competent we are to give counsel and help in a day of trial. It showed the shallowness of leaders; the divergence of parties from their alleged grounds; showed that men would not stick to what they had said, that the resolutions of public bodies, or the pledges never so often given and put on record of public men, will not bind them. The fact comes out more plainly that you cannot rely on any man for the defence of truth, who is not constitutionally or by blood and temperament on that side. A man of a greedy and unscrupulous selfishness may maintain morals when they are in fashion: but he will not stick. . . . The popular assumption that all men loved freedom, and believed in the Christian religion, was found hollow American brag; only persons who were known and tried benefactors are found standing for freedom: the sentimentalists went downstream. I question the value of our civilization, when I see that the public mind had never less hold of the strongest of all truths. The sense of injustice is blunted,—a sure sign of the shallowness of our intellect. I cannot accept the railroad and telegraph in exchange for reason and charity. It is not skill in iron locomotives that makes so fine civility, as the jealousy of liberty. I cannot think the most judicious tubing a compensation for metaphysical debility. What is the use of admirable law-forms, and political forms, if a hurricane of party feeling and a combination of monied interests can beat them to the ground? What is the use of courts, if judges only quote authorities, and no judge exerts original jurisdiction, or recurs to first principles? What is the use of a Federal Bench, if its opinions are the political breath of the hour? And what is the use of constitutions, if all the guaranties provided by the jealousy of ages for the protection of liberty are made of no effect, when a bad act of Congress finds a willing commissioner? The levity of the public mind has been shown in the past year by the most extravagant actions. Who could have believed it, if foretold that a hundred guns would be fired in Boston on the passage of the Fugitive Slave Bill? Nothing proves the want of all thought, the absence of standard in men's minds, more than the dominion of party. Here are humane people who have tears for misery, an open purse for want; who should have been the defenders of the poor man, are found his embittered enemies, rejoicing in his rendition,—merely from party ties. I thought none, that was not ready to go on all fours, would back this law. And yet here are upright men, *compotes mentis*, husbands, fathers, trustees, friends, open, generous, brave, who can see nothing in this claim for bare humanity, and the health and honor of their native State, but canting fanaticism, sedition and "one idea." Because of this preoccupied mind, the whole wealth and power of Boston— two hundred thousand souls, and one hundred and eighty millions of money—are thrown into the scale of crime: and the poor black boy, whom the fame of Boston had reached in the recesses of a vile swamp, or in the alleys of Savannah, on arriving here finds all this force employed to catch him. The famous town of Boston is his master's hound. The learning of the universities, the culture of elegant society, the acumen of lawyers, the majesty of the Bench, the eloquence of the Christian pulpit, the stoutness of Democracy, the respectability of the Whig party are all combined to kidnap him.

The crisis is interesting as it shows the self-protecting nature of the world and of the Divine laws. It is the law of the world,—as much immorality as there is, so much misery. The greatest prosperity will in vain resist the greatest calamity. You borrow the succour of the devil and he must have his fee. He was never known to abate a penny of his rents. In every nation all the immorality that exists breeds plagues. But of the corrupt society that exists we have never been able to combine any pure prosperity. There is always something in the very advantages of a condition which hurts it. Africa has its malformation; England has its Ireland; Germany its hatred of classes; France its love of gunpowder; Italy its Pope; and America, the most prosperous country in the Universe, has the greatest calamity in the Universe, negro slavery.

Let me remind you a little in detail how the natural retribution acts in reference to the statute which Congress passed a year ago. For these few months have shown very conspicuously its nature and impracticability. It is contravened:

1. By the sentiment of duty. An immoral law makes it a man's duty to break it, at every hazard. For virtue is the very self of every man. It is therefore a principle of law that an immoral contract is void, and that an immoral statute is void. For, as laws do not make right, and are simply declaratory of a right which already existed, it is not to be presumed that they can so stultify themselves as to command injustice.

It is remarkable how rare in the history of tyrants is an immoral law. Some color, some indirection was always used. If you take up the volumes of the "Universal History," you will find it difficult searching. The precedents are few. It is not easy to parallel the wickedness of this American law. And that is the head and body of this discontent, that the law is immoral.

Here is a statute which enacts the crime of kidnapping,—a crime on one footing with arson and murder. A man's right to liberty is as inalienable as his right to life.

Pains seem to have been taken to give us in this statute a wrong pure from any mixture of right. If our resistance to this law is not right, there is no right. This is not meddling with other people's affairs: this is hindering other people from meddling with us. This is not going crusading into Virginia and Georgia after slaves, who, it is alleged, are very comfortable where they are:—that amiable argument falls to the ground; but this is befriending in our own State, on our own farms, a man who has taken the risk of being shot, or burned alive, or cast into the sea, or starved to death, or suffocated in a wooden box, to get away from his driver: and this man who has run the gauntlet of a thousand miles for his freedom, the statute says, you men of Massachusetts shall hunt, and catch, and send back again to the dog-hutch he fled from.

It is contrary to the primal sentiment of duty, and therefore all men that are born are, in proportion to their power of thought and their moral sensibility, found to be the natural enemies of this law. The resistance of all moral beings is secured to it. I had thought, I confess, what must come at last would come at first, a banding of all men against the authority of this statute. I thought it a point on which all sane men were agreed, that the law must respect the public morality. I thought that all men of all conditions had been made sharers of a certain experience, that in certain rare and retired moments they had been made to see how man is man, or what makes the essence of rational beings, namely, that whilst animals have to do with eating the fruits of the ground, men have to do with rectitude, with benefit, with truth, with something which is, independent of appearances: and that this tie makes the substantiality of life, this, and not their ploughing, or sailing, their trade or the breeding of families. I thought that every time a man goes back to his own thoughts, these angels receive him, talk with him, and that, in the best hours, he is uplifted in virtue of this essence, into a peace and into a power which the material world cannot give: that these moments counterbalance the years of drudgery, and that this owning of a law, be it called morals, religion, or godhead, or what you will, constituted the explanation of life, the excuse and indemnity for the errors and calamities which sadden it. In long years consumed in trifles, they remember these moments, and are consoled. I thought it was this fair mystery, whose foundations are hidden in eternity, which made the basis of human society, and of law; and that to pretend anything else, as that the acquisition of property was the end of living, was to confound all distinctions, to make the world a greasy hotel, and, instead of noble motives and inspirations, and a heaven of companions and angels around and before us, to leave us in a grimacing menagerie of monkeys and idiots. All arts, customs, societies, books, and laws, are good as they foster and concur with this spiritual element: all men are beloved as they raise us to it; hateful as they deny or resist it. The laws especially draw their obligation only from their concurrence with it. . . .

2. It is contravened by all the sentiments. How can a law be enforced that fines pity, and imprisons charity? As long as men have bowels, they will disobey. You know that the Act of Congress of September 18, 1850, is a law which every one of you will break on the earliest occasion. There is not a manly Whig, or a manly Democrat, of whom, if a slave were hidden in one of our houses from the hounds, we should not ask with confidence to lend his wagon in aid of his escape, and he would lend it. The man would be too strong for the partisan.

And here I may say that it is absurd, what I often hear, to accuse the friends of freedom in the North with being the occasion of the new stringency of the Southern slave-laws. If you starve or beat the orphan, in my presence, and I accuse your cruelty, can I help it? In the words of Electra in the Greek tragedy, " 'Tis you that say it, not I. You do the deeds, and your ungodly deeds find me the words." Will you blame the ball for rebounding from the floor, blame the air for rushing in where a vacuum is made or the boiler for exploding under pressure of steam? These facts are after laws of the world, and so is it law, that, when justice is violated, anger begins. The very defence which the God of Nature has provided for the innocent against cruelty is the sentiment of indignation and pity in the bosom of the beholder. Mr. Webster tells the President that "he has been in the North, and he has found no man, whose opinion is of any weight, who is opposed to the law." Oh, Mr. President, trust not the information! The gravid old Universe goes spawning on; the womb conceives and the breasts give suck to thousands and millions of hairy babes formed not in the image of your statute, but in the image of the Universe; too many to be bought off; too many than they can be rich, and therefore peaceable; and necessitated to express first or last every feeling of the heart. You can keep no secret, for whatever is true some of them will unreasonably say. You can commit no crime, for they are created in their sentiments conscious of and hostile to it; and unless you can suppress the newspaper, pass a law against book-shops, gag the English tongue in America, all short of this is futile. This dreadful English Speech is saturated with songs, proverbs and speeches that flatly contradict and defy every line of Mr. Mason's statute. Nay, unless you can draw a sponge over those seditious Ten Commandments which are the root of our European and American civilization; and over that eleventh commandment, "Do unto others as you would have them do to you," your labor is vain.

3. It is contravened by the written laws themselves, because the sentiments, of course, write the statutes. Laws are merely declaratory of the natural sentiments of mankind, and the language of all permanent laws will be in contradiction to any immoral enactment. And thus it happens here: Statute fights against Statute. By the law of Congress March 2, 1807, it is piracy and murder, punishable with death, to enslave a man on the coast of Africa. By law of Congress September, 1850, it is a high crime and misdemeanor, punishable with fine and imprisonment, to resist the reënslaving a man on the coast of America. Off soundings, it is piracy and murder to enslave him. On soundings, it is fine and prison not to reënslave. What kind of legislation is this? What kind of constitution which covers it? And yet the crime which the second law ordains is greater than the crime which the first law forbids under penalty of the gibbet. For it is a greater crime to reënslave a man who has shown himself fit for freedom, than to enslave him at first, when it might be pretended to be a mitigation of his lot as a captive in war.

4. It is contravened by the mischiefs it operates. A wicked law cannot be executed by good men, and must be by bad. Flagitious men must be employed, and every act of theirs is a stab at the public peace. It cannot be executed at such a cost, and so it brings a bribe in its hand. This law comes with infamy in it, and out of it. It offers a bribe in its own clauses for the consummation of the crime. To serve it, low and mean people are found by the groping of the government. No government ever found it hard to pick up tools for base actions. If you cannot find them in the huts of the poor, you shall find them in the palaces of the rich. Vanity can buy some, ambition others, and money others. The first execution of the law, as was inevitable, was a little hesitating; the second was easier; and the glib officials became, in a few weeks, quite practised and handy at stealing men. But worse, not the officials alone are bribed, but the whole community is solicited. The scowl of the community is attempted to be averted by the mischievous whisper, "Tariff and Southern market, if you will be

quiet: no tariff and loss of Southern market, if you dare to murmur."
I wonder that our acute people who have learned that the cheapest
police is dear schools, should not find out that an immoral law costs
more than the loss of the custom of a Southern city.

The humiliating scandal of great men warping right into wrong
was followed up very fast by the cities. New York advertised in
Southern markets that it would go for slavery, and posted the names
of merchants who would not. Boston, alarmed, entered into the same
design. Philadelphia, more fortunate, had no conscience at all, and, in
this auction of the rights of mankind, rescinded all its legislation
against slavery. And the Boston "Advertiser," and the "Courier," in
these weeks, urge the same course on the people of Massachusetts.
Nothing remains in this race of roguery but to coax Connecticut or
Maine to outbid us all by adopting slavery into its constitution.

Great is the mischief of a legal crime. Every person who touches this
business is contaminated. There has not been in our lifetime another
moment when public men were personally lowered by their political
action. But here are gentlemen whose believed probity was the confidence and fortification of multitudes, who, by fear of public opinion, or
through the dangerous ascendancy of Southern manners, have been
drawn into the support of this foul business. We poor men in the country who might once have thought it an honor to shake hands with them,
or to dine at their boards, would now shrink from their touch, nor could
they enter our humblest doors. You have a law which no man can obey,
or abet the obeying, without loss of self-respect and forfeiture of the
name of gentlemen. What shall we say of the functionary by whom the
recent rendition was made? If he has rightly defined his powers, and
has no authority to try the case, but only to prove the prisoner's identity, and remand him, what office is this for a reputable citizen to hold?
No man of honor can sit on that bench. It is the extension of the
planter's whipping- post; and its incumbents must rank with a class
from which the turnkey, the hangman and the informer are taken, necessary functionaries, it may be, in a state, but to whom the dislike and
the ban of society universally attaches.

5. These resistances appear in the history of the statute, in the ret-
ributions which speak so loud in every part of this business, that I
think a tragic poet will know how to make it a lesson for all ages. Mr.
Webster's measure was, he told us, final. It was a pacification, it was

a suppression, a measure of conciliation and adjustment. These were his words at different times: "there was to be no parleying more;" it was "irrepealable." Does it look final now? His final settlement has dislocated the foundations. The state-house shakes like a tent. His pacification has brought all the honesty in every house, all scrupulous and good-hearted men, all women, and all children, to accuse the law. It has brought United States swords into the streets, and chains round the court-house. "A measure of pacification and union." What is its effect? To make one sole subject for conversation and painful thought throughout the continent, namely, slavery. There is not a man of thought or of feeling but is concentrating his mind on it. There is not a clerk but recites its statistics; not a politician but is watching its incalculable energy in the elections; not a jurist but is hunting up precedents; not a moralist but is prying into its quality; not an economist but is computing its profit and loss: Mr. Webster can judge whether this sort of solar microscope brought to bear on his law is likely to make opposition less. The only benefit that has accrued from the law is its service to education. It has been like a university to the entire people. It has turned every dinner-table into a debating-club, and made every citizen a student of natural law. When a moral quality comes into politics, when a right is invaded, the discussion draws on deeper sources: general principles are laid bare, which cast light on the whole frame of society. And it is cheering to behold what champions the emergency called to this poor black boy; what subtlety, what logic, what learning, what exposure of the mischief of the law; and, above all, with what earnestness and dignity the advocates of freedom were inspired. It was one of the best compensations of this calamity.

But the Nemesis works underneath again. It is a power that makes noonday dark, and draws us on to our undoing; and its dismal way is to pillory the offender in the moment of his triumph. The hands that put the chain on the slave are in that moment manacled. Who has seen anything like that which is now done? The words of John Randolph, wiser than he knew, have been ringing ominously in all echoes for thirty years, words spoken in the heat of the Missouri debate. "We do not govern the people of the North by our black slaves, but by their own white slaves. We know what we are doing. We have conquered you once, and we can and will conquer you

THERE IS INFAMY IN THE AIR   57

again. Ay, we will drive you to the wall, and when we have you there
once more, we will keep you there and nail you down like base
money." These words resounding ever since from California to Oregon, from Cape Florida to Cape Cod, come down now like the cry of
Fate, in the moment when they are fulfilled. By white slaves, by a
white slave, are we beaten. Who looked for such ghastly fulfillment,
or to see what we see? Hills and Halletts, servile editors by the hundred, we could have spared. But him, our best and proudest, the first
man of the North, in the very moment of mounting the throne, irre-
sistibly taking the bit in his mouth and the collar on his neck, and har-
nessing himself to the chariot of the planters.

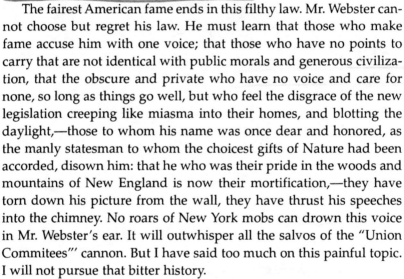

The fairest American fame ends in this filthy law. Mr. Webster cannot choose but regret his law. He must learn that those who make
fame accuse him with one voice; that those who have no points to
carry that are not identical with public morals and generous civilization, that the obscure and private who have no voice and care for
none, so long as things go well, but who feel the disgrace of the new
legislation creeping like miasma into their homes, and blotting the
daylight,—those to whom his name was once dear and honored, as
the manly statesman to whom the choicest gifts of Nature had been
accorded, disown him: that he who was their pride in the woods and
mountains of New England is now their mortification,—they have
torn down his picture from the wall, they have thrust his speeches
into the chimney. No roars of New York mobs can drown this voice
in Mr. Webster's ear. It will outwhisper all the salvos of the "Union
Commitees'" cannon. But I have said too much on this painful topic.
I will not pursue that bitter history.

But passing from the ethical to the political view, I wish to place
this statute, and we must use the introducer and substantial author
of the bill as an illustration of the history. I have as much charity for
Mr. Webster, I think, as any one has. I need not say how much I have
enjoyed his fame. Who has not helped to praise him? Simply he was
the one eminent American of our time, whom we could produce as a
finished work of Nature. We delighted in his form and face, in his
voice, in his eloquence, in his power of labor, in his concentration, in
his large understanding, in his daylight statement, simple force; the
facts lay like the strata of a cloud, or like the layers of the crust of the
globe. He saw things as they were, and he stated them so. He has

been by his clear perceptions and statements in all these years the best head in Congress, and the champion of the interests of the Northern seaboard: but as the activity and growth of slavery began to be offensively felt by his constituents, the senator became less sensitive to these evils. They were not for him to deal with: he was the commercial representative. He indulged occasionally in excellent expression of the known feeling of the New England people: but, when expected and when pledged, he omitted to speak, and he omitted to throw himself into the movement in those critical moments when his leadership would have turned the scale. At last, at a fatal hour, this sluggishness accumulated to downright counteraction, and, very unexpectedly to the whole Union, on the 7th March, 1850, in opposition to his education, association, and to all his own most explicit language for thirty years, he crossed the line, and became the head of the slavery party in this country.

Mr. Webster perhaps is only following the laws of his blood and constitution. I suppose his pledges were not quite natural to him. Mr. Webster is a man who lives by his memory, a man of the past, not a man of faith or of hope. He obeys his powerful animal nature;—and his finely developed understanding only works truly and with all its force, when it stands for animal good; that is, for property. He believes, in so many words, that government exists for the protection of property. He looks at the Union as an estate, a large farm, and is excellent in the completeness of his defence of it so far. He adheres to the letter. Happily he was born late,—after the independence had been declared, the Union agreed to, and the constitution settled. What he finds already written, he will defend. Lucky that so much had got well written when he came. For he has no faith in the power of self-government; none whatever in extemporizing a government. Not the smallest municipal provision, if it were new, would receive his sanction. In Massachusetts, in 1776, he would, beyond all question, have been a refugee. He praises Adams and Jefferson, but it is a past Adams and Jefferson that his mind can entertain. A present Adams and Jefferson he would denounce. So with the eulogies of liberty in his writings,—they are mentalism and youthful rhetoric. He can celebrate it, but it means as much from him as from Metternich or Talleyrand. This is all inevitable from his constitution. All the drops of his blood have eyes that look downward. It is neither praise

nor blame to say that he has no moral perception, no moral sentiment, but in that region—to use the phrase of the phrenologists—a
hole in the head. The scraps of morality to be gleaned from his
speeches are reflections of the mind of others; he says what he hears
said, but often makes signal blunders in their use. In Mr. Webster's
imagination the American Union was a huge Prince Rupert's drop,[1]
which, if so much as the smallest end be shivered off, the whole will
snap into atoms. Now the fact is quite different from this. The people
are loyal, law-loving, law-abiding. They prefer order, and have no
taste for misrule and uproar.

The destiny of this country is great and liberal, and is to be greatly
administered. It is to be administered according to what is, and is to
be, and not according to what is dead and gone. The union of this
people is a real thing, an alliance of men of one flock, one language,
one religion, one system of manners and ideas. I hold it to be a real
and not a statute union. The people cleave to the Union, because they
see their advantage in it, the added power of each.

I suppose the Union can be left to take care of itself. As much real
union as there is, the statutes will be sure to express; as much disunion as there is, no statute can long conceal. Under the Union I suppose the fact to be that there are really two nations, the North and the
South. It is not slavery that severs them, it is climate and temperament. The South does not like the North, slavery or no slavery, and
never did. The North likes the South well enough, for it knows its
own advantages. I am willing to leave them to the facts. If they continue to have a binding interest, they will be pretty sure to find it out:
if not, they will consult their peace in parting. But one thing appears
certain to me, that, as soon as the constitution ordains an immoral
law, it ordains disunion. The law is suicidal, and cannot be obeyed.
The Union is at an end as soon as an immoral law is enacted. And he
who writes a crime into the statute-book digs under the foundations
of the Capitol to plant there a powder-magazine, and lays a train.

I pass to say a few words to the question, What shall we do?

1. What in our federal capacity is our relation to the nation?

2. And what as citizens of a state?

---

[1] A glass bulb which, if struck a sharp but slight blow, will shatter into many
pieces. [Editor's note.]

I am an Unionist as we all are, or nearly all, and I strongly share the hope of mankind in the power, and therefore, in the duties of the Union; and I conceive it demonstrated,—the necessity of common sense and justice entering into the laws. What shall we do? First, abrogate this law; then, proceed to confine slavery to slave states, and help them effectually to make an end of it. Or shall we, as we are advised on all hands, lie by, and wait the progress of the census? But will Slavery lie by? I fear not. She is very industrious, gives herself no holidays. No proclamations will put her down. She got Texas and now will have Cuba, and means to keep her majority. The experience of the past gives us no encouragement to lie by. Shall we call a new Convention, or will any expert statesman furnish us a plan for the summary or gradual winding up of slavery, so far as the Republic is its patron? Where is the South itself? Since it is agreed by all sane men of all parties (or was yesterday) that slavery is mischievous, why does the South itself never offer the smallest counsel of her own? I have never heard in twenty years any project except Mr. Clay's. Let us hear any project with candor and respect. Is it impossible to speak of it with reason and good nature? It is really the project fit for this country to entertain and accomplish. Everything invites emancipation. The grandeur of the design, the vast stake we hold; the national domain, the new importance of Liberia; the manifest interest of the slave states; the religious effort of the free states; the public opinion of the world;—all join to demand it.

We shall one day bring the States shoulder to shoulder and the citizens man to man to exterminate slavery. Why in the name of common sense and the peace of mankind is not this made the subject of instant negotiation and settlement? Why not end this dangerous dispute on some ground of fair compensation on one side, and satisfaction on the other to the conscience of the free states? It is really the great task fit for this country to accomplish, to buy that property of the planters, as the British nation bought the West Indian slaves. I say buy,—never conceding the right of the planter to own, but that we may acknowledge the calamity of his position, and bear a countryman's share in relieving him; and because it is the only practicable course, and is innocent. Here is a right social or public function, which one man cannot do, which all men must do. 'Tis said it will cost two thousand millions of dollars. Was there ever any contribution that was so enthusiastically paid as this will be? We will have a chimney-tax. We will give up our coaches, and wine, and watches. The churches will melt their plate. The father of his country shall wait, well pleased, a little longer for his monument; Franklin for his, the Pilgrim Fathers for theirs, and the patient Columbus for his. The mechanics will give, the needlewomen will give; the children will have cent-societies. Every man in the land will give a week's work to dig away this accursed mountain of sorrow once and forever out of the world.

Nothing is impracticable to this nation, which it shall set itself to do. Were ever men so endowed, so placed, so weaponed? Their power of territory seconded by a genius equal to every work. By new arts the earth is subdued, roaded, tunnelled, telegraphed, gas-lighted; vast amounts of old labor disused; the sinews of man being relieved by sinews of steam. We are on the brink of more wonders. The sun paints; presently we shall organize the echo, as now we do the shadow. Chemistry is extorting new aids. The genius of this people, it is found, can do anything which can be done by men. These thirty nations are equal to any work, and are every moment stronger. In twenty-five years they will be fifty millions. Is it not time to do something besides ditching and draining, and making the earth mellow and friable? Let them confront this mountain of poison,—bore, blast, excavate, pulverize and shovel it once for all, down into the bottomless pit. A thousand millions were cheap.

But grant that the heart of financiers, accustomed to practical figures, shrinks within them at these colossal amounts, and the embarrassments which complicate the problem; granting that these contingencies are too many to be spanned by any human geometry, and that these evils are to be relieved only by the wisdom of God working in ages,—and by what instrument, whether Liberia, whether flax-cotton, whether the working out this race by Irish and Germans, none can tell, or by what sources God has guarded his law; still the question recurs, What must we do? One thing is plain, we cannot answer for the Union, but we must keep Massachusetts true. It is of unspeakable importance that she play her honest part. She must follow no vicious examples. Massachusetts is a little state: countries have been great by ideas. Europe is little compared with Asia and Africa; yet Asia and Africa are its ox and its ass. Europe, the least of all the continents, has almost monopolized for twenty centuries the genius and power of them all. Greece was the least part of Europe. Attica a little part of that,—one tenth of the size of Massachusetts. Yet that district still rules the intellect of men. Judaea was a petty country. Yet these two, Greece and Judaea, furnish the mind and the heart by which the rest of the world is sustained; and Massachusetts is little, but, if true to itself, can be the brain which turns about the behemoth.

I say Massachusetts, but I mean Massachusetts in all the quarters of her dispersion; Massachusetts, as she is the mother of all the New England states, and as she sees her progeny scattered over the face of the land, in the farthest South, and the uttermost West. The immense power of rectitude is apt to be forgotten in politics. But they who have brought the great wrong on the country have not forgotten it. They avail themselves of the known probity and honor of Massachusetts, to endorse the statute. The ancient maxim still holds that never was any injustice effected except by the help of justice. The great game of the government has been to win the sanction of Massachusetts to the crime. Hitherto they have succeeded only so far as to win Boston to a certain extent. The behavior of Boston was the reverse of what it should have been: it was supple and officious, and it put itself into the base attitude of pander to the crime. It should have placed obstruction at every step. Let the attitude of the states be firm. Let us respect the Union to all honest ends. But also respect an older and wider union, the law of Nature and rectitude. Massachusetts is as strong as the Universe, when it does that. We will never intermeddle with your slavery,—but you can in no wise be suffered to bring it to Cape Cod and Berkshire. This law must be made inoperative. It must be abrogated and wiped out of the statute-book; but whilst it stands there, it must be disobeyed. We must make a small state great, by making every man in it true. It was the praise of Athens, "She could not lead countless armies into the field, but she knew how with a little band to defeat those who could." Every Roman reckoned himself at least a match for a Province. Every Dorian did. Every Englishman in Australia, in South Africa, in India, or in whatever barbarous country their forts and factories have been set up, represents London, represents the art, power and law of Europe. Every man educated at the Northern school carries the like advantages into the South. For it is confounding distinctions to speak of the geographic sections of this country as of equal civilization. Every nation and every man bows, in spite of himself, to a higher mental and moral existence; and the sting of the late disgraces is that this royal position of Massachusetts was foully lost, that the well-known sentiment of her people was not expressed. Let us correct this error. In this one fastness let truth be spoken and right done. Here let there be no confusion in our ideas. Let us not lie, not steal, nor help to steal, and let us not call stealing by any fine name, such as "Union" or "Patriotism." Let us know that not by the public, but by ourselves, our safety must be bought. That is the secret of Southern power, that they rest not on meetings, but on private heats and courages.

It is very certain from the perfect guaranties in the constitution, and the high arguments of the defenders of liberty, which the occasion called out, that there is sufficient margin in the statute and the law for the spirit of the Magistrate to show itself, and one, two, three occasions have just now occurred, and past, in either of which, if one man had felt the spirit of Coke or Mansfield or Parsons, and read the law with the eye of freedom, the dishonor of Massachusetts had been prevented, and a limit set to these encroachments forever.

CHAPTER 3

A WHITE ABOLITIONIST VIEW OF SLAVERY

Harriet Beecher Stowe: Uncle Tom's Cabin

*I*n 1852 the most controversial work of the inflamed pre-Civil War decade was published by Harriet Beecher Stowe (1811–1896). Uncle Tom's Cabin; or, Life Among the Lowly, *originally serialized in the abolitionist National Era in 1851, created an immediate sensation. Within a year's time over 300,000 copies were sold. Mrs. Stowe, the wife of a teacher at the Lane Seminary in Cincinnati, was almost wholly untrained as a writer, yet she possessed the zeal of the reformer. Her long residence in Cincinnati had brought her into contact with fugitive slaves and made her acutely aware of the conditions that existed under slavery south of the Ohio River. The passage of the Fugitive Slave Law of 1850 and the disorders that followed aroused her to write* Uncle Tom's Cabin. *The book represented the degree to which the sectional issues had become emotionalized and dramatized. The South was whipped into a furor of indignation by its appearance; in the North, the book helped to set the stage for the appearance of the anti-slavery Republican party two years later. The gulf of misunderstanding between the two sections was widened. The object of her book, Mrs. Stowe wrote, was to "awaken sympathy and feeling for the African race" and to show the "wrongs and sorrows" that existed under the "cruel and unjust" system of slavery. In achieving her object, she continued, she disclaimed any "invidious feeling" toward those Southerners who, through no fault of their own, had become involved with the institution. The book, however, failed as a rational appeal to moderate thinking Americans; instead it contributed to the heightening emotional atmosphere that would make a rational solution to the nation's problems impossible. When Mrs. Stowe visited Abraham Lincoln later in the White House, he referred to her as the "little woman who wrote the book that made this great war."*

Chapter V—Showing the Feelings of Living Property on Changing Owners

Mr. and Mrs. Shelby had retired to their apartment for the night. He was lounging in a large easy-chair, looking over some letters that had come in the afternoon mail, and she was standing before her mirror, brushing out the complicated braids and curls in which Eliza had arranged her hair; for, noticing her pale cheeks and haggard eyes, she had excused her attendance that night, and ordered her to bed. The employment, naturally enough, suggested her conversation with the girl in the morning; and, turning to her husband, she said, carelessly,

"By the by, Arthur, who was that low-bred fellow that you lugged in to our dinner-table to-day?"

"Haley is his name," said Shelby, turning himself rather uneasily in his chair, and continuing with his eyes fixed on a letter.

"Haley! Who is he, and what may be his business here, pray?"

"Well, he's a man that I transacted some business with, last time I was at Natchez," said Mr. Shelby.

"And he presumed on it to make himself quite at home, and call and dine here, ay?"

"Why, I invited him; I had some accounts with him," said Shelby.

"Is he a negro-trader?" said Mrs. Shelby, noticing a certain embarrassment in her husband's manner.

"Why, my dear, what put that into your head?" said Shelby, looking up.

"Nothing,—only Eliza came in here, after dinner, in a great worry, crying and taking on, and said you were talking with a trader, and that she heard him make an offer for her boy—the ridiculous little goose!"

"She did, hey?" said Mr. Shelby, returning to his paper, which he seemed for a few moments quite intent upon, not perceiving that he was holding it bottom upwards.

"It will have to come out," said he, mentally; "as well now as ever."

"I told Eliza," said Mrs. Shelby, as she continued brushing her hair, "that she was a little fool for her pains, and that you never had anything to do with that sort of persons. Of course, I knew you never meant to sell any of our people,—least of all, to such a fellow."

"Well, Emily," said her husband, "so I have always felt and said; but the fact is that my business lies so that I cannot get on without. I shall have to sell some of my hands."

"To that creature? Impossible! Mr. Shelby, you cannot be serious."

"I'm sorry to say that I am," said Mr. Shelby. "I've agreed to sell Tom."

"What! our Tom?—that good, faithful creature!—been your faithful servant from a boy! O, Mr. Shelby!—and you have promised him his freedom, too,—you and I have spoken to him a hundred times of it. Well, I can believe anything now,—I can believe *now* that you could sell little Harry, poor Eliza's only child!" said Mrs. Shelby, in a tone between grief and indignation.

"Well, since you must know all, it is so. I have agreed to sell Tom and Harry both; and I don't know why I am to be rated, as if I were a monster, for doing what every one does every day."

"But why, of all others, choose these?" said Mrs. Shelby. "Why sell them, of all on the place, if you must sell at all?"

"Because they will bring the highest sum of any,—that's why. I could choose another, if you say so. The fellow made me a high bid on Eliza, if that would suit you any better," said Mr. Shelby.

"The wretch!" said Mrs. Shelby, vehemently.

"Well, I didn't listen to it, a moment,—out of regard to your feelings, I wouldn't;—so give me some credit."

"My dear," said Mrs. Shelby, recollecting herself, "forgive me. I have been hasty. I was surprised, and entirely unprepared for this;—but surely you will allow me to intercede for these poor creatures. Tom is a noble-hearted, faithful fellow, if he is black. I do believe, Mr. Shelby, that if he were put to it, he would lay down his life for you."

"I know it,—I dare say;—but what's the use of all this? I can't help myself."

"Why not make a pecuniary sacrifice? I'm willing to bear my part of the inconvenience. O, Mr. Shelby, I have tried—tried most faithfully, as a Christian woman should—to do my duty to these poor, simple, dependent creatures. I have cared for them, instructed them, watched over them, and known all their little cares and joys, for years; and how can I ever hold up my head again among them, if, for the sake of a little paltry gain, we sell such a faithful, excellent, confiding creature as poor Tom, and tear from him in a moment all we have taught him to love and value? I have taught them the duties of the family, of parent and child, and husband and wife; and how can I bear to have this open acknowledgment that we care for no tie, no duty, no relation, however sacred, compared with money? I have talked with Eliza about her boy—her duty to him as a Christian mother, to watch over him, pray for him, and bring him up in a Christian way; and now what can I say, if you tear him away, and sell him, soul and body, to a profane, unprincipled man, just to save a little money? I have told her that one soul is worth more than all the money in the world; and how will she believe me when she sees us turn round and sell her child?—sell him, perhaps, to certain ruin of body and soul!"

"I'm sorry you feel so about it, Emily,—indeed I am," said Mr. Shelby; "and I respect your feelings, too, though I don't pretend to share them to their full extent; but I tell you now, solemnly, it's of no use—I can't help myself. I didn't mean to tell you this, Emily; but, in plain words, there is no choice between selling these two and selling everything. Either they must go, or *all* must. Haley has come into possession of a mortgage, which, if I don't clear off with him directly, will take everything before it. I've raked, and scraped, and borrowed, and all but begged,—and the price of these two was needed to make up the balance, and I had to give them up. Haley fancied the child; he agreed to settle the matter that way, and no other. I was in his power, and *had* to do it. If you feel so to have them sold, would it be any better to have *all* sold?"

Mrs. Shelby stood like one stricken. Finally, turning to her toilet, she rested her face in her hands, and gave a sort of groan.

"This is God's curse on slavery!—a bitter, bitter, most accursed thing!—a curse to the master and a curse to the slave! I was a fool to think I could make anything good out of such a deadly evil. It is a sin to hold a slave under laws like ours,—I always felt it was,—I always thought so when I was a girl,—I thought so still more after I joined the church; but I thought I could gild it over,—I thought, by kindness, and care, and instruction, I could make the condition of mine better than freedom—fool that I was!"

"Why, wife, you are getting to be an abolitionist, quite."

"Abolitionist! if they knew all I know about slavery they *might* talk! We don't need them to tell us; you know I never thought that slavery was right—never felt willing to own slaves."

"Well, therein you differ from many wise and pious men," said Mr. Shelby. "You remember Mr. B.'s sermon, the other Sunday?"

"I don't want to hear such sermons; I never wish to hear Mr. B. in our church again. Ministers can't help the evil, perhaps, can't cure it, any more than we can,—but defend it!—it always went against my common sense. And I think you didn't think much of that sermon, either."

"Well," said Shelby, "I must say these ministers sometimes carry matters further than we poor sinners would exactly dare to do. We men of the world must wink pretty hard at various things, and get used to a deal that isn't the exact thing. But we don't quite fancy, when women and ministers come out broad and square, and go beyond us in matters of either modesty or morals, that's a fact. But now, my dear, I trust you see the necessity of the thing, and you see that I have done the very best that circumstances would allow."

"O yes, yes!" said Mrs. Shelby, hurriedly and abstractedly fingering her gold watch,—"I haven't any jewelry of any amount," she added, thoughtfully; "but would not this watch do something?—it was an expensive one, when it was bought. If I could only at least save Eliza's child, I would sacrifice anything I have."

"I'm sorry, very sorry, Emily," said Mr. Shelby, "I'm sorry this takes hold of you so; but it will do no good. The fact is, Emily, the thing's done; the bills of sale are already signed, and in Haley's hands; and you must be thankful it is no worse. That man has had it in his power to ruin us all,—and now he is fairly off. If you knew the man as I do, you'd think that we had had a narrow escape."

"Is he so hard, then?"

"Why, not a cruel man, exactly, but a man of leather,—a man alive to nothing but trade and profit,—cool, and unhesitating, and unrelenting, as death and the grave. He'd sell his own mother at a good per centage—not wishing the old woman any harm, either."

"And this wretch owns that good, faithful Tom, and Eliza's child!"

"Well, my dear, the fact is that this goes rather hard with me; it's a thing I hate to think of. Haley wants to drive matters, and take possession to-morrow. I'm going to get out my horse bright and early, and be off. I can't see Tom, that's a fact; and you had better arrange a drive somewhere, and carry Eliza off. Let the thing be done when she is out of sight."

"No, no," said Mrs. Shelby; "I'll be in no sense accomplice or help in this cruel business. I'll go and see poor old Tom, God help him, in his distress! They shall see, at any rate, that their mistress can feel for and with them. As to Eliza, I dare not think about it. The Lord forgive us! What have we done, that this cruel necessity should come on us?"

There was one listener to this conversation whom Mr. and Mrs. Shelby little suspected.

Communicating with their apartment was a large closet, opening by a door into the outer passage. When Mrs. Shelby had dismissed Eliza for the night, her feverish and excited mind had suggested the idea of this closet; and she had hidden herself there, and, with her ear pressed close against the crack of the door, had lost not a word of the conversation.

When the voices died into silence, she rose and crept stealthily away. Pale, shivering, with rigid features and compressed lips, she looked an entirely altered being from the soft and timid creature she had been hitherto. She moved cautiously along the entry, paused one moment at her mistress' door, and raised her hands in mute appeal to Heaven, and then turned and glided into her own room. It was a quiet, neat apartment, on the same floor with her mistress. There was the pleasant sunny window, where she had often sat singing at her sewing; there a little case of books, and various little fancy articles, ranged by them, the gifts of Christmas holidays; there was her simple wardrobe in the closet and in the drawers:—here was, in short, her home; and, on the whole, a happy one it had been to her. But there, on the bed, lay her slumbering boy, his long curls falling negligently around his unconscious face, his rosy mouth half open, his little fat hands thrown out over the bedclothes, and a smile spread like a sunbeam over his whole face.

"Poor boy! poor fellow!" said Eliza; "they have sold you! but your mother will save you yet!"

No tear dropped over that pillow; in such straits as these, the heart has no tears to give,—it drops only blood, bleeding itself away in silence. She took a piece of paper and a pencil, and wrote, hastily,

"O, Missis! dear Missis! don't think me ungrateful,—don't think hard of me, any way,—I heard all you and master said to-night. I am going to try to save my boy—you will not blame me! God bless and reward you for all your kindness!"

Hastily folding and directing this, she went to a drawer and made up a little package of clothing for her boy, which she tied with a hand-kerchief firmly round her waist; and, so fond is a mother's remem-brance, that, even in the terrors of that hour, she did not forget to put in the little package one or two of his favorite toys, reserving a gayly painted parrot to amuse him, when she should be called on to awaken him. It was some trouble to arouse the little sleeper; but, after some effort, he sat up, and was playing with his bird, while his mother was putting on her bonnet and shawl.

"Where are you going, mother?" said he, as she drew near the bed, with his little coat and cap.

His mother drew near, and looked so earnestly into his eyes, that he at once divined that something unusual was the matter.

"Hush, Harry," she said; "mustn't speak loud, or they will hear us. A wicked man was coming to take little Harry away from his mother, and carry him 'way off in the dark; but mother won't let him—she's going to put on her little boy's cap and coat, and run off with him, so the ugly man can't catch him."

Saying these words, she had tied and buttoned on the child's sim-ple outfit, and, taking him in her arms, she whispered to him to be very still; and, opening a door in her room which led into the outer verandah, she glided noiselessly out.

It was a sparkling, frosty, star-light night, and the mother wrapped the shawl close round her child, as, perfectly quiet with vague terror, he clung round her neck.

Old Bruno, a great Newfoundland, who slept at the end of the porch, rose, with a low growl, as she came near. She gently spoke his name, and the animal, an old pet and playmate of hers, instantly, wagging his tail, prepared to follow her, though apparently revolving much, in his simple dog's head, what such an indiscreet midnight promenade might mean. Some dim ideas of imprudence or impro-priety in the measure seemed to embarrass him considerably; for he often stopped, as Eliza glided forward, and looked wistfully, first at her and then at the house, and then, as if reassured by reflection, he pattered along after her again. A few minutes brought them to the window of Uncle Tom's cottage, and Eliza, stopping, tapped lightly on the window-pane.

The prayer-meeting at Uncle Tom's had, in the order of hymn-singing, been protracted to a very late hour; and, as Uncle Tom had indulged himself in a few lengthy solos afterwards, the consequence was, that, although it was now between twelve and one o'clock, he and his worthy helpmeet were not yet asleep.

"Good Lord! what's that?" said Aunt Chloe, starting up and hastily drawing the curtain. "My sakes alive, if it an't Lizy! Get on your clothes, old man, quick!—there's old Bruno, too, a pawin' round; what on airth! I'm gwine to open the door."

And, suiting the action to the word, the door flew open, and the light of the tallow candle, which Tom had hastily lighted, fell on the haggard face and dark, wild eyes of the fugitive.

"Lord bless you! —I'm skeered to look at ye, Lizy! Are ye tuck sick, or what's come over ye?"

"I'm running away—Uncle Tom and Aunt Chloe—carrying off my child—Master sold him!"

"Sold him?" echoed both, lifting up their hands in dismay.

"Yes, sold him!" said Eliza, firmly; "I crept into the closet by Mistress' door to-night, and I heard Master tell Missis that he had sold my Harry, and you, Uncle Tom, both, to a trader; and that he was going off this morning on his horse, and that the man was to take possession to-day."

Tom had stood, during this speech, with his hands raised, and his eyes dilated, like a man in a dream. Slowly and gradually, as its meaning came over him, he collapsed, rather than seated himself, on his old chair, and sunk his head down upon his knees.

"The good Lord have pity on us!" said Aunt Chloe. "O! it don't seem as if it was true! What has he done, that Mas'r should sell *him?*"

"He hasn't done anything,—it isn't for that. Master don't want to sell; and Missis—she's always good. I heard her plead and beg for us; but he told her 'twas no use; that he was in this man's debt, and that this man had got the power over him; and that if he didn't pay him off clear, it would end in his having to sell the place and all the people, and move off. Yes, I heard him say there was no choice between selling these two and selling all, the man was driving him so hard. Master said he was sorry; but oh, Missis—you ought to have heard her talk! If she an't a Christian and an angel, there never was one. I'm a wicked girl to leave her so; but, then, I can't help it. She said, herself, one soul was worth more than the world; and this boy has a soul, and if I let him be carried off, who knows what'll become of it? It must be right: but, if it an't right, the Lord forgive me, for I can't help doing it!"

"Well, old man!" said Aunt Chloe, "why don't you go, too? Will you wait to be toted down river, where they kill niggers with hard work and starving? I'd a heap rather die than go there, any day! There's time for ye,—be off with Lizy,—you've got a pass to come and go any time. Come, bustle up, and I'll get your things together."

Tom slowly raised his head, and looked sorrowfully but quietly around, and said,

"No, no—I an't going. Let Eliza go—it's her right! I wouldn't be the one to say no—tan't in *natur* for her to stay; but you heard what she said! If I must be sold, or all the people on the place, and everything go to rack, why, let me be sold. I s'pose I can b'ar it as well as any on 'em," he added, while something like a sob and a sigh shook his broad, rough chest convulsively. "Mas'r always found me on the spot—he always will. I never have broke trust, nor used my pass no ways contrary to my word, and I never will. It's better for me alone to go, than to break up the place and sell all. Mas'r an't to blame, Chloe, and he'll take care of you and the poor—"

Here he turned to the rough trundle-bed full of little woolly heads, and broke fairly down. He leaned over the back of the chair, and covered his face with his large hands. Sobs, heavy, hoarse and loud, shook the chair, and great tears fell through his fingers on the floor: just such tears, sir, as you dropped into the coffin where lay your first-born son; such tears, woman, as you shed when you heard the cries of your dying babe. For, sir, he was a man,—and you are but another man. And, woman, though dressed in silk and jewels, you are but a woman, and, in life's great straits and mighty griefs, ye feel but one sorrow!

"And now," said Eliza, as she stood in the door, "I saw my husband only this afternoon, and I little knew then what was to come. They have pushed him to the very last standing place, and he told me, to-day, that he was going to run away. Do try, if you can, to get word to him. Tell him how I went, and why I went; and tell him I'm going to try and find Canada. You must give my love to him, and tell him, if I never see him again,"—she turned away, and stood with her back to them for a moment, and then added, in a husky voice, "tell him to be as good as he can, and try and meet me in the kingdom of heaven."

"Call Bruno in there," she added. "Shut the door on him, poor beast! He mustn't go with me!"

A few last words and tears, a few simple adieus and blessings, and, clasping her wondering and affrighted child in her arms, she glided noiselessly away.

CHAPTER 4

A BLACK ABOLITIONIST VIEW
OF SLAVERY

Frederick Douglass:
"What to the Slave Is the Fourth of July?"

*F*rederick Douglass (1817–1895) was born a slave in Maryland. As a
household servant during childhood, he learned to read. Later his owner
sent him to Baltimore as apprentice to a ship caulker. In 1838, he made an
attempt to escape, his second, and this time he succeeded, disguising himself
as a sailor and finding his way to New York. Douglass began lecturing about
slavery, impressing crowds with his persuasive rhetoric and oratorical ability. In 1845 he published an autobiography entitled Narrative of the Life of
Frederick Douglass, an American Slave. *Making his home in Rochester,
New York, he began a newspaper called* North Star. *By the 1850s Douglass
was the most famous black man in America. In this speech, delivered to the
Rochester Ladies Anti-Slavery Society in 1852, Douglass used a holiday
white Americans hold as sacred and pointed out the mockery that slavery
made of Jefferson's natural rights philosophy.*

. . . [T]he 4th of July. It is the birthday of your National Independence,
and of your political freedom. This, to you, is what the Passover was
to the emancipated people of God. It carries your minds back to the
day, and to the act of your great deliverance; and to the signs, and to
the wonders, associated with that act, and that day. This celebration
also marks the beginning of another year of your national life; and
reminds you that the Republic of America is now 76 years old. I am
glad, fellow-citizens, that your nation is so young. Seventy-six years,
though a good old age for a man, is but a mere speck in the life of a
nation. Three score years and ten is the allotted time for individual
men; but nations number their years by thousands. According to this
fact, you are, even now, only in the beginning of your national career,
still lingering in the period of childhood. I repeat, I am glad this is so.

There is hope in the thought, and hope is much needed, under the dark clouds which lower above the horizon. The eye of the reformer is met with angry flashes, portending disastrous times; but his heart may well beat lighter at the thought that America is young, and that she is still in the impressible stage of her existence. May he not hope that high lessons of wisdom, of justice and of truth, will yet give direction to her destiny? Were the nation older, the patriot's heart might be sadder, and the reformer's brow heavier. Its future might be shrouded in gloom, and the hope of its prophets go out in sorrow. There is consolation in the thought that America is young. . . .

Fellow-citizens, I shall not presume to dwell at length on the associations that cluster about this day. The simple story of it is that, 76 years ago, the people of the country were British subjects. The style and title of your "sovereign people" (in which you now glory) was not then born. You were under the British Crown. . . . But, your fathers, who had not adopted the fashionable idea of this day, of the infallibility of government and the absolute character of its acts, presumed to differ from the home government in respect to the wisdom and the justice of some of those burdens and restraints. They went so far in their excitement as to pronounce the measures of government unjust, unreasonable, and oppressive, and altogether such as ought not to be quietly submitted to. I scarcely need say, fellow-citizens, that my opinion of those measures fully accords with that of your fathers. . . .

Feeling themselves harshly and unjustly treated by the home government, your fathers, like men of honesty, and men of spirit, earnestly sought redress. They petitioned and remonstrated; they did so in a decorous, respectful, and loyal manner. Their conduct was wholly unexceptionable. This, however, did not answer the purpose. They saw themselves treated with sovereign indifference, coldness and scorn. Yet they persevered. They were not the men to look back. . . .

Oppression makes a wise man mad. Your fathers were wise men, and if they did not go mad, they became restive under this treatment. They felt themselves the victims of grievous wrongs, wholly incurable in the colonial capacity. With brave men there is always a remedy for oppression. Just here, the idea of a total separation of the colonies from the crown was born! It was a startling idea, much more so, than we, at this distance of time, regard it. The timid and the prudent (as has been intimated) of that time, were, of course, shocked and alarmed by it. . . .

On the 2d of July, 1776, the old Continental Congress, to the dismay of the lovers of ease, and the worshippers of property, clothed that dreadful idea with the authority of national sanction. . . . They succeeded; and to-day you reap the fruits of their success. The freedom gained is yours; and you, therefore, may properly celebrate this anniversary.

Fellow Citizens, I am not wanting in respect for the fathers of this republic. The signers of the Declaration of Independence were brave men. They were great men too—great enough to give fame to a great age. It does not often happen to a nation to raise, at one time, such a number of truly great men. . . . They were statesmen, patriots and heroes, and for the good they did, and the principles they contended for, I will unite with you to honor their memory. . . .

THE PRESENT

My business, if I have any here to-day, is with the present. The accepted time with God and his cause is the ever-living now. . . . We have to do with the past only as we can make it useful to the present and to the future. . . .

Fellow-citizens, pardon me, allow me to ask, why am I called upon to speak here to-day? . . .

I am not included within the pale of this glorious anniversary! Your high independence only reveals the immeasurable distance between us. The blessings in which you, this day, rejoice, are not enjoyed in common. The rich inheritance of justice, liberty, prosperity and independence, bequeathed by your fathers, is shared by you, not by me. The sunlight that brought life and healing to you, has brought stripes and death to me. This Fourth [of] July is *yours*, not *mine*. *You* may rejoice, *I* must mourn. To drag a man in fetters into the grand illuminated temple of liberty, and call upon him to join you in joyous anthems, were inhuman mockery and sacrilegious irony. . . .

Fellow-citizens; above your national, tumultuous joy, I hear the mournful wail of millions! whose chains, heavy and grievous yesterday, are, to-day, rendered more intolerable by the jubilee shouts that reach them. If I do forget, if I do not faithfully remember those bleeding children of sorrow this day, "may my right hand forget her cunning, and may my tongue cleave to the roof of my mouth!" To forget them, to pass lightly over their wrongs, and to chime in with the popular theme, would be treason most scandalous and shocking, and would make me a reproach before God and the world. My subject, then fellow-citizens, is AMERICAN SLAVERY. I shall see, this day, and its popular characteristics, from the slave's point of view. Standing there, identified with the American bondsman, making his wrongs mine, I do not hesitate to declare, with all my soul, that the character and conduct of this nation never looked blacker to me than on this 4th of July! Whether we turn to the declarations of the past, or to the professions of the present, the conduct of the nation seems equally hideous and revolting. America is false to the past, false to the present, and solemnly binds herself to be false to the future. Standing with God and the crushed and bleeding slave on this occasion, I will, in the name of humanity which is outraged, in the name of liberty which is fettered, in the name of the constitution and the Bible, which are disregarded and trampled upon, dare to call in question and to denounce, with all the emphasis I can command, everything that serves to perpetuate slavery—the great sin and shame of America! "I will not equivocate; I will not excuse;" I will use the severest language I can command; and yet no one word shall escape me that any man, whose judgement is not blinded by prejudice, or who is not at heart a slaveholder, shall not confess to be right and just.

But I fancy I hear some one of my audience say, it is just in this circumstance that you and your brother abolitionists fail to make a favorable impression on the public mind. Would you argue more, and denounce less, would you persuade more, and rebuke less, your cause would be much more likely to succeed. But, I submit, where all is plain there is nothing to be argued. What point in the anti-slavery creed would you have me argue? On what branch of the subject do the people of this country need light? Must I undertake to prove that the slave is a man? This point is conceded already. Nobody doubts it. The slaveholders themselves acknowledge it in the enactment of laws for their government. . . .

What, am I to argue that it is wrong to make men brutes, to rob them of their liberty, to work them without wages, to keep them ignorant of their relations to their fellow men, to beat them with sticks, to flay their flesh with the lash, to load their limbs with irons, to hunt them with dogs, to sell them at auction, to sunder their families, to knock out their teeth, to burn their flesh, to starve them into obedience and submission to their masters? Must I argue that a system thus marked with blood, and stained with pollution, is *wrong*? No! I will not. I have better employments for my time and strength, than such arguments would imply.

What, then, remains to be argued? Is it that slavery is not divine; that God did not establish it; that our doctors of divinity are mistaken? There is blasphemy in the thought. That which is inhuman, cannot be divine! *Who* can reason on such a proposition? They that can, may; I cannot. The time for such argument is past.

At a time like this, scorching irony, not convincing argument, is needed. O! had I the ability, and could I reach the nation's ear, I would, to-day, pour out a fiery stream of biting ridicule, blasting reproach, withering sarcasm, and stern rebuke. For it is not light that is needed, but fire; it is not the gentle shower, but thunder. We need the storm, the whirlwind, and the earthquake. The feeling of the nation must be quickened; the conscience of the nation must be roused; the propriety of the nation must be startled; the hypocrisy of the nation must be exposed; and its crimes against God and man must be proclaimed and denounced.

What, to the American slave, is your 4th of July? I answer: a day that reveals to him, more than all other days in the year, the gross injustice and cruelty to which he is the constant victim. To him, your celebration is a sham; your boasted liberty, an unholy license; your national greatness, swelling vanity; your sounds of rejoicing are empty and heartless; your denunciations of tyrants, brass fronted impudence; your shouts of liberty and equality, hollow mockery; your prayers and hymns, your sermons and thanksgivings, and all your religious parade, and solemnity, are, to him, mere bombast, fraud, deception, impiety, and hypocrisy—a thin veil to cover up crimes which would disgrace a nation of savages. There is not a nation on earth guilty of practices, more shocking and bloody, than are the people of these United States, at this very hour.

Go where you may, search where you will, roam through all the monarchies and despotisms of the old world, travel through South America, search out every abuse, and when you have found the last, lay your facts by the side of the everyday practices of this nation, and you will say with me, that, for revolting barbarity and shameless hypocrisy, America reigns without rival.

The Internal Slave Trade

Take the American slave-trade, which, we are told by the papers, is especially prosperous just now. . . . Behold the practical operation of the internal slave-trade, the American slave-trade, sustained by American politics and American religion. Here you will see men and women reared like swine for the market. You know what is a swine-drover? I will show you a man-drover. They inhabit all our Southern States. They perambulate the country, and crowd the highways of the nation, with droves of human stock. You will see one of these human flesh-jobbers, armed with a pistol, whip and bowie-knife, driving a company of a hundred men, women, and children, from the Potomac to the slave market at New Orleans. . . .

I was born amid such sights and scenes. To me the American slave-trade is a terrible reality. When a child, my soul was often pierced with a sense of its horrors. I lived on Philpot Street, Fell's Point, Baltimore, and have watched from the wharves, the slave ships in the Basin, anchored from the shore, with their cargoes of human flesh, waiting for favorable winds to waft them down the Chesapeake. There was, at that time, a grand slave mart kept at the head of Pratt Street, by Austin Woldfolk. His agents were sent into every town and county in Maryland, announcing their arrival, through the papers, and on flaming *"hand-bills,"* headed Cash for Negroes. These men were generally well dressed men, and very captivating in their manners. Ever ready to drink, to treat, and to gamble. The fate of many a slave has depended upon the turn of a single card; and many a child has been snatched from the arms of its mother by bargains arranged in a state of brutal drunkenness.

The flesh-mongers gather up their victims by dozens, and drive them, chained, to the general depot at Baltimore. When a sufficient number have been collected here, a ship is chartered, for the purpose of conveying the forlorn crew to Mobile, or to New Orleans. From the slave prison to the ship, they are usually driven in the darkness of night; for since the anti-slavery agitation, a certain caution is observed.

In the deep still darkness of midnight, I have been often aroused by the dead heavy footsteps, and the piteous cries of the chained gangs

that passed our door. The anguish of my boyish heart was intense. . . .
Fellow-citizens, this murderous traffic is, to-day, in active operation
in this boasted republic. In the solitude of my spirit, I see clouds of
dust raised on the highways of the South; I see the bleeding footsteps;
I hear the doleful wail of fettered humanity, on the way to the slave-
markets, where the victims are to be sold like *horses, sheep,* and *swine,*
knocked off to the highest bidder. . . .

By an act of the American Congress, not yet two years old, slavery
has been nationalized in its most horrible and revolting form. By that
act, Mason & Dixon's line has been obliterated. . . . The Fugitive Slave
Law makes MERCY TO THEM, A CRIME; and bribes the judge who tries
them. . . . The oath of any two villains is sufficient, under this hell-
black enactment, to send the most pious and exemplary black man
into the remorseless jaws of slavery! His own testimony is nothing.
He can bring no witnesses for himself. The minister of American justice is bound by law to hear but *one* side; and *that* side, is the side of
the oppressor. . . .

THE CHURCH RESPONSIBLE

But the church of this country is not only indifferent to the wrongs
of the slave, it actually takes sides with the oppressors. It has made
itself the bulwark of American slavery, and the shield of American
slave-hunters. Many of its most eloquent Divines, who stand as the
very lights of the church, have shamelessly given the sanction of religion and the Bible to the whole slave system. They have taught that
man may, properly, be a slave; that the relation of master and slave is
ordained of God; that to send back an escaped bondman to his master
is clearly the duty of all the followers of the Lord Jesus Christ; and this
horrible blasphemy is palmed off upon the world for Christianity. . . .

Let the religious press, the pulpit, the Sunday school, the conference meeting, the great ecclesiastical, missionary, Bible and tract
associations of the land array their immense powers against slavery
and slave-holding; and the whole system of crime and blood would
be scattered to the winds; and that they do not do this involves them
in the most awful responsibility of which the mind can conceive. . . .

Americans! your republican politics, not less than your republican
religion, are flagrantly inconsistent. You boast of your love of liberty,
your superior civilization, and your pure Christianity, while the whole

political power of the nation (as embodied in the two great political parties), is solemnly pledged to support and perpetuate the enslavement of three millions of your countrymen. You hurl your anathemas at the crowned headed tyrants of Russia and Austria, and pride yourselves on your Democratic institutions, while you yourselves consent to be the mere *tools* and *bodyguards* of the tyrants of Virginia and Carolina. . . . You declare, before the world, and are understood by the world to declare, that you *"hold these truths to be self evident, that all men are created equal"* . . . and yet, you hold securely, in a bondage which, according to your own Thomas Jefferson, *"is worse than ages of that which your fathers rose in rebellion to oppose," a seventh part* of the inhabitants of your country.

Fellow-citizens! I will not enlarge further on your national inconsistencies. The existence of slavery in this country brands your republicanism as a sham, your humanity as a base pretense, and your Christianity as a lie. It destroys your moral power abroad; it corrupts your politicians at home. It saps the foundation of religion; it makes your name a hissing, and a by-word to a mocking earth. It is the antagonistic force in your government, the only thing that seriously disturbs and endangers your *Union.* . . .

THE CONSTITUTION

But it is answered in reply to all this, that precisely what I have now denounced is, in fact, guaranteed and sanctioned by the Constitution of the United States; that the right to hold and to hunt slaves is a part of that Constitution framed by the illustrious Fathers of this Republic. . . . Fellow-citizens! there is no matter in respect to which, the people of the North have allowed themselves to be so ruinously imposed upon, as that of the pro-slavery character of the Constitution. In *that* instrument I hold there is neither warrant, license, nor sanction of the hateful thing; but, interpreted as it *ought* to be interpreted, the CONSTITUTION IS A GLORIOUS LIBERTY DOCUMENT. Read its preamble, consider its purposes. Is slavery among them? Is it at the gateway? or is it in the temple? It is neither. While I do not intend to argue this question on the present occasion, let me ask, if it be not somewhat singular that, if the Constitution were intended to be, by its framers and adopters, a slave-holding instrument, why neither *slavery, slaveholding,* nor *slave* can anywhere be found in it. . . .

Now, take the Constitution according to its plain reading, and I defy the presentation of a single pro-slavery clause in it. On the other hand it will be found to contain principles and purposes, entirely hostile to the existence of slavery. . . .

Allow me to say, in conclusion, notwithstanding the dark picture I have this day presented of the state of the nation, I do not despair of this country. There are forces in operation, which must inevitably work the downfall of slavery. *"The arm of the Lord is not shortened,"* and the doom of slavery is certain. I, therefore, leave off where I began, with *hope*. While drawing encouragement from the Declaration of Independence, the great principles it contains, and the genius of American Institutions . . . .

CHAPTER 5

Popular Sovereignty
or Congressional Dictation

Stephen A. Douglas:
Speech on the Kansas-Nebraska Bill

*S*tephen *A. Douglas (1813–1861) was not only the most prominent but
also the most controversial of America's political leaders in the decade
preceding the Civil War. Elected to Congress from Illinois in 1843 and elevated to the United States Senate four years later, Douglas became the leading figure in the Democratic Party during the last years of sectional conflict.
As chairman of the committee on territories in both House and Senate, he
became directly involved in the explosive issue of slavery and expansion.
Douglas's solution to the slavery question was popular sovereignty—the
people of each territory should decide for themselves whether or not they
should have slavery. He played an important role in the passage of the Compromise of 1850 and was successful in applying popular sovereignty to Utah
and New Mexico territories. In 1854 Douglas introduced the Kansas-
Nebraska Act, organizing those territories out of the vast area west of Missouri and Iowa according to his principle of popular sovereignty. Because the
territories lay in the area covered by the old Missouri Compromise of 1820,
Douglas's act explicitly repealed that former legislation. His action immediately aroused the bitter hostility of anti-slavery men in the North who
regarded the repeal as the betrayal of a sacred compact. Among those who
assailed Douglas were several senators and congressmen, including Charles
Sumner and Salmon P. Chase, who issued the "Appeal of the Independent
Democrats" shortly after Douglas introduced his bill. On January 30, 1854,
Douglas answered their attack in the selection that follows.*

M r. President, when I proposed on Tuesday last that the Senate
should proceed to the consideration of the bill to organize the
Territories of Nebraska and Kansas, it was my purpose only to
occupy ten or fifteen minutes in explanation of its provisions. I

desired to refer to two points: first, as to those provisions relating to the Indians; and second, to those which might be supposed to bear upon the question of slavery.

The committee, in drafting this bill, had in view the great anxiety which had been expressed by some members of the Senate to protect the rights of the Indians, and prevent infringements upon them. By the provisions of the bill, I think we have so clearly succeeded in that respect as to obviate all possible objection upon that score. The bill itself provides that it shall not operate upon any of the rights of the lands of the Indians; nor shall they be included within the limits of those Territories, until they shall, by treaty with the United States, expressly consent to come under the operations of the act, and be incorporated within the limits of the Territories. This provision certainly is broad enough, clear enough, explicit enough, to protect all the rights of the Indians as to their persons and their property.

Upon the other point—that pertaining to the question of slavery in the Territories—it was the intention of the committee to be equally explicit. We took the principles established by the compromise act of 1850 as our guide, and intended to make each and every provision of the bill accord with those principles. Those measures established and rest upon the great principle of self-government—that the people should be allowed to decide the questions of their domestic institutions for themselves, subject only to such limitations and restrictions as are imposed by the Constitution of the United States, instead of having them determined by an arbitrary or geographical line.

The original bill reported by the committee, as a substitute for the bill introduced by the Senator from Iowa (Mr. Dodge) was believed to have accomplished this object. The amendment which was subsequently reported by us was only designed to render that clear and specific which seemed, in the minds of some, to admit of doubt and misconstruction. In some parts of the country the original substitute was deemed and construed to be an annulment or a repeal of what has been known as the Missouri compromise, while in other parts it was otherwise construed. As the object of the committee was to conform to the principles established by the compromise measures of 1850, and to carry those principles into effect in the Territories, we thought it was better to recite in the bill precisely what we understood to have been accomplished by those measures, viz.: That the

Missouri compromise, having been superseded by the legislation of 1850, has become inoperative, and hence we propose to leave the question to the people of the States and the Territories, subject only to the limitations and provisions of the Constitution.

Sir, this is all that I intended to say, if the question had been taken up for consideration on Tuesday last; but since that time occurrences have transpired which compel me to go more fully into the discussion. It will be borne in mind that the Senator from Ohio (Mr. Chase) then objected to the consideration of the bill, and asked for its postponement until this day, on the ground that there had not been time to understand and consider its provisions; and the Senator from Massachusetts (Mr. Sumner) suggested that the postponement should be for one week, for that purpose. These suggestions seeming to be reasonable to Senators around me, I yielded to their request, and consented to the postponement of the bill until this day.

Sir, little did I suppose at the time that I granted that act of courtesy to those two Senators, that they had drafted and published to the world a document, over their own signatures, in which they arraigned me as having been guilty of a criminal betrayal of my trust, as having been guilty of an act of bad faith, and been engaged in an atrocious plot against the cause of free government. Little did I suppose that those two Senators had been guilty of such conduct when they called upon me to grant that courtesy, to give them an opportunity of investigating the substitute reported from the committee. I have since discovered that on that very morning the *National Era*, the Abolition organ in this city, contained an address, signed by certain Abolition confederates, to the people, in which the bill is grossly misrepresented, in which the action of the members of the committee is grossly falsified, in which our motives are arraigned, and our characters calumniated. And, sir, what is more, I find that there was a postscript added to the address, published that very morning, in which the principal amendment reported by the committee was set out, and then coarse epithets applied to me by name. Sir, had I known those facts at the time I granted that act of indulgence, I should have responded to the request of those Senators in such terms as their conduct deserved, so far as the rules of the Senate, and a respect for my own character, would have permitted me to do. . . .

The argument of this manifesto is predicated upon the assumption that the policy of the fathers of the Republic was to prohibit slavery in all the territory ceded by the old States to the Union and made United States territory, for the purpose of being organized into new States. I take issue upon that statement. Such was not the practice in the early history of the Government. It is true that in the territory northwest of the Ohio river slavery was prohibited by the ordinance of 1787; but it is also true that in the territory south of the Ohio river, to wit, the Territory of Tennessee, slavery was permitted and protected; and it is also true, that in the organization of the Territory of Mississippi, in 1798, the provisions of the ordinance of 1787 were applied to it, with the exception of the sixth article, which prohibited slavery. Then, sir, you find upon the statute-books under Washington and the early Presidents, provisions of law showing that in the southwestern territories the right to hold slaves was clearly implied or recognized, while in the northwest territories it was prohibited. The only conclusion that can be fairly and honestly drawn from that legislation is, that it was the policy of the fathers of the Republic to prescribe a line of demarkation between free territories and slaveholding territories by a natural or a geographical line, being sure to make that line correspond, as near as might be, to the laws of climate, of production, and probably of all those other causes that would control the institution and make it either desirable or undesirable to the people inhabiting the respective territories.

Sir, I wish you to bear in mind, too, that this geographical line established by the founders of the Republic, between free Territories and slave Territories, extended as far westward as our territory then reached, the object being to avoid all agitation upon the slavery question by settling that question forever, so far as our territory extended, which was then to the Mississippi river.

When, in 1803, we acquired from France the Territory known as Louisiana, it became necessary to legislate for the protection of the inhabitants residing therein. It will be seen by looking into the bill establishing the territorial government in 1805 for the Territory of New Orleans, embracing the same country now known as the State of Louisiana, that the ordinance of 1787 was expressly extended to that Territory, excepting the sixth section, which prohibited slavery. Then that act implied that the Territory of New Orleans was to be a slaveholding Territory by making that exception in the law. But, Sir, when they came to form what was then called the Territory of Louisiana, subsequently known as the Territory of Missouri, north of the thirty-third parallel, they used different language. They did not extend the ordinance of 1787 to it at all. They first provided that it should be governed by laws made by the governor and the judges; and when, in 1812, Congress gave to that Territory, under the name of the Territory of Missouri, a territorial government, the people were allowed to do as they pleased upon the subject of slavery, subject only to the limitations of the Constitution of the United States. Now, what is the inference from that legislation? That slavery was, by implication, recognized South of the thirty-third parallel, and north of that the people were left to exercise their own judgment and do as they pleased upon the subject, without any implication for or against the existence of the institution.

This continued to be the condition of the country in the Missouri Territory up to 1820, when the celebrated act which is now called the Missouri compromise act was passed. Slavery did not exist in, nor was it excluded from, the country now known as Nebraska. There was no code of laws upon the subject of slavery either way: First, for the reason that slavery had never been introduced into Louisiana, and established by positive enactment. It had grown up there by a sort of common law, and been supported and protected. When a common law grows up, when an institution becomes established under a usage, it carries it so far as that usage actually goes, and no further. If it had been established by direct enactment, it might have carried it so far as the political jurisdiction extended; but, be that as it may, by the act of 1812, creating the Territory of Missouri, that Territory was allowed to legislate upon the subject of slavery as it saw proper, subject only to the limitations which I have stated; and the country not inhabited or thrown open to settlement was set apart as Indian country, and rendered subject to Indian laws. Hence the local legislation of the State of Missouri did not reach into that Indian country, but was excluded from it by the Indian code and Indian laws. The municipal regulations of Missouri could not go there until the Indian title had been extinguished, and the country thrown open to settlement. Such being the case, the only legislation in existence in

Nebraska Territory at the time that the Missouri act passed, namely, the 6th of March, 1820, was a provision in effect, that the people should be allowed to do as they pleased upon the subject of slavery.

The Territory of Missouri having been left in that legal condition, positive opposition was made to the bill to organize a State government, with a view to its admission into the Union; and a Senator from my State, Mr. Jesse B. Thomas, introduced an amendment, known as the eighth section of the bill, in which it was provided that slavery should be prohibited north of 36° 30′ north latitude, in all that country which we had acquired from France. What was the object of the enactment of that eighth section? Was it not to go back to the original policy of prescribing boundaries to the limitation of free institutions, and of slave institutions, by a geographical line, in order to avoid all controversy in Congress upon the subject? Hence they extended that geographical line through all the territory purchased from France, which was as far as our possessions then reached. It was not simply to settle the question on that piece of country, but it was to carry out a great principle, by extending that dividing line as far west as our territory went, and running it onward on each new acquisition of territory. True, the express enactment of the eighth section of the Missouri act, now called the Missouri compromise act, only covered the territory acquired from France; but the principles of the act, the objects of its adoption, the reasons in its support, required that it should be extended indefinitely westward, so far as our territory might go, whenever new purchases should be made.

Thus stood the question up to 1845, when the joint resolution for the annexation of Texas passed. There was inserted in that a provision, suggested in the first instance and brought before the House of Representatives by myself, extending the Missouri compromise line indefinitely westward through the territory of Texas. Why did I bring forward that proposition? Why did the Congress of the United States adopt it? Not because it was of the least practical importance, so far as the question of slavery within the limits of Texas was concerned, for no man ever dreamed that it had any practical effect there. Then why was it brought forward? It was for the purpose of preserving the principle, in order that it might be extended still further westward, even to the Pacific Ocean, whenever we should acquire the country that far. I will here read that clause in the joint resolution for the annexation of Texas. . . .

It will be seen that that contains a very remarkable provision, which is, that when States lying north of 36° 30′ apply for admission, slavery shall be prohibited in their constitutions. I presume no one pretends that Congress could have power thus to fetter a State applying for admission into this Union; but it was necessary to preserve the principle of the Missouri compromise line in order that it might afterwards be extended; and it was supposed that while Congress had no power to impose any such limitation, yet as that was a compact with the State of Texas, that State could consent for herself that, when any portion of her own territory, subject to her own jurisdiction and control, applied for a constitution, it should be in a particular form; but that provision would not be binding on the new State one day after it was admitted into the Union. The other provision was, that such States as should lie south of 36° 30′ should come into the Union, with or without slavery, as each should decide in its constitution. Then, by that act the Missouri compromise was extended indefinitely westward, so far as the State of Texas went, that is, to the Rio Del Norte; for our Government at the time recognized the Rio Del Norte as its boundary. We recognized in many ways, and among them by even paying Texas for it, in order that it might be included in and form a portion of, the Territory of New Mexico.

Then, sir, in 1848 we acquired from Mexico the country between the Rio Del Norte and the Pacific ocean. Immediately after that acquisition, the Senate, on my own motion, voted into a bill a provision to extend the Missouri compromise indefinitely westward to the Pacific ocean, in the same sense, and with the same understanding with which it was originally adopted. That provision passed this body by a decided majority—I think by ten at least—and went to the House of Representatives, and was there defeated by northern votes.

Now, sir, let us pause and consider for a moment. The first time that the principles of the Missouri compromise were ever abandoned, the first time they were ever rejected by Congress, was by the defeat of that provision in the House of Representatives in 1848. By whom was that defeat effected? By northern votes, with Free-Soil proclivities. It was the defeat of that Missouri compromise that reopened the slavery agitation with all its fury. It was the defeat of that Missouri compromise that created the tremendous struggle of 1850. It was the defeat of that Missouri compromise that created the necessity for making a new compromise in 1850. Had we been faithful to the principles of the Missouri compromise in 1848, this question would not have arisen. Who was it that was faithless? I undertake to say it was the very men who now insist that the Missouri compromise was a solemn compact, and should never be violated or departed from. Every man who is now assailing the principle of the bill under consideration, so far as I am advised, was opposed to the Missouri compromise in 1848. The very men who now arraign me for a departure from the Missouri compromise, are the men who successfully violated it, repudiated it, and caused it to be superseded by the compromise measures of 1850. Sir, it is with rather bad grace that the men who proved false themselves, should charge upon me and others, who were ever faithful, the responsibilities and consequences of their own treachery.

Then, Sir, as I before remarked, the defeat of the Missouri compromise in 1848 having created the necessity for the establishment of a new one in 1850, let us see what that compromise was.

The leading feature of the compromise of 1850 was congressional non-intervention as to slavery in the Territories; that the people of the Territories, and of all the States, were to be allowed to do as they pleased upon the subject of slavery, subject only to the provisions of the Constitution of the United States.

That, Sir, was the leading feature of the compromise measures of 1850. Those measures therefore, abandoned the idea of a geographical line as the boundary between free States and slave States; abandoned it because compelled to do it from an inability to maintain it; and in lieu of that, substituted a great principle of self-government, which would allow the people to do as they thought proper. Now, the question is, when that new compromise, resting upon that great fundamental principle of freedom, was established, was it not an abandonment of the old one—the geographical line? Was it not a supersedure of the old one within the very language of the substitute for the bill which is now under consideration? I say it did supersede it, because it applied its provisions as well to the north as to the south of 36° 30'. It established a principle which was equally applicable to the country north as well as south of the parallel of 36° 30′—a principle of universal application. . . .

I say, therefore, that a close examination of this act clearly establishes the fact that it was the intent as well as the legal effect of the compromise measures of 1850 to supersede the Missouri compromise, and all geographical and territorial lines.

Sir, in order to avoid any misconstruction, I will state more distinctly what my precise idea is upon this point. So far as the Utah and New Mexico bills included the territory which had been subject to the Missouri compromise provision, to that extent they absolutely annulled the Missouri compromise. As to the unorganized territory not covered by those bills, it was superseded by the principles of the compromise of 1850. We all know that the object of the compromise measures of 1850 was to establish certain great principles, which would avoid the slavery agitation in all time to come. Was it our object simply to provide for a temporary evil? Was it our object just to heal over an old sore, and leave it to break out again? Was it our object to adopt a mere miserable expedient to apply to that territory, and that alone, and leave ourselves entirely at sea without compass when new territory was acquired, or new territorial organizations were to be made? Was that the object for which the eminent and venerable Senator from Kentucky (Mr. Clay) came here and sacrificed even his last energies upon the altar of his country? Was that the object for which WEBSTER, CLAY, CASS, and all the patriots of that day, struggled so long and so strenuously? Was it merely the application of a temporary expedient in agreeing to stand by past and dead legislation that the Baltimore platform pledged us to sustain the compromise of 1850? Was it the understanding of the Whig party, when they adopted the compromise measures of 1850 as an article of political faith, that they were only agreeing to that which was past, and had no reference to the future? If that was their meaning—if that was their object—they palmed off an atrocious fraud upon the American people. Was it the meaning of the Democratic party, when we pledged ourselves to stand by the compromise of 1850, that we spoke only of the past, and had no reference to the future? If so, it was then a fraud. When we pledged our President to stand by the compromise measures, did we not understand that we pledged him as to his future action? Was it as to his past conduct? If it had been in relation to past conduct only, the pledge would have been untrue as to a very large portion of the Democratic party. Men went into that convention who had been opposed to the compromise measures—men who abhorred those measures when they were pending—men who never would have voted affirmatively on them. But inasmuch as those measures had been passed, and the country had acquiesced in them, and it was important to preserve the principle in order to avoid agitation in the future, these men said, we waive our past objections, and we will stand by you and with you in carrying out these principles in the future.

Such I understood to be the meaning of the two great parties at Baltimore. Such I understand to have been the effect of their pledges. If they did not mean this, they meant merely to adopt resolutions which were never to be carried out, and which were designed to mislead and deceive the people for the mere purpose of carrying an election.

I hold, then, that as to the territory covered by the Utah and New Mexico bills, there was an express annulment of the Missouri compromise; and as to all the other unorganized territories, it was superseded by the principles of that legislation, and we are bound to apply those principles in the organization of all new Territories, to all which we now own, or which we may hereafter acquire. If this construction be given, it makes that compromise a final adjustment. No other construction can possibly impart finality to it. By any other construction the question is to be reopened the moment you ratify a new treaty acquiring an inch of country from Mexico. By any other construction you reopen the issue every time you make a new territorial government. But, sir, if you treat the compromise measures of 1850 in the light of great principles, sufficient to remedy temporary evils, at the same time that they prescribe rules of action applicable everywhere in all time to come, then you avoid the agitation forever, if you observe good faith to the provisions of these enactments, and the principles established by them.

Mr. President, I repeat, that so far as the question of slavery is concerned, there is nothing in the bill under consideration which does not carry out the principle of the compromise measures of 1850, by leaving the people to do as they please, subject only to the provisions of the Constitution of the United States. If that principle is wrong, the bill is wrong. If that principle is right, the bill is right. It is unnecessary to quibble about phraseology or words; it is not the mere words, the mere phraseology, that our constituents wish to judge by. They wish to know the legal effect of our legislation.

The legal effect of this bill, if it be passed as reported by the Committee on Territories, is neither to legislate slavery into these Territories nor out of them, but to leave the people do as they please, under the provisions and subject to the limitations of the Constitution of the United States. Why should not this principle prevail? Why should any man, North or South, object to it? I will especially address the argument to my own section of country, and ask why should any northern man object to this principle? If you will review the history of the slavery question in the United States, you will see that all the great results in behalf of free institutions which have been worked out, have been accomplished by the operation of this principle, and by it alone.

When these States were colonies of Great Britain, every one of them was a slaveholding province. When the Constitution of the United States was formed, twelve out of the thirteen were slaveholding States. Since that time six of those States have become free. How has this been effected? Was it by virtue of abolition agitation in Congress? Was it in obedience to the dictates of the Federal Government? Not at all; but they have become free States under the silent but sure and irresistible working of that great principle of self-government which teaches every people to do that which the interests of themselves and their posterity morally and pecuniarily may require.

Under the operation of this principle New Hampshire became free, while South Carolina continued to hold slaves; Connecticut abolished slavery, while Georgia held on to it; Rhode Island abandoned the institution, while Maryland preserved it; New York, New Jersey, and Pennsylvania abolished slavery, while Virginia, North Carolina, and Kentucky retained it. Did they do it at your bidding? Did they do it at the dictation of the Federal Government? Did they do it in obedience to any of your Wilmot provisoes or ordinances of '87? Not at all; they did it by virtue of their right as freemen under the Constitution of the United States, to establish and abolish such institutions as they thought their own good required.

Let me ask you where have you succeeded in excluding slavery by an act of Congress from one inch of the American soil? You may tell me that you did it in the northwest territory by the ordinance of 1787. I will show you by the history of the country that you did not accomplish any such thing. You prohibited slavery there by law, but you did not exclude it in fact. Illinois was a part of the northwest territory. With the exception of a few French and white settlements, it was a vast wilderness, filled with hostile savages, when the ordinance of 1787 was adopted. Yet, sir, when Illinois was organized into a territorial government it established and protected slavery, and maintained it in spite of your ordinance, and in defiance of its express prohibition. It is a curious fact, that so long as Congress said the territory of Illinois should not have slavery, she actually had it; and on the very day when you withdrew your congressional prohibition, the people of Illinois of their own free will and accord, provided for a system of emancipation.

Thus you did not succeed in Illinois Territory with your ordinance or your Wilmot Proviso, because the people there regarded it as an invasion of their rights. They regarded it as a usurpation on the part of the Federal Government. They regarded it as violative of the great principles of self-government, and they determined that they would never submit even to have freedom so long as you forced it upon them.

Nor must it be said that slavery was abolished in the constitution of Illinois in order to be admitted into the Union as a State, in compliance with the ordinance of 1787, for they did no such thing. In the constitution with which the people of Illinois were admitted into the Union, they absolutely violated, disregarded, and repudiated your ordinance. The ordinance said that slavery should be forever prohibited in that country. The constitution with which you received them into the Union as a State said that all slaves then in the State should remain slaves for life, and that all persons born of slave parents after a certain day should be free at a certain age, and that all persons born in the State after a certain other day should be free from the time of their birth. Thus their State constitution, as well as their territorial legislation, repudiated your ordinance. Illinois, therefore, is a case in point to prove that whenever you have attempted to dictate institutions to any part of the United States, you have failed. The same is true, though not to the same extent, with reference to the Territory of Indiana, where there were many slaves during the time of its territorial existence; and I believe also there were a few in the Territory of Ohio.

But, sir, these Abolition confederates in their manifesto, have also referred to the wonderful results of their policy in the State of Iowa and the Territory of Minnesota. Here again they happen to be in fault as to the laws of the land. The act to organize the Territory of Iowa did not prohibit slavery, but the people of Iowa were allowed to do as they pleased under the territorial government; for the sixth section of that act provided that the legislative authority should extend to all rightful subjects of legislation, except as to the disposition of the public lands, and taxes in certain cases, but not excepting slavery. It may, however, be said by some that slavery was prohibited in Iowa by virtue of that clause in the Iowa act which declared the laws of Wisconsin to be in force therein, inasmuch as the ordinance of 1787 was one of the laws of Wisconsin. If, however, they say this, they defeat their object, because the very clause which transfers the laws of Wisconsin to Iowa, and makes them of force therein, also provides that those laws are subject to be altered, modified or repealed by the Territorial Legislature of Iowa. Iowa, therefore, was left to do as she pleased. Iowa, when she came to form a constitution and State government, preparatory to admission into the Union, considered the subject of free and slave institutions calmly, dispassionately, without any restraint or dictation, and determined that it would be to the interest of her people in their climate, and with their productions, to prohibit slavery, and hence Iowa became a free State by virtue of this great principle of allowing the people to do as they please, and not in obedience to any federal command.

The Abolitionists are also in the habit of referring to Oregon as another instance of the triumph of their abolition policy. There again they have overlooked or misrepresented the history of the country. Sir, it is well known, or if it is not, it ought to be, that for about twelve years you failed to give Oregon any government or any protection; and during that period the inhabitants of that country established a government of their own, and by virtue of their own laws, passed by their own representatives before you extended your jurisdiction over them, prohibited slavery by a unanimous vote. Slavery was prohibited there by the action of the people themselves, and not by virtue of any legislation of Congress.

It is true that in the midst of the tornado which swept over the country in 1848, 1849, and 1850, a provision was forced into the Oregon bill prohibiting slavery in that Territory; but that only goes to show that the object of those who pressed it was not so much to establish free institutions as to gain a political advantage by giving an ascendancy to their peculiar doctrines, in the laws of the land; for slavery having been already prohibited there, and no man proposing to establish it, what was the necessity for insulting the people of Oregon by saying in your law that they should not do that which they had unanimously said they did not wish to do? That was the only effect of your legislation, so far as the Territory of Oregon was concerned.

How was it in regard to California? Every one of these abolition confederates who have thus arraigned me and the Committee on Territories before the country, who have misrepresented our position, and misquoted the law and the fact, predicted that unless Congress interposed by law, and prohibited slavery in California, it would inevitably become a slaveholding State. Congress did not interfere; Congress did not prohibit slavery. There was no enactment upon the subject; but the people formed a State constitution, and then prohibited slavery.

MR. WELLER. The vote was unanimous in the convention of California for prohibition.

MR. DOUGLAS. So it was in regard to Utah and New Mexico. In 1850, we who resisted any attempt to force institutions upon the people of those Territories, inconsistent with their wishes and their right to decide for themselves, were denounced as slavery propagandists. Every one of us who was in favor of the Compromise measures of 1850 was arraigned for having advocated a principle proposing to introduce slavery into those Territories; and the people were told, and made to believe, that unless we prohibited it by act of Congress, slavery would necessarily and inevitably be introduced into these Territories. . . .

I know of but one Territory of the United States where slavery does exist, and that one is where you have prohibited it by law, and it is this very Nebraska Territory. In defiance of the eighth section of the act of 1820, in defiance of Congressional dictation, there have been, not many, but a few slaves introduced. I heard a minister of the

Gospel the other day conversing with a member of the Committee on Territories upon this subject. This preacher was from that country; and a member put this question to him: "Have you any negroes out there?" He said there were a few held by the Indians. I asked him if there were not some held by white men? He said there were a few, under peculiar circumstances, and he gave an instance: An abolition missionary, a very good man, had gone there from Boston, and he took his wife with him. He got out into the country, but could not get any help; hence he, being a kind-hearted man, went down to Missouri, and gave $1,000 for a negro, and took him up there as "help." [Laughter.] So, under peculiar circumstances, when these Free-Soil and Abolition preachers and missionaries go into the country, they can buy a negro for their own use, but they do not like to allow any one else to do the same thing. [Renewed laughter.] I suppose the fact of the matter is simply this: there the people can get no servants—no "help," as they are called in the section of country where I was born—and, from the necessity of the case, they must do the best they can, and for this reason, a few slaves have been taken there. I have no doubt that whether you organize the Territory of Nebraska or not this will continue for sometime to come. It certainly does exist, and it will increase as long as the Missouri compromise applies to the Territory; and I suppose it will continue for a little while during their territorial condition, whether a prohibition is imposed or not. But when settlers rush in—when labor becomes plenty, and therefore cheap, in that climate, with its productions, it is worse than folly to think of its being a slaveholding country. I do not believe there is a man in Congress who thinks it could be permanently a slaveholding country. I have no idea that it could. All I have to say on that subject is, that when you create them into a Territory, you thereby acknowledge that they ought to be considered a distinct political organization. And when you give them in addition a Legislature, you thereby confess that they are competent to exercise the powers of legislation. If they wish slavery they have a right to it. If they do not want it they will not have it, and you should not force it upon them.

I do not like, I never did like, the system of legislation on our part, by which a geographical line, in violation of the laws of nature, and climate, and soil, and of the laws of God, should be run to establish institutions for a people; yet, out of a regard for the peace and quiet of the country, out of respect for past pledges, and out of a desire to adhere faithfully to all compromises, I sustained the Missouri compromise so long as it was in force, and advocated its extension to the Pacific. Now, when that has been abandoned, when it has been superseded, when a great principle of self-government has been substituted for it, I choose to cling to that principle, and abide in good faith, not only by the letter, but by the spirit of the last compromise.

Sir, I do not recognize the right of the Abolitionists of this country to arraign me for being false to sacred pledges, as they have done in their proclamation. Let them show when and where I have ever proposed to violate a compact. I have proved that I stood by the compact of 1820 and 1845, and proposed its continuance and observance in 1848. I have proved that the Free-Soilers and Abolitionists were the guilty parties who violated that compromise then. I should like to compare notes with these Abolition confederates about adherence to compromises. When did they stand by or approve of any one that was ever made?

Did not every Abolitionist and Free-Soiler in America denounce the Missouri compromise in 1820? Did they not for years hunt down ravenously for his blood every man who assisted in making that compromise? Did they not in 1845, when Texas was annexed, denounce all of us who went for the annexation of Texas, and for the continuation of the Missouri compromise line through it? Did they not in 1848 denounce me as a slavery propagandist for standing by the principles of the Missouri compromise, and proposing to continue the Missouri compromise line to the Pacific ocean? Did they not themselves violate and repudiate it then? Is not the charge of bad faith true as to every Abolitionist in America, instead of being true as to me and the committee, and those who advocate this bill?

They talk about the bill being a violation of the compromise measures of 1850. Who can show me a man in either House of Congress who was in favor of the compromise measures of 1850, and who is not now in favor of leaving the people of Nebraska and Kansas to do as they please upon the subject of slavery according to the provisions of my bill? Is there one? If so, I have not heard of him. This tornado has been raised by Abolitionists, and Abolitionists alone. They have made an impression upon the public mind in the way in which I have mentioned, by a falsification of the law and the facts; and this whole organization against the compromise measures of 1850 is an Abolition movement. . . .

Now, I ask the friends and the opponents of this measure to look at it as it is. Is not the question involved the simple one, whether the people of the Territories shall be allowed to do as they please upon the question of slavery, subject only to the limitations of the Constitution? That is all the bill provides; and it does so in clear, explicit, and unequivocal terms. I know there are some men, Whigs and Democrats, who, not willing to repudiate the Baltimore platform of their own party, would be willing to vote for this principle, provided they could do so in such equivocal terms that they could deny that it means what it was intended to mean in certain localities. I do not wish to deal in any equivocal language. If the principle is right, let it be avowed and maintained. If it is wrong, let it be repudiated. Let all this quibbling about the Missouri compromise, about the territory acquired from France, about the act of 1820, be cast behind you; for the simple question is, will you allow the people to legislate for themselves upon the subject of slavery? Why should you not?

When you propose to give them a territorial government do you not acknowledge that they ought to be erected into a political organization; and when you give them a Legislature do you not acknowledge that they are capable of self-government? Having made that acknowledgement, why should you not allow them to exercise the rights of legislation? Oh, these Abolitionists say they are entirely willing to concede all this, with one exception. They say they are willing to trust the Territorial Legislature, under the limitations of the Constitution, to legislate upon the rights of inheritance, to legislate in regard to religion, education, and morals, to legislate in regard to the relations of husband and wife, of parent and child, of guardian and ward, upon everything pertaining to the dearest rights and interests of white men, but they are not willing to trust them to legislate in regard to a few miserable negroes. That is their single exception. They acknowledge that the people of the Territories are capable of deciding for themselves concerning white men, but not in relation to negroes. The real gist of the matter is this: Does it require any higher degree of civilization, and intelligence, and learning, and sagacity, to legislate for negroes than for white men? If it does, we ought to adopt the abolition doctrine, and go with them against this bill. If it does not—if we are willing to trust the people with the great, sacred, fundamental right of prescribing their own institutions, consistent with the Constitution of the country, we must vote for this bill as reported by the Committee on Territories. That is the only question involved in the bill. I hope I have been able to strip it of all the misrepresentation, to wipe away all of that mist and obscurity with which it has been surrounded by this Abolition address.

I have now said all I have to say upon the present occasion. For all, except the first ten minutes of these remarks, the Abolition confederates are responsible. My object, in the first place, was only to explain the provisions of the bill, so that they might be distinctly understood. I was willing to allow its assailants to attack it as much as they pleased, reserving to myself the right, when the time should approach for taking the vote, to answer, in a concluding speech, all the arguments which might be urged against it. I still reserve—what I believe common courtesy and parliamentary usage awards to the chairman of a committee and the author of a bill—the right of summing up, after all shall have been said which has to be said against this measure. . . .

We intend to stand by the principle of the compromise measures of 1850—that principle which lost the Presidency to the Senator from Michigan (Mr. Cass) in 1848, but which triumphed in 1850, although he had been a martyr in the cause—that principle to which the Democracy are pledged, not merely by the Baltimore platform, but by a higher and a more solemn obligation, to which they are pledged by the love and affection which they have for that great fundamental principle of Democracy and free institutions which lies at the basis of our creed, and gives every political community the right to govern itself in obedience to the Constitution of the country.

CHAPTER 6

SLAVERY JUSTIFIED

George Fitzhugh: Sociology for the South, or the Failure of Free Society

George Fitzhugh (1806–1881), a native of tidewater Virginia, became one of the South's leading apologists for slavery. Although trained in the law, he spent most of his antebellum career writing pamphlets on slavery and the race question. During the 1850s he served as contributing editor to two Richmond newspapers and engaged in extensive speaking assignments, on one occasion debating the question of slavery with the abolitionist Wendell Phillips before a New England audience. Fitzhugh published two important books during the decade, Sociology for the South, or the Failure of Free Society *(1854) and* Cannibals All! or Slaves Without Masters *(1857), in which he argued the social advantages of slavery and arraigned the society of the North. His arguments were part of a growing body of literature in defense of the South's "peculiar institution." As the attacks on slavery by Northern antislavery and abolitionist groups increased and as the question became hopelessly entangled with national politics, Southern spokesmen were moved to find new justifications for their social order. Preachers, scientists, and professors joined publicists like Fitzhugh to counter the Northern attacks. Slavery, which had been regarded in the South as a necessary, but immoral, institution not long before, soon came to be viewed as a positive good, as a Christianizing and civilizing influence. The selection that follows, "Slavery Justified," first appeared as a pamphlet in 1849, but was reprinted in 1854 as an appendix to Fitzhugh's book,* Sociology for the South. *Appearing in the same year as Douglas's introduction of the Kansas-Nebraska Act and the formation of the Republican Party, the essay became an important expression of a Southern point of view toward slavery, although some of Fitzhugh's ideas often seemed too extreme even for all Southerners to accept.*

Liberty and equality are new things under the sun. The free states of antiquity abounded with slaves. The feudal system that supplanted Roman institutions changed the form of slavery, but brought with it neither liberty nor equality. France and the Northern States of our Union have alone fully and fairly tried the experiment of a social organization founded upon universal liberty and equality of rights. England has only approximated to this condition in her commercial and manufacturing cities. The examples of small communities in Europe are not fit exponents of the working of the system. In France and in our Northern States the experiment has already failed, if we are to form our opinions from the discontent of the masses, or to believe the evidence of the Socialists, Communists, Anti-Renters, and a thousand other agrarian sects that have arisen in these countries, and threaten to subvert the whole social fabric. The leaders of these sects, at least in France, comprise within their ranks the greater number of the most cultivated and profound minds in the nation, who have made government their study. Add to the evidence of these social philosophers, who, watching closely the working of the system, have proclaimed to the world its total failure, the condition of the working classes, and we have conclusive proof that liberty and equality have not conduced to enhance the comfort or the happiness of the people. Crime and pauperism have increased. Riots, trades unions, strikes for higher wages, discontent breaking out into revolution, are things of daily occurrence, and show that the poor see and feel quite as clearly as the philosophers, that their condition is far worse under the new than under the old order of things. Radicalism and Chartism in England owe their birth to the free and equal institutions of her commercial and manufacturing districts, and are little heard of in the quiet farming districts, where remnants of feudalism still exist in the relation of landlord and tenant, and in the laws of entail and primogeniture.

So much for experiment. We will now endeavor to treat the subject theoretically, and to show that the system is on its face self-destructive and impracticable. When we look to the vegetable, animal and human kingdoms, we discover in them all a constant conflict, war, or race of competition, the result of which is, that the weaker or less healthy genera, species and individuals are continually displaced and exterminated by the stronger and more hardy. It is a means by which some contend Nature is perfecting her own work. We, however, witness the war, but do not see the improvement. Although from the earliest date of recorded history, one race of plants has been eating out and taking the place of another, the stronger or more cunning animals been destroying the feebler, and man exterminating and supplanting his fellow, still the plants, the animals and the men of to-day seem not at all superior, even in those qualities of strength and hardihood to which they owe their continued existence, to those of thousands of years ago. To this propensity of the strong to oppress and destroy the weak, government owes its existence. So strong is this propensity, and so destructive to human existence, that man has never yet been found so savage as to be without government. Forgetful of this important fact, which is the origin of all governments, the political economists and the advocates of liberty and equality propose to enhance the well being of man by trammeling his conduct as little as possible, and encouraging what they call FREE COMPETITION. Now, free competition is but another name for liberty and equality, and we must acquire precise and accurate notions about it in order to ascertain how free institutions will work. It is, then, that war or conflict to which Nature impels her creatures, and which government was intended to restrict. It is true, it is that war somewhat modified and restricted, for the warmest friends of freedom would have some government. The question is, whether the proposed restrictions are sufficient to neutralize the self-destructive tendencies which nature impresses on society. We proceed to show that the war of the wits, of mind with mind, which free competition or liberty and equality beget and encourage, is quite as oppressive, cruel and exterminating, as the war of the sword, of theft, robbery, and murder, which it forbids. It is only substituting strength of mind for strength of body. Men are told it is their duty to compete, to endeavor to get ahead of and supplant their fellow men, by the exercise of all the intellectual and moral strength with which nature and education have endowed them. "Might makes right," is the order of creation, and this law of nature, so far as mental might is concerned, is restored by liberty to man. The struggle to better one's condition, to pull others down or supplant them, is the great organic law of free society. All men being equal, all aspire to the highest honors and the largest possessions. Good men and bad men teach their children one and the same lesson—"Go ahead, push your way in the world." In such society, virtue, if virtue there be, loses all her loveliness because of her selfish aims. None but the selfish virtues are encouraged, because none other aid a man in the race of Free Competition. Good men and bad men have the same end in view, are in pursuit of the same object—self-promotion, self-elevation. The good man is prudent, cautious, and cunning of fence; he knows well the arts (the virtues, if you please), which will advance his fortunes and enable him to depress and supplant others; he bides his time, takes advantage of the follies, the improvidence, and vices of others, and makes his fortune out of the misfortunes of his fellow men. The bad man is rash, hasty, and unskillful. He is equally selfish, but not half so cunning. Selfishness is almost the only motive of human conduct with good and bad in free society, where every man is taught that he may change and better his condition. A vulgar adage, "Every man for himself, and devil take the hindmost," is the moral which liberty and free competition inculcate. Now, there are no more honors and wealth in proportion to numbers, in this generation, than in the one which preceded it; population fully keeps pace with the means of subsistence; hence, those who better their condition or rise to higher places in society, do so generally by pulling down others or pushing them from their places. Where men of strong minds, of strong wills, and of great self-control, come into free competition with the weak and improvident, the latter soon become the inmates of jails and penitentiaries.

The statistics of France, England and America show that pauperism and crime advance *pari passu* with liberty and equality. How can it be otherwise, when all society is combined to oppress the poor and weak minded? The rich man, however good he may be, employs the laborer who will work for the least wages. If he be a good man, his punctuality enables him to cheapen the wages of the poor man. The poor war with one another in the race of competition, in order to get employment, by underbidding; for laborers are more abundant than employers. Population increases faster than capital. Look to the situation of woman when she is thrown into this war of competition, and has to support herself by her daily wages. For the same or equally valuable services she gets not half the pay that man does, simply because the modesty of her sex prevents her from resorting to all the arts and means of competition which men employ. He who would emancipate woman, unless he could make her as coarse and strong in mind and body as man, would be her worst enemy; her subservience to and dependence on man, is necessary to her very existence. She is not a soldier fitted to enlist in the war of free competition. We do not set children and women free because they are not capable of taking care of themselves, not equal to the constant struggle of society. To set them free would be to give the lamb to the wolf to take care of. Society would quickly devour them. If the children of ten years of age were remitted to all the rights of person and property which men enjoy, all can perceive how soon ruin and penury would overtake them. But half of mankind are but grown-up children, and liberty is as fatal to them as it would be to children.

We will cite another familiar instance to prove and illustrate the destructive effects of liberty or free competition. It is that where two races of men of different capacity are brought into juxtaposition. It is the boast of the Anglo-Saxon, that by the arts of peace under the influence of free trade he can march to universal conquest. However true this may be, all know that if Englishmen or Americans settle among inferior races, they soon become the owners of the soil, and gradually extirpate or reduce to poverty the original owners. They are the wiregrass of nations. The same law of nature which enables and impels the stronger race to oppress and exterminate the weaker, is constantly at work in the bosom of every society, between its stronger and weaker members. Liberty and equality rather encourage than restrict this law in its deadly operation. A Northern gentleman, who was both statesman and philosopher, once told us, that his only objection to domestic slavery was, that it would perpetuate an inferior race, who, under the influence of free trade and free competition, would otherwise disappear from the earth. China and Japan acted wisely to anticipate this new philosophy and exclude Europeans.

One step more, and that the most difficult in this process of reasoning and illustration, and we have done with this part of our subject. Liberty and equality throw the whole weight of society on its weakest members; they combine all men in oppressing precisely that part of mankind who most need sympathy, aid and protection. The very astute and avaricious man, when left free to exercise his facul-

ties, is injured by no one in the field of competition, but levies a tax
on all with whom he deals. The sensible and prudent, but less astute
man, is seldom worsted in competing with his fellow men, and generally benefited. The very simple and improvident man is the prey of
every body. The simple man represents a class, the common day
laborers. The employer cheapens their wages, and the retail dealer
takes advantage of their ignorance, their inability to visit other markets, and their want of credit, to charge them enormous profits. They
bear the whole weight of society on their shoulders; they are the pro-
ducers and artificers of all the necessaries, the comforts, the luxuries,
the pomp and splendor of the world; they create it all, and enjoy none
of it; they are the muzzled ox that treadeth out the straw; they are at
constant war with those above them, asking higher wages but getting
lower; for they are also at war with each other, underbidding to get
employment. This process of underbidding never ceases so long as
employers want profits or laborers want employment. It ends when
wages are reduced too low to afford subsistence, in filling poor-
houses, and jails, and graves. It has reached that point already in
France, England and Ireland. A half million died of hunger in one
year in Ireland—they died because in the eye of the law they were the
equals, and liberty had made them the enemies, of their landlords
and employers. Had they been vassals or serfs, they would have been
beloved, cherished and taken care of by those same landlords and
employers. Slaves never die of hunger, scarcely ever feel want.

The bestowing upon men equality of rights, is but giving license to
the strong to oppress the weak. It begets the grossest inequalities of
condition. Menials and day laborers are and must be as numerous as
in a land of slavery. And these menials and laborers are only taken
care of while young, strong and healthy. If the laborer gets sick, his
wages cease just as his demands are greatest. If two of the poor get
married, who being young and healthy, are getting good wages, in a
few years they may have four children. Their wants have increased,
but the mother has enough to do to nurse the four children, and the
wages of the husband must support six. There is no equality, except in
theory, in such society, and there is no liberty. The men of property,
those who own lands and money, are masters of the poor; masters,
with none of the feelings, interests or sympathies of masters; they
employ them when they please, and for what they please, and may

leave them to die in the highway, for it is the only home to which the poor in free countries are entitled. They (the property holders) beheaded Charles Stuart and Louis Capet, because these kings asserted a divine right to govern wrong, and forgot that office was a trust to be exercised for the benefit of the governed; and yet they seem to think that property is of divine right, and that they may abuse its possession to the detriment of the rest of society, as much as they please. A pretty exchange the world would make, to get rid of kings who often love and protect the poor, and get in their place a million of pelting, petty officers in the garb of money-changers and land-owners, who think that as they own all the property, the rest of mankind have no right to a living, except on the conditions they may prescribe. "'Tis better to fall before the lion than the wolf," and modern liberty has substituted a thousand wolves for a few lions. The vulgar landlords, capitalists and employers of to-day, have the liberties and lives of the people more completely in their hands, than had the kings, barons and gentlemen of former times; and they hate and oppress the people as cordially as the people despise them. But these vulgar parvenus, these psalm-singing regicides, these worshipers of mammon, "have but taught bloody instructions, which being taught, return to plague the inventor." The king's office was a trust, so are your lands, houses and money. Society permits you to hold them, because private property well administered conduces to the good of all society. *This is your only title;* you lose your right to your property, as the king did to his crown, so soon as you cease faithfully to execute your trust; you can't make commons and forests of your lands and starve mankind; you must manage your lands to produce the most food and raiment for mankind, or you forfeit your title; you may not understand this philosophy, but you feel that it is true, and are trembling in your seats as you hear the murmurings and threats of the starving poor.

The moral effect of free society is to banish Christian virtue, that virtue which bids us love our neighbor as ourself, and to substitute the very equivocal virtues proceeding from mere selfishness. The intense struggle to better each one's pecuniary condition, the rivalries, the jealousies, the hostilities which it begets, leave neither time nor inclination to cultivate the heart or the head. Every finer feeling of our nature is chilled and benumbed by its selfish atmosphere; affection is under the ban, because affection makes us less regardful of mere self; hospitality is considered criminal waste, chivalry a stumbling-block, and the code of honor foolishness; taste, sentiment, imagination, are forbidden ground, because no money is to be made by them. Gorgeous pageantry and sensual luxury are the only pleasures indulged in, because they alone are understood and appreciated, and they are appreciated just for what they cost in dollars and cents. What makes money, and what costs money, are alone desired. Temperance, frugality, thrift, attention to business, industry, and skill in making bargains are virtues in high repute, because they enable us to supplant others and increase our own wealth. The character of our Northern brethren, and of the Dutch, is proof enough of the justice of these reflections. The Puritan fathers had lived in Holland, and probably imported Norway rats and Dutch morality in the Mayflower.

Liberty and equality are not only destructive to the morals, but to the happiness of society. Foreigners have all remarked on the careworn, thoughtful, unhappy countenances of our people, and the remark only applies to the North, for travellers see little of us at the South, who live far from highways and cities, in contentment on our farms.

The facility with which men may improve their condition would, indeed, be a consideration much in favor of free society, if it did not involve as a necessary consequence the equal facility and liability to lose grade and fortune. As many fall as rise. The wealth of society hardly keeps pace with its numbers. All cannot be rich. The rich and the poor change places oftener than where there are fixed hereditary distinctions; so often, that the sense of insecurity makes every one unhappy; so often, that we see men clutching at security through means of Odd Fellows, Temperance Societies, &c., which provide for members when sick, and for the families of deceased members; so often, that almost every State in the Union has of late years enacted laws or countenanced decisions giving more permanency to property. Entails and primogeniture are as odious to us as kings were to the Romans; but their object—to keep property in our families—is as dear to us as to any people on earth, because we love our families as much. Hence laws to exempt small amounts of personal property from liability to debt are daily enacted, and hence Iowa or Wisconsin has a provision in her constitution, that the homestead of some forty acres shall be exempt from execution. Hence, also, the mighty impulse of late in favor of woman's rights. Legislatures and courts are vieing with each other which shall do most to secure married women's rights to them. The ruin of thousands upon thousands of families in the revulsion of 1837, taught the necessity of this new species of entail, this new way of keeping property in the family. The ups and downs of life became too rapid to be agreeable to any who had property to lose or a family to provide for. We have not yet quite cooled down from the fervor of the Revolution. We have been looking to one side only of our institutions. We begin to feel, however, that there is another and a dark side,—a side where all are seen going down the hill of fortune. Let us look closely and fearlessly at this feature of free society, so much lauded and so little understood. What object more laudable, what so dear to a man's heart, as to continue a competency of property, refinement of mind and morals, to his posterity? What nobler incentive to virtuous conduct, than the belief that such conduct will redound to the advantage of our descendants? What reflection so calculated to make men reckless, wretched and immoral, as the conviction that the means they employ to improve the moral, mental and pecuniary condition of their offspring, are, in this land of ups and downs, the very means to make them the prey of the cunning, avaricious and unprincipled, who have been taught in the school of adversity and poverty? We constantly boast that the wealthy and powerful of to-day are the sons of the weak, ignorant and destitute of yesterday. It is the other side of the picture that we want moral courage to look at. We are dealing now with figures of arithmetic, not of rhetoric. Those who rise, pull down a class as numerous, and often more worthy than themselves, to the abyss of misery and penury. Painful as it may be, the reader shall look with us at this dark side of the picture; he shall view the vanquished as well as the victors on this battleground of competition; he shall see those who were delicately reared, taught no tricks of trade, no shifts of thrifty avarice, spurned, insulted, down-trodden by the coarse and vulgar, whose wits and whose appetites had been sharpened by necessity. If he can sympathize with fallen virtue or detest successful vice, he will see nothing in this picture to admire.

The wide fields of the newly rich will cease to excite pleasure in the contemplation; they will look like Golgothas covered with human bones. Their coarse and boisterous joys, while they revel in their spoils, will not help to relieve the painful sympathies for their victims.

But these parvenus are men with all the feelings of men, though somewhat blunted by the race for wealth; they love their children, and would have them unlike themselves, moral, refined, and educated—above the necessities and tricks of their parents. They rear them as gentlemen, to become the victims in their turn of the children of fallen gentlemen of a past generation—these latter having learned in the school of adversity the path to fortune. In Heaven's name, what is human life worth with such prospects ahead? Who would not rather lie down and die than exert himself to educate and make fortunes for his children, when he has reason to fear that by so doing he is to heap coals of fire on their heads. And yet this is an exact picture of the prospect which universal liberty holds out to its votaries. It is true it hides with a veil the agonies of the vanquished, and only exhibits the vulgar mirth of the victors. We have lifted the veil.

In Boston, a city famed for its wealth and the prudence of its inhabitants, nine-tenths of the men in business fail. In the slaveholding South, except in new settlements, failures are extremely rare; small properties descend from generation to generation in the same family; there is as much stability and permanency of property as is compatible with energy and activity in society; fortunes are made rather by virtuous industry than by tricks, cunning and speculation.

We have thus attempted to prove from theory and from actual experiment, that a society of universal liberty and equality is absurd and impracticable. We have performed our task, we know, indifferently, but hope we have furnished suggestions that may be profitably used by those more accustomed to authorship.

We now come in the order of our subject to treat of the various new sects of philosophers that have appeared of late years in France and in our free States, who, disgusted with society as it exists, propose to re-organize it on entirely new principles. We have never heard of a convert to any of these theories in the slave States. If we are not all contented, still none see evils of such magnitude in society as to require its entire subversion and reconstruction. We shall group all these sects together, because they all concur in the great truth that free competition is the bane of free society; they all concur, too, in modifying or wholly destroying the institution of private property.

Many of them, seeing that property enables its owners to exercise a more grinding oppression than kings ever did, would destroy its tenure altogether. In France, especially, these sects are headed by men of great ability, who saw the experiment of liberty and equality fairly tested in France after the revolution of 1792. They saw, as all the world did, that it failed to promote human happiness or well-being.

France found the Consulate and the Empire havens of bliss compared with the stormy ocean of liberty and equality on which she had been tossed. Wise, however, as these Socialists and Communists of France are, they cannot create a man, a tree, or a new system of society; these are God's works, which man may train, trim and modify, but cannot create. The attempt to establish government on purely theoretical abstract speculation, regardless of circumstance and experience, has always failed; never more signally than with the Socialists. . . .

The sufferings of the Irish, and the complaints of the Radicals and Chartists, have given birth to a new party in England, called Young England. This party saw in the estrangement and hostility of classes, and the sufferings of the poor, the same evils of free competition that had given rise to Socialism in France; though less talented than the Socialists, they came much nearer discovering the remedy for these evils.

Young England belongs to the most conservative wing of the tory party; he inculcates strict subordination of rank; would have the employer kind, attentive and paternal, in his treatment of the operative. The operative, humble, affectionate and obedient to his employer. He is young, and sentimental, and would spread his doctrines in tracts, sonnets and novels; but society must be ruled by sterner stuff than sentiment. Self-interest makes the employer and free laborer enemies. The one prefers to pay low wages, the other needs high wages. War, constant war, is the result, in which the operative perishes, but is not vanquished; he is hydra-headed, and when he dies two take his place. But numbers diminish his strength. The competition among laborers to get employment begets an intestine war, more destructive than the war from above. There is but one remedy for this evil, so inherent in free society, and that is, to identify the interests of the weak and the strong, the poor and the rich. Domestic Slavery does this far better than any other institution. Feudalism only answered the purpose in so far as Feudalism retained the features of slavery. To it (slavery) Greece and Rome, Egypt and Judea, and all the other distinguished States of antiquity, were indebted for their great prosperity and high civilization; a prosperity and a civilization which appear almost miraculous, when we look to their ignorance of the physical sciences. In the moral sciences they were our equals, in the fine arts vastly our superiors. Their poetry, their painting, their sculpture, their drama, their elocution, and their architecture, are models which we imitate, but never equal. In the science of government and of morals, in pure metaphysics, and in all the walks of intellectual philosophy, we have been beating the air with our wings or revolving in circles, but have not advanced an inch. . . .

But this high civilization and domestic slavery did not merely co-exist, they were cause and effect. Every scholar whose mind is at all imbued with ancient history and literature, sees that Greece and Rome were indebted to this institution alone for the taste, the leisure and the means to cultivate their heads and their hearts; had they been tied down to Yankee notions of thrift, they might have produced a Franklin, with his "penny saved is a penny gained;" they might have had utilitarian philosophers and invented the spinning jenny, but they never would have produced a poet, an orator, a sculptor or an architect; they would never have uttered a lofty sentiment, achieved a glorious feat in war, or created a single work of art.

A modern Yankee, or a Dutchman, is the fair result of liberty and equality. French character has not yet been subdued and tamed into insignificance by their new institutions; and besides, the pursuit of arms elevates and purifies the sentiments of Frenchmen. In what is the Yankee or Dutchman comparable to the Roman, Athenian or Spartan? In nothing save his care of his pelf and his skill in driving a bargain. The ruins of Thebes, of Nineveh, and of Balbec, the obelisks and pyramids of Egypt, the lovely and time-defying relics of Roman and Grecian art, the Doric column and the Gothic spire, alike attest the taste, the genius and the energy of society where slavery existed. . . .

And now Equality where are thy monuments? And Echo answers where! Echo deep, deep, from the bowels of the earth, where women and children drag out their lives in darkness, harnessed like horses to heavy cars loaded with ore. Or, perhaps, it is an echo from some grand, gloomy and monotonous factory, where pallid children work fourteen hours a day, and go home at night to sleep in damp cellars. It may be too, this cellar contains aged parents too old to work, and cast off by their employer to die. Great railroads and mighty steamships too, thou mayest boast, but still the operatives who construct them are beings destined to poverty and neglect. Not a vestige of art canst thou boast; not a ray of genius illumes thy handiwork. The sordid spirit of mammon presides o'er all, and from all proceed the sighs and groans of the oppressed.

Domestic slavery in the Southern States has produced the same results in elevating the character of the master that it did in Greece and Rome. He is lofty and independent in his sentiments, generous, affectionate, brave and eloquent; he is superior to the Northerner in every thing but the arts of thrift. History proves this. A Yankee sometimes gets hold of the reins of State, attempts Apollo, but acts Phaeton. Scipio and Aristides, Calhoun and Washington, are the noble results of domestic slavery. Like Egyptian obelisks 'mid the waste of time—simple, severe, sublime,—they point ever heavenward, and lift the soul by their examples. Adams and Van Buren, cunning, complex and tortuous, are fit exponents of the selfish system of universal liberty. Coriolanus, marching to the gates of Rome with dire hate and deadly indignation, is grand and noble in his revenge. Adams and Van Buren, insidiously striking with reptile fangs at the South, excite in all bosoms hatred and contempt; but we will not indulge in sweeping denunciation. In public and in private life, the North has many noble and generous souls. Men who, like Webster and Cass, Dickinson and Winthrop, can soar in lofty eloquence beyond the narrow prejudices of time and place, see man in all his relations, and contemn the narrow morality which makes the performance of one duty the excuse for a thousand crimes. We speak only of the usual and common effects of slavery and of equality. The Turk, half civilized as he is, exhibits the manly, noble and generous traits of character peculiar to the slave owner; he is hospitable, generous, truthful, brave, and strictly honest. In many respects, he is the finest specimen of humanity to be found in the world.

But the chief and far most important enquiry is, how does slavery affect the condition of the slave? One of the wildest sects of Communists in France proposes not only to hold all property in common, but

to divide the profits, not according to each man's in-put and labor,
but according to each man's wants. Now this is precisely the system
of domestic slavery with us. We provide for each slave, in old age and
in infancy, in sickness and in health, not according to his labor, but
according to his wants. The master's wants are more costly and
refined, and he therefore gets a larger share of the profits. A Southern
farm is the beau ideal of Communism; it is a joint concern, in which
the slave consumes more than the master, of the coarse products, and
is far happier, because although the concern may fail, he is always
sure of a support; he is only transferred to another master to participate in the profits of another concern; he marries when he pleases,
because be knows he will have to work no more with a family than
without one, and whether he live or die, that family will be taken care
of; he exhibits all the pride of ownership, despises a partner in a
smaller concern, "a poor man's negro," boasts of "our crops, horses,
fields and cattle;" and is as happy as a human being can be. And why
should he not?—he enjoys as much of the fruits of the farm as he is
capable of doing, and the wealthiest can do no more. Great wealth
brings many additional cares, but few additional enjoyments. Our
stomachs do not increase in capacity with our fortunes. We want no
more clothing to keep us warm. We may create new wants, but we
cannot create new pleasures. The intellectual enjoyments which
wealth affords are probably balanced by the new cares it brings along
with it.

There is no rivalry, no competition to get employment among
slaves, as among free laborers. Nor is there a war between master and
slave. The master's interest prevents his reducing the slave's
allowance or wages in infancy or sickness, for he might lose the slave
by so doing. His feeling for his slave never permits him to stint him in
old age. The slaves are all well fed, well clad, have plenty of fuel, and
are happy. They have no dread of the future—no fear of want. A state
of dependence is the only condition in which reciprocal affection can
exist among human beings—the only situation in which the war of
competition ceases, and peace, amity and good will arise. A state of
independence always begets more or less of jealous rivalry and hostility. A man loves his children because they are weak, helpless and
dependent; he loves his wife for similar reasons. When his children
grow up and assert their independence, he is apt to transfer his affec-

tion to his grand-children. He ceases to love his wife when she becomes masculine or rebellious; but slaves are always dependent, never the rivals of their master. Hence, though men are often found at variance with wife or children, we never saw one who did not like his slaves, and rarely a slave who was not devoted to his master. "I am thy servant!" disarms me of the power of master. Every man feels the beauty, force and truth of this sentiment of Sterne. But he who acknowledges its truth, tacitly admits that dependence is a tie of affection, that the relation of master and slave is one of mutual good will. Volumes written on the subject would not prove as much as this single sentiment. It has found its way to the heart of every reader, and carried conviction along with it. The slave-holder is like other men; he will not tread on the worm nor break the bruised reed. The ready submission of the slave, nine times out of ten, disarms his wrath even when the slave has offended. The habit of command may make him imperious and fit him for rule; but he is only imperious when thwarted or crossed by his equals; he would scorn to put on airs of command among blacks, whether slaves or free; he always speaks to them in a kind and subdued tone. We go farther, and say the slave-holder is better than others because he has greater occasion for the exercise of the affections. His whole life is spent in providing for the minutest wants of others, in taking care of them in sickness and in health. Hence he is the least selfish of men. Is not the old bachelor who retires to seclusion, always selfish? Is not the head of a large family almost always kind and benevolent? And is not the slave-holder the head of the largest family? Nature compels master and slave to be friends; nature makes employers and free laborers enemies.

The institution of slavery gives full development and full play to the affections. Free society chills, stints and eradicates them. In a homely way the farm will support all, and we are not in a hurry to send our children into the world, to push their way and make their fortunes, with a capital of knavish maxims. We are better husbands, better fathers, better friends, and better neighbors than our Northern brethren. The tie of kindred to the fifth degree is often a tie of affection with us. First cousins are scarcely acknowledged at the North, and even children are prematurely pushed off into the world. Love for others is the organic law of our society, as self-love is of theirs.

Every social structure must have its substratum. In free society this substratum, the weak, poor and ignorant, is borne down upon and oppressed with continually increasing weight by all above. We have solved the problem of relieving this substratum from the pressure from above. The slaves are the substratum, and the master's feelings and interests alike prevent him from bearing down upon and oppressing them. With us the pressure on society is like that of air or water, so equally diffused as not anywhere to be felt. With them it is the pressure of the enormous screw, never yielding, continually increasing. Free laborers are little better than trespassers on this earth given by God to all mankind. The birds of the air have nests, and the foxes have holes, but they have not where to lay their heads. They are driven to cities to dwell in damp and crowded cellars, and thousands are even forced to lie in the open air. This accounts for the rapid growth of Northern cities. The feudal Barons were more generous and hospitable and less tyrannical than the petty land-holders of modern times. Besides, each inhabitant of the barony was considered as having some right of residence, some claim to protection from the Lord of the Manor. A few of them escaped to the municipalities for purposes of trade, and to enjoy a larger liberty. Now penury and the want of a home drive thousands to towns. The slave always has a home, always an interest in the proceeds of the soil.

An intelligent New Englander, who was much opposed to negro slavery, boasting of his own country, told us that native New Englanders rarely occupied the place of domestic or body servants, or that of hired day laborers on public works. Emigrants alone served as menials, cleansed the streets, and worked on railroads and canals. New England is busy importing white free laborers for the home market, and catching negroes in Africa for the Brazilian market. Some of the negroes die on the passage, but few after they arrive in Brazil. The masters can't afford to neglect them. Many of the white laborers die on the passage of cholera and other diseases occasioned by filth and crowding—a fourth of them probably in the first year after they arrive, for the want of employment or the neglect of employers. The horrors of the middle passage are nothing to the horrors of a deck passage up the Mississippi when cholera prevails, or the want, penury and exposure that emigrants are subjected to in our large cities. England, too, has a tender conscience about slavery, but she is importing captured African slaves into her colonies to serve as apprentices, and extending this new species of slave trade even to Asia. "Expel nature with a fork, she will soon return." Slavery is natural and necessary, and will in some form insinuate itself into all civilized society. The domestic slave trade is complained of, and justly too, because it severs family ties. It is one of the evils of slavery, and no institution is without its evils. But how is it with New England? Are none of the free, the delicately reared and enlightened forced to quit the domestic hearth and all its endearments, to seek a living among strangers? Delicacy forbids our dwelling on this painful topic. The instances are before our eyes. What would induce a Virginian, rich or poor, to launch such members of his family unattended on the cold world.

More than half of the white citizens of the North are common laborers, either in the field, or as body or house servants. They perform the same services that our slaves do. They serve their employers for hire; they have quite as little option whether they shall so serve, or not, as our slaves, for they cannot live without their wages. Their hire or wages, except with the healthy and able-bodied, are not half what we allow our slaves, for it is wholly insufficient for their comfortable maintenance, whilst we always keep our slaves in comfort, in return for their past, present, or expected labor. The socialists say wages is slavery. It is a gross libel on slavery. Wages are given in time of vigorous health and strength, and denied when most needed, when sickness or old age has overtaken us. The slave is never without a master to maintain him. The free laborer, though willing to work, cannot always find an employer. He is then without a home and without wages! In a densely peopled country, where the supply of laborers exceeds the demand, wages is worse than slavery. Oh! Liberty and Equality, to what a sad pass do you bring your votaries! This is the exact condition to which the mass of society is reduced in France and England, and to which it is rapidly approximating in our Northern States. This state of things brought about the late revolution in France. The Socialist rulers undertook to find employment, put the laborers of Paris to work, transplanting trees and digging the earth. This experiment worked admirably in all but one respect. The government could find employment, but could not find wages. THE RIGHT TO EMPLOYMENT! Frenchmen deluged Paris with fraternal gore to vindicate this right. The right to live when you are strong enough to work, for it is then only you want employment. Poor as this boon would be, it is one which Liberty and Equality cannot confer. If it were conferred, the free laborer's condition would still be below the slave's, for the wages of the slave are paid whether he is fit for employment or not.

Oh carry, carry me back to old Virginia shore,
For I am old and feeble grown,
And cannot work any more.

Liberty and Equality, thou art humble in thy pretensions; thou askest little. But that little inexorable fate denies thee. Literally and truly, "darkness, death and black despair surround thee."

In France, England, Scotland and Ireland, the genius of famine hovers o'er the land. Emigrants, like a flock of hungry pigeons or Egyptian locusts, are alighting on the North. Every green thing will soon be consumed. The hollow, bloated prosperity which she now enjoys is destined soon to pass away. Her wealth does not increase with her numbers; she is dependent for the very necessaries of life on the slaveholding States. If those States cut off commercial intercourse with her, as they certainly will do if she does not speedily cease interference with slavery, she will be without food or clothing for her overgrown population. She is already threatened with a social revolution. The right to separate property in land is not only questioned by many, but has been successfully denied in the case of the Anti-Renters. Judges and Governors are elected upon pledges that they will sustain those who deny this right and defy the law. The editor of the most influential paper in the North, lately a member of Congress, is carrying on open war, not only against the right of property, but against every institution held sacred by society. A people who can countenance and patronise such doctrines, are almost ripe to carry those doctrines into practice. An insurrection of the poor against the rich may happen speedily among them. Should it occur, they have no means of suppressing it. No standing army, no efficient militia, no strength in their State governments. Society is hurrying on to the gulf of agrarianism, and no port of safety is in sight; no remedy for the evils with which it is beset has been suggested, save the remedies of the Socialists; remedies tried in France and proved to be worthless.

Population is too dense to introduce negro slaves. White men will not submit to be slaves, and are not fitted for slavery if they would. To the European race some degree of liberty is necessary, though famine stare them in the face. We are informed in Holy Writ, that God ordained certain races of men for slaves. The wisest philosopher of ancient times, with the experience of slavery before his eyes, proclaimed the same truth. Modern Abolitionists, wiser than Moses and Aristotle, have discovered that all men should be free. They have yet to discover the means of sustaining their lives in a state of freedom.

At the slaveholding South all is peace, quiet, plenty and contentment. We have no mobs, no trades unions, no strikes for higher wages, no armed resistance to the law, but little jealousy of the rich by the poor. We have but few in our jails, and fewer in our poor houses. We produce enough of the comforts and necessaries of life for a population three or four times as numerous as ours. We are wholly exempt from the torrent of pauperism, crime, agrarianism, and infidelity which Europe is pouring from her jails and alms houses on the already crowded North. Population increases slowly, wealth rapidly. In the tide water region of Eastern Virginia, as far as our experience extends, the crops have doubled in fifteen years, whilst the population has been almost stationary. In the same period the lands, owing to improvements of the soil and the many fine houses erected in the country, have nearly doubled in value. This ratio of improvement has been approximated or exceeded wherever in the South slaves are numerous. We have enough for the present, and no Malthusian spectres frightening us for the future. Wealth is more equally distributed than at the North, where a few millionaires own most of the property of the country. (These millionaires are men of cold hearts and weak minds; they know how to make money, but not how to use it, either for the benefit of themselves or of others.) High intellectual and moral attainments, refinement of head and heart, give standing to a man in the South, however poor he may be. Money is, with few exceptions, the only thing that ennobles at the North. We have poor among us, but none who are over-worked and under-fed. We do not crowd cities because lands are abundant and their owners kind, merciful and hospitable. The poor are as hospitable as the rich, the negro as the white man. Nobody dreams of turning a friend, a relative, or a stranger from

his door. The very negro who deems it no crime to steal, would scorn
to sell his hospitality. We have no loafers, because the poor relative or
friend who borrows our horse, or spends a week under our roof, is a
welcome guest. The loose economy, the wasteful mode of living at the
South, is a blessing when rightly considered; it keeps want, scarcity
and famine at a distance, because it leaves room for retrenchment. The
nice, accurate economy of France, England and New England, keeps
society always on the verge of famine, because it leaves no room to
retrench, that is to live on a part only of what they now consume. Our
society exhibits no appearance of precocity, no symptoms of decay. A
long course of continuing improvement is in prospect before us, with
no limits which human foresight can descry. Actual liberty and equality with our white population has been approached much nearer than
in the free States. Few of our whites ever work as day laborers, none
as cooks, scullions, ostlers, body servants, or in other menial capacities. One free citizen does not lord it over another; hence that feeling
of independence and equality that distinguishes us; hence that pride
of character, that self-respect, that gives us ascendancy when we come
in contact with Northerners. It is a distinction to be a Southerner, as it
was once to be a Roman citizen.

In Virginia we are about to reform our constitution. A fair opportunity will be afforded to draw a wider line of distinction between
freemen and slaves, to elevate higher the condition of the citizen, to
inspire every white man with pride of rank and position. We should
do more for education. We have to educate but half of society, at the
North they attempt to educate all. Besides, here all men have time for
self-education, for reading and reflection. Nobody works long hours.
We should prohibit the exercise of mechanic arts to slaves (except on
their master's farm) and to free negroes. We should extend the right
of suffrage to all native Virginians, and to Southerners who move to
Virginia, over twenty-one years of age. We should permit no for-
eigner and no Northerner, who shall hereafter remove to the State, to
vote in elections. We should have a small, well drilled, paid militia,
to take the place of the patrol and the present useless militia system.
All men of good character should serve on juries without regard to
property qualifications. Thus we should furnish honorable occupation to all our citizens, whilst we cultivated and improved their
minds by requiring them all to take part in the administration of jus-

tice and of government. We should thus make poverty as honorable as it was in Greece and Rome; for to be a Virginian would be a higher distinction than wealth or title could bestow. We should cease to be a bye-word and reproach among nations for our love of the almighty dollar. We should be happy in the confidence that our posterity would never occupy the place of slaves, as half mankind must ever do in free society. Until the last fifteen years, our great error was to imitate Northern habits, customs and institutions. Our circumstances are so opposite to theirs, that whatever suits them is almost sure not to suit us. Until that time, in truth, we distrusted our social system. We thought slavery morally wrong, we thought it would not last, we thought it unprofitable. The Abolitionists assailed us; we looked more closely into our circumstances; became satisfied that slavery was morally right, that it would continue ever to exist, that it was as profitable as it was humane. This begat self-confidence, self-reliance. Since then our improvement has been rapid. Now we may safely say, that we are the happiest, most contented and prosperous people on earth. The intermeddling of foreign pseudo-philanthropists in our affairs, though it has occasioned great irritation and indignation, has been of inestimable advantage in teaching us to form a right estimate of our condition. This intermeddling will soon cease; the poor at home in thunder tones demand their whole attention and all their charity. Self-preservation will compel them to listen to their demands. Moreover, light is breaking in upon us from abroad. All parties in England now agree that the attempt to put down the slave trade has greatly aggravated its horrors, without at all diminishing the trade itself. It is proposed to withdraw her fleet from the African coast. France has already given notice that she will withdraw hers. America will follow the example. The emancipation of the slaves in the West Indies is admitted to have been a failure in all respects. The late masters have been ruined, the liberated slaves refuse to work, and are fast returning to the savage state, and England herself has sustained a severe blow in the present diminution and prospective annihilation of the once enormous imports from her West Indian colonies.

In conclusion, we will repeat the propositions, in somewhat different phraseology, with which we set out. First—That Liberty and Equality, with their concomitant Free Competition, beget a war in society that is as destructive to its weaker members as the custom of exposing the deformed and crippled children. Secondly—That slavery protects the weaker members of society just as do the relations of parent, guardian and husband, and is as necessary, as natural, and almost as universal as those relations. Is our demonstration imperfect? Does universal experience sustain our theory? Should the conclusions to which we have arrived appear strange and startling, let them therefore not be rejected without examination. The world has had but little opportunity to contrast the working of Liberty and Equality with the old order of things, which always partook more or less of the character of domestic slavery. The strong prepossession in the public mind in favor of the new system, makes it reluctant to attribute the evil phenomena which it exhibits, to defects inherent in the system itself. That these defects should not have been foreseen and pointed out by any process of *a priori* reasoning, is but another proof of the fallibility of human sagacity and foresight when attempting to foretell the operation of new institutions. It is as much as human reason can do, when examining the complex frame of society, to trace effects back to their causes—much more than it can do, to foresee what effects new causes will produce. We invite investigation.

CHAPTER 7

RESISTANCE TO THE EXTENSION OF SLAVERY

Proceedings of the Republican Convention at Pittsburgh, February 22, 1856

The passage of the Kansas-Nebraska Act in 1854 ushered in a period of party realignment in American politics. The opposition to the repeal of the Missouri Compromise and the application of popular sovereignty to the new territories resulted in the formation of a new party. The turmoil and confusion that existed in Kansas after the passage of the act stimulated this opposition movement. Known at first as the Anti-Nebraska Party, the new organization had its inception in several spontaneous protest meetings held throughout the North. The name Republican Party (chosen to enhance an identification with Thomas Jefferson) gradually supplanted the earlier label. Made up of old-line Whigs, Know-Nothings and Free-Soil Democrats, the Party included many diverse elements; unity was provided by a common opposition to the spread of slavery to the Western territories. On February 22, 1856, representatives of the new party met in Pittsburgh, Pennsylvania, to perfect their national organization for the pending Presidential election. An address to the people of the United States (the selection which follows) was issued and a national nominating convention was scheduled to meet in Philadelphia the following June.

TO THE PEOPLE OF THE UNITED STATES

Having met in convention in the city of Pittsburgh, in the State of Pennsylvania, this 22d day of February, 1856, as the representatives of people in various sections of the Union, to consult upon the political evils by which the country is menaced, and the political action by which those evils may be averted, we address to you this Declaration of our Principles, and of the purposes which we seek to promote.

We declare, in the first place, our fixed and unalterable devotion to the Constitution of the United States, to the ends for which it was established, and to the means which it provided for their attainment. We accept the solemn protestation of the people of the United States, that they ordained it, "in order to form a more perfect Union, establish justice, ensure domestic tranquility, provide for the common defence, promote the general welfare, and secure the blessings of liberty to themselves and their posterity." We believe that the powers which it confers upon the Government of the United States are ample for the accomplishment of these objects; and that if these powers are exercised in the spirit of the Constitution itself, they cannot lead to any other result. We respect those great rights which the Constitution declares to be inviolable, freedom of speech and of the Press, the free exercise of religious belief, and the right of the people peaceably to assemble and to petition the Government for a redress of grievances. We would preserve those great safeguards of civil freedom, the *habeas corpus,* the right of trial by jury, and the right of personal liberty, unless deprived thereof for crime by due process of law. We declare our purpose to obey in all things, the requirements of the Constitution, and of all laws enacted in pursuance thereof. We cherish a profound reverence for the wise and patriotic men by whom it was framed, and a lively sense of the blessings it has conferred upon our country, and upon mankind throughout the world. In every crisis of difficulty and of danger, we shall invoke its spirit, and proclaim the supremacy of its authority.

In the next place, we declare our ardent and unshaken attachment to this Union of American States, which the Constitution created, and has thus far preserved. We revere it as the purchase of the blood of our forefathers, as the condition of our national renown, and as the guardian and guarantee of that Liberty which the Constitution was designed to secure. We will defend and protect it against all its enemies. We will recognise no geographical divisions, no local interests, no narrow or sectional prejudices, in our endeavors to preserve the Union of these States against foreign aggression and domestic strife. What we claim for ourselves, we claim for all. The rights, privileges, and liberties, which we demand as our inheritance, we concede as their inheritance to all the citizens of this Republic.

Holding these opinions, and animated by these sentiments, we declare our conviction that the Government of the United States is not administered in accordance with the Constitution, or for the preservation or prosperity of the American Union; but that its powers are systematically wielded *For The Promotion And Extension Of The Interests Of Slavery,* in direct hostility to the letter and spirit of the Constitution, in flagrant disregard of other great interests of the country, and in open contempt of the public sentiment of the American people and of the Christian world. We proclaim our belief that the policy which has for years past been adopted in the administration of the General Government, tends to the utter subversion of each of the great ends for which the Constitution was established; and that, unless it shall be arrested by the prompt interposition of the people, the hold of the Union upon their loyalty and affection will be relaxed, the domestic tranquility will be disturbed, and all constitutional securities, for the blessings of liberty to ourselves and our posterity, will be destroyed. The slaveholding interest cannot be made permanently paramount in the General Government, without involving consequences fatal to free institutions. We acknowledge that it is large and powerful; that in the States where it exists, it is entitled, under the Constitution, like all other local interests, to immunity from the interference of the General Government, and that it must necessarily exercise, through its representatives, a considerable share of political power. But there is nothing in its position, as there is certainly nothing in its character, to sustain the supremacy which it seeks to establish. There is not a State in the Union in which the slaveholders number *one-tenth* part of the free white population—nor in the aggregate do they number *one-fiftieth* part of the white population of the United States. The annual productions of the other classes in the Union far exceed the total value of all the slaves. To say nothing, therefore, of the questions of natural justice and of political economy which Slavery involves, neither its magnitude, nor the number of those by whom it is represented, entitle it to *one-tenth* part of the political powers conferred upon the Federal Government by the Constitution. Yet we see it seeking, and at this moment wielding, all the functions of government—executive, legislative, and judicial—and using them for the augmentation of its powers and the establishment of its ascendency.

From this ascendency, the principles of the Constitution, the rights of the several States, the safety of the Union, and the welfare of the People of the United States, demand that it should be dislodged. . . .

The first contest concerning the admission of a new State, which turned upon the question of Slavery, occurred in 1819, when Missouri, formed out of territory purchased from France in 1803, applied to Congress for admission to the Union as a slaveholding State. The application was strenuously resisted by the people of the free States. It was everywhere felt that the decision involved consequences of the last importance to the welfare of the country, and that, if the progress of Slavery was ever to be arrested, that was the time to arrest it. The slaveholding interest demanded its admission as a right, and denied the power of Congress to impose conditions upon new States applying to be admitted into the Confederacy. The power rested with the free States, and Missouri was denied admission. But the subject was reviewed. The slaveholding interest, with characteristic and timely sagacity, abated something of its pretensions, and settled the controversy on the basis of compromise. Missouri was admitted into the Union, by an act bearing date March 6, 1820, in which it was also declared that "in all that territory ceded by France to the United States, under the name of Louisiana, which lies north of 36° 30′ of north latitude, not included within the limits of the State of Missouri, SLAVERY AND INVOLUNTARY SERVITUDE otherwise than in the punishment of crimes whereof the parties shall have been duly convicted, SHALL BE, AND IS HEREBY, FOREVER PROHIBITED." In each house of Congress, a majority of the members from the slaveholding States voted in favor of the bill with this provision—thus declaring and exercising, by their votes, the constitutional power of Congress to prohibit Slavery even in Territories where it had been permitted by the law of France, at the date of their cession to the United States. A new slave State, Arkansas, formed out of that portion of this Territory lying south of 36° 30′, to which the prohibition was not extended, was admitted to the Union in 1836. Two slave States thus came into the Confederacy by virtue of this arrangement; while Freedom gained nothing by it but the prohibition of Slavery from a vast region which civilization had made no attempt to penetrate.

Thus ended the first great contest of Freedom and Slavery for position and power in the General Government. The slaveholding interest had achieved a virtual victory. It secured all the immediate results for which it struggled; it acquired the power of offsetting, in the Federal Senate, two of the free States of the Confederacy; and the time could not be foreseen when, in the fulfillment of its compact, it would yield any positive and practical advantage to the interests of Freedom. Neither then, nor for many years thereafter, did any statesman dream that, when the period should arrive, the slaveholding interest would trample on its bond, and fling its faith to the winds.

A quarter of a century elapsed before the annexation of Texas. Slavery bad been active, meantime, in fastening its hold upon the Government, in binding political parties to its chariot, and in seeking in Congress to stifle the right of petition, and to crush all freedom of speech and of the press. In every slaveholding State, none but slaveholders, or those whose interests are identified with Slavery, were admitted to fill any office, or exercise any authority, civil or political. The whites, not slaveholders, in their presence, or in the midst of their society, were reduced to a vassalage little less degrading than that of the slaves themselves. Even at this day, although the white population of the slaveholding States is more than six millions, of whom but 347,525, or less than *one-seventeenth*, are the owners of slaves, none but a slaveholder, or one who will act with exclusive reference to Slavery, is ever allowed to represent the State in any National Convention, in either branch of Congress, or in any high position of civil trust and political power. The slaveholding class, small as it is, is the governing class, and shapes legislation and guides all public action for the advancement of its own interests and the promotion of its own ends. During all that time, and from that time even to the present, all slaveholding delegates in National Conventions, upon whatever else they may differ, always concur in imposing upon the convention assent to their requisitions in regard to Slavery, as the indispensable condition of their support. Holding thus in their hands power to decide the result of the election, and using that power, undeviatingly and sternly, for the extortion of their demands, they have always been able to control the nominations of both parties, and thus, whatever may be the issue, to secure a President who is sure to be the instrument of their behests. Thus has it come to pass that, for twenty years, we have never had a President who would appoint to the humblest office within his gift, in any section of the Union, any man known to hold opinions hostile to Slavery, or to be active in resisting its aggressions and usurpations of power. Men, the most upright and the most respectable, in States where Slavery is only known by name, have been ineligible to the smallest trust—have been held unfit to distribute letters from the Federal post-office to their neighbors, or trim the lamps of a lighthouse upon the remotest point of our extended coast. Millions of our citizens have been thus disfranchised for their opinions concerning Slavery, and the vast patronage of the General Government has been systematically wielded in its service, and for the promotion of its designs.

It was by such discipline, and under such influences, that the Government and the country were prepared for the second great stride of Slavery towards new dominion, and for the avowal of motives by which it was attended. . . .

Texas was admitted into the Union on the 29th December, 1845, with a Constitution forbidding the abolition of Slavery, and a stipulation that *four more* States should become members of the Confederacy, whenever they might be formed within her limits, and with or without Slavery, as their inhabitants might decide. The General Government then made virtual provision for the addition of *five* new slave States to the Union—practically securing to the slaveholding interest ten additional members in the Senate—representing States, it might be, with less than a million inhabitants, and out-voting five of the old States, with an aggregate population of eleven millions. The corrupt and tyrannical Kings of England, when votes were needed in the House of Lords to sustain them against the people, created Peers as the emergency required. Is there in this anything in more flagrant contradiction to the principles of Republican Freedom, or more dangerous to the public liberties, than in the system practised by the slaveholding interest represented in the General Government?

But a third opportunity was close at hand, and Slavery made a third struggle for the extension of its domain and the enlargement of its power.

The annexation of Texas involved us in war with Mexico. The war was waged on our part with vigor, skill, and success. It resulted in the cession to the United States of New Mexico, California, and Deseret, vast territories over which was extended by Mexican law a prohibition of Slavery. The slaveholders demanded access to them all, resisted the admission of California and New Mexico, which the energy of freemen, outstripping in its activity the Government, and even the slaveholding interest, had already converted into free States, and treasonably menaced Congress and the Union with overthrow, if its demands were not conceded. The free spirit of the country was roused with indignation by these pretensions, and for a time the whole nation roused to the tempest which they had created. Untoward events aided the wrong. The death of the President threw the whole power of the Administration into timid and faithless hands. Party resentments and party ambitions interposed against the right. Great men, leaders of the people, from whom, in better days, the people had learned lessons of principles and patriotism, yielded to the howlings of the storm, and sought shelter, in submission, from its rage. The slaveholding interest was again victorious. California, with her free constitution, was indeed admitted into the Union; but New Mexico, with her constitution forbidding Slavery within her borders, was denied admission, and remanded to the condition of a Territory; and while Congress refused to enact a positive prohibition of Slavery in the Territories of New Mexico and Deseret, it was provided that, when they should apply for admission as States, they should come in with or without Slavery, as their inhabitants might decide. Additional concessions were made to the Slave Power—the General Government assumed the recapture of fugitive slaves, and passed laws for the accomplishment of that end, subversive at once of State sovereignty, and of the established safeguard of civil freedom. Then the country again had rest. Wearied with its efforts, or content with their success, the slaveholding interest proclaimed a truce.

When Franklin Pierce, on the 4th of March, 1853, became President of the United States, no controversy growing out of Slavery was agitating the country. Established laws, some of them enacted with unusual solemnity, and under circumstances which made them of more than ordinary obligation, had fixed the character of all the States, and ended the contest concerning the Territories. Sixteen States were free States, and fifteen States were Slave States. By the Missouri Compromise of 1820, Slavery was forever prohibited from all the Louisiana Territory lying north of the line of 36° 30′; while over that Territory lying south of that line, and over the Territories of New Mexico and Deseret, no such prohibition had been extended. The whole country reposed upon this arrangement. All sections and all interests, whether approving it or not, seemed to acquiesce in its terms. The slaveholding interest, through all its organs, and especially through the General Government, proclaimed that this was a final and irrepealable adjustment of the struggle between Freedom and Slavery for political power; that it had been effected by mutual concessions, and in the spirit of compromise; and that it should be as enduring as the Union, and as sacred as the Constitution itself. Both political parties gave it their sanction in their National Conventions; the whole country assented to its validity; and President Pierce, in his first official message to Congress, pledged himself to use all the power of his position to prevent it from being disturbed.

But all these protestations proved delusive, and the acquiescence and contentment which they produced afforded the opportunity, not only for new aggressions on the part of Slavery, but for the repudiation of engagements into which its agents had solemnly entered. Less than a year had elapsed before these pledges were broken, and the advantages which they secured to Freedom withdrawn by the slaveholding power. . . .

In the course of time and the natural progress of population, that portion of the Louisiana Territory lying west of the Mississippi river, and north of the line of 36° 30′, came to be desired for occupation; and on the 24th of March, 1854, an act was passed erecting upon it the two Territories of Kansas and Nebraska, and organizing Governments for them both. From this whole region, the slaveholding interest, thirty-four years before, had agreed that "Slavery and involuntary servitude, otherwise than in the punishment of crime, should be forever prohibited," and had received, as the price of this agreement, the admission of Missouri, and, subsequently, the admission of Arkansas, into the Union. By the Kansas and Nebraska bill, this prohibition was declared to be "inoperative and void;" and the intent and meaning of the bill was further declared to be, "not to legislate Slavery into any Territory or State, nor to exclude it therefrom, but to leave the people thereof perfectly free to form and regulate their domestic institutions in their own way, subject only to the Constitution of the

United States." Thus, without a single petition for such action from any quarter of the Union, but against the earnest remonstrances of thousands of our citizens against the settled and profound convictions of the great body of the people in every portion of the country, and in wanton disregard of the obligations of justice and of good faith, the Missouri Compromise of 1820 was repealed, and the seal which had guaranteed Freedom to that vast Territory which the United States had purchased from France was snatched from the bond. Oregon, Washington, New Mexico, Deseret, and the new State acquired from Texas north of 36° 30', by compact, were all opened up to Slavery, and those who might first become the inhabitants thereof were authorized to make laws for its establishment and perpetuation. . . .

Nor did the slaveholding interest stop here in its crusade of injustice and wrong. The first election of members for the Territorial Legislature of Kansas was fixed for the 30th of March, 1855, and the law of Congress prescribed that at that election none but "actual residents of the Territory" should be allowed to vote. Yet, to prevent people of the Territory themselves from exercising the right to prohibit Slavery, which the act of Congress had conferred upon them, the slaveholding interest sent armed bands of men from the neighboring State of Missouri, who entered the Territory on the day of election, took possession of the polls, excluded the legal voters, and proceeded themselves to elect members of the Legislature, without the slightest regard to the qualifications prescribed by law. The judges of election, appointed under authority of the Administration at Washington, aided and abetted in the perpetration of the outrages upon the rights of the people of Kansas, and the President of the United States removed from office the Governor whom he had himself appointed, but who refused to acknowledge the Legislature which the slaveholding invaders from Missouri had thus imposed upon the Territory.

That Legislature met on the 2d of July, 1855. Its first act was to exclude those members, duly elected, who would not consent to the enactment of laws for the admission of Slavery into the Territory. Having thus silenced all opposition to its behests, the Legislature proceeded to the enactment of laws for the government of Kansas upon the subject of Slavery. The laws of Missouri in regard to it were at first extended over the Territory. It was then enacted, that every person who should raise an insurrection or rebellion of negroes in the

Territory; every person who should entice away a slave, with intent
to procure his freedom; every person who should aid or assist in so
enticing away a slave within the Territory; and every person who
should entice or carry away a slave from any other State or Territory
of the Union, and bring him within the Territory of Kansas, with the
intent to effect or procure his freedom, upon the conviction thereof
should suffer DEATH. It was further enacted, that if any person should
write, print, or publish any book, paper, argument, opinion, advice,
or inuendo, calculated to produce a disorderly, dangerous, or rebellious disaffection among the slaves in the Territory, or to induce them
to escape from their masters, he should be deemed guilty of FELONY,
and be punished by imprisonment at hard labor for a term not less
than FIVE YEARS; and that if any free person, by speaking or writing
should assert or maintain that persons have not the right to hold
slaves in that Territory; or should introduce or circulate any book,
paper, pamphlet, or circular, containing any such denial of the right
of persons to hold slaves in that Territory, he should be deemed
guilty of felony, and be punished by IMPRISONMENT at hard labor for a
term not less than TWO YEARS. It was still further enacted, by the same
Legislature, that every free white male citizen of the United States,
and inhabitant of the Territory, who should pay a tax of one dollar,
and take an oath to support the Constitution of the United States, the
act organizing the Territory of Kansas, the Territorial law, and the act
for the recapture of fugitive slaves, should be entitled to vote at any
election in said Territory—thus making citizens of Missouri, or of any
other State, legal voters in Kansas, upon their presentation at the
polls, upon taking the oaths prescribed, and upon the payment of one
dollar—in direct violation of the spirit of the act of Congress, and in
open disregard of the rights of the people of the Territory. And having made these enactments for the establishment of Slavery, the Legislature appointed Sheriffs, Judges, and other officers of the Territory,
for their enforcement—thus depriving the people of all power over
the enactment of their own laws, and the choice of officers for their
execution.

That these despotic acts, even if they had been passed by a Legislature duly elected by the people of the Territory, would have been
null and void, inasmuch as they are plainly in violation of the Federal
Constitution, is too clear for argument. Congress itself is expressly for-

bidden by the Constitution of the United States to make any laws abridging the freedom of speech and of the press; and it is absurd to suppose that a Territorial Legislature, deriving all its power from Congress, should not be subject to the same restrictions. But these laws were not enacted by the people of Kansas. They were imposed upon them by an armed force. Yet the President of the United States, in a special message sent to Congress on the 24th of January, 1856, declares that they have been enacted by the duly-constituted authorities of the Territory, and that they are of binding obligation upon the people thereof. And on the 12th of February, 1856, he issued his proclamation, denouncing any attempt to resist or subvert these barbarous and void enactments, and warning all persons engaged in such attempts, that they will be opposed, not only by the local militia, but by any available forces belonging to the regular army of the United States. Thus has the Federal Government solemnly recognised the usurpation set up in Kansas by invaders from Missouri, and pledged all the power of the United States to its support. American history furnishes no parallel to the cruelty and tyranny of these acts of the present Administration. The expulsion of aliens, and the penalties inflicted upon citizens for exercising freedom of speech and of the press, under the alien and sedition laws, which were overthrown by the Republican party of 1798, were lenient and mild when compared with the outrages perpetrated upon the people of Kansas, under color of law, by the usurping invaders, sustained by the Federal Government.

With a full sense of the importance of the declaration, we affirm that the execution of these threats by the President of the United States, upon the people of Kansas, would be an unconstitutional exercise of Executive power, presenting a case of intolerable tyranny; that American citizens cannot submit to it, and remain free; and that if blood shall be shed in the prosecution of so unlawful a purpose, those by whose agency it may be spilt will be held to a strict and stern account by the freemen of the Republic. So plain, palpable, and deliberate a violation of the Constitution, would justify the interposition of the States, whose duty it would be, by all the constitutional means in their power, to vindicate the rights and liberties of the citizen against the power of the Federal Government; and we take this occasion to express to our fellow-citizens in Kansas, against whom these unconstitutional acts are directed, our profound sympathy with them in the resistance which it is their right and their duty to make to them, and our determination to make that sympathy efficient by all the means which we may lawfully employ.

Thus, for a period of twenty-five years, has slavery been contending, under various pretexts, but with constant success, against the tendencies of civilization and the spirit of our institutions, for the extension and perpetuation of its power. The degree in which the General Government has aided its efforts may be traced in the successive steps it has taken. In 1787, all the States in the Confederacy united in ordaining that Slavery should be forever prohibited from all the territory belonging to the United States. In 1789, the first Congress of the United States passed a law reaffirming this ordinance, and re-enacting the prohibition of Slavery which it contained. In 1820, the slaveholding interest secured the admission of Missouri, as a slave State, into the Union, by acceding to a similar prohibition of Slavery from the Louisiana Territory lying north of 36° 30'. In 1854, that prohibition was repealed, and the people of the Territory were left free to admit or exclude Slavery, in their own discretion. In 1856, the General Government proclaims its determination to use all the power of the United States to enforce upon the people obedience to laws imposed upon them by armed invaders, establishing Slavery, and visiting with terrible penalties their exercise of freedom of speech and of the press upon that subject. While two-thirds of the American people live in States where Slavery is forbidden by law, and while five-sixths of the capital, enterprise, and productive industry of the country rests upon Freedom as their basis, Slavery thus controls all departments of their common Government, and wields their powers on its own behalf. . . .

As a matter of course, for all these acts, and for all the outrages by which they have been attended, the slaveholding interest pretends to find a warrant in the Constitution of the United States. All usurpation, in countries professing to be free, must have the color of law for its support. No outrage, committed by Power upon Popular Rights, is left without some attempt at vindication. The partition of Poland, the overthrow of the Constitution of Hungary, the destruction of Irish independence, like the repeal of the Missouri Compromise and the conquest of Kansas, were consummated with a scrupulous observance of the forms of law. . . .

I. The repeal of the Missouri Compromise, it is urged on behalf of those by whom it was effected, involved no violation of good faith, because that Compromise was merely an act of Congress, and as such repealable at pleasure. Regarded as a legal technicality, we are not disposed to contest this plea. The Compromise was undoubtedly embodied in a Congressional enactment, subject to repeal. But in this case, by the very nature of the transaction, the faith of the parties was pledged that this enactment *should not be* repealed. The spirit of the law, whatever its form, was the spirit of a compact. Its enactment was secured by an exchange of equivalents. The slaveholding interest procured the admission of Missouri into the Union, by consenting and voting, through its Representatives in Congress, that north of its southern line, in the Territory of Louisiana, Slavery should be prohibited *forever.* Without that consent and that vote, the admission of Missouri could not have been secured; nor would the prohibition of Slavery until 1854, or until any other date, or for any other time than that specified in the act—namely, *forever*—have purchased the assent of the free States to the admission of Missouri as a Slave State into the Union. The word *forever,* therefore, was a part of the law, and of the consideration for its enactment. Such a law may be repealed; but its repeal is the rupture of a compact—the repudiation of a solemn covenant. The Missouri Compromise has been regarded as such a compact, from the date of its enactment, in all sections and by all the people of the country. Successive Presidents have invoked for it a respect and an obligation scarcely inferior to that of the Constitution itself; and Senator Douglas himself, as late as 1845, declared that it had been "canonized in the hearts of the American people, as a sacred thing, which no ruthless hand would ever be reckless enough to disturb." Whatever, therefore, the mere form of the bond may have permitted, good faith on the part of the representatives of the slaveholding interest required that it should be kept inviolate.

II. Nor is this charge of bad faith, brought against the slaveholding interest for having repealed the Missouri Compromise, answered or evaded by the pleas argued in its defence, that originally it was forcibly imposed by the free States upon the slave States, without their consent; that it was subsequently violated by the free States, in their refusal to extend its provisions over New Mexico and Utah; or that its repeal, having been offered by the free States themselves, could not be resisted or refused by the representatives of Slavery. (1.) Even if it were true that the prohibition of Slavery north of 36° 30′ was originally enacted by the free States, against the votes of the South, the fact that the admission of Missouri was accepted as the price of that prohibition would have made the slaveholding interest a party to the transaction, assenting to its terms, and bound by its obligations. But the fact is not so. The act of March 6, 1820, which admitted Missouri, and prohibited Slavery in the Louisiana Territory north of 36° 30′, received in the Senate the vote of *fourteen* members from slaveholding States, while only *eight* were cast against it; and in the House of Representatives, *thirty-eight* members from the slave States voted for it, and *thirty-seven* against it. A majority of the votes from slaveholding States, in each branch of Congress, were thus given for the bill; and so far were the representatives of Slavery from regarding it as having been forced upon them, that Charles Pinckney, one of their greatest and ablest leaders, declared, on the night of its passage, that *"it was regarded in the slaveholding States as a triumph."* (2.) Still more absurd is it to say that the refusal of the North to extend the provisions of the Compromise over other regions, was a violation of its terms, or in any way released the parties to it from their obligation to abide by its requirements. (3.) It is true that the ostensible author of the proposition to repeal it was a Senator from a free State; but the fact did not authorize the inference that the sentiment of the free States was justly and truly represented by his action. There was, indeed, no room to doubt that it was condemned by the unanimous voice of the free States, and that it would be regarded by them, and by the country at large, as a very gross and wanton violation of obligations which had been voluntarily assumed. No matter from what geographical quarter of the Union it came, it was brought forward in the interest and on behalf of the slaveholders. This indeed, is among the worst of the effects of Slavery, and among the most signal proofs of its ascendency, that able and ambitious men should enlist in its service, and volunteer to perform offices on its behalf which its representatives would scorn to perform themselves—from the conviction that by that path the honors and dignities of the General Government are to be secured. The slaveholding interest owed it to honor and good faith to resist the temptation which such men might hold out for the repudiation of its obligations. . . .

III. But it is urged that the original enactment of the Missouri Compromise, by which Slavery was prohibited from entering a portion of the territory of the United States, was a violation of the Constitution; that Congress has no rightful power to make such a prohibition; but that into any territory over which the Constitution is extended, the slaveholder has a right, by virtue of its provisions, to take his slaves.

In reply to this, we answer:

First—That, whether the plea be true or false, it comes too late; that the slaveholding interest conceded the constitutionality of the prohibition, by assenting to its enactment, and aiding it by the votes of its representatives.

Second—That, if the plea were true, the enactment was null and void, by reason of its unconstitutionality, and its repeal, therefore, was a needless ostentation of bad faith; and,

Third—That the plea is not true, but is directly contrary to the plain letter as well as to the spirit of the Constitution, and to the uniform practice of Government from its foundation.

The Constitution declares that "the Congress shall have power to make all needful rules and regulations respecting the Territories or other property belonging to the United States." This language is very plain and very broad. It imposes no limitation upon the power of Congress to make rules and regulations respecting the Territories, except that they shall be such as are "needful;" and this, of course, lies in the discretion of power to determine. It assumes that power to legislate for the Territories, which are the common property of the Union, must exist somewhere; and also that it may most justly, and most safely, be placed in the common Government of the Union. The authority of Congress over the Territories is therefore without any other limit than such as its judgment of what is "needful," of what will best promote their welfare, and that of the whole country to which they belong, may impose. If Congress, therefore, deem it expedient to make a rule and regulation which shall prohibit Slavery from any Territory, we find nothing in the Constitution which removes such a prohibition from the sphere of its authority. The power of Congress over the Territories of the United States is as complete and as full as that possessed by any State Legislature over territory belonging to that State; and if the latter may prohibit Slavery within its territory, so may the former also.

It has been urged, we are aware, that the rules and regulations which Congress is authorized to make respecting the Territories are restricted to them and regarded as property; and that this clause of the Constitution confers no governmental power over them whatever. But this cannot be so, because it is under this clause that Congress does govern the Territories—that it organizes their Governments and provides for their ultimate admission as States. There is no other clause of the Constitution from which this power of government can be inferred; as it unquestionably exists, therefore it must rest upon this provision. But from whatever source it may be derived, the authority to govern necessarily implies the right to decide what policy and what laws will best promote the welfare of those on whose behalf that authority is exercised. If Congress, therefore, believes that the well-being of the Territories and of the country at large will be promoted by excluding Slavery from them, it has, beyond all question, the right thus to prohibit and exclude it.

This view of the authority of Congress over the Territories of the United States is sustained by other clauses of the Constitution. In the ninth section of the first article, it is declared that "the migration or importation of such persons as any of the States *now existing* may think proper to admit, shall not be prohibited by Congress prior to the year 1808." This is not a grant of power. On the contrary, it is a restriction imposed upon power assumed to exist. The language of the clause takes it for granted that Congress had power to prohibit the migration and the importation of slaves—a power doubtless conferred by the authority "to regulate commerce with foreign nations and among the several States;" for, whether slaves are to be regarded as persons or as property, commerce of necessity relates to both. This clause of the Constitution, therefore, imposes upon the authority of Congress to prohibit the migration or importation of slaves a specific and a limited restriction—namely that this power should not be exercised over any of the States *then existing*, prior to the year 1808. Over any State *not* then existing, and, by still stronger implication, over any *Territories* of the United States, the exercise of its authority was unrestricted; and it might prohibit the migration or importation of slaves into them, at any time, in its own discretion.

Nor do any considerations connected with alleged rights of property in slaves contravene the existence or the exercise of this authority.

The Constitution does not recognise slaves as property, in any instance, or to any extent. In the clause already cited, they are called "persons." In the clause respecting their escape into other States, they are to be returned, not as property, but as "persons held to service or labor." And in the apportionment of representation and of direct taxes, it is provided by the Constitution that to the whole number of free persons are to be added three-fifths of all other "persons." In all its provisions which have reference to slaves, they are described and regarded as persons. The idea of their being property is carefully and intentionally excluded. If they are property at all, therefore, it is not by virtue of the Constitution, but of local laws, and only within their jurisdiction. The local laws of any State are excluded from the Territories of the United States, by the necessity of the case as well as by the exclusive sovereignty conferred upon Congress. . . .

Failing thus to establish the right of the slaveholder to carry his slaves as property, by virtue of the Constitution, into territory belonging to the United States, the slaveholding interest has been compelled to claim, for the inhabitants of the Territories themselves, the right to provide for excluding or admitting Slavery, as a right inherent in their sovereignty over their own affairs. This principle of popular sovereignty, as it is styled, was embodied in the bills for organizing New Mexico and Utah, and is made the substitute for the prohibition of Slavery in the Missouri Compromise, which it repealed; and the slaveholding interest is now sustained by the Federal Government in this new position, as it has been in all the positions it has successively assumed. The principle of popular sovereignty is fundamental in our institutions. No one doubts that the people are sovereign over all the Territories, as well as over all the States of the Confederacy. But this sovereignty is subject to limitation and definition, and can only exist within the limitations of the Constitution. The People are sovereign in the House of Representatives; but their sovereignty may be overruled by the Senate, or defeated by the veto of the President. The States are sovereign; but only within certain limits, and in subordination to the sovereignty of the nation. Two sovereignties over the same country, and on the same subject, it is manifest, cannot co-exist; one must of necessity exclude the other. But the Constitution, in express and unmistakeable terms, makes Congress sovereign over the Territories, by conferring upon it power to make "*all* needful rules and regulations respecting them." The doctrine of popular sovereignty in the people of the Territories finds no warrant or support in the Constitution. In the language of Mr. Calhoun, "it involves an absurdity; if the sovereignty over the Territories be in their inhabitants, instead of the United States, they would cease to be Territories of the United States, the moment we permit them to be inhabited." So long as they remain Territories, they are the possession and under the exclusive dominion of the United States; and it is for the General Government to make such laws for them as their welfare, and that of the nation, may require.

We deny that Congress may abdicate a portion of its authority, and commit to the inhabitants of a Territory powers conferred upon it by the Constitution. Such an abdication is an abandonment of duty, and cannot be justified on the pretended principle of popular sovereignty. That principle, indeed, is discarded in the very act of Congress in which it is claimed to be embodied. If sovereignty exists, it must be exercised through the organized departments of Government—the legislative, executive, and judicial. But the act to organize the Territories of Kansas and Nebraska prescribes the requisites of citizenship and the qualifications of voters, confers upon the President and Senate the appointment of a Governor, who is clothed with the veto power, and of judges by whom the common law shall be interpreted. Each department of the Government thus rests virtually in the power of the President of the United States. To style the small remnant of power which such a law leaves to the people "popular sovereignty," is an abuse of language, and an insult to common sense. Yet even this has been effectually destroyed, by the invasion of armed men, sustained by the General Government in their high-handed endeavor to force Slavery into Kansas, against the will of the hardy settlers who have made it their home.

This whole system of doctrine by which Slavery seeks possession of the Territories of the United States, either by asserting the sovereignty of their inhabitants, or by denying the power of Congress to exclude and prohibit Slavery from them, is novel and alien to the principles and the administration of our Government. Congress has always asserted and exercised the right of prohibition. It was exercised by the vote of the First Congress, in 1789, reaffirming the ordinance of the old Confederacy by which Slavery was prohibited from the Territory northwest of the Ohio river. It was exercised in 1820, in the prohibition of Slavery from the Louisiana Territory north of 36° 30'. It was exercised in 1848, when Slavery was prohibited from the Territory of Oregon.

Nor is it in the least degree impaired by the argument that these Territories, when they become States, and are admitted into the Union, can establish or prohibit Slavery, in their discretion. Their rights as States do not begin until their obligations as Territories end. The Constitution knows nothing of "inchoate States." Congress has power to make "all needful rules and regulations" for them as Territories, until they are admitted into the Union as members of the common Confederacy. . . .

In all these successive acts, in the admission of Missouri and of Arkansas, in the annexation of Texas, and the provision for admitting four new States from her territory in the war with Mexico and the conquest of her provinces, in the repeal of the Missouri Compromise, and in the cruel war now waged against the people of Kansas for the extension of Slavery into that Territory, we trace the footsteps of a powerful interest, aiming at absolute political power, and striding onward to a complete ascendency over the General Government. It finds powerful allies, and an open field in the political arena, for the prosecution of its purposes. Always acting as a compact unit, it finds its opponents divided by a variety of interests. Partisan alliances and personal ambitions have hitherto prevented any union against its aggressions; and not feeling or fearing the displeasure of their constituents, Representatives from the free States have been induced to aid in the promotion of its designs. All other interests have been compelled to give way before it. The representatives of Freedom on the floors of Congress have been treated with contumely, if they resist or question the right to supremacy of the slaveholding class. The labor and the commerce of sections where Slavery does not exist obtain tardy and inadequate recognition from the General Government, which is swayed by its influence, and for the accomplishment of its ends. The Executive of the nation is the willing servant of its behests, and sacrifices to its favor the rights and the interests of the country. The purse and the sword of the nation are at its command. A hundred millions of dollars were expended in the annexation of Texas, and the war with Mexico, which was a part of its price. Two hundred millions have been offered for Cuba, and war with all Europe is threatened, if necessary, to prevent the emancipation of its slaves. Thus is the decision of great questions of public policy, touching vast interests and vital rights—questions even of peace and of war—made to turn, not upon the requirements of justice and honor, but upon its relation to the subject of Slavery—upon the effect it will have upon the interest of the slaveholding class.

The people of the free States have cherished the hope that the efforts made to extend Slavery, which have fallen under their notice, were accidental, and indicative of weakness rather than ambition. They have trusted that the sagacious statesmen of the slaveholding States would gradually perceive and acknowledge the inconvenience and danger of Slavery, and would take such measures as they might deem wise and safe for its ultimate removal. They have feared the effect of agitation upon this subject, relied upon the good faith and honor of the slaveholding States, and believed that time, the natural growth of population, and the recognised laws of political and social economy, would gradually and peacefully work out the extinction of a system so repugnant to justice and the national character and welfare. It has seemed to them incredible, that in this late age, when Christianity has for near two thousand years been filling the world with its light, and when almost every nation on earth but our own has abolished chattel slavery, the effort should be made, or the wish cherished, by any portion of our people, to make the interest of Slavery predominant, and to convert this Republic, the only Government which professes to be founded upon human rights, into the mightiest slave empire the world has ever seen. But it is impossible to deceive ourselves longer. The events of the past two years have disclosed the designs of the slave power, and the desperate means it is prepared to use for their accomplishment. We cannot shut our eyes longer to the fact that the slaveholding interest is determined to counteract the tendencies of time and of civilization, by its own energy, by its bold appropriation of all the powers and agencies of the Government, and by the violation, if need be, of the most sacred compacts and compromises. It is resolved that Slavery shall be under the protection of the national flag—that it shall no longer be the creature of local law, but that it shall stand clothed with all the sanctions, and sustained by all the power of this great Republic. It is determined that the President shall do its bidding, and that Congress shall legislate according to its decrees. It is resolved upon the dethronement of the principles of Republicanism, and the establishment, in their stead, of an OLIGARCHY, bound together by a common interest in the ownership of slaves.

Nor have we any reason to believe that Slavery will be content with this absolute supremacy over the Federal Government, which it has already so well-nigh achieved. On the contrary, the dark shadow of its sceptre falls upon the sovereignty of the several States, and menaces them with dire disaster. South Carolina, abandoning her once-cherished doctrine of State Rights, asserts the Federal supremacy over laws made by States, exclusively for the protection of their citizens. The State of Virginia is contesting in courts of law the right of the State of New York to forbid the existence of Slavery within her limits. A Federal Court in Pennsylvania has denied the right of that State to decree freedom to slaves brought by their masters within her borders, and has proclaimed that Slavery exists by the law of nations. The division of California, and the organization of a slave State within her limits, have been proposed. A Senator on the floor of Congress has urged that the Government of the United States should no longer restrain, by its naval power, the African slave trade, and the demand for its restoration is openly made by Southern journals and by leading public men in the Southern States.

When these great objects shall have been accomplished—when the States, as well as the General Government, shall have become subject to the law of Slavery, and when three hundred and fifty thousand slaveholders shall hold despotic rule over the millions of this Republic, Slavery cannot fail, from the necessity of its nature, to attempt outrages which will awaken storms that will sweep it in carnage from the face of the earth. The longer tyranny is practiced unresisted, the fiercer and the more dreadful is the resistance which in the end it provokes. History is full of instances to prove that nothing is so dangerous as a wrong long unredressed—that evils, which at the outset it would have been easy to remove, by sufferance become fatal to those through whose indifference and toleration they have increased. The tendencies of the measures adopted by the slaveholding interests to secure its own extension through the action of the Federal Government, is to give to Congress jurisdiction of the general subject; and its representatives must be sagacious enough to perceive, that if they establish the principle that Congress may interfere with Slavery for its protection, it may interfere with it also for its destruction. If, therefore, they succeed in such an enlargement of the power of Congress—having already discarded the principle of compromise from legislation—they must foresee that the natural effect of their encroachments upon the rights and liberties of the non-slaveholding population of the country will be to arouse them to the direct exercise of the power thus placed in their hands. Whether it is safe or wise for that interest to invite such a contest, we need not here consider.

The time draws nigh, fellow-countrymen, when you will be called upon to decide upon the policy and the principles of the General Government. Your votes at the approaching Presidential election will determine whether Slavery shall continue to be the paramount and controlling influence in the Federal Administration, or whether other rights and other interests shall resume the degree of consideration to which they are entitled. The issue is upon us by no act of ours, and it cannot be evaded. Under a profound conviction of impending dangers, the grounds whereof we have now set forth, we call upon you to deliver the Constitution and the Union from the subjugation which threatens both. Holding, with the late Mr. Calhoun, that "the obligation to repel aggression is not much less solemn than that of abstaining from making aggression, and that the party which submits to it, when it can be resisted, is not much less guilty and responsible for consequences than that which makes it," we invoke a surrender of all party prejudices and all personal feelings, and a cordial and earnest union for the vindication of rights and liberties which we cannot surrender without degradation and shame. We summon you to send delegates, in numbers three times as large as your representation in Congress, to meet in Convention at Philadelphia, on the 17th day of June next, to nominate candidates for the Presidency and Vice-Presidency of the United States. Let them come prepared to surrender all personal preferences, and all sectional or local views—resolved only to make such nominations and to take such action as shall advance the principles we hold and the purposes we seek to promote. Disclaiming any intention to interfere with Slavery in the States where it exists, or to invalidate those portions of the Constitution by which it is removed from the national control, let us prevent the General Government from its ascendency, bring back its administration to the principles and the practice of its wise and illustrious founders, and thus vindicate the Constitution and the Union, and secure the blessings of liberty to ourselves and our posterity.

We do, therefore, declare to the people of the United States, as objects for which we unite in political action:

1. We demand and shall attempt to secure the repeal of all laws which allow the introduction of Slavery into Territories once consecrated to Freedom, and will resist by every constitutional means the existence of Slavery in any of the Territories of the United States.

2. We will support by every lawful means our brethren in Kansas in their constitutional and manly resistance to the usurped authority of their lawless invaders, and will give the full weight of our political power in favor of the immediate admission of Kansas to the Union as a free, sovereign, and independent State.

3. Believing that the present National Administration has shown itself to be weak and faithless, and that its continuance in power is identified with the progress of the slave power to national supremacy, with the exclusion of Freedom from the Territory, and with increasing civil discord, it is a leading purpose of our organization to oppose and overthrow it.

CHAPTER 8

SPOKESMAN FOR THE MORAL ISSUE

Abraham Lincoln: Address at Cooper Institute, February 27, 1860

A braham Lincoln (1809–1865) became one of the most popular speakers and spokesmen of the Republican Party following his nationally publicized debates with Stephen A. Douglas in 1858. During the next two years he spoke extensively in such states as Ohio, Wisconsin, and Kansas. On February 27, 1860 Lincoln delivered one of his most significant speeches at the Cooper Institute (now Cooper Union) in New York City. Thoroughly political in nature, the address did a great deal to raise Lincoln's stature among Easterners and was an important step toward his nomination for the Presidency by the Republican Party. The preceding months had been crucial ones to the sectional conflict, and Lincoln's speech reflected the growing tension between North and South. Douglas had published his most complete exposition of popular sovereignty in Harper's Magazine *for September, 1859, claiming for his doctrine both a constitutional and historical justification. Not long afterward, John Brown's raid at Harper's Ferry, Virginia, sent a wave of fear through the slaveholding states, and instilled in the Southern mind an attitude toward the North and the Republican Party that could not easily be erased. During these same months, some Southern States reacted to the growing possibility that a Republican would be elected to the Presidency in 1860 by threatening a dissolution of the Union. Lincoln's speech at Cooper Institute was, to a large degree, directed to these developments.*

MR. PRESIDENT AND FELLOW-CITIZENS OF NEW-YORK:

The facts with which I shall deal this evening are mainly old and familiar; nor is there anything new in the general use I shall make of them. If there shall be any novelty, it will be in the mode of presenting the facts, and the inferences and observations following that presentation.

In his speech last autumn, at Columbus, Ohio, as reported in "The New-York Times," Senator Douglas said:

"Our fathers, when they framed the Government under which we live, understood this question just as well, and even better, than we do now."

I fully indorse this, and I adopt it as a text for this discourse. I so adopt it because it furnishes a precise and an agreed starting point for a discussion between Republicans and that wing of the Democracy headed by Senator Douglas. It simply leaves the inquiry: *"What was the understanding those fathers had of the question mentioned?"*

What is the frame of Government under which we live?

The answer must be: "The Constitution of the United States." That Constitution consists of the original, framed in 1787, (and under which the present government first went into operation,) and twelve subsequently framed amendments, the first ten of which were framed in 1789.

Who were our fathers that framed the Constitution? I suppose the "thirty-nine" who signed the original instrument may be fairly called our fathers who framed that part of the present Government. It is almost exactly true to say they framed it, and it is altogether true to say they fairly represented the opinion and sentiment of the whole nation at that time. Their names, being familiar to nearly all, and accessible to quite all, need not now be repeated.

I take these "thirty-nine" for the present, as being "our fathers who framed the Government under which we live."

What is the question which, according to the text, those fathers understood "just as well, and even better than we do now?"

It is this: Does the proper division of local from federal authority, or anything in the Constitution, forbid *our Federal Government* to control as to slavery in *our Federal Territories?*

Upon this, Senator Douglas holds the affirmative, and Republicans the negative. This affirmation and denial form an issue; and this issue—this question—is precisely what the text declares our fathers understood "better than we."

Let us now inquire whether the "thirty-nine," or any of them, ever acted upon this question; and if they did, how they acted upon it— how they expressed that better understanding?

In 1784, three years before the Constitution—the United States then owning the Northwestern Territory, and no other, the Congress of the Confederation had before them the question of prohibiting slavery in that Territory; and four of the "thirty-nine," who afterward framed the Constitution, were in that Congress, and voted on that question. Of these, Roger Sherman, Thomas Mifflin, and Hugh Williamson voted for the prohibition, thus showing that, in their understanding, no line dividing local from federal authority, nor anything else, properly forbade the Federal Government to control as to slavery in federal territory. The other of the four—James M'Henry—voted against the prohibition, showing that, for some cause, he thought it improper to vote for it.

In 1787, still before the Constitution, but while the Convention was in session framing it, and while the Northwestern Territory still was the only territory owned by the United States, the same question of prohibiting slavery in the territory again came before the Congress of the Confederation; and two more of the "thirty-nine" who afterward signed the Constitution, were in that Congress, and voted on the question. They were William Blount and William Few; and they both voted for the prohibition—thus showing that, in their understanding, no line dividing local from federal authority, nor anything else, properly forbade the Federal Government to control as to slavery in federal territory. This time the prohibition became a law, being part of what is now well known as the Ordinance of '87

The question of federal control of slavery in the territories, seems not to have been directly before the Convention which framed the original Constitution; and hence it is not recorded that the "thirty-nine," or any of them, while engaged on that instrument, expressed any opinion of that precise question.

In 1789, by the first Congress which sat under the Constitution, an act was passed to enforce the Ordinance of '87, including the prohibition of slavery in the Northwestern Territory. The bill for this act was reported by one of the "thirty-nine," Thomas Fitzsimmons, then a member of the House of Representatives from Pennsylvania. It went through all its stages without a word of opposition, and finally passed both branches without yeas and nays, which is equivalent to an unanimous passage. In this Congress there were sixteen of the thirty-nine fathers who framed the original Constitution. They were

John Langdon, Nicholas Gilman, Wm. S. Johnson, Roger Sherman, Robert Morris, Thos. Fitzsimmons, William Few, Abraham Baldwin, Rufus King, William Paterson, George Clymer, Richard Bassett, George Read, Pierce Butler, Daniel Carroll, James Madison.

This shows that, in their understanding, no line dividing local from federal authority, nor anything in the Constitution, properly forbade Congress to prohibit slavery in the federal territory; else both their fidelity to correct principle, and their oath to support the Constitution, would have constrained them to oppose the prohibition.

Again, George Washington, another of the "thirty-nine," was then President of the United States, and, as such, approved and signed the bill; thus completing its validity as a law, and thus showing that, in his understanding, no line dividing local from federal authority, nor anything in the Constitution, forbade the Federal Government, to control as to slavery in federal territory.

No great while after the adoption of the original Constitution, North Carolina ceded to the Federal Government the country now constituting the State of Tennessee; and a few years later Georgia ceded that which now constitutes the States of Mississippi and Alabama. In both deeds of cession it was made a condition by the ceding States that the Federal Government should not prohibit slavery in the ceded country. Besides this, slavery was then actually in the ceded country. Under these circumstances, Congress, on taking charge of these countries, did not absolutely prohibit slavery within them. But they did interfere with it—take control of it—even there, to a certain extent. In 1798, Congress organized the Territory of Mississippi. In the act of organization, they prohibited the bringing of slaves into the Territory, from any place without the United States, by fine, and giving freedom to slaves so brought. This act passed both branches of Congress without yeas and nays. In that Congress were three of the "thirty-nine" who framed the original Constitution. They were John Langdon, George Read and Abraham Baldwin. They all, probably, voted for it. Certainly they would have placed their opposition to it upon record, if, in their understanding, any line dividing local from federal authority, or anything in the Constitution, properly forbade the Federal Government to control as to slavery in federal territory.

In 1803, the Federal Government purchased the Louisiana country. Our former territorial acquisitions came from certain of our own

States; but this Louisiana country was acquired from a foreign nation. In 1804, Congress gave a territorial organization to that part of it which now constitutes the State of Louisiana. New Orleans, lying within that part, was an old and comparatively large city. There were other considerable towns and settlements, and slavery was extensively and thoroughly intermingled with the people. Congress did not, in the Territorial Act, prohibit slavery; but they did interfere with it—take control of it—in a more marked and extensive way than they did in the case of Mississippi. The substance of the provision therein made, in relation to slaves, was:

First. That no slave should be imported into the territory from foreign parts.

Second. That no slave should be carried into it who had been imported into the United States since the first day of May, 1798.

Third. That no slave should be carried into it, except by the owner, and for his own use as a settler; the penalty in all the cases being a fine upon the violator of the law, and freedom to the slave.

This act also was passed without yeas and nays. In the Congress which passed it, there were two of the "thirty-nine." They were Abraham Baldwin and Jonathan Dayton. As stated in the case of Mississippi, it is probable they both voted for it. They would not have allowed it to pass without recording their opposition to it, if, in their understanding, it violated either the line properly dividing local from federal authority, or any provision of the Constitution.

In 1819–20, came and passed the Missouri question. Many votes were taken, by yeas and nays, in both branches of Congress, upon the various phases of the general question. Two of the "thirty-nine"— Rufus King and Charles Pinckney—were members of that Congress. Mr. King steadily voted for slavery prohibition and against all compromises, while Mr. Pinckney as steadily voted against slavery prohibition and against all compromises. By this, Mr. King showed that, in his understanding, no line dividing local from federal authority, nor anything in the Constitution, was violated by Congress prohibiting slavery in federal territory; while Mr. Pinckney, by his votes, showed that, in his understanding, there was some sufficient reason for opposing such prohibition in that case.

The cases I have mentioned are the only acts of the "thirty-nine," or of any of them, upon the direct issue, which I have been able to discover.

To enumerate the persons who thus acted, as being four in 1784, two in 1787, seventeen in 1789, three in 1798, two in 1804, and two in 1819–20—there would be thirty of them. But this would be counting John Langdon, Roger Sherman, William Few, Rufus King, and George Read, each twice, and Abraham Baldwin, three times. The true number of those of the "thirty-nine" whom I have shown to have acted upon the question, which, by the text, they understood better than we, is twenty-three, leaving sixteen not shown to have acted upon it in any way.

Here, then, we have twenty-three out of our thirty-nine fathers "who framed the Government under which we live," who have, upon their official responsibility and their corporal oaths, acted upon the very question which the text affirms they "understood just as well, and even better than we do now;" and twenty-one of them—a clear majority of the whole "thirty-nine"—so acting upon it as to make them guilty of gross political impropriety and wilful perjury, if, in their understanding, any proper division between local and federal authority, or anything in the Constitution they had made themselves, and sworn to support, forbade the Federal Government to control as to slavery in the federal territories. Thus the twenty-one acted; and, as actions speak louder than words, so actions, under such responsibility, speak still louder.

Two of the twenty-three voted against Congressional prohibition of slavery in the federal territories, in the instances in which they acted upon the question. But for what reasons they so voted is not known. They may have done so because they thought a proper division of local from federal authority, or some provision or principle of the Constitution, stood in the way; or they may, without any such question, have voted against the prohibition, on what appeared to them to be sufficient grounds of expediency. No one who has sworn to support the Constitution, can conscientiously vote for what he understands to be an unconstitutional measure, however expedient he may think it; but one may and ought to vote against a measure which he deems constitutional, if, at the same time, he deems it inexpedient. It, therefore, would be unsafe to set down even the two who voted against the prohibition, as having done so because, in their understanding, any proper division of local from federal authority, or anything in the Constitution, forbade the Federal Government to control as to slavery in federal territory.

The remaining sixteen of the "thirty-nine," so far as I have discovered, have left no record of their understanding upon the direct question of federal control of slavery in the federal territories. But there is much reason to believe that their understanding upon that question would not have appeared different from that of their twenty-three compeers, had it been manifested at all.

For the purpose of adhering rigidly to the text, I have purposely omitted whatever understanding may have been manifested by any person, however distinguished, other than the thirty-nine fathers who framed the original Constitution; and, for the same reason, I have also omitted whatever understanding may have been manifested by any of the "thirty-nine" even, on any other phase of the general question of slavery. If we should look into their acts and declarations on those other phases, as the foreign slave trade, and the morality and policy of slavery generally, it would appear to us that on the direct question of federal control of slavery in federal territories, the sixteen, if they had acted at all, would probably have acted just as the twenty-three did. Among that sixteen were several of the most noted anti-slavery men of those times—as Dr. Franklin, Alexander Hamilton and Gouverneur Morris—while there was not one now known to have been otherwise, unless it may be John Rutledge, of South Carolina.

The sum of the whole is, that of our thirty-nine fathers who framed the original Constitution, twenty-one—a clear majority of the whole—certainly understood that no proper division of local from federal authority, nor any part of the Constitution, forbade the Federal Government to control slavery in the federal territories; while all the rest probably had the same understanding. Such, unquestionably, was the understanding of our fathers who framed the original Constitution; and the text affirms that they understood the question "better than we."

But, so far, I have been considering the understanding of the question manifested by the framers of the original Constitution. In and by the original instrument, a mode was provided for amending it; and, as I have already stated, the present frame of "the Government under which we live" consists of that original, and twelve amendatory articles framed and adopted since. Those who now insist that federal control of slavery in federal territories violates the Constitution, point us to the provisions which they suppose it thus violates; and, as I understand, they all fix upon provisions in these amendatory articles, and not in the original instrument. The Supreme Court, in the Dred Scott case, plant themselves upon the fifth amendment, which provides that no person shall be deprived of "life, liberty or property without due process of law;" while Senator Douglas and his peculiar adherents plant themselves upon the tenth amendment, providing that "the powers not delegated to the United States by the Constitution," "are reserved to the States respectively, or to the people."

Now, it so happens that these amendments were framed by the first Congress which sat under the Constitution—the identical Congress which passed the act already mentioned, enforcing the prohibition of slavery in the Northwestern Territory. Not only was it the same Congress, but they were the identical, same individual men who, at the same session, and at the same time within the session, had under consideration, and in progress toward maturity, these Constitutional amendments, and this act prohibiting slavery in all the territory the nation then owned. The Constitutional amendments were introduced before, and passed after the act enforcing the Ordinance of '87; so that, during the whole pendency of the act to enforce the Ordinance, the Constitutional amendments were also pending.

The seventy-six members of that Congress, including sixteen of the framers of the original Constitution, as before stated, were preeminently our fathers who framed that part of "the Government under which we live," which is now claimed as forbidding the Federal Government to control slavery in the federal territories.

Is it not a little presumptuous in any one at this day to affirm that the two things which that Congress deliberately framed, and carried to maturity at the same time, are absolutely inconsistent with each other? And does not such affirmation become impudently absurd when coupled with the other affirmation from the same mouth, that those who did the two things, alleged to be inconsistent, understood whether they really were inconsistent better than we—better than he who affirms that they are inconsistent?

It is surely safe to assume that the thirty-nine framers of the original Constitution, and the seventy-six members of the Congress which framed the amendments thereto, taken together, do certainly include those who may be fairly called "our fathers who framed the Government under which we live." And so assuming, I defy any man to show that any one of them ever, in his whole life, declared that, in his understanding, any proper division of local from federal authority, or any part of the Constitution, forbade the Federal Government to control as to slavery in the federal territories. I go a step further. I defy any one to show that any living man in the whole world ever did, prior to the beginning of the present century, (and I might almost say prior to the beginning of the last half of the present century,) declare that, in his understanding, any proper division of local from federal authority, or any part of the Constitution, forbade the Federal Government to control as to slavery in the federal territories. To those who now so declare, I give, not only "our fathers who framed the Government under which we live," but with them all other living men within the century in which it was framed, among whom to search, and they shall not be able to find the evidence of a single man agreeing with them.

Now, and here, let me guard a little against being misunderstood. I do not mean to say we are bound to follow implicitly in whatever our fathers did. To do so, would be to discard all the lights of current experience—to reject all progress—all improvement. What I do say is, that if we would supplant the opinions and policy of our fathers in any case, we should do so upon evidence so conclusive, and argument so clear, that even their great authority, fairly considered and weighed, cannot stand; and most surely not in a case whereof we ourselves declare they understood the question better than we.

If any man at this day sincerely believes that a proper division of local from federal authority, or any part of the Constitution, forbids the Federal Government to control as to slavery in the federal territories, he is right to say so, and to enforce his position by all truthful evidence and fair argument which he can. But he has no right to mislead others, who have less access to history, and less leisure to study it, into the false belief that "our fathers, who framed the Government under which we live," were of the same opinion—thus substituting falsehood and deception for truthful evidence and fair argument. If any man at this day sincerely believes "our fathers who framed the Government under which we live," used and applied principles, in other cases, which ought to have led them to understand that a proper division of local from federal authority or some part of the Constitution, forbids the Federal Government to control as to slavery in the federal territories, he is right to say so. But he should, at the same time, brave the responsibility of declaring that, in his opinion, be understands their principles better than they did themselves; and especially should he not shirk that responsibility by asserting that they "understood the question just as well, and even better, than we do now."

But enough! *Let all who believe that "our fathers, who framed the Government under which we live, understood this question just as well, and even better, than we do now," speak as they spoke, and act as they acted upon it. This is all Republicans ask—all Republicans desire—in relation to slavery. As those fathers marked it, so let it be again marked, as an evil not to be extended, but to be tolerated and protected only because of and so far as its actual presence among us makes that toleration and protection a necessity. Let all the guaranties those fathers gave it, be, not grudgingly, but fully and fairly maintained.* For this Republicans contend, and with this, so far as I know or believe, they will be content.

And now, if they would listen—as I suppose they will not—I would address a few words to the Southern people.

I would say to them:—You consider yourselves a reasonable and a just people; and I consider that in the general qualities of reason and justice you are not inferior to any other people. Still, when you speak of us Republicans, you do so only to denounce us as reptiles, or, at the best, as no better than outlaws. You will grant a hearing to pirates or murderers, but nothing like it to "Black Republicans." In all your contentions with one another, each of you deems an unconditional condemnation of "Black Republicanism" as the first thing to be attended to. Indeed, such condemnation of us seems to be an indispensable prerequisite—license, so to speak—among you to be admitted or permitted to speak at all. Now, can you, or not, be prevailed upon to pause and to consider whether this is quite just to us, or even to yourselves? Bring forward your charges and specifications, and then be patient long enough to hear us deny or justify.

You say we are sectional. We deny it. That makes an issue; and the burden of proof is upon you. You produce your proof; and what is it? Why, that our party has no existence in your section—gets no votes in your section. The fact is substantially true; but does it prove the issue? If it does, then in case we should, without change of principle, begin to get votes in your section, we should thereby cease to be sectional. You cannot escape this conclusion; and yet, are you willing to abide by it? If you are, you will probably soon find that we have ceased to be sectional, for we shall get votes in your section this very year. You will then begin to discover, as the truth plainly is, that your proof does not touch the issue. The fact that we get no votes in your section, is a fact of your making, and not of ours. And if there be fault in that fact, that fault is primarily yours, and remains so until you show that we repel you by some wrong principle or practice. If we do repel you by any wrong principle or practice, the fault is ours; but this brings you to where you ought to have started—to a discussion of the right or wrong of our principle. If our principle, put in practice, would wrong your section for the benefit of ours, or for any other object, then our principle, and we with it, are sectional, and are justly opposed and denounced as such. Meet us, then, on the question of whether our principle, put in practice, would wrong your section; and so meet us as if it were possible that something may be said on our side. Do you accept the challenge? No! Then you really believe that the principle which "our fathers who framed the Government under which we live" thought so clearly right as to adopt it, and indorse it again and again, upon their official oaths, is in fact so clearly wrong as to demand your condemnation without a moment's consideration.

Some of you delight to flaunt in our faces the warning against sectional parties given by Washington in his Farewell Address. Less than eight years before Washington gave that warning, he had, as President of the United States, approved and signed an act of Congress, enforcing the prohibition of slavery in the Northwestern Territory, which act embodied the policy of the Government upon that subject up to and at the very moment he penned that warning; and about one year after he penned it, he wrote La Fayette that he considered that prohibition a wise measure, expressing in the same connection his hope that we should at some time have a confederacy of free States.

Bearing this in mind, and seeing that sectionalism has since arisen upon this same subject, is that warning a weapon in your hands against us, or in our hands against you? Could Washington himself speak, would he cast the blame of that sectionalism upon us, who sustain his policy, or upon you who repudiate it? We respect that warning of Washington, and we commend it to you, together with his example pointing to the right application of it.

But you say you are conservative—eminently conservative—while we are revolutionary, destructive, or something of the sort. What is conservatism? Is it not adherence to the old and tried, against the new and untried? We stick to, contend for, the identical old policy on the point in controversy which was adopted by "our fathers who framed the Government under which we live;" while you with one accord reject, and scout, and spit upon that old policy, and insist upon substituting something new. True, you disagree among yourselves as to what that substitute shall be. You are divided on new propositions and plans, but you are unanimous in rejecting and denouncing the old policy of the fathers. Some of you are for reviving the foreign slave trade; some for a Congressional Slave-Code for the Territories; some for Congress forbidding the Territories to prohibit Slavery within their limits; some for maintaining Slavery in the Territories through the judiciary; some for the "gur-reat pur-rinciple" that "if one man would enslave another, no third man should object," fantastically called "Popular Sovereignty;" but never a man among you in favor of federal prohibition of slavery in federal territories, according to the practice of "our fathers who framed the Government under which we live." Not one of all your various plans can show a precedent or an advocate in the century within which our Government originated. Consider, then, whether your claim of conservatism for yourselves, and your charge of destructiveness against us, are based on the most clear and stable foundations.

Again, you say we have made the slavery question more prominent than it formerly was. We deny it. We admit that it is more prominent, but we deny that we made it so. It was not we, but you, who discarded the old policy of the fathers. We resisted, and still resist, your innovation; and thence comes the greater prominence of the question. Would you have that question reduced to its former proportions? Go back to that old policy. What has been will be again, under the same conditions. If you would have the peace of the old times, readopt the precepts and policy of the old times.

You charge that we stir up insurrections among your slaves. We deny it; and what is your proof? Harper's Ferry! John Brown!! John Brown was no Republican; and you have failed to implicate a single Republican in his Harper's Ferry enterprise. If any member of our party is guilty in that matter, you know it or you do not know it. If you do know it, you are inexcusable for not designating the man and proving the fact. If you do not know it, you are inexcusable for asserting it, and especially for persisting in the assertion after you have tried and failed to make the proof. You need not be told that persisting in a charge which one does not know to be true, is simply malicious slander.

Some of you admit that no Republican designedly aided or encouraged the Harper's Ferry affair; but still insist that our doctrines and declarations necessarily lead to such results. We do not believe it. We know we hold to no doctrine, and make no declaration, which were not held to and made by "our fathers who framed the Government under which we live." You never dealt fairly by us in relation to this affair. When it occurred, some important State elections were near at hand, and you were in evident glee with the belief that, by charging the blame upon us, you could get an advantage of us in those elections. The elections came, and your expectations were not quite fulfilled. Every Republican man knew that, as to himself at least, your charge was a slander, and he was not much inclined by it to cast his vote in your favor. Republican doctrines and declarations are accompanied with a continual protest against any interference whatever with your slaves, or with you about your slaves. Surely, this does not encourage them to revolt. True, we do, in common with "our fathers, who framed the Government under which we live," declare our belief that slavery is wrong; but the slaves do not hear us declare even this. For anything we say or do, the slaves would scarcely know there is a Republican party. I believe they would not, in fact, generally know it but for your misrepresentations of us, in their hearing. In your political contests among yourselves, each faction charges the other with sympathy with Black Republicanism; and then, to give point to the charge, defines Black Republicanism to simply be insurrection, blood and thunder among the slaves.

Slave insurrections are no more common now than they were before the Republican party was organized. What induced the Southampton insurrection, twenty-eight years ago, in which, at least, three times as many lives were lost as at Harper's Ferry? You can scarcely stretch your very elastic fancy to the conclusion that Southampton was "got up by Black Republicanism." In the present state of things in the United States, I do not think a general, or even a very extensive slave insurrection, is possible. The indispensable concert of action cannot be attained. The slaves have no means of rapid communication; nor can incendiary freemen, black or white, supply it. The explosive materials are everywhere in parcels; but there neither are, nor can be supplied, the indispensable connecting trains.

Much is said by Southern people about the affection of slaves for their masters and mistresses; and a part of it, at least, is true. A plot for an uprising could scarcely be devised and communicated to twenty individuals before some one of them, to save the life of a favorite master or mistress, would divulge it. This is the rule; and the slave revolution in Hayti was not an exception to it, but a case occurring under peculiar circumstances. The gunpowder plot of British history, though not connected with slaves, was more in point. In that case, only about twenty were admitted to the secret; and yet one of them, in his anxiety to save a friend, betrayed the plot to that friend, and, by consequence, averted the calamity. Occasional poisonings from the kitchen, and open or stealthy assassinations in the field, and local revolts extending to a score or so, will continue to occur as the natural results of slavery; but no general insurrection of slaves, as I think, can happen in this country for a long time. Whoever much fears, or much hopes for such an event, will be alike disappointed.

In the language of Mr. Jefferson, uttered many years ago, "It is still in our power to direct the process of emancipation, and deportation, peaceably, and in such slow degrees, as that the evil will wear off insensibly; and their places be, *pari passu*, filled up by free white laborers. If, on the contrary, it is left to force itself on, human nature must shudder at the prospect held up."

Mr. Jefferson did not mean to say, nor do I, that the power of emancipation is in the Federal Government. He spoke of Virginia; and, as to the power of emancipation, I speak of the slaveholding States only. The Federal Government, however, as we insist, has the power of restraining the extension of the institution—the power to insure that a slave insurrection shall never occur on any American soil which is now free from slavery.

John Brown's effort was peculiar. It was not a slave insurrection. It was an attempt by white men to get up a revolt among slaves, in which the slaves refused to participate. In fact, it was so absurd that the slaves, with all their ignorance, saw plainly enough it could not succeed. That affair, in its philosophy, corresponds with the many attempts, related in history, at the assassination of kings and emperors. An enthusiast broods over the oppression of a people till he fancies himself commissioned by Heaven to liberate them. He ventures the attempt, which ends in little else than his own execution. Orsini's attempt on Louis Napoleon, and John Brown's attempt at Harper's Ferry were, in their philosophy, precisely the same. The eagerness to cast blame on old England in the one case, and on New England in the other, does not disprove the sameness of the two things.

And how much would it avail you, if you could, by the use of John Brown, Helper's Book, and the like, break up the Republican organization? Human action can be modified to some extent, but human nature cannot be changed. There is a judgment and a feeling against slavery in this nation, which cast at least a million and a half of votes. You cannot destroy that judgment and feeling—that sentiment—by breaking up the political organization which rallies around it. You can scarcely scatter and disperse an army which has been formed into order in the face of your heaviest fire; but if you could, how much would you gain by forcing the sentiment which created it out of the peaceful channel of the ballot-box, into some other channel? What would that other channel probably be? Would the number of John Browns be lessened or enlarged by the operation?

But you will break up the Union rather than submit to a denial of your Constitutional rights.

That has a somewhat reckless sound; but it would be palliated, if not fully justified, were we proposing, by the mere force of numbers, to deprive you of some right, plainly written down in the Constitution. But we are proposing no such thing.

When you make these declarations, you have a specific and well-understood allusion to an assumed Constitutional right of yours, to take slaves into the federal territories, and to hold them there as property. But no such right is specifically written in the Constitution. That instrument is literally silent about any such right. We, on the contrary, deny that such a right has any existence in the Constitution, even by implication.

Your purpose, then, plainly stated, is, that you will destroy the Government, unless you be allowed to construe and enforce the Constitution as you please, on all points in dispute between you and us. You will rule or ruin in all events.

This, plainly stated, is your language. Perhaps you will say the Supreme Court has decided the disputed Constitutional question in your favor. Not quite so. But waiving the lawyer's distinction between dictum and decision, the Court have decided the question for you in a sort of way. The Court have substantially said, it is your Constitutional right to take slaves into the federal territories, and to hold them there as property. When I say the decision was made in a sort of way, I mean it was made in a divided Court, by a bare majority of the Judges, and they not quite agreeing with one another in the reasons for making it; that it is so made as that its avowed supporters disagree with one another about its meaning, and that it was mainly based upon a mistaken statement of fact—the statement in the opinion that "the right of property in a slave is distinctly and expressly affirmed in the Constitution."

An inspection of the Constitution will show that the right of property in a slave is not "*distinctly* and *expressly* affirmed" in it. Bear in mind, the Judges do not pledge their judicial opinion that such right is *impliedly* affirmed in the Constitution; but they pledge their veracity that it is "*distinctly* and *expressly*" affirmed there—"distinctly," that is, not mingled with anything else—"expressly," that is, in words meaning just that, without the aid of any inference, and susceptible of no other meaning.

If they had only pledged their judicial opinion that such right is affirmed in the instrument by implication, it would be open to others to show that neither the word "slave" nor "slavery" is to be found in the Constitution, nor the word "property" even, in any connection with language alluding to the things slave, or slavery, and that wherever in that instrument the slave is alluded to, he is called a "person;"—and wherever his master's legal right in relation to him is alluded to, it is spoken of as "service or labor which may be due,"—as a debt payable in service or labor. Also, it would be open to show, by contemporaneous history, that this mode of alluding to slaves and slavery, instead of speaking of them, was employed on purpose to exclude from the Constitution the idea that there could be property in man.

To show all this, is easy and certain.

When this obvious mistake of the Judges shall be brought to their notice, is it not reasonable to expect that they will withdraw the mistaken statement, and reconsider the conclusion based upon it?

And then it is to be remembered that "our fathers, who framed the Government under which we live"—the men who made the Constitution—decided this same Constitutional question in our favor, long ago—decided it without division among themselves, when making the decision; without division among themselves about the meaning of it after it was made, and, so far as any evidence is left, without basing it upon any mistaken statement of facts.

Under all these circumstances, do you really feel yourselves justified to break up this Government, unless such a court decision as yours is, shall be at once submitted to as a conclusive and final rule of political action? But you will not abide the election of a Republican President! In that supposed event, you say, you will destroy the Union; and then, you say, the great crime of having destroyed it will be upon us! That is cool. A highwayman holds a pistol to my ear, and mutters through his teeth, "Stand and deliver, or I shall kill you, and then you will be a murderer!"

To be sure, what the robber demanded of me—my money—was my own; and I had a clear right to keep it; but it was no more my own than my vote is my own; and the threat of death to me, to extort my money, and the threat of destruction to the Union, to extort my vote, can scarcely be distinguished in principle.

A few words now to Republicans. *It is exceedingly desirable that all parts of this great Confederacy shall be at peace, and in harmony, one with another. Let us Republicans do our part to have it so. Even though much provoked, let us do nothing through passion and ill temper. Even though the southern people will not so much as listen to us, let us calmly consider their demands, and yield to them if, in our deliberate view of our duty, we possibly can.* Judging by all they say and do, and by the subject and nature of their controversy with us, let us determine, if we can, what will satisfy them.

Will they be satisfied if the Territories be unconditionally surrendered to them? We know they will not. In all their present complaints against us, the Territories are scarcely mentioned. Invasions and insurrections are the rage now. Will it satisfy them, if, in the future, we have nothing to do with invasions and insurrections? We know it will not. We so know, because we know we never had anything to do with invasions and insurrections; and yet this total abstaining does not exempt us from the charge and the denunciation.

The question recurs, what will satisfy them? Simply this: We must not only let them alone, but we must, somehow, convince them that we do let them alone. This, we know by experience, is no easy task. We have been so trying to convince them from the very beginning of our organization, but with no success. In all our platforms and speeches we have constantly protested our purpose to let them alone; but this has had no tendency to convince them. Alike unavailing to convince them, is the fact that they have never detected a man of us in any attempt to disturb them.

These natural, and apparently adequate means all failing, what will convince them? This, and this only: cease to call slavery *wrong*, and join them in calling it *right*. And this must be done thoroughly— done in *acts* as well as in *words*. Silence will not be tolerated—we must place ourselves avowedly with them. Senator Douglas's new sedition law must be enacted and enforced, suppressing all declarations that slavery is wrong, whether made in politics, in presses, in pulpits, or in private. We must arrest and return their fugitive slaves with greedy pleasure. We must pull down our Free State constitutions. The whole atmosphere must be disinfected from all taint of opposition to slavery, before they will cease to believe that all their troubles proceed from us.

I am quite aware they do not state their case precisely in this way. Most of them would probably say to us, "Let us alone, *do* nothing to us, and *say* what you please about slavery." But we do let them alone—have never disturbed them—so that, after all, it is what we say, which dissatisfies them. They will continue to accuse us of doing, until we cease saying.

I am also aware they have not, as yet, in terms, demanded the overthrow of our Free-State Constitutions. Yet those Constitutions declare the wrong of slavery, with more solemn emphasis, than do all other sayings against it; and when all these other sayings shall have been silenced, the overthrow of these Constitutions will be demanded, and nothing be left to resist the demand. It is nothing to the contrary, that they do not demand the whole of this just now. Demanding what they do, and for the reason they do, they can voluntarily stop nowhere short of this consummation. Holding, as they do, that slavery is morally right, and socially elevating, they cannot cease to demand a full national recognition of it, as a legal right, and a social blessing.

Nor can we justifiably withhold this, on any ground save our conviction that slavery is wrong. If slavery is right, all words, acts, laws, and constitutions against it, are themselves wrong, and should be silenced, and swept away. If it is right, we cannot justly object to its nationality—its universality; if it is wrong, they cannot justly insist upon its extension—its enlargement. All they ask, we could readily grant, if we thought slavery right; all we ask, they could as readily grant, if they thought it wrong. Their thinking it right, and our thinking it wrong, is the precise fact upon which depends the whole controversy. Thinking it right, as they do, they are not to blame for desiring its full recognition, as being right; but, thinking it wrong, as we do, can we yield to them? Can we cast our votes with their view, and against our own? In view of our moral, social, and political responsibilities, can we do this?

Wrong as we think slavery is, we can yet afford to let it alone where it is, because that much is due to the necessity arising from its actual presence in the nation; but can we, while our votes will prevent it, allow it to spread into the National Territories, and to overrun us here in these Free States? If our sense of duty forbids this, then let us stand by our duty, fearlessly and effectively. Let us be diverted by none of those sophistical contrivances wherewith we are so industriously plied and belabored—contrivances such as groping for some middle ground between the right and the wrong, vain as the search for a man who should be neither a living man nor a dead man—such as a policy of "don't care" on a question about which all true men do care—such as Union appeals beseeching true Union men to yield to Disunionists, reversing the divine rule, and calling, not the sinners, but the righteous to repentance—such as invocations to Washington, imploring men to unsay what Washington said, and undo what Washington did.

Neither let us be slandered from our duty by false accusations against us, nor frightened from it by menaces of destruction to the Government nor of dungeons to ourselves. LET US HAVE FAITH THAT RIGHT MAKES MIGHT, AND IN THAT FAITH, LET US, TO THE END, DARE TO DO OUR DUTY AS WE UNDERSTAND IT.

CHAPTER 9

OUR CAUSE IS JUST AND HOLY

Jefferson Davis: Message to the Confederate Congress, April 29, 1861

Relying on historical evidence (like Lincoln @ Cooper's Union)

*F*ollowing the fall of Fort Sumter in mid-April, 1861, President Lincoln *issued a proclamation calling for 75,000 volunteer troops to suppress the "rebellion." Jefferson Davis, President of the Confederate States of America, immediately convened the Confederate Congress, and on April 29 delivered the following message, in which he reviewed the events which had resulted in an outbreak of hostilities. Davis (1808–1889) had been a member of the United States Senate when his home state of Mississippi seceded from the Union in January, 1861. Resigning from the Senate (where he had become the leading champion of the Southern interest during the sectional conflict), Davis was shortly afterward chosen to lead the newly organized Southern nation. In addition to detailing the events which shattered the peace, his message to the Confederate Congress in April presented the official Southern version of the causes of the Civil War. Lincoln's proclamation was considered a "declaration of war" against the Confederacy; the efforts of the Southern government to avert hostilities and to establish peaceful relations with the United States were emphasized, and the guilt for initiating civil war was placed on Lincoln.*

*I*t is my pleasing duty to announce to you that the Constitution framed for the establishment of a permanent Government for the Confederate States has been ratified by conventions in each of those States to which it was referred. To inaugurate the Government in its full proportions and upon its own substantial basis of the popular will, it only remains that elections should be held for the designation of the officers to administer it. There is every reason to believe that at no distant day other States, identified in political principles and community of interests with those which you represent, will join this Confederacy, giving to its typical constellation increased splendor, to its Government of free, equal, and sovereign States a wider sphere of usefulness, and to the friends of constitutional liberty a greater security for its harmonious and perpetual existence. It was not, however, for the purpose of making this announcement that I have deemed it my duty to convoke you at an earlier day than that fixed by yourselves for your meeting. The declaration of war made against this Confederacy by Abraham Lincoln, the President of the United States, in his proclamation issued on the 15th day of the present month, rendered it necessary, in my judgment, that you should convene at the earliest practicable moment to devise the measures necessary for the defense of the country. The occasion is indeed an extraordinary one. It justifies me in a brief review of the relations heretofore existing between us and the States which now unite in warfare against us and in a succinct statement of the events which have resulted in this warfare, to the end that mankind may pass intelligent and impartial judgment on its motives and objects. During the war waged against Great Britain by her colonies on this continent a common danger impelled them to a close alliance and to the formation of a Confederation, by the terms of which the colonies, styling themselves States, entered "severally into a firm league of friendship with each other for their common defense, the security of their liberties, and their mutual and general welfare, binding themselves to assist each other against all force offered to or attacks made upon them, or any of them, on account of religion, sovereignty, trade, or any other pretense whatever." In order to guard against any misconstruction of their compact, the several States made explicit declaration in a distinct article—that "each State retains its sovereignty, freedom, and independence, and every power, jurisdiction, and right which is not by this Confederation expressly delegated to the United States in Congress assembled."

Under this contract of alliance, the war of the Revolution was successfully waged, and resulted in the treaty of peace with Great Britain in 1783, by the terms of which the several States were *each by name* recognized to be independent. The Articles of Confederation contained a clause whereby all alterations were prohibited unless confirmed by the Legislatures of *every State* after being agreed to by the Congress; and in obedience to this provision, under the resolution of Congress of the 21st of February, 1787, the several States appointed delegates who attended a convention "for the *sole and express purpose* of revising the Articles of Confederation and reporting to Congress and the several Legislatures such alterations and provisions therein as shall, when agreed to in Congress *and confirmed by the States,* render the Federal Constitution adequate to the exigencies of Government and the preservation of the Union." It was by the delegates chosen by the *several States* under the resolution just quoted that the Constitution of the United States was framed in 1787 and submitted to the *several States* for ratification, as shown by the seventh article, which is in these words: "The ratification of the *conventions of nine States* shall be sufficient for the establishment of this Constitution *between the States* so ratifying the same." I have italicized certain words in the quotations just made for the purpose of attracting attention to the singular and marked caution with which the States endeavored in every possible form to exclude the idea that the separate and independent sovereignty of each State was merged into one common government and nation, and the earnest desire they evinced to impress on the Constitution its true character—that of a *compact between* independent States. The Constitution of 1787, having, however, omitted the clause already recited from the Articles of Confederation, which provided in explicit terms that each State *retained* its sovereignty and independence, some alarm was felt in the States, when invited to ratify the Constitution, lest this omission should be construed into an abandonment of their cherished principle, and they refused to be satisfied until amendments were added to the Constitution placing beyond any pretense of doubt the reservation by the States of all their sovereign rights and powers not expressly delegated to the United States by the Constitution.

Strange, indeed, must it appear to the impartial observer, but it is none the less true that all these carefully worded clauses proved unavailing to prevent the rise and growth in the Northern States of a political school which has persistently claimed that the government thus formed was not a compact *between* States, but was in effect a national government, set up *above* and *over* the States. An organization created by the States to secure the blessings of liberty and independence against *foreign* aggression, has been gradually perverted into a machine for their control in their *domestic* affairs. The *creature* has been exalted above its *creators;* the *principals* have been made subordinate to

historical evidence

the *agent* appointed by themselves. The people of the Southern States, whose almost exclusive occupation was agriculture, early perceived a tendency in the Northern States to render the common government subservient to their own purposes by imposing burdens on commerce as a protection to their manufacturing and shipping interests. Long and angry controversies grew out of these attempts, often successful, to benefit one section of the country at the expense of the other. And the danger of disruption arising from this cause was enhanced by the fact that the Northern population was increasing, by immigration and other causes, in a greater ratio than the population of the South. By degrees, as the Northern States gained preponderance in the National Congress, self-interest taught their people to yield ready assent to any plausible advocacy of their right as a majority to govern the minority without control. They learned to listen with impatience to the suggestion of any constitutional impediment to the exercise of their will, and so utterly have the principles of the Constitution been corrupted in the Northern mind that, in the inaugural address delivered by President Lincoln in March last, he asserts as an axiom, which he plainly deems to be undeniable, that the theory of the Constitution requires that in all cases the majority shall govern; and in another memorable instance the same Chief Magistrate did not hesitate to liken the relations between a State and the United States to those which exist between a county and the State in which it is situated and by which it was created. This is the lamentable and fundamental error on which rests the policy that has culminated in his declaration of war against these Confederate States. In addition to the long-continued and deep-seated resentment felt by the Southern States at the persistent abuse of the powers they had delegated to the Congress, for the purpose of enriching the manufacturing and shipping classes of the North at the expense of the South, there has existed for nearly half a century another subject of discord, involving interests of such transcendent magnitude as at all times to create the apprehension in the minds of many devoted lovers of the Union that its permanence was impossible. When the several States delegated certain powers to the United States Congress, a large portion of the laboring population consisted of African slaves imported into the colonies by the mother country. In twelve out of the thirteen States negro slavery existed, and the right of property in slaves was protected by law. This property was recognized in the Constitution, and provision was made against its loss by the escape of the slave. The increase in the number of slaves by further importation from Africa was also secured by a clause forbidding Congress to prohibit the slave trade anterior to a certain date, and in no clause can there be found any delegation of power to the Congress authorizing it in any manner to legislate to the prejudice, detriment, or discouragement of the owners of that species of property, or excluding it from the protection of the Government.

The climate and soil of the Northern States soon proved unpropitious to the continuance of slave labor, whilst the converse was the case at the South. Under the unrestricted free intercourse between the two sections, the Northern States consulted their own interests by selling their slaves to the South and prohibiting slavery within their limits. The South were willing purchasers of a property suitable to their wants, and paid the price of the acquisition without harboring a suspicion that their quiet possession was to be disturbed by those who were inhibited not only by want of constitutional authority, but by good faith as vendors, from disquieting a title emanating from themselves. As soon, however, as the Northern States that prohibited African slavery within their limits had reached a number sufficient to give their representation a controlling voice in the Congress, a persistent and organized system of hostile measures against the rights of the owners of slaves in the Southern States was inaugurated and gradually extended. A continuous series of measures was devised and prosecuted for the purpose of rendering insecure the tenure of property in slaves. Fanatical organizations, supplied with money by voluntary subscriptions, were assiduously engaged in exciting amongst the slaves a spirit of discontent and revolt; means were furnished for their escape from their owners, and agents secretly employed to entice them to abscond; the constitutional provision for their rendition to their owners was first evaded, then openly denounced as a violation of conscientious obligation and religious duty; men were taught that it was a merit to elude, disobey, and violently oppose the execution of the laws enacted to secure the performance of the promise contained in the constitutional compact; owners of slaves were mobbed and even murdered in open day solely for applying to a magistrate for the arrest of a fugitive slave; the dogmas of these voluntary organizations soon obtained control of the Legislatures of many of the Northern States, and laws were passed providing for the punishment, by ruinous fines and long-continued imprisonment in jails and penitentiaries, of citizens of the Southern States who should dare to ask aid of the officers of the law for the recovery of their property. Emboldened by success, the theater of agitation and aggression against the clearly expressed constitutional rights of the Southern States was transferred to the Congress; Senators and Representatives were sent to the common councils of the nation, whose chief title to this distinction consisted in the display of a spirit of ultra fanaticism, and whose business was not "to promote the general welfare or insure domestic tranquillity," but to awaken the bitterest hatred against the citizens of sister States by violent denunciation of their institutions; the transaction of public affairs was impeded by repeated efforts to usurp powers not delegated by the Constitution, for the purpose of impairing the security of property in slaves, and reducing those States which held slaves to a condition of inferiority. Finally a great party was organized for the purpose of obtaining the administration of the Government, with the avowed object of using its power for the total exclusion of the slave States from all participation in the benefits of the public domain acquired by all the States in common, whether by conquest or purchase; of surrounding them entirely by States in which slavery should be prohibited; of thus rendering the property in slaves so insecure as to be comparatively worthless, and thereby annihilating in effect property worth thousands of millions of dollars. This party, thus organized, succeeded in the month of November last in the election of its candidate for the Presidency of the United States.

In the meantime, under the mild and genial climate of the Southern States and the increasing care and attention for the well-being and comfort of the laboring class, dictated alike by interest and humanity, the African slaves had augmented in number from about 600,000, at the date of the adoption of the constitutional compact, to upward of 4,000,000. In moral and social condition they had been elevated from brutal savages into docile, intelligent, and civilized agricultural laborers, and supplied not only with bodily comforts but with careful religious instruction. Under the supervision of a superior race their labor had been so directed as not only to allow a gradual and marked amelioration of their own condition, but to convert

hundreds of thousands of square miles of the wilderness into cultivated lands covered with a prosperous people; towns and cities had
sprung into existence, and had rapidly increased in wealth and population under the social system of the South; the white population of
the Southern slaveholding States had augmented from about
1,250,000 at the date of the adoption of the Constitution to more than
8,500,000 in 1860; and the productions of the South in cotton, rice,
sugar, and tobacco, for the full development and continuance of
which the labor of African slaves was and is indispensable, had
swollen to an amount which formed nearly three-fourths of the
exports of the whole United States and had become absolutely necessary to the wants of civilized man. With interests of such overwhelming magnitude imperiled, the people of the Southern States
were driven by the conduct of the North to the adoption of some
course of action to avert the danger with which they were openly
menaced. With this view the Legislatures of the several States invited
the people to select delegates to conventions to be held for the purpose of determining for themselves what measures were best
adopted to meet so alarming a crisis in their history. Here it may be
proper to observe that from a period as early as 1798 there had
existed in all of the States of the Union a party almost uninterrupt-
edly in the majority based upon the creed that each State was, in the
last resort, the sole judge as well of its wrongs as of the mode and
measure of redress. Indeed, it is obvious that under the law of nations
this principle is an axiom as applied to the relations of independent
sovereign States, such as those which had united themselves under
the constitutional compact. The Democratic party of the United
States repeated, in its successful canvass in 1856, the declaration
made in numerous previous political contests, that it would "faithfully abide by and uphold the principles laid down in the Kentucky
and Virginia resolutions of 1798, and in the report of Mr. Madison to
the Virginia Legislature in 1799; and that it adopts those principles as
constituting one of the main foundations of its political creed." The
principles thus emphatically announced embrace that to which I
have already adverted—the right of each State to judge of and
redress the wrongs of which it complains. These principles were
maintained by overwhelming majorities of the people of all the States
of the Union at different elections, especially in the elections of Mr.

Jefferson in 1805, Mr. Madison in 1809, and Mr. Pierce in 1852. In the exercise of a right so ancient, so well-established, and so necessary for self-preservation, the people of the Confederate States, in their conventions, determined that the wrongs which they had suffered and the evils with which they were menaced required that they should revoke the delegation of powers to the Federal Government which they had ratified in their several conventions. They consequently passed ordinances resuming all their rights as sovereign and independent States and dissolved their connection with the other States of the Union.

Having done this, they proceeded to form a new compact amongst themselves by new articles of confederation, which have been also ratified by the conventions of the several States with an approach to unanimity far exceeding that of the conventions which adopted the Constitution of 1787. They have organized their new Government in all its departments; the functions of the executive, legislative, and judicial magistrates are performed in accordance with the will of the people, as displayed not merely in a cheerful acquiescence, but in the enthusiastic support of the Government thus established by themselves; and but for the interference of the Government of the United States in this legitimate exercise of the right of a people to self-government, peace, happiness, and prosperity would now smile on our land. That peace is ardently desired by this Government and people has been manifested in every possible form. Scarce had you assembled in February last when, prior even to the inauguration of the Chief Magistrate you had elected, you passed a resolution expressive of your desire for the appointment of commissioners to be sent to the Government of the United States "for the purpose of negotiating friendly relations between that Government and the Confederate States of America, and for the settlement of all questions of disagreement between the two Governments upon principles of right, justice, equity, and good faith." It was my pleasure as well as my duty to cooperate with you in this work of peace. . . . It was in furtherance of these accordant views of the Congress and the Executive that I made choice of three discreet, able, and distinguished citizens, who repaired to Washington. Aided by their cordial cooperation and that of the Secretary of State, every effort compatible with self-respect and the dignity of the Confederacy was exhausted before

I allowed myself to yield to the conviction that the Government of the United States was determined to attempt the conquest of this people and that our cherished hopes of peace were unattainable.

On the arrival of our commissioners in Washington on the 5th of March they postponed, at the suggestion of a friendly intermediary, doing more than giving informal notice of their arrival. This was done with a view to afford time to the President, who had just been inaugurated, for the discharge of other pressing official duties in the organization of his Administration before engaging his attention in the object of their mission. It was not until the 12th of the month that they officially addressed the Secretary of State, informing him of the purpose of their arrival, and stating, in the language of their instructions, their wish. . . .

To this communication no formal reply was received until the 8th of April. During the interval the commissioners had consented to waive all questions of form. With the firm resolve to avoid war if possible, they went so far even as to hold during that long period unofficial intercourse through an intermediary, whose high position and character inspired the hope of success, and through whom constant assurances were received from the Government of the United States of peaceful intentions; of the determination to evacuate Fort Sumter; and further, that no measure changing the existing status prejudicially to the Confederate States, especially at Fort Pickens, was in contemplation, but that in the event of any change of intention on the subject, notice would be given to the commissioners. The crooked paths of diplomacy can scarcely furnish an example so wanting in courtesy, in candor, and directness as was the course of the United States Government toward our commissioners in Washington. . . .

Early in April the attention of the whole country, as well as that of our commissioners, was attracted to extraordinary preparations for an extensive military and naval expedition in New York and other Northern ports. These preparations commenced in secrecy, for an expedition whose destination was concealed, only became known when nearly completed, and on the 5th, 6th, and 7th of April transports and vessels of war with troops, munitions, and military supplies sailed from Northern ports bound southward. Alarmed by so extraordinary a demonstration, the commissioners requested the delivery of an answer to their official communication of the 12th of March, and thereupon received on the 8th of April a reply, dated on the 15th of the previous month, from which it appears that during the whole interval, whilst the commissioners were receiving assurances calculated to inspire hope of the success of their mission, the Secretary of State and the President of the United States had already determined to hold no intercourse with them whatever; to refuse even to listen to any proposals they had to make, and had profited by the delay created by their own assurances in order to prepare secretly the means for effective hostile operations. That these assurances were given has been virtually confessed by the Government of the United States by its sending a messenger to Charleston to give notice of its purpose to use force if opposed in its intention of supplying Fort Sumter. No more striking proof of the absence of good faith in the conduct of the Government of the United States toward this Confederacy can be required than is contained in the circumstances which accompanied this notice. . . .

A heavy tempest delayed the arrival of the expedition and gave time to the commander of our forces at Charleston to ask and receive the instructions of this Government. Even then, under all the provocation incident to the contemptuous refusal to listen to our commissioners, and the tortuous course of the Government of the United States, I was sincerely anxious to avoid the effusion of blood, and directed a proposal to be made to the commander of Fort Sumter, who had avowed himself to be nearly out of provisions, that we would abstain from directing our fire on Fort Sumter if he would promise not to open fire on our forces unless first attacked. This proposal was refused and the conclusion was reached that the design of the United States was to place the besieging force at Charleston between the simultaneous fire of the fleet and the fort. There remained, therefore, no alternative but to direct that the fort should at once be reduced. This order was executed by General Beauregard with the skill and success which were naturally to be expected from the well-known character of that gallant officer; and although the bombardment lasted but thirty-three hours our flag did not wave over its battered walls until after the appearance of the hostile fleet off Charleston. Fortunately, not a life was lost on our side, and we were gratified in being spared the necessity of a useless effusion of blood, by the prudent caution of the officers who commanded the fleet in abstaining from the evidently futile effort to enter the harbor for the relief of Major Anderson. . . .

Scarcely had the President of the United States received intelligence of the failure of the scheme which he had devised for the reënforcement of Fort Sumter, when he issued the declaration of war against this Confederacy which has prompted me to convoke you. In the extraordinary production that high functionary affects total ignorance of the existence of an independent Government, which, possessing the entire and enthusiastic devotion of its people, is exercising its functions without question over seven sovereign States, over more than 5,000,000 of people, and over a territory whose area exceeds half a million of square miles. . . .

In conclusion, I congratulate you on the fact that in every portion of our country there has been exhibited the most patriotic devotion to our common cause. Transportation companies have freely tendered the use of their lines for troops and supplies. The presidents of the railroads of the Confederacy, in company with others who control lines of communication with States that we hope soon to greet as sisters, assembled in convention in this city, and not only reduced largely the rates heretofore demanded for mail service and conveyance of troops and munitions, but voluntarily proffered to receive their compensation, at these reduced rates, in the bonds of the Confederacy, for the purpose of leaving all the resources of the Government at its disposal for the common defense. Requisitions for troops have been met with such alacrity that the numbers tendering their services have in every instance greatly exceeded the demand. Men of the highest official and social position are serving as volunteers in the ranks. The gravity of age and the zeal of youth rival each other in the desire to be foremost for the public defense; and though at no other point than the one heretofore noticed have they been stimulated by the excitement incident to actual engagement and the hope of distinction for individual achievement, they have borne what for new troops is the most severe ordeal—patient toil and constant vigil, and all the exposure and discomfort of active service, with a resolution and fortitude such as to command approbation and justify the highest expectation of their conduct when active valor shall be required in place of steady endurance. A people thus united and resolved cannot shrink from any sacrifice which they may be called on to make, nor can there be a reasonable doubt of their final success, however long and severe may be the test of their determination to maintain their birthright of freedom and equality as a trust which it is their first duty to transmit undiminished to their posterity. A bounteous Providence cheers us with the promise of abundant crops. The fields of grain which will within a few weeks be ready for the sickle give assurance of the amplest supply of food for man; whilst the corn, cotton, and other staple productions of our soil afford abundant proof that up to this period the season has been propitious. We feel that our cause is just and holy; we protest solemnly in the face of mankind that we desire peace at any sacrifice save that of honor and independence; we seek no conquest, no aggrandizement, no concession of any kind from the States with which we were lately confederated; all we ask is to be let alone; that those who never held power over us shall not now attempt our subjugation by arms. This we will, this we must, resist to the direst extremity. The moment that this pretension is abandoned the sword will drop from our grasp, and we shall be ready to enter into treaties of amity and commerce that cannot but be mutually beneficial. So long as this pretension is maintained, with a firm reliance on that Divine Power which covers with its protection the just cause, we will continue to struggle for our inherent right to freedom, independence, and self-government. . . .

CHAPTER 10

THIS IS ESSENTIALLY
A PEOPLE'S CONTEST

Abraham Lincoln: Message to Congress, July 4, 1861

Following the fall of Fort Sumter, on April 15, 1861, when Lincoln issued his proclamation calling for seventy-five-thousand troops, he also summoned Congress into special session, to meet on July 4. On the opening day of the session, Lincoln delivered his message (the selection which follows), setting forth the official Northern interpretation of the events leading to the outbreak of war. Lincoln's message and that of Jefferson Davis in April (the preceding selection) constituted the first official statements on the character of the Civil War from the Northern and Southern points of view.

Having been convened on an extraordinary occasion, as authorized by the Constitution, your attention is not called to any ordinary subject of legislation.

At the beginning of the present Presidential term, four months ago, the functions of the Federal Government were found to be generally suspended within the several States of South Carolina, Georgia, Alabama, Mississippi, Louisiana, and Florida, excepting only those of the Post Office Department.

Within these States, all the Forts, Arsenals, Dock-yards, Custom-houses, and the like, including the movable and stationary property in, and about them, had been seized, and were held in open hostility to this Government, excepting only Forts Pickens, Taylor, and Jefferson, on, and near the Florida coast, and Fort Sumter, in Charleston harbor, South Carolina. The Forts thus seized had been put in improved condition; new ones had been built; and armed forces had been organized, and were organizing, all avowedly with the same hostile purpose.

The Forts remaining in the possession of the Federal government, in, and near, these States, were either besieged or menaced by warlike preparations; and especially Fort Sumter was nearly surrounded by well-protected hostile batteries, with guns equal in quality to the best of its own, and outnumbering the latter as perhaps ten to one. A disproportionate share of the Federal muskets and rifles, had somehow found their way into these States, and had been seized, to be used against the government. Accumulations of the public revenue, lying within them, had been seized for the same object. The Navy was scattered in distant seas; leaving but a very small part of it within the immediate reach of the government. Officers of the Federal Army and Navy, had resigned in great numbers; and, of those resigning, a large proportion had taken up arms against the government. Simultaneously, and in connection, with all this, the purpose to sever the Federal Union, was openly avowed. In accordance with this purpose, an ordinance had been adopted in each of these States, declaring the States, respectively, to be separated from the National Union. A formula for instituting a combined government of these states had been promulgated; and this illegal organization in the character of confederate States was already invoking recognition, aid, and intervention, from Foreign Powers.

Finding this condition of things, and believing it to be an imperative duty upon the incoming Executive, to prevent, if possible, the consummation of such attempt to destroy the Federal Union, a choice of means to that end became indispensable. This choice was made; and was declared in the Inaugural address. The policy chosen looked to the exhaustion of all peaceful measures, before a resort to any stronger ones. It sought only to hold the public places and property, not already wrested from the Government, and to collect the revenue; relying for the rest, on time, discussion, and the ballot-box. It promised a continuance of the mails, at government expense, to the very people who were resisting the government; and it gave repeated pledges against any disturbance to any of the people, or any of their rights. Of all that which a president might constitutionally, and justifiably, do in such a case, everything was foreborne, without which, it was believed possible to keep the government on foot.

On the 5th of March, (the present incumbent's first full day in office) a letter of Major Anderson, commanding at Fort Sumter, written on the 28th of February, and received at the War Department on the 4th of March, was, by that Department, placed in his hands. This letter expressed the professional opinion of the writer, that re-inforcements could not be thrown into that Fort within the time for his relief, rendered necessary by the limited supply of provisions, and with a view of holding possession of the same, with a force of less than twenty thousand good, and well-disciplined men. This opinion was concurred in by all the officers of his command; and their *memoranda* on the subject, were made enclosures of Major Anderson's letter. The whole was immediately laid before Lieutenant General Scott, who at once concurred with Major Anderson in opinion. On reflection, however, he took full time, consulting with other officers, both of the Army and the Navy; and, at the end of four days, came reluctantly, but decidedly, to the same conclusion as before. He also stated at the same time that no such sufficient force was then at the control of the Government, or could be raised, and brought to the ground, within the time when the provisions in the Fort would be exhausted. In a purely military point of view, this reduced the duty of the administration, in the case, to the mere matter of getting the garrison safely out of the Fort.

It was believed, however, that to so abandon that position, under the circumstances, would be utterly ruinous; that the *necessity* under which it was to be done, would not be fully understood—that, by many, it would be construed as a part of a *voluntary* policy—that, at home, it would discourage the friends of the Union, embolden its adversaries, and go far to insure to the latter, a recognition abroad— that, in fact, it would be our national destruction consummated. This could not be allowed. Starvation was not yet upon the garrison; and ere it would be reached, *Fort Picken*s might be reinforced. This last, would be a clear indication of *policy*, and would better enable the country to accept the evacuation of Fort Sumter, as a military *necessity*. An order was at once directed to be sent for the landing of the troops from the Steamship Brooklyn, into Fort Pickens. This order could not go by land, but must take the longer, and slower route by sea. The first return news from the order was received just one week before the fall of Fort Sumter. The news itself was, that the officer

commanding the Sabine, to which vessel the troops had been transferred from the Brooklyn, acting upon some *quasi* armistice of the late
administration, (and of the existence of which, the present administration, up to the time the order was despatched, had only too vague
and uncertain rumors, to fix attention) had refused to land the troops.
To now re-inforce Fort Pickens, before a crisis would be reached at
Fort Sumter was impossible—rendered so by the near exhaustion of
provisions in the latter-named Fort. In precaution against such a con-
jucture, the government had, a few days before, commenced preparing an expedition, as well adapted as might be, to relieve Fort Sumter,
which expedition was intended to be ultimately used, or not, according to circumstances. The strongest anticipated case, for using it, was
now presented; and it was resolved to send it forward. As had been
intended, in this contingency, it was also resolved to notify the Governor of South Carolina, that he might expect an attempt would be
made to provision the Fort; and that, if the attempt should not be
resisted, there would be no effort to throw in men, arms, or ammunition, without further notice, or in case of an attack upon the Fort. This
notice was accordingly given; whereupon the Fort was attacked, and
bombarded to its fall, without even awaiting the arrival of the provi-
sioning expedition.

It is thus seen that the assault upon, and reduction of, Fort Sumter,
was, in no sense, a matter of self defence on the part of the assailants.
They well knew that the garrison in the Fort could, by no possibility,
commit aggression upon them. They knew—they were expressly
notified—that the giving of bread to the few brave and hungry men
of the garrison, was all which would on that occasion be attempted,
unless themselves, by resisting so much, should provoke more. They
knew that this Government desired to keep the garrison in the Fort,
not to assail them, but merely to maintain visible possession, and
thus to preserve the Union from actual, and immediate dissolution—
trusting, as herein-before stated, to time, discussion, and the ballot-
box, for final adjustment; and they assailed, and reduced the Fort, for
precisely the reverse object—to drive out the visible authority of the
Federal Union, and thus force it to immediate dissolution.

That this was their object, the Executive well understood; and
having said to them in the inaugural address, "You can have no conflict without being yourselves the aggressors," he took pains, not

only to keep this declaration good, but also to keep the case so free from the power of ingenious sophistry, as that the world should not be able to misunderstand it. By the affair at Fort Sumter, with its surrounding circumstances, that point was reached. Then, and thereby, the assailants of the Government, began the conflict of arms, without a gun in sight, or in expectancy, to return their fire, save only the few in the Fort, sent to that harbor, years before, for their own protection, and still ready to give that protection, in whatever was lawful. In this act, discarding all else, they have forced upon the country, the distinct issue: "Immediate dissolution, or blood."

And this issue embraces more than the fate of these United States. It presents to the whole family of man, the question, whether a constitutional republic, or a democracy—a government of the people, by the same people—can, or cannot, maintain its territorial integrity, against its own domestic foes. It presents the question, whether discontented individuals, too few in numbers to control administration, according to organic law, in any case, can always, upon the pretences made in this case, or on any other pretences, or arbitrarily, without any pretence, break up their Government, and thus practically put an end to free government upon the earth. It forces us to ask: "Is there, in all republics, this inherent, and fatal weakness?" "Must a government, of necessity, be too strong for the liberties of its own people, or too weak to maintain its own existence?"

So viewing the issue, no choice was left but to call out the war power of the Government; and so to resist force, employed for its destruction, by force, for its preservation. . . .

It is now recommended that you give the legal means for making this contest a short, and a decisive one; that you place at the control of the government, for the work, at least four hundred thousand men, and four hundred millions of dollars. That number of men is about one tenth of those of proper ages within the regions where, apparently, *all* are willing to engage; and the sum is less than a twenty third part of the money value owned by the men who seem ready to devote the whole. A debt of six hundred millions of dollars *now*, is a less sum per head, than was the debt of our revolution, when we came out of that struggle; and the money value in the country now, bears even a greater proportion to what it was *then*, than does the population. Surely each man has as strong a motive *now*, to preserve our *liberties*, as each had *then*, to *establish* them.

A right result, at this time, will be worth more to the world, than ten times the men, and ten times the money. The evidence reaching us from the country, leaves no doubt, that the material for the work is abundant; and that it needs only the hand of legislation to give it legal sanction, and the hand of the Executive to give it practical shape and efficiency. One of the greatest perplexities of the government, is to avoid receiving troops faster than it can provide for them. In a word, the people will save their government, if the government itself, will do its part, only indifferently well.

It might seem, at first thought, to be of little difference whether the present movement at the South be called "secession" or "rebellion." The movers, however, well understand the difference. At the beginning, they knew they could never raise their treason to any respectable magnitude, by any name which implies *violation* of law. They knew their people possessed as much of moral sense, as much of devotion to law and order, and as much pride in, and reverence for, the history, and government, of their common country, as any other civilized, and patriotic people. They knew they could make no advancement directly in the teeth of these strong and noble sentiments. Accordingly they commenced by an insidious debauching of the public mind. They invented an ingenious sophism, which, if conceded, was followed by perfectly logical steps, through all the incidents, to the complete destruction of the Union. The sophism itself is, that any state of the Union may, *consistently* with the national Constitution, and therefore *lawfully*, and *peacefully*, withdraw from the Union, without the consent of the Union, or of any other state. The little disguise that the supposed right is to be exercised only for just cause, themselves to be the sole judge of its justice, is too thin to merit any notice.

With rebellion thus sugar-coated, they have been drugging the public mind of their section for more than thirty years; and, until at length, they have brought many good men to a willingness to take up arms against the government the day *after* some assemblage of men have enacted the farcical pretence of taking their State out of the Union, who could have been brought to no such thing the day *before*.

This sophism derives much—perhaps the whole—of its currency, from the assumption, that there is some omnipotent, and sacred supremacy, pertaining to a *State*—to each State of our Federal Union. Our States have neither more, nor less power, than that reserved to them, in the Union, by the Constitution—no one of them ever having been a State *out* of the Union. The original ones passed into the Union even *before* they cast off their British colonial dependence; and the new ones each came into the Union directly from a condition of dependence, excepting Texas. And even Texas, in its temporary independence, was never designated a State. The new ones only took the designation of States, on coming into the Union, while that name was first adopted for the old ones, in, and by, the Declaration of Independence. Therein the "United Colonies" were declared to be "Free and Independent States;" but, even then, the object plainly was not to declare their independence of *one another*, or of the *Union;* but directly the contrary, as their mutual pledge, and their mutual action, before, at the time, and afterwards, abundantly show. The express plighting of faith, by each and all of the original thirteen, in the Articles of Confederation, two years later, that the Union shall be perpetual, is most conclusive. Having never been States, either in substance, or in name, *outside* of the Union, whence this magical omnipotence of "State rights," asserting a claim of power to lawfully destroy the Union itself? Much is said about the "sovereignty" of the States; but the word, even, is not in the national Constitution; nor, as is believed, in any of the State constitutions. What is a "sovereignty," in the political sense of the term? Would it be far wrong to define it "A political community, without a political superior?" Tested by this, no one of our States, except Texas, ever was a sovereignty. And even Texas gave up the character on coming into the Union; by which act, she acknowledged the Constitution of the United States, and the laws and treaties of the United States made in pursuance of the Constitution, to be, for her, the supreme law of the land. The States have their *status* IN the Union, and they have no other *legal status*. If they break from this, they can only do so against law, and by revolution. The Union, and not themselves separately, procured their independence, and their liberty. By conquest, or purchase, the Union gave each of them, whatever of independence, and liberty, it has. The Union is older than any of the States; and, in fact, it created them as States. Originally, some dependent colonies made the Union; and, in turn, the Union threw off their old dependence, for them, and made them States, such as they are. Not one of them ever had a State constitution, independent of the Union. Of course, it is not forgotten that all the new States framed their constitutions, before they entered the Union; nevertheless, dependent upon, and preparatory to, coming into the Union.

Unquestionably the States have the powers, and rights, reserved to them in, and by the National Constitution; but among these, surely, are not included all conceivable powers, however mischievous, or destructive; but, at most, such only, as were known in the world, at the time, as governmental powers; and certainly, a power to destroy the government itself, had never been known as a governmental—as a merely administrative power. This relative matter of National power, and State rights, as a principle, is no other than the principle of *generality,* and *locality.* Whatever concerns the whole, should be confined to the whole—to the general government; while, whatever concerns *only* the State, should be left exclusively, to the State. This is all there is of original principle about it. Whether the National Constitution, in defining boundaries between the two, has applied the principle with exact accuracy, is not to be questioned. We are all bound by that defining, without question.

What is now combatted, is the position that secession is *consistent* with the Constitution—is *lawful,* and *peaceful.* It is not contended that there is any express law for it; and nothing should ever be implied as law, which leads to unjust, or absurd consequences. . . .

The seceders insist that our Constitution admits of secession. They have assumed to make a National Constitution of their own, in which, of necessity, they have either *discarded,* or *retained,* the right of secession, as they insist, it exists in ours. If they have discarded it, they thereby admit that, on principle, it ought not to be in ours. If they have retained it, by their own construction of ours they show that to be consistent they must secede from one another, whenever they shall find it the easiest way of settling their debts, or effecting any other selfish, or unjust object. The principle itself is one of disintegration, and upon which no government can possibly endure.

If all the States, save one, should assert the power to drive that one out of the Union, it is presumed the whole class of seceder politicians would at once deny the power, and denounce the act as the greatest outrage upon State rights. But suppose that precisely the same act, instead of being called "driving the one out," should be called "the seceding of the others from that one," it would be exactly what the seceders claim to do; unless, indeed, they make the point, that the one, because it is a minority, may rightfully do, what the others, because they are a majority, may not rightfully do. These politicians are subtle, and profound, on the rights of minorities. They are not partial to that power which made the Constitution, and speaks from the preamble, calling itself "We, the People."

It may well be questioned whether there is, to-day, a majority of the legally qualified voters of any State, except perhaps South Carolina, in favor of disunion. There is much reason to believe that the Union men are the majority in many, if not in every other one, of the so-called seceded States. The contrary has not been demonstrated in any one of them. It is ventured to affirm this, even of Virginia and Tennessee; for the result of an election, held in military camps, where the bayonets are all on one side of the question voted upon, can scarcely be considered as demonstrating popular sentiment. At such an election, all that large class who are, at once, *for* the Union, and against coercion, would be coerced to vote *against* the Union.

It may be affirmed, without extravagance, that the free institutions we enjoy, have developed the powers, and improved the condition, of our whole people, beyond any example in the world. Of this we now have a striking, and an impressive illustration. So large an army as the government has now on foot, was never before known, without a soldier in it, but who had taken his place there, of his own free choice. But more than this: there are many single Regiments whose members, one and another, possess full practical knowledge of all the arts, sciences, professions, and whatever else, whether useful or elegant, is known in the world; and there is scarcely one, from which there could not be selected, a President, a Cabinet, a Congress, and perhaps a Court, abundantly competent to administer the government itself. Nor do I say this is not true, also, in the army of our late friends, now adversaries, in this contest; but if it is, so much better the reason why the government, which has conferred such benefits on both them and us, should not be broken up. Whoever, in any section, proposes to abandon such a government, would do well to consider, in deference to what principle it is, that he does it—what better he is likely to get in its stead—whether the substitute will give, or be intended to give, so much of good to the people. There are some foreshadowings on this subject. Our adversaries have adopted some Declarations of Independence; in which, unlike the good old one, penned by Jefferson, they omit the words "all men are created equal." Why? They have adopted a temporary national constitution, in the preamble of which, unlike our good old one, signed by Washington, they omit "We, the People," and substitute "We, the deputies of the sovereign and independent States." Why? Why this deliberate pressing out of view, the rights of men, and the authority of the people?

This is essentially a People's contest. On the side of the Union, it is a struggle for maintaining in the world, that form, and substance of government, whose leading object is, to elevate the condition of men—to lift artificial weights from all shoulders—to clear the paths of laudable pursuit for all—to afford all, an unfettered start, and a fair chance, in the race of life. Yielding to partial, and temporary departures, from necessity, this is the leading object of the government for whose existence we contend.

I am most happy to believe that the plain people understand, and appreciate this. It is worthy of note, that while in this, the government's hour of trial, large numbers of those in the Army and Navy, who have been favored with the offices, have resigned, and proved false to the hand which had pampered them, not one common soldier, or common sailor is known to have deserted his flag.

Great honor is due to those officers who remain true, despite the example of their treacherous associates; but the greatest honor, and most important fact of all, is the unanimous firmness of the common soldiers, and common sailors. To the last man, so far as known, they have successfully resisted the traitorous efforts of those, whose commands, but an hour before, they obeyed as absolute law. This is the patriotic instinct of the plain people. They understand, without an argument, that destroying the government, which was made by Washington, means no good to them.

Our popular government has often been called an experiment. Two points in it, our people have already settled—the successful *establishing*, and the successful *administering* of it. One still remains— its successful *maintenance* against a formidable [internal] attempt to overthrow it. It is now for them to demonstrate to the world, that

those who can fairly carry an election, can also suppress a rebellion—
that ballots are the rightful, and peaceful, successors of bullets; and
that when ballots have fairly, and constitutionally, decided, there can
be no successful appeal, back to bullets; that there can be no successful appeal, except to ballots themselves, at succeeding elections. Such
will be a great lesson of peace; teaching men that what they cannot
take by an election, neither can they take it by a war—teaching all, the
folly of being the beginners of a war.

Lest there be some uneasiness in the minds of candid men, as to
what is to be the course of the government, towards the Southern
States, *after* the rebellion shall have been suppressed, the Executive
deems it proper to say, it will be his purpose then, as ever, to be
guided by the Constitution, and the laws; and that he probably will
have no different understanding of the powers, and duties of the Federal government, relatively to the rights of the States, and the people,
under the Constitution, than that expressed in the inaugural address.

He desires to preserve the government, that it may be administered for all, as it was administered by the men who made it. Loyal
citizens everywhere, have the right to claim this of their government;
and the government has no right to withhold, or neglect it. It is not
perceived that, in giving it, there is any coercion, any conquest, or
any subjugation, in any just sense of those terms.

The Constitution provides, and all the States have accepted the
provision, that "The United States shall guarantee to every State in
this Union a republican form of government." But, if a State may lawfully go out of the Union, having done so, it may also discard the
republican form of government; so that to prevent its going out, is an
indispensable *means*, to the *end*, of maintaining the guaranty mentioned; and when an end is lawful and obligatory, the indispensable
means to it, are also lawful, and obligatory.

It was with the deepest regret that the Executive found the duty
of employing the war-power, in defence of the government, forced
upon him. He could but perform this duty, or surrender the existence
of the government. No compromise, by public servants, could, in this
case, be a cure; not that compromises are not often proper, but that no
popular government can long survive a marked precedent, that those
who carry an election, can only save the government from immediate destruction, by giving up the main point, upon which the people

gave the election. The people themselves, and not their servants, can safely reverse their own deliberate decisions. As a private citizen, the Executive could not have consented that these institutions shall perish; much less could he, in betrayal of so vast, and so sacred a trust, as these free people had confided to him. He felt that he had no moral right to shrink; nor even to count the chances of his own life, in what might follow. In full view of his great responsibility, he has, so far, done what he has deemed his duty. You will now, according to your own judgment, perform yours. He sincerely hopes that your views, and your action, may so accord with his, as to assure all faithful citizens, who have been disturbed in their rights, of a certain, and speedy restoration to them, under the Constitution, and the laws.

And having thus chosen our course, without guile, and with pure purpose, let us renew our trust in God, and go forward without fear, and with manly hearts.

CHAPTER 11

SOLDIERING IN WARTIME

Private John O. Casler:
"Four Years in the Stonewall Brigade"

In the early twentieth century, Private John O. Casler published a memoir of his experiences as a Confederate soldier. Casler joined the 33rd Virginia Regiment, Army of Northern Virginia, shortly after the war began and remained a soldier throughout the conflict. When joined with the Virginia 2d, 4th, 5th, and 27th, it became known as the "Stonewall Brigade," for its first commander, Thomas J. Jackson. This unit saw some of the fiercest fighting in the war, including Bull Run in 1861, the Shenandoah Valley campaign, Seven Days' battles, Cedar Mountain, Groveton, Second Bull Run, Antietam, and Fredericksburg in 1862, and Chancellorsville in 1863, where the Stonewall Brigade suffered its highest losses, with nearly five hundred casualties, including Jackson himself. This excerpt includes Casler's thoughts about many aspects of soldiering, including his reasons for enlistment, attitudes toward officers, and military discipline. He also reveals his thoughts about camaraderie among soldiers, combat, and the deaths of friends. The death of Stonewall Jackson, described by Casler at the end of this document, caused an enormous outpouring of grief throughout the Confederacy. Robert E. Lee told his son, "It is a terrible loss. I do not know how to replace him." With Jackson's death, Lee had lost his most aggressive and most successful general.

I was born in Gainsboro, Frederick County, Virginia, nine miles northwest of Winchester, on the first day of December, 1838. My mother's maiden name was Heironimus, an old family name of that county, dating back of the Revolutionary war. When I was three years old my father removed to Springfield, Hampshire County (in what is now West Virginia), an adjoining county, where I spent my boyhood days as most other boys do, in learning a trade and going to school, where I received a fair English education for those days.

In March, 1859, when I was in my 21st year, I cut loose from the parental roof and took Horace Greeley's advice to "Go West and grow up with the country." I landed in Cass County, Missouri, in which state I remained, living in different counties, until the spring of 1861, when the signs of the times indicated war, and I concluded to go back to old Virginia. I left Sedalia, Mo., the 8th day of April, 1861, and returned to Frederick County, Virginia, where my father was engaged in farming, having moved back to that county during my absence.

After leaving Sedalia I went to St. Louis, and there got on board a steamboat bound for Pittsburgh, Pa. After passing Cairo, Ill., we heard of the firing on Fort Sumter, and saw bills posted at the different towns we passed calling for 75,000 troops for ninety days to protect Washington and put down the rebellion. Then we knew that war had commenced.

Various opinions were indulged in by the passengers, some saying that the North did not need that many troops, and that it would all be settled in less than ninety days. But, alas! vain hope! How little we knew of the struggle that was before us. I parted with my fellow passengers at Parkersburg, W. Va. Some were going into the Union army, and some of us into the Southern army.

I arrived at home and remained there a short time. At that time the Governor of Virginia was calling for volunteers. There had been a company raised at Springfield, my native town, and they were in service and camped at Blue's Gap, fifteen miles east of Romney, on the road leading to Winchester. As I had but fifteen miles to go to reach them, I bade farewell to my parents and sisters and went to the company, and arrived that evening in camp.

I met old schoolmates and acquaintances whom I had parted from two years before in the school room, and now found them in arms. I signed my name to the muster-roll, put on the uniform of the gray, and was mustered into service for one year. The name of the company was "Potomac Guards," Captain P. T. Grace commanding. . . . The next morning, which was the 19th of June [1861], we were ordered to fall in, and marched to Romney. The day was hot and the road dusty, and marching went quite hard with us, especially myself, who had never marched a day in my life; but I kept ranks, for, "Who would not a soldier be, and with the soldiers march?" Arriving in Romney about 3 P.M., we quartered in an old building, took a good wash, had some refreshments, and felt like soldiers indeed, with our clothes covered with brass buttons and the ladies smiling at us and cheering us on. . . .

On the 15th of July our regiment was marched one mile north of Winchester and permanently attached to General T[homas] J. Jackson's Brigade, consisting of the 2d, 4th, 5th and 27th Virginia Regiments. Ours, not being full yet, was not numbered, but called Colonel Cummings' Regiment. . . . July 18th we marched through Winchester and took the road leading to Berry's Ferry, on the Shenandoah river, about eighteen miles distant. The citizens were much grieved to see us leave, for fear the enemy would be in town, as there were no troops left but a few militia and Colonel Turner Ashby's cavalry.

After marching a few miles we halted, and the Adjutant read us orders that the enemy were about to overpower General [Pierre G. T.] Beauregard at Manasses Junction, and we would have to make a forced march. It was General [Joseph E.] Johnston's wish that all the men would keep in ranks and not straggle, if possible. Then we started on a quick march, marched all day and nearly all night, wading the Shenandoah river about 12 o'clock at night, halted at a small village called Paris about two hours, then resumed the march about daylight, and arrived at Piedmont Station, on the Manasses Gap railroad.

Our brigade was in the advance on the march, and when we arrived at the station the citizens for miles around came flocking to see us. . . . The next day, the 20th of July, we marched about four miles down Bull Run, to where General Beauregard had engaged the enemy on the 18th, and repulsed their advance. There we joined the brigade. We lay on our arms all night. We tore all the feathers out of our hats, because we heard the Yanks had feathers in theirs, and we might be fired on by mistake, as our company was the only one that had black plumes in their hats. We could hear pickets firing at intervals, and did not know what minute we would be rushed into action.

My particular friend and messmate, William I. Blue, and myself lay down together, throwing a blanket over us, and talked concerning our probable fate the next day. We had been in [the] line of battle several times, and had heard many false alarms, but we all knew there was no false alarm this time; that the two armies lay facing each other, and that a big battle would be fought the next day; that we were on the eve of experiencing the realties of war in its most horrible form—

brother against brother, father against son, kindred against kindred, and our own country torn to pieces by civil war.

While lying thus, being nearly asleep, he roused me up and said that he wanted to make a bargain with me, which was, if either of us got killed the next day the one who survived should see the other buried, if we kept possession of the battle-field.

I told him I would certainly do that, and we pledged ourselves accordingly. . . . July 21st dawned clear and bright (and for the last time on many a poor soldier), and with it the sharpshooters in front commenced skirmishing. We were ordered to "fall in," and were marching up the run about four miles, and then ordered back to "Blackburn's Ford." Our company and the "Hardy Greys" were thrown out as skirmishers, opposite the ford, in a skirt of woods commanding a full view of the ford, and ordered to fire on the enemy if they attempted to cross the run. While we were lying in that position heavy firing was heard on our left, both infantry and artillery. In a few moments we were ordered from there to join the regiment, and went "double quick" up the run to where the fighting was going on. The balance of the brigade was in line of battle behind the brow of a small ridge. We were halted at the foot of this ridge and Colonel Cummings told us that it was General Jackson's command that our regiment should depend principally on the bayonet that day, as it was a musket regiment.

Some of the boys were very keen for a fight, and while we were down in the run they were afraid it would be over before we got into it. One in particular, Thomas McGraw, was very anxious to get a shot at the "bluecoats," and when the Colonel read us the order about the bayonet I asked Tom how he liked that part of the programme. He said that was closer quarters than he had anticipated.

Our regiment marched up the hill and formed "left in front," on the left of the brigade, and on the entire left of our army. As we passed by the other regiments the shells were bursting and cutting down the pines all around us. . . . At this time our troops were falling aback, but in good order, fighting every inch of the way, but were being overpowered and flanked by superior numbers. . . . It was there and at this time that General Jackson received the name of "Stonewall," and the brigade the ever memorable name of "Stonewall Brigade." General Barnard E. Bee, riding up to General Jackson, who sat on his horse calm and unmoved, though severely wounded in the hand, exclaimed in a voice of anguish: "General, they are beating us back!"

Turning to General Bee, he said calmly: "Sir, we'll give them the bayonet."

Hastening back to his men, General Bee cried enthusiastically, as he pointed to Jackson: "Look yonder! There is Jackson and his brigade standing like a stone wall. Let us determine to die here and we will conquer. Rally behind them!"

They passed through our brigade and formed in the rear. I knew they were South Carolinians by the "Palmetto tree" on their caps. General Bee and Colonel Bartow fell, mortally wounded. . . .

That morning we had been given a signal to use in time of battle, to distinguish friend from foe, which was to throw the right hand to the forehead, palm outward, and say, "Sumter." When this regiment (which was the 14th Brooklyn, N.Y.), appeared in view Colonel Cummings gave the signal, and it was returned by one of the officers, but how they got it was a mystery. So, when the scattering shots were fired by some of our regiment, Colonel Cummings exclaimed: "Cease firing, you are firing on friends!" And the volley came from them at the same time, and I know I remarked, "Friends, hell! That looks like it."

Colonel Cummings, seeing his mistake, and also seeing a battery of artillery taking position and unlimbering, in close proximity and in a place where it could enfilade our troops, determined to capture it before it could do any damage. I don't think he had any orders from any superior officer, but took the responsibility on himself. Then came the command: "Attention! Forward march! Charge bayonets! Double quick!" And away we went, sweeping everything before us; but the enemy broke and fled.

We were soon in possession of the guns, killed nearly all the horses, and a great portion of the men were killed or wounded; and we were none too soon, for one minute more and four guns would have belched forth into our ranks, carrying death and destruction, and perhaps been able to have held their position. As it was, the guns were rendered useless, and were not used any more that day. . . .

[I] saw my friend William I. Blue, lying on his face, dead. . . . He must have been killed instantly, for he was in the act of loading his gun. One hand was grasped around his gun, in the other he held a cartridge, with one end of it in his mouth, in the act of tearing it off.

I sat down by him and took a hearty cry, and then, thinks I, "It does not look well for a soldier to cry," but I could not help it. . . . My company only numbered fifty-five rank and file, when we went into service, but, so many having the measles and other ailments, we went into the fight with only twenty-seven men, and out of that number we lost five killed and six wounded. The killed were William I. Blue, Thomas Furlough, James Adams, John W. Marker and Amos Hollenback. . . . We worked nearly all night taking care of the wounded, for nearly all of the enemy's wounded were left in our hands. I took a short sleep on the battle-field. The next day was rainy and muddy. The regiment was ordered to "fall in," but not knowing where they were going, I did not want to leave until I had buried my friend, according to promise. When they marched off I hid behind a wagon, and Sergeant Daily, seeing me, ordered me to come on. I told him never would I leave that field until I had buried my friend, unless I was put under arrest. He then left me, and I looked around for some tools to dig a grave. I found an old hoe and spade, and commenced digging the grave under an apple tree. . . . While I was at work a Georgian came to me and wanted the tools as soon as I was done with them. He said he wanted to bury his brother, and asked if I was burying a brother.

"No," I replied, "but dear as a brother" . . . and thus ended the first battle of "Bull Run," and the first big battle of the war. . . .

On the 4th of October [1861] General Jackson was promoted to Major General [commanding a division that included the Stonewall Brigade], and ordered to Winchester, to take command of the forces then in the Shenandoah Valley, and he had his brigade paraded to bid them farewell. We all had the blues, for we did not want to part with him as our commander. . . .

General R. B. Garnett, commanding our brigade, was relieved of his command by General Jackson for some mismanagement at the battle of Kernstown [March 23, 1862]. I never heard exactly what it was; but General C. S. Winder took command of our brigade. He was an old United States officer, and very strict. General Garnett afterwards commanded a brigade in Pickett's Division, and was killed at Gettysburg.

We had heretofore always had a large wagon train to haul of our cooking utensils, mess chests, tents and blankets, but were here ordered to reduce the train, use fewer cooking utensils, and dispense with the mess chests and tents, and every man to carry his knapsack and blankets. If found in the wagons they were to be thrown away. So we started on the march up the Shenandoah river under the new tactics, through the rain and mud; and, as we had a good many blankets and an overcoat apiece, it was a hard task, and a great many blankets were thrown away. I suppose the order was from [General Jackson's] headquarters, but General Winder had just taken the command of the brigade, and, as this order came at the same time, we all thought he was the cause of it.

As he was a kind of fancy General, and seemed to put on a good many airs, and was a very strict disciplinarian, the boys all took a dislike to him from the start, and never did like him afterwards. Whenever he would pass the brigade on the march we would sing out, "More baggage, more baggage," until he got tired of it. He wheeled suddenly around one day and told my Captain to arrest the men for such conduct. I was one of the men, but it was like "hunting for a needle in a haystack" to find out who we were, so we escaped. . . .

General Winder . . . issued orders . . . that when the regiments halted to camp, and stacked arms, the roll should be called, and all who were absent should be bucked the next day from sunrise to sunset; that he was determined to break up straggling in the brigade. As I and my friend [Tom] Powell were not there in time to answer the roll call we were included in the number to be bucked.

Now, bucking a soldier is tying his hands together at the wrists and slipping them down over his knees and then running a stick through under the knees and over the arms. Gagging is placing a bayonet in the mouth and tying it with a string behind his neck.

Some of the officers complained to General Winder about the severity of the order and tried to get him to revoke it; but it was no use—it had to be done. Accordingly about thirty belonging to the brigade were taken out in the woods the next morning, placed under guard, and bucked from sunrise to sunset. It was a tiresome and painful situation, as we had to sit cramped up all day in one position, and if a fellow happened to fall over one of the guards would have to sit him up.

We were all as mad as fury about it, for it was a punishment that had never been inflicted in our brigade before. That night, after we were released, about one-half of the number deserted. . . . I told my Captain I did not intend to answer to roll call that evening, and if I was bucked again for straggling it would be the last time; that I would never shoulder my musket again for a cause that would treat soldiers in that manner.

Some of the officers then went to General Jackson and made complaint about Winder's order. He sent Winder word that he did not want to hear of any more bucking in that brigade for straggling. That was the last of it, and the only time it was ever done. General Winder would often have some of the men tied up by the thumbs at his headquarters all day for some small offense.

He was a good General and a brave man, and knew how to handle troops in battle; but was very severe, and very tyrannical. . . . [Later in the war] General Winder was killed. . . .

We marched on and crossed the Blue Ridge to the east by Brown's Gap, and continue[d] until we reached the Virginia Central railroad, at Mechum's river, when we got on the cars and went by rail to Staunton. . . . The enemy retreated about one mile and went into camp, we thought, for they built a great many fires, but the next morning they were gone. They had been retreating all night, leaving some baggage and a good many wounded in camp. We were on the march early next morning, but did not overtake them until we got near Franklin, Pendleton County, a distance of forty miles, where they met reinforcements, and made another stand.

We were drawn up in line of battle, and lay there all day, skirmishing some with them, but had no general engagement. At dark we retired from their front, went into camp, cooked rations, and the next morning started back. We marched east until near Staunton, when we turned down the Valley, marching north, passing by Stribling Springs, Mount Solon, Bridgewater and Dayton, on to Harrisonburg, where we were ordered to pile away our knapsacks in the courthouse. We knew there was some game on hand then, for when General Jackson ordered knapsacks to be left behind he meant business.

We marched on at a quick march down the Valley to Newmarket, where we turned east, crossed the Massanutton mountain, and over into the Page Valley, on down Page Valley until we arrived at Front Royal.

Now, [Union] General [Nathaniel] Banks, of commissary fame, had a considerable army at Front Royal and Strasburg, and we had been re-enforced by General [Richard] Ewell's Division. Our advance [on May 23, 1862] surprised the enemy at both places, and got in between the two armies. We had some sharp fighting for a while, but we got them cut off, and captured a great many, besides wagons, artillery, etc., and the rout became general. The roads to Winchester, a distance of eighteen miles, showed wreckage of all kinds of baggage and commissary stores. We followed the retreating army all that night. Their rear guard would sometimes take advantage of the darkness and lay in ambush for us, but we would soon outflank them and move on. My company and Company F were in advance, and we had several men wounded.

When we got to Winchester, at daylight, they had made another stand in the fortifications around the town [May 25, 1862], and we had to form a line around them and charge. . . . They hotly contested the place, but finally gave way at all points, and the rout became general. . . . We captured a great amount of commissary stores, ammunition and baggage of all kinds, also all the sutler stores in Winchester, and, I think, about 5,000 prisoners. The enemy had set fire to a part of the town in order to burn up their stores, but we were too close on them and extinguished the fire, so there were only two or three buildings burnt. . . . Previous to this time we had fared very well in the way of rations, clothing, etc. We had the usual army rations: one pound and two ounces of flour; three-fourths of a pound of bacon, or one and one-fourth pounds of beef; coffee, rice, beans, sugar, molasses, etc.; but on account of transportation and blockade, it soon came down to meat and bread, with occasional sprinklings of the others. So, whenever we made such a haul as we did from Banks we fared sumptuously until the quartermasters got it in their clutches. That would be the last of it, especially the sutler stores. Therefore, the soldiers began to appropriate anything in the way of grub, such as hogs, chickens, apples, corn, etc., to their own use. We would not allow any man's chickens to run out into the road and bite us as we marched along. We would not steal them! No! Who ever heard of a soldier stealing? But simply take them.

Some wag in the brigade had gotten up a nick-name for every regiment in the brigade. The 2d was called "The Innocent 2d," because they never stole anything; the 4th, "The Harmless 4th," because they had no fights in camp; the 5th, "The Fighting 5th," because it was the largest regiment and would have some rows in camp; the 27th, "The Bloody 27th," as there were several Irish companies in it, and the 33d (my regiment), was "The Lousy 33d," because it was the first regiment in the brigade that found any lice on them. So this is the way it went from camp to camp: "The Innocent 2d," "The Harmless 4th," "The Fighting 5th," "The Bloody 27th," and "The Lousy 33d." . . .

After this severe campaign and the battles of Manassas [in August 1862] I found myself completely used up. I had slept but little for six days and nights, and was suffering with sore feet and hemorrhoids. I had been worrying night and day with my Lieutenant, who died, and could go no further. I, therefore, reported to our surgeon, as the army started on the march again, and he sent me to the field hospital near the battle ground. When I got there I found a great many tents filled with sick and wounded—more than the surgeons and nurses could attend to. I thought it was a poor place to recruit; but upon looking around I found a great many farmers there with their wagons, who brought in supplies for the wounded, such as butter, milk, chickens, vegetables, etc. As one of them, a fatherly-looking old man, was about starting home I went to him and told him my condition and asked him if he would not take me home with him and take care of me until I got well. He was much pleased to do so, and would willingly have taken a wagon load if the doctors would consent to it; but the wounded had to remain in their charge until properly cared for.

I proceeded home with my farmer, whose name was Lee. He lived about ten miles from the hospital in Loudoun County. He and his family treated me very kindly and gave me every attention. In about a week I felt like a new man. General Lee's army had crossed the Potomac into Maryland, and as none of our troops except a few cavalry were in this part of Virginia it was open to the enemy from Alexandria, and the sick and wounded were being removed to Winchester. After remaining at my friend Lee's ten days, I went to the hospital at Aldie, and was sent from there to Winchester, but was as well as ever. When we were within a few miles of Winchester I left the main road, "flanked" around Winchester and went home. I remained at home until General

Lee's army came back from Maryland into Virginia, and camped a few miles north of Winchester at a small place called Bunker's Hill, when I left home and reported to my regiment. . . .

On the 29th of April, 1863, we left our winter quarters and marched up the river to Hamilton's Crossing, near Fredericksburg, about twelve miles from Chancellorsville.

We found the whole army on the move, and formed in line of battle. General Joe Hooker (Fighting Joe), commanding the Federal army, was threatening to cross the river and some artillery and skirmish fighting was going on. . . . In the morning, on the 2d of May, our army was lying in line of battle in front of General Hooker, near Chancellorsville, facing westward. . . . We soon got the blockade open and all the artillery through. We then came to another blockade and soon opened that. I heard two or three shells come tearing up the road from the enemy, but heard nothing else from them until we got to Chancellorsville after dark.

It was a running fight for three miles. We took them completely by surprise, and our three divisions got merged into one line of battle, all going forward at full speed. Our artillery did not have time to unlimber and fire; they had to keep in a trot to keep up with the infantry. We ran through the enemy's camps where they were cooking supper. Tents were standing, and camp-kettles were on the fire full of meat. I saw a big Newfoundland dog lying in one tent as quietly as if nothing had happened. We had a nice chance to plunder their camps and search the dead; but the men were afraid to stop, as they had to keep with the artillery and were near a good many officers, who might whack them over the head with their swords if they saw them plundering; but the temptation was too great, and sometimes they would run their hands in some dead men's pockets as they hurried along, but seldom procured anything of value. . . .

It was the 11th United States Corps that we first attacked and demoralized. Another corps, the 5th, was sent to their assistance, but were likewise repulsed. Our army did not halt until dark, when we came to the enemy's fortified position in and around Chancellorsville.

Our officers then commenced forming the men in line, and getting them in some kind of order, but the men kept up a terrible noise and confusion, hallooing for this regiment and that regiment, until it seemed that there were not more than three or four of any regiment together. They were all mixed up in one confused mass. The enemy could hear us distinctly by the noise we made. They located us precisely, and immediately opened on us with twenty pieces of artillery, at short range, and swept the woods and road with the most terrific and destructive shelling that we were subjected to during the war.

Charlie Cross, Sam Nunnelly, Jake Fogle and myself were together when the shelling commenced. We stepped to one side and happened to find a sink, or low place, where a tree had blown down some time in the past, and laid down in it. We filled it up even with the ground, and it seemed as if the shells did not miss us more than six inches. Some would strike in front of us, scattering the dirt all over us. I believe if I had stuck my head up a few inches I would have been killed.

We could hear some one scream out every second in the agonies of death. Jake Fogle kept praying all the time. Every time a shell would pass directly over us Jake would say: "Lord, save us this time!" "Lord, save us this time!" Sam Nunnelly, a wild, reckless fellow, would laugh at him and say: "Pray on Jake! Pray on Jake!" and the two kept that up as long as the shelling lasted. Cross and I tried to get Sam to hush, but it was no use. . . . If the enemy had known our situation, and the good range they had on us, and had kept it up, they would literally have torn us to pieces and nearly annihilated our corps that night. It was fortunate for us that they kept it up no longer; but it was fearful while it lasted. It was some time during the shelling that General Jackson was wounded, which resulted in his death one week afterwards. . . .

Our pioneer corps then went to work burying the dead, when I witnessed the most horrible sight my eyes ever beheld. On the left of our line, where the Louisiana Brigade had fought the last evening of the battle, and where they drove the enemy about one mile through the woods, and then in turn fell back to their own position, the scene beggars description. The dead and badly wounded from both sides were lying where they fell. The woods, taking fire that night from the shells, burnt rapidly and roasted the wounded men alive. As we went to bury them we could see where they had tried to keep the fire from them by scratching the leaves away as far as they could reach. But it availed not; they were burnt to a crisp. The only way we could tell to which army they belonged was by turning them over and examining their clothing where they lay close to the ground. There we would usually find some of the clothing that was not burned, so we could see whether they wore the blue or gray. We buried them all alike by covering them up with dirt where they lay. It was the most sickening sight I saw during the war and I wondered whether the American people were civilized or not, to butcher one another in that manner; and I came to the conclusion that we were barbarians North and South alike. . . .

Our loss was estimated at ten thousand five hundred; the enemy's at eighteen thousand; but we lost Jackson, who was a whole corps in himself. . . .The news of the wounding of General Jackson filled the army with the most profound and undisguised grief. His men loved him devotedly, and he was the idol of the whole army.

CHAPTER 12

A PRISONER OF WAR AT ANDERSONVILLE

Sergeant-Major Robert H. Kellogg: "Can This Be Hell?"

Union soldier Robert H. Kellogg published Life and Death in Andersonville Prison *in 1867. A member of the 16th Connecticut Regiment, Kellogg had the misfortune of being captured and incarcerated, an experience he shared with one in seven soldiers during this war. Kellogg's experience was worse than most, for he was sent to Andersonville, the most infamous of Civil War prisons. Located in south Georgia and constructed in 1864 to house 15,000, Andersonville soon held a population more than twice that number. Thirteen thousand men died, the highest prison mortality rate of the war. Kellogg's vivid descriptions of camp life and his discussion of ways that soldiers coped with prison life make this an important source of information. Although he speaks somewhat sympathetically of Commandant Henry Wirz in the excerpt, Kellogg testified against Wirz at his war crimes trial. Wirz was the only Confederate to be tried and executed for war crimes after the war.*

. . . This place, so notorious in the history of the war, is situated in Sumter Co., about sixty-five miles southwest from Macon, and fifty from the Alabama state line. We were counted as we left the cars, and then marched a short distance from the depot, where we remained all night, surrounded by a line of fires and a heavy guard. Here we heard terrible stories of small-pox being prevalent in the prison, and also about the *"dead line,"* which was death to any one who should step over it, but even then we thought they might be trying to frighten us.

We were aroused from our slumbers the next morning at an early hour, and called to submit to the orders of a bustling officer, dressed in Captain's uniform, who did his work with a great deal of swearing and threatening, dividing us into messes of ninety men each, each mess to be in charge of a sergeant, who should call the roll every morning, draw the rations, and receive an extra one himself for his trouble. Three "nineties" constituted a detachment, which was also in charge of a sergeant. Thus classed, and our names taken, we were marched off to the prison. As we came near it, we found it to consist of twelve or fifteen acres of ground, enclosed by a high stockade of hewed pine logs, closely guarded by numerous sentinels, who stood in elevated boxes overlooking the camp.

As we entered the place a spectacle met our eyes that almost froze our blood with horror, and made our hearts fail within us. Before us were forms that had once been active and erect;—*stalwart men*, now nothing but mere walking skeletons, covered with filth and vermin. Many of our men, in the heat and intensity of their feeling, exclaimed with earnestness, "Can this be hell?" "God protect us!" and thought that *He* alone could bring them out alive from so terrible a place. In the center of the whole was a swamp, occupying about three or four acres of the narrowed limits, and a part of this marshy place had been used by the prisoners as a sink, and excrement covered the ground, the scent arising from which was suffocating. This ground allotted to our ninety was near the edge of this plague-spot, and how we were to live through the warm summer weather in the midst of such fearful surroundings, was more than we cared to think of just then.

Along the edge of the swamp, from one side of the camp to the other, ran a little shallow brook, three or four feet wide, and this, with a few small springs, were to furnish our water for the season. . . . No shelter was provided for us by the rebel authorities, and we therefore went to work to provide for ourselves. Eleven of us combined to form a *"family."* For the small sum of two dollars in greenbacks we purchased eight small saplings about eight or nine feet long; these we bent and made fast in the ground, and covering them with our blankets, made a tent with an oval roof, about thirteen feet long. We needed the blankets for our protection from the cold at night, but of the two, we concluded it to be quite as essential to our comfort to shut out the rain. In the afternoon we drew rations, each man getting a pint and a half of coarse corn meal, about two ounces of bacon, a little salt, and also a little soap. We baked a cake of the meal for our supper, and being very weary we laid ourselves down upon the cold ground to sleep. It was very cold, and our hard couch, without any covering to wrap about us, made it comfortless indeed.

There were ten deaths on our side of the camp that night. The old prisoners called it *"being exchanged,"* and truly it was a blessed transformation to those who went from such a miserable existence on earth, to a glorious one above. We could not weep for such, but only rejoice that their cares and toils were ended. . . .

. . . [W]e had some communication with the outside world, through the ARRIVAL OF PRISONERS, who were coming into camp in greater or less numbers almost every day. A squad of eighteen or twenty came in on the afternoon of the twelfth, all of them from [General William T.] Sherman's army, with the exception of two or three from Currituck, N. C., near our place of capture. The boys from Dalton [Georgia] brought us cheering news from our forces at that place, telling us that our brave General was in the rear of the rebel army and giving them what we were pleased to denominate *"particular fits."* . . .

. . . [A] rebel publication fell into our hands, printed at Richmond, and called "The Second Year of the War." It was a very one-sided affair, full of misrepresentations, making everything Southern about perfect, and all action on the corresponding side unworthy and barbarous. I finished its perusal, ending with thorough disgust, and wondering if that was the kind of trash the Southern people would have to accept as *history.* . . .

None can tell our intense longings to know the *real* condition of affairs in the field. Reports in regard to operations were various. At times we would feel remarkably cheerful over the good news brought in by the prisoners, and were content to remain in our wretched quarters longer, if we could only know Uncle Sam's armies were steadily accomplishing the desired result. . . .

The rapid influx of prisoners made an enlargement of our prison limits necessary, and a number of men were taken out to do the work. They had extra rations as an inducement, and better treatment in every respect, as the reward for their labor. I hardly knew what to think about it, whether it was right or wrong. . . .

About the middle of the month things seemed to be growing worse and worse. Twenty-three hundred prisoners came in, in two days . . . partly from [Ulysses S.] Grant's army, but more from

[Benjamin] Butler's. *"Poor fellows!"* we said silently, as they came in, "it is an awful place for you to come into just now." It was bad enough at any time, but worse than ever then, because of the mud and filth which everywhere covered the ground. . . . We were actually suffering from *hunger*. When I attempted to arise from a sitting posture I would find myself dizzy and *blind* for a few moments, and I could attribute it to nothing but our exceedingly meagre diet. It was poor in *quantity* and miserable in *quality*. At this time we had just wood enough to cook a little rice for breakfast, and we could have nothing more the remainder of the day. Let the intensity of our *cravings* be ever so great, there was no remedy. Six of our *"ninety"* were at length permitted to gather their *"handful of sticks,"* that we might cook our cake of meal on the morrow, and truly men must be of the *true metal* to remain *staunch and true* through all this. That they did the following little incident will testify. A YANKEE TRAITOR who works in Americus, making shoes for the Jeff Davis government, said to be first and foremost in the shop, came into camp and was caught trying to entice out others to work with him. It excited the indignation of many, and as a fit punishment for what was esteemed his villainy, he was taken and half his head shaved, and then left to make his way out, hooted and jeered at by the whole crowd, but even then it was considered altogether too slight for one who would dare tamper with their *loyalty*. . . .

. . . The twenty-third was a warm, bright day, and three hundred more prisoners marked their entrance into prison then; not a very desirable era in their history, as they will soon find out, we thought. They were from the 2d corps, and were captured at Petersburg, Va., about a week before. They reported our forces close upon that city then, and we fancied it already *ours*. . . . It gave us courage to hear from them that Grant's army was in excellent condition, and constantly receiving reinforcements. Hope was slightly confirmed, also, by the assertion that a copy of the *New York Herald* was in circulation through the prison, in which it was stated that *"exchange"* was to commence on the 7th of the coming July, and that transports had already left that city for Savannah, with that end in view. We longed to know if it was *really* so, for the suspense we were in was terrible, and this, combined with the actual privation we were constantly enduring, made the days seem insufferably long. That night we had no bacon with our rations at all,—nothing but a pint and a half of corn meal, and a little salt, for twenty-four hours. Many of the men would eat up what they received at a single meal, and then go hungry until the next issue. The morning following this, we had some fresh meat, from which the orderly and myself made a pretty good soup. That which came to our part of the detachment was very good, but much of it was miserable, being badly *tainted* and *full of maggots*. . . .

It again came my turn to go out with the squad after wood. We obtained our scanty supply, and were on our way back to prison, when we stopped for a few moments to rest. I improved the opportunity to dig all the *red root* that I could, as it was a valuable remedy for *diarrhea*, which was distressingly prevalent in camp. The sergeant in charge of the guard was rather cross and surly, and allowed us but a little time to get breath, and then ordered us on again. In my haste I left my knife upon the ground, and did not discover my loss until I was nearly back to the stockade. The sergeant then refused to let me return for it. I was just giving it up for lost, when Captain [Henry] Wirz came riding along, and as a last resort I appealed to him. For a wonder he told me to go with him, and, walking his horse, he went with me to the spot where I had used the knife, and thus I recovered it. If I had failed to find it, he would have doubtless thought I was guilty of deception, and shot me through without any remorse whatever. . . .

The next day our *forces* numbered seventy more, who had been captured near Atlanta. They were bearers of *positive* news, to the effect that two corps of Gen. Sherman's army had crossed the Chattahoochee river, and that Atlanta itself, and [General Joseph] Johnston's army, were in a *tight place*. Such information we were always glad to receive. . . .

. . . [O]ur *"ninety"* had had no wood given them by the *"rebs"* since the 30th of June [1864], or *nearly a month*, and *uncooked* rations had been distributed to us many times. About the only variety we had in those days was a little *sorghum molasses* with our corn meal. *Salt*, we concluded, was a scarce article in the confederacy, since we would pass four whole days in succession without seeing any. While our *temporal* wants were thus poorly supplied, we were not wholly denied *spiritual* food. . . . We had *preaching*. Elder Shephard, a Sergeant in the 97th Ohio Reg't, and a prisoner with us, officiated. Just after one of our quiet sunsets, we gathered together and he gave us a splendid discourse upon the text, "Fight the good fight of faith." He drew a comparison between the *Christian* and the *soldier*, and carried it through in an admirable manner. . . .

. . . My strength was failing, owing in great measure to the miserable and insufficient fare, and a change of food seemed absolutely necessary. I thought of my *gold pen*, that had done me daily service, and resolved to sell that. Thus decided, I went forth to see if I could raise money for my need in this way, but the first day my efforts were all unavailing. . . . I finally succeeded in selling it to a Rebel Lieutenant for *three bars of soap*. I then sold the soap for five dollars and twenty cents in "greenbacks," retaining a good sized piece for my own use. The following morning I went over to the Rebel Sutler's, bright and early, and invested my little fortune in beans and salt, and for that day I had something good to eat, in comparison with my usual food. I felt much better [in] every way. . . . We could hope for little improvement where we were, but as diversion of mind often tends to physical advantage, we availed ourselves of everything that was offered, to secure this. One of my comrades, by some means, became the possessor of "Woodbury's Shorter Course in German," and I began to study that language, or rather, re-commenced it, as I had been engaged in its acquisition at the time of our capture. This book was a perfect treasure, and with it I passed many an otherwise dull hour, agreeably and profitably. . . .

Quite a number of letters came in on the 1st of September [1864], for the boys of our regiment. They were all from home, but contained nothing but domestic news. One of our number passed beyond the boundaries of time in the morning: G——, of Co. A. His brother, an old prisoner, who belonged to another regiment, died a few days before. The next day, still another died after a long sickness. The boys who carried out his body to the dead-house, learned that another of the same company was also lying dead. Our regiment was getting sadly thinned, and we said in our sorrow, "God only knows how many of us will live to tell the sad tale." The charge of the "ninety" devolved upon me, as the other sergeants had become too feeble to discharge their wonted duties. It would keep me busy nearly the whole day drawing rations and cooking for the poor sick boys who were unable to cook for themselves. As if we had not enough already, some sick and wounded ones were sent in from Macon, and a few so-called convalescents were sent in from the hospital to the prison, that room might be made for them there. . . .

. . . It was the general expectation, when any went into the hospital, that it was the last of earth for them. . . . [E]maciated, pain-racked frames had no place to rest but upon the cold, hard ground, and in the numberless instances their heads were pillowed upon nothing softer than a stick of wood. . . . We must see our men pine away and die, while we were utterly powerless to help them. . . .

About the first of June, the hospital was completed outside the stockade. This was situated about one hundred rods from the entrance to the latter place, and occupied quite a pleasant position. Some of the trees had been left standing, and furnished quite an agreeable shade. It was enclosed by a board fence about six feet high, and contained about four acres of ground. This was laid out in streets and wards, and now and then a tent was to be seen, but most of them were nothing but square pieces of canvas spread over a pole, which formed a roof but left it all open below, so that the patients were exposed constantly to the rain, sun, and night dews. . . .

A person . . . unused to the horrors of prison life, would have turned pale at the sickening sight before him. He would have *felt* things unutterable in view of these half-starved, half-clothed, diseased and wretched beings. . . .

The horrors of scurvy none can know but those who have witnessed them. It appeared in different forms. Sometimes it would appear in the limbs, and the cords would be so drawn up they could not walk. The flesh would become discolored as if they had been beaten with clubs, and so soft, the impress of the fingers would remain as they pressed upon it. Sometimes it would be confined to the bones, and not show itself outside at all. In such cases it would be attended with the most intense pain. At other times it would be in the mouth, and the gums would become separated from the teeth, and finally they would drop out altogether, and not a tooth be left in the jaw. I have seen hundreds of cases in this disease, where the men have *actually starved to death*, because they were unable to eat the coarse food that was furnished them by the Confederates. . . .

In the month of June it rained twenty-one days in succession, and it was not strange that disease should multiply and assume every imaginable form. There were fifteen thousand men in the stockade, without shelter of any kind, and it might be expected that the hospital would be rapidly peopled from their ranks. Indeed the latter place was hardly any better. During the warm season it was dreadful. The men scarcely ever wore any clothing at all, but a shirt, that they might keep as free as possible from the lice, which covered all their clothing. It was three hours' work every day, in my comparatively healthful condition, to keep my own body tolerably free from them, and the poor, sick men, who were too feeble to help themselves, would actually find their life-blood taken away from them in this way. Many men have died apparently from no other cause than that of being overrun with lice. I have had men's hair cut, when, if these had been measured, there would have been in bulk a half pint of them, and in size about a quarter of an inch. Mosquitoes, too, were terrible. A man who could not, through weakness, defend himself, looked as if he had the measles, so completely would his face be covered with their bites, and fleas without number vied with these to torment the poor prisoner, sick or well. It is hardly possible to conceive a greater accumulation of woes to come upon mortal men, than fell to the lot of our prisoners at Andersonville. . . .

As a sad consequence of all this, *thirteen thousand* of our brave boys lie buried in that ever-to-be-remembered place. . . . After death, the men were carried to the gate and laid inside the stockade, next to the dead line, where they often remained in the hot sun until the next morning. They were then taken by our own men, who had been paroled for the purpose, and carried outside to a DEAD HOUSE, made of pine boughs, which formed a kind of screen. After all had been collected at this place, they were carried out unto the place of burial. I have seen one hundred bodies in a row, and some of them so decomposed as to fall to pieces on being removed. Large quantities of whisky were given to the men who attended to the burial of these. . . .

After the death of the men, they were numbered, and their names written on a piece of paper and pinned to their clothing. They were then taken to the dead-house. . . . The place of burial was about half a mile from the hospital. It was situated on high ground, being level, and surrounded with pine forests, which made it very pleasant. It is emphatically a *Soldiers' Cemetery*, and a fearful comment upon Southern cruelty.

But for their wretched system of treatment, the earth would not have held in its embrace so many of our brave boys; but for this, so many of the survivors would not carry with them broken constitutions and maimed bodies, as they must now do.

CHAPTER 13

THE REAL WAR WILL NEVER GET IN THE BOOKS

Walt Whitman on the "War of Attempted Secession"

W*alt Whitman (1819–1892), America's greatest poet of the nineteenth century, was a participant in the Civil War, which he frequently called the "War of Attempted Secession," as well as one of its most sensitive commentators. He made his home in Brooklyn, New York, where he had earlier served as editor of the Brooklyn* Daily Eagle *and the Brooklyn* Freeman, *the latter a free-soil journal. In 1855, he published his first collection of poetry in* Leaves of Grass, *and by 1860, the collection had gone through three editions. In 1862, Whitman volunteered as a nurse, and for the next three years, he served in army hospitals, both in the field and in and around Washington, D.C. During these years he kept a notebook of his impressions of the war and its soldiers, the jottings of which formed the basis for much of his Civil War writing. At the end of the war, he published* Drum Taps, *a collection of Civil War poetry, and later incorporated into his prose work,* Specimen Days, *the story of his experiences in the hospitals. Whitman viewed the war in its human aspects and came closer to capturing the suffering, despair and heartbreak of the conflict than any other writer. To Whitman, not only the unity of the nation was threatened by the war but also the cause of liberty and equality everywhere. From the war emerged a "great homogeneous Nation," prepared to embark upon its "genuine career in history." The selection that follows is taken from* Specimen Days.

OPENING OF THE SECESSION WAR

News of the attack on fort sumter and the *flag* at Charleston harbor, S. C., was receiv'd in New York city late at night (13th April, 1861,) and was immediately sent out in extras of the newspapers. I had been to the opera in Fourteenth street that night, and after the performance was walking down Broadway toward twelve o'clock, on my way to Brooklyn, when I heard in the distance the loud cries of the newsboys,

212

who came presently tearing and yelling up the street, rushing from side to side even more furiously than usual. I bought an extra and cross'd to the Metropolitan hotel (Niblo's) where the great lamps were still brightly blazing, and, with a crowd of others, who gather'd impromptu, read the news, which was evidently authentic. For the benefit of some who had no papers, one of us read the telegram aloud, while all listen'd silently and attentively. No remark was made by any of the crowd, which had increas'd to thirty or forty, but all stood a minute or two, I remember, before they dispers'd. I can almost see them there now, under the lamps at midnight again.

NATIONAL UPRISING AND VOLUNTEERING

I have said somewhere that the three Presidentiads preceding 1861 show'd how the weakness and wickedness of rulers are just as eligible here in America under republican, as in Europe under dynastic influences. But what can I say of that prompt and splendid wrestling with secession slavery, the arch-enemy personified, the instant he unmistakably show'd his face? The volcanic upheaval of the nation, after that firing on the flag at Charleston, proved for certain something which had been previously in great doubt, and at once substantially settled the question of disunion. In my judgment it will remain as the grandest and most encouraging spectacle yet vouchsafed in any age, old or new, to political progress and democracy. It was not for what came to the surface merely—though that was important—but what it indicated below, which was of eternal importance. Down in the abysms of New World humanity there had form'd and harden'd a primal hard-pan of national Union will, determin'd and in the majority, refusing to be tamper'd with or argued against, confronting all emergencies, and capable at any time of bursting all surface bonds, and breaking out like an earthquake. It is, indeed, the best lesson of the century, or of America, and it is a mighty privilege to have been part of it. (Two great spectacles, immortal proofs of democracy, unequall'd in all the history of the past, are furnish'd by the secession war—one at the beginning, the other at its close. Those are, the general, voluntary, arm'd upheaval, and the peaceful and harmonious disbanding of the armies in the summer of 1865.)

CONTEMPTUOUS FEELING

Even after the bombardment of Sumter, however, the gravity of the revolt, and the power and will of the slave States for a strong and continued military resistance to national authority, were not at all realized at the North, except by a few. Nine-tenths of the people of the free States look'd upon the rebellion, as started in South Carolina, from a feeling one-half of contempt, and the other half composed of anger and incredulity. It was not thought it would be join'd in by Virginia, North Carolina, or Georgia. A great and cautious national official predicted that it would blow over "in sixty days," and folks generally believ'd the prediction. I remember talking about it on a Fulton ferryboat with the Brooklyn mayor, who said he only "hoped the Southern fire-eaters would commit some overt act of resistance, as they would then be at once so effectually squelch'd, we would never hear of secession again—but he was afraid they never would have the pluck to really do anything." I remember, too, that a couple of companies of the Thirteenth Brooklyn, who rendezvou'd at the city armory, and started thence as thirty days' men, were all provided with pieces of rope, conspicuously tied to their musket-barrels, with which to bring back each man a prisoner from the audacious South, to be led in a noose, on our men's early and triumphant return!

BATTLE OF BULL RUN, JULY, 1861

All this sort of feeling was destin'd to be arrested and revers'd by a terrible shock—the battle of first Bull Run—certainly, as we now know it, one of the most singular fights on record. (All battles, and their results, are far more matters of accident than is generally thought; but this was throughout a casualty, a chance. Each side supposed it had won, till the last moment. One had, in point of fact, just the same right to be routed as the other. By a fiction, or series of fictions, the national forces at the last moment exploded in a panic and fled from the field.) The defeated troops commenced pouring into Washington over the Long Bridge at daylight on Monday, 22d—day drizzling all through with rain. The Saturday and Sunday of the battle (20th, 21st,) had been parch'd and hot to an extreme—the dust, the grime and smoke, in layers, sweated in, follow'd by other layers again sweated in, absorb'd by those excited souls—their clothes all saturated with the clay-powder filling the air—stirr'd up everywhere on the dry roads and trodden fields by the regiments, swarming wagons, artillery, &c.—all the men with this coating of murk and sweat and rain, now recoiling back, pouring over the Long Bridge—a horrible march of twenty miles, returning to Washington baffled, humiliated, panic-struck. Where are the vaunts, and the proud boasts with which you went forth? Where are your banners, and your bands of music, and your ropes to bring back your prisoners? Well, there isn't a band playing—and there isn't a flag but clings ashamed and lank to its staff.

The sun rises, but shines not. The men appear, at first sparsely and shame-faced enough, then thicker, in the streets of Washington—appear in Pennsylvania avenue, and on the steps and basement entrances. They come along in disorderly mobs, some in squads, stragglers, companies. Occasionally, a rare regiment, in perfect order, with its officers (some gaps, dead, the true braves,) marching in silence, with lowering faces, stern, weary to sinking, all black and dirty, but every man with his musket, and stepping alive; but these are the exceptions. Sidewalks of Pennsylvania avenue, Fourteenth street, &c., crowded, jamm'd with citizens, darkies, clerks, everybody, lookers-on; women in the windows, curious expressions from faces, as those swarms of dirt-cover'd return'd soldiers there (will they never end?) move by; but nothing said, no comments; (half our lookers-on secesh of the most venomous kind—they say nothing; but the devil snickers in their faces.) During the forenoon Washington gets all over motley with these defeated soldiers—queer-looking objects, strange eyes and faces, drench'd (the steady rain drizzles on all day) and fearfully worn, hungry, haggard, blister'd in the feet. Good people (but not over-many of them either,) hurry up something for their grub. They put wash-kettles on the fire, for soup, for coffee. They set tables on the side-walks—wagon-loads of bread are purchas'd, swiftly cut in stout chunks. Here are two aged ladies, beautiful, the first in the city for culture and charm, they stand with store of eating and drink at an improvis'd table of rough plank, and give food, and have the store replenish'd from their house every half-hour all that day; and there in the rain they stand, active, silent, white-hair'd, and give food, though the tears stream down their cheeks,

almost without intermission, the whole time. Amid the deep excitement, crowds and motion, and desperate eagerness, it seems strange
to see many, very many, of the soldiers sleeping—in the midst of all,
sleeping sound. They drop down anywhere, on the steps of houses,
up close by the basements or fences, on the sidewalk, aside on some
vacant lot, and deeply sleep. A poor seventeen or eighteen year old
boy lies there, on the stoop of a grand house; he sleeps so calmly, so
profoundly. Some clutch their muskets firmly even in sleep. Some in
squads; comrades, brothers, close together—and on them, as they lay,
sulkily drips the rain.

As afternoon pass'd, and evening came, the streets, the barrooms,
knots everywhere, listeners, questioners, terrible yarns, bugaboo,
mask'd batteries, our regiment all cut up, &c.—stories and story-
tellers, windy, bragging, vain centres of street-crowds. Resolution,
manliness, seem to have abandon'd Washington. The principal hotel,
Willard's, is full of shoulder-straps—thick, crush'd, creeping with
shoulder-straps. (I see them, and must have a word with them. There
you are, shoulder-straps!—but where are your companies? where are
your men? Incompetents! never tell me of chances of battle, of getting
stray'd, and the like. I think this is your work, this retreat, after all.
Sneak, blow, put on airs there in Willard's sumptuous parlors and
barrooms, or anywhere—no explanation shall save you. Bull Run is
your work; had you been half or one-tenth worthy your men, this
would never have happen'd.)

Meantime, in Washington, among the great persons and their
entourage, a mixture of awful consternation, uncertainty, rage,
shame, helplessness, and stupefying disappointment. The worst is
not only imminent, but already here. In a few hours—perhaps before
the next meal—the secesh generals, with their victorious hordes, will
be upon us. The dream of humanity, the vaunted Union we thought
so strong, so impregnable—lo! it seems already smash'd like a china
plate. One bitter, bitter hour—perhaps proud America will never
again know such an hour. She must pack and fly—no time to spare.
Those white palaces—the dome-crown'd capitol there on the hill, so
stately over the trees —shall they be left—or destroy'd first? For it is
certain that the talk among certain of the magnates and officers and
clerks and officials everywhere, for twenty-four hours in and around
Washington after Bull Run, was loud and undisguised for yielding

out and out, and substituting the southern rule, and Lincoln promptly abdicating and departing. If the secesh officers and forces had immediately follow'd, and by a bold Napoleonic movement had enter'd Washington the first day, (or even the second,) they could have had things their own way, and a powerful faction north to back them. One of our returning colonels express'd in public that night, amid a swarm of officers and gentlemen in a crowded room, the opinion that it was useless to fight, that the southerners had made their title clear, and that the best course for the national government to pursue was to desist from any further attempt at stopping them, and admit them again to the lead, on the best terms they were willing to grant. Not a voice was rais'd against this judgment, amid that large crowd of officers and gentlemen. (The fact is, the hour was one of the three or four of those crises we had then and afterward, during the fluctuations of four years, when human eyes appear'd at least just as likely to see the last breath of the Union as to see it continue.)

THE STUPOR PASSES—SOMETHING ELSE BEGINS

But the hour, the day, the night pass'd, and whatever returns, an hour, a day, a night like that can never again return. The President, recovering himself, begins that very night—sternly, rapidly sets about the task of reorganizing his forces, and placing himself in positions for future and surer work. If there were nothing else of Abraham Lincoln for history to stamp him with, it is enough to send him with his wreath to the memory of all future time, that he endured that hour, that day, bitterer than gall—indeed a crucifixion day—that it did not conquer him—that he unflinchingly stemm'd it, and resolv'd to lift himself and the Union out of it.

Then the great New York papers at once appear'd, (commencing that evening, and following it up the next morning, and incessantly through many days afterwards,) with leaders that rang out over the land with the loudest, most reverberating ring of clearest bugles, full of encouragement, hope, inspiration, unfaltering defiance. Those magnificent editorials! they never flagg'd for a fortnight. The "Herald" commenced them—I remember the articles well. The "Tribune" was equally cogent and inspiriting—and the "Times," "Evening Post," and other principal papers, were not a whit behind. They came in good time, for they were needed. For in the humiliation of Bull

Run, the popular feeling north, from its extreme of superciliousness, recoil'd to the depth of gloom and apprehension.

(Of all the days of the war, there are two especially I can never forget. Those were the day following the news, in New York and Brooklyn, of that first Bull Run defeat, and the day of Abraham Lincoln's death. I was home in Brooklyn on both occasions. The day of the murder we heard the news very early in the morning. Mother prepared breakfast—and other meals afterward—as usual; but not a mouthful was eaten all day by either of us. We each drank half a cup of coffee; that was all. Little was said. We got every newspaper morning and evening, and the frequent extras of that period, and pass'd them silently to each other.

DOWN AT THE FRONT

FALMOUTH, VA., *opposite Fredericksburgh, December 21, 1862.*—Begin my visits among the camp hospitals in the army of the Potomac. Spend a good part of the day in a large brick mansion on the banks of the Rappahannock, used as a hospital since the battle—seems to have receiv'd only the worst cases. Out doors, at the foot of a tree, within ten yards of the front of the house, I notice a heap of amputated feet, legs, arms, hands, &c., a full load for a one-horse cart. Several dead bodies lie near, each cover'd with its brown woolen blanket. In the door-yard, towards the river, are fresh graves, mostly of officers, their names on pieces of barrel-staves or broken boards, stuck in the dirt. (Most of these bodies were subsequently taken up and transported north to their friends.) The large mansion is quite crowded upstairs and down, everything impromptu, no system, all bad enough, but I have no doubt the best that can be done; all the wounds pretty bad, some frightful, the men in their old clothes, unclean and bloody. Some of the wounded are rebel soldiers and officers, prisoners. One, a Mississippian, a captain, hit badly in leg, I talk'd with some time; he ask'd me for papers, which I gave him. (I saw him three months afterward in Washington, with his leg amputated, doing well.) I went through the rooms, downstairs and up. Some of the men were dying. I had nothing to give at that visit, but wrote a few letters to folks home, mothers, &c. Also talk'd to three or four, who seem'd most susceptible to it, and needing it.

AFTER FIRST FREDERICKSBURG

December 23 to 31—The results of the late battle are exhibited everywhere about here in thousands of cases, (hundreds die every day,) in the camp, brigade, and division hospitals. These are merely tents, and sometimes very poor ones, the wounded lying on the ground, lucky if their blankets are spread on layers of pine or hemlock twigs, or small leaves. No cots; seldom even a mattress. It is pretty cold. The ground is frozen hard, and there is occasional snow. I go around from one case to another. I do not see that I do much good to these wounded and dying; but I cannot leave them. Once in a while some youngster holds on to me convulsively, and I do what I can for him; at any rate, stop with him and sit near him for hours, if he wishes it.

Besides the hospitals, I also go occasionally on long tours through the camps, talking with the men, &c. Sometimes at night among the groups around the fires, in their shebang enclosures of bushes. These are curious shows, full of characters and groups. I soon get acquainted anywhere in camp, with officers or men, and am always well used. Sometimes I go down on picket with the regiments I know best. As to rations, the army here at present seems to be tolerably well supplied, and the men have enough, such as it is, mainly salt pork and hard tack. Most of the regiments lodge in the flimsy little shelter-tents. A few have built themselves huts of logs and mud, with fire-places.

BACK TO WASHINGTON

January, '63.—Left camp at Falmouth, with some wounded, a few days since, and came here by Aquia creek railroad, and so on government steamer up the Potomac. Many wounded were with us on the cars and boat. The cars were just common platform ones. The railroad journey of ten or twelve miles was made mostly before sunrise. The soldiers guarding the road came out from their tents or shebangs of bushes with rumpled hair and half-awake look. Those on duty were walking their posts, some on banks over us, others down far below the level of the track. I saw large cavalry camps off the road. At Aquia creek landing were numbers of wounded going north. While I waited some three hours, I went around among them. Several wanted word sent home to parents, brothers, wives, &c., which I did for them, (by mail the next day from Washington.) On the boat I had my hands full. One poor fellow died going up.

I am now remaining in and around Washington, daily visiting the hospitals. Am much in Patent-office, Eighth street, H street, Armory-Square, and others. Am now able to do a little good, having money, (as almoner of others home,) and getting experience. To-day, Sunday afternoon and till nine in the evening, visited Campbell hospital; attended specially to one case in ward 1, very sick with pleurisy and typhoid fever, young man, farmer's son, D. F. Russell, company E, 60th New York, downhearted and feeble; a long time before he would take any interest; wrote a letter home to his mother, in Malone, Franklin county, N. Y., at his request; gave him some fruit and one or two other gifts; envelop'd and directed his letter, &c. Then went thoroughly through ward 6, observ'd every case in the ward, without, I think, missing one; gave perhaps from twenty to thirty persons, each one some little gift, such as oranges, apples, sweet crackers, figs, &c.

Thursday, Jan. 21—Devoted the main part of the day to Armory-square hospital; went pretty thoroughly through wards F, G, H, and I; some fifty cases in each ward. In ward F supplied the men throughout with writing paper and stamp'd envelope each; distributed in small portions, to proper subjects, a large jar of first-rate preserv'd berries, which had been donated to me by a lady—her own cooking. Found several cases I thought good subjects for small sums of money, which I furnish'd. (The wounded men often come up broke, and it helps their spirits to have even the small sum I give them.) My paper and envelopes all gone, but distributed a good lot of amusing reading matter; also, as I thought judicious, tobacco, oranges, apples, &c. Interesting cases in ward I; Charles Miller, bed 19, company D, 53d Pennsylvania, is only sixteen years of age, very bright, courageous boy, left leg amputated below the knee; next bed to him, another young lad very sick; gave each appropriate gifts. In the bed above, also, amputation of the left leg; gave him a little jar of raspberries; bed 1, this ward, gave a small sum; also to a soldier on crutches, sitting on his bed near. . . . (I am more and more surprised at the very great proportion of youngsters from fifteen to twenty-one in the army. I afterwards found a still greater proportion among the southerners.)

Evening, same day, went to see D. F. R., before alluded to; found him remarkably changed for the better; up and dress'd—quite a triumph; he afterwards got well, and went back to his regiment. Distributed in the wards a quantity of note-paper, and forty or fifty stamp'd envelopes, of which I had recruited my stock, and the men were much in need.

FIFTY HOURS LEFT WOUNDED ON THE FIELD

Here is a case of a soldier I found among the crowded cots in the Patent-office. He likes to have some one to talk to, and we will listen to him. He got badly hit in his leg and side at Fredericksburgh that eventful Saturday, 13th of December. He lay the succeeding two days and nights helpless on the field, between the city and those grim terraces of batteries; his company and regiment had been compell'd to leave him to his fate. To make matters worse, it happen'd he lay with his head slightly down hill, and could not help himself. At the end of some fifty hours he was brought off, with other wounded, under a flag of truce. I ask him how the rebels treated him as he lay during those two days and nights within reach of them—whether they came to him—whether they abused him? He answers that several of the rebels, soldiers and others, came to him at one time and another. A couple of them, who were together, spoke roughly and sarcastically, but nothing worse. One middle-aged man, however, who seem'd to be moving around the field, among the dead and wounded, for benevolent purposes, came to him in a way he will never forget; treated our soldier kindly, bound up his wounds, cheer'd him, gave him a couple of biscuits and a drink of whiskey and water; asked him if he could eat some beef. This good secesh, however, did not change our soldier's position, for it might have caused the blood to burst from the wounds, clotted and stagnated. Our soldier is from Pennsylvania; has had a pretty severe time; the wounds proved to be bad ones. But he retains a good heart, and is at present on the gain. (It is not uncommon for the men to remain on the field this way, one, two, or even four or five days.) . . .

A NIGHT BATTLE, OVER A WEEK SINCE

May 12.—There was part of the late battle at Chancellorsville, (second Fredericksburgh,) a little over a week ago, Saturday, Saturday night and Sunday, under Gen. Joe Hooker, I would like to give just a glimpse of—(a moment's look in a terrible storm at sea—of which a few suggestions are enough, and full details impossible.) The fighting had been very hot during the day, and after an intermission the latter part, was resumed at night, and kept up with furious energy till 3 o'clock in the morning. That afternoon (Saturday) an attack sudden and strong by Stonewall Jackson had gain'd a great advantage to the southern army, and broken our lines, entering us like a wedge, and leaving things in that position at dark. But Hooker at 11 at night made a desperate push, drove the secesh forces back, restored his original lines, and resumed his plans. This night scrimmage was very exciting, and afforded countless strange and fearful pictures. The fighting had been general both at Chancellorsville and northeast at Fredericksburgh. (We hear of some poor fighting, episodes, skedaddling on our part. I think not of it. I think of the fierce bravery, the general rule.) One corps, the 6th, Sedgewick's, fights four dashing and bloody battles in thirty-six hours, retreating in great jeopardy, losing largely but maintaining itself, fighting with the sternest desperation under all circumstances, getting over the Rappahannock only by the skin of its teeth, yet getting over. It lost many, many brave men, yet it took vengeance, ample vengeance.

But it was the tug of Saturday evening, and through the night and Sunday morning, I wanted to make a special note of. It was largely in the woods, and quite a general engagement. The night was very pleasant, at times the moon shining out full and clear, all Nature so calm in itself, the early summer grass so rich, and foliage of the trees—yet there the battle raging, and many good fellows lying helpless, with new accessions to them, and every minute amid the rattle of muskets and crash of cannon, (for there was an artillery contest too,) the red life-blood oozing out from heads or trunks or limbs upon that green and dew-cool grass. Patches of the woods take fire, and several of the wounded, unable to move, are consumed—quite large spaces are swept over, burning the dead also—some of the men have their hair and beards singed—some, burns on their faces and hands—others holes burnt in their clothing. The flashes of fire from the cannon, the quick flaring flames and smoke, and the immense roar—the musketry so general, the light nearly bright enough for each side to see the other—the crashing, tramping of men—the yelling—close quarters—we hear the secesh yells—our men cheer loudly back, especially if Hooker is in sight—hand to hand conflicts, each side stands up to it, brave, determin'd as demons, they often charge upon us—a thousand deeds are done worth to write newer greater poems on—and still the woods on fire—still many are not only scorch'd—-too many, unable to move, are burn'd to death.

Then the camps of the wounded—O heavens, what scene is this?—is this indeed *humanity*—these butchers' shambles? There are several of them. There they lie, in the largest, in an open space in the woods, from 200 to 300 poor fellows—the groans and screams—the odor of blood, mixed with the fresh scent of the night, the grass, the trees—that slaughter-house! O well is it their mothers, their sisters cannot see them—cannot conceive, and never conceiv'd, these things. One man is shot by a shell, both in the arm and leg—both are amputated—there lie the rejected members. Some have their legs blown off—some bullets through the breast—some indescribably horrid wounds in the face or head, all mutilated, sickening, torn, gouged out—some in the abdomen—some mere boys—many rebels, badly hurt—they take their regular turns with the rest, just the same as any—the surgeons use them just the same. Such is the camp of the wounded—such a fragment, a reflection afar off of the bloody scene—while over all the clear, large moon comes out at times softly, quietly shining. Amid the woods, that scene of flitting souls—amid the crack and crash and yelling sounds—the impalpable perfume of the woods—and yet the pungent, stifling smoke—the radiance of the moon, looking from heaven at intervals so placid—the sky so heavenly—the clear-obscure up there, those buoyant upper oceans—a few large placid stars beyond, coming silently and languidly out, and then disappearing—the melancholy, draperied night above, around. And there, upon the roads, the fields, and in those woods, that contest, never one more desperate in any age or land—both parties now in force—masses—no fancy battle, no semi-play, but fierce and savage demons fighting there—courage and scorn of death the rule, exceptions almost none.

What history, I say, can ever give—for who can know—the mad, determin'd tussle of the armies, in all their separate large and little squads—as this—each steep'd from crown to toe in desperate, mortal purports? Who know the conflict, hand-to-hand—the many con-

flicts in the dark, those shadowy—tangled, flashing-moonbeam'd
woods—the writhing groups and squads—the cries, the din, the
cracking guns and pistols—the distant cannon—the cheers and calls
and threats and awful music of the oaths—the indescribable mix—
the officers' orders, persuasions, encouragements—the devils fully
rous'd in human hearts—the strong shout, *Charge, men, charge*—the
flash of the naked sword, and rolling flame and smoke? And still the
broken, clear and clouded heaven—and still again the moonlight
pouring silvery soft its radiant patches over all. Who paint the scene,
the sudden partial panic of the afternoon, at dusk? Who paint the
irrepressible advance of the second division of the Third corps, under
Hooker himself, suddenly order'd up—those rapid-filing phantoms
through the woods? Who show what moves there in the shadows,
fluid and firm—to save, (and it did save,) the army's name, perhaps
the nation? as there the veterans hold the field. (Brave Berry falls not
yet—but death has mark'd him—soon he falls.)

UNNAMED REMAINS THE BRAVEST SOLDIER

Of scenes like these, I say, who writes—whoe'er can write the
story? Of many a score—aye, thousands, north and south, of unwrit
heroes, unknown heroisms, incredible, impromptu, first-class desper-
ations—who tells? No history ever—no poem sings, no music sounds,
those bravest men of all—those deeds. No formal general's report, nor
book in the library, nor column in the paper, embalms the bravest,
north or south, east or west. Unnamed, unknown, remain, and still
remain, the bravest soldiers. Our manliest—our boys—our hardy dar-
lings; no picture gives them. Likely, the typic one of them (standing,
no doubt, for hundreds, thousands,) crawls aside to some bush-
clump, or ferny tuft, on receiving his death-shot—there sheltering a
little while, soaking roots, grass and soil, with red blood—the battle
advances, retreats, flits from the scene, sweeps by—and there, haply
with pain and suffering (yet less, far less, than is supposed,) the last
lethargy winds like a serpent round him—the eyes glaze in death—
none recks—perhaps the burial-squads, in truce, a week afterwards,
search not the secluded spot—and there, at last, the Bravest Soldier
crumbles in mother earth, unburied and unknown. . . .

DOWN AT THE FRONT

CULPEPPER, VA., *Feb. '64.*—Here I am pretty well down toward the extreme front. Three or four days ago General S., who is now in chief command, (I believe Meade is absent, sick,) moved a strong force southward from camp as if intending business. They went to the Rapidan; there has since been some manoeuvring and a little fighting, but nothing of consequence. The telegraphic accounts given Monday morning last, make entirely too much of it, I should say. What General S. intended we here know not, but we trust in that competent commander. We were somewhat excited, (but not so very much either,) on Sunday, during the day and night, as orders were sent out to pack up and harness, and be ready to evacuate, to fall back towards Washington. But I was very sleepy and went to bed. Some tremendous shouts arousing me during the night, I went forth and found it was from the men above mention'd, who were returning. I talk'd with some of the men; as usual I found them full of gayety, endurance, and many fine little outshows, the signs of the most excellent good manliness of the world. It was a curious sight to see those shadowy columns moving through the night.

I stood unobserv'd in the darkness and watch'd them long. The mud was very deep. The men had their usual burdens, overcoats, knapsacks, guns and blankets. Along and along they filed by me, with often a laugh, a song, a cheerful word, but never once a murmur. It may have been odd, but I never before so realized the majesty and reality of the American people *en masse.* It fell upon me like a great awe. The strong ranks moved neither fast nor slow. They had march'd seven or eight miles already through the slipping unctuous mud. The brave First corps stopt here. The equally brave Third corps moved on to Brandy station. The famous Brooklyn 14th are here, guarding the town. You see their red legs actively moving everywhere. Then they have a theatre of their own here. They give musical performances, nearly everything done capitally. Of course the audience is a jam. It is good sport to attend one of these entertainments of the 14th. I like to look around at the soldiers, and the general collection in front of the curtain, more than the scene on the stage. . . .

THE MILLION DEAD, TOO, SUMM'D UP

The dead in this war—there they lie, strewing the fields and woods and valleys and battle-fields of the south—Virginia, the Peninsula—Malvern hill and Fair Oaks—the banks of the Chicka-hominy—the terraces of Fredericksburgh— Antietam bridge—the grisly ravines of Manassas—the bloody promenade of the Wilder-ness—the varieties of the *strayed dead*, (the estimate of the War department is 25,000 national soldiers kill'd in battle and never buried at all, 5,000 drown'd—15,000 inhumed by strangers, or on the march in haste, in hitherto unfound localities—2,000 graves cover'd by sand and mud by Mississippi freshets, 3,000 carried away by caving-in of banks, &c.,)—Gettysburgh, the West, Southwest—Vicksburgh—Chattanooga—the trenches of Petersburgh—the num-berless battles, camps, hospitals everywhere—the crop reap'd by the mighty reapers, typhoid, dysentery, inflammations—and blackest and loathesomest of all, the dead and living burial-pits, the prison-pens of Andersonville, Salisbury, Belle-Isle, &c., (not Dante's pictured hell and all its woes, its degradations, filthy torments, excell'd those prisons)—the dead, the dead, the dead—*our* dead—or South or North, ours all, (all, all, all, finally dear to me)—or East or West—Atlantic coast or Mississippi valley—somewhere they crawl'd to die, alone, in bushes, low gullies, or on the sides of hills—(there, in secluded spots, their skeletons, bleach'd bones, tufts of hair, buttons, fragments of clothing, are occasionally found yet)—our young men once so handsome and so joyous, taken from us—the son from the mother, the husband from the wife, the dear friend from the dear friend—the clusters of camp graves, in Georgia, the Carolinas, and in Tennessee—the single graves left in the woods or by the road-side, (hundreds, thousands, obliterated)—the corpses floated down the rivers, and caught and lodged, (dozens, scores, floated down the upper Potomac, after the cavalry engagements, the pursuit of Lee, following Gettysburgh)—some lie at the bottom of the sea—the gen-eral million, and the special cemeteries in almost all the States—the infinite dead—(the land entire saturated, perfumed with their impal-pable ashes' exhalation in Nature's chemistry distill'd, and shall be so forever, in every future grain of wheat and ear of corn, and every flower that grows, and every breath we draw)—not only Northern dead leavening Southern soil—thousands, aye tens of thousands, of Southerners, crumble to-day in Northern earth.

And everywhere among these countless graves—everywhere in the many soldier Cemeteries of the Nation, (there are now, I believe, over seventy of them)—as at the time in the vast trenches, the depositories of slain, Northern and Southern, after the great battles—not only where the scathing trail passed those years, but radiating since in all the peaceful quarters of the land—we see, and ages yet may see, on monuments and gravestones, singly or in masses, to thousands or tens of thousands, the significant word Unknown.

(In some of the cemeteries nearly *all* the dead are unknown. At Salisbury, N. C., for instance, the known are only 85, while the unknown are 12,027, and 11,700 of these are buried in trenches. A national monument has been put up here, by order of Congress, to mark the spot—but what visible, material monument can ever fittingly commemorate that spot?)

THE REAL WAR WILL NEVER GET IN THE BOOKS

And so good-bye to the war. I know not how it may have been, or may be, to others—to me the main interest I found, (and still, on recollection, find,) in the rank and file of the armies, both sides, and in those specimens amid the hospitals, and even the dead on the field. To me the points illustrating the latent personal character and eligibilities of these States, in the two or three millions of American young and middle-aged men, North and South, embodied in those armies—and especially the one-third or one-fourth of their number, stricken by wounds or disease at some time in the course of the contest—were of more significance even than the political interests involved. (As so much of a race depends on how it faces death, and how it stands personal anguish and sickness. As, in the glints of emotions under emergencies, and the indirect traits and asides in Plutarch, we get far profounder clues to the antique world than all its more formal history.)

Future years will never know the seething hell and the black infernal background of countless minor scenes and interiors, (not the official surface-courteousness of the Generals, not the few great battles) of the Secession war; and it is best they should not—the real war will never get in the books. In the mushy influences of current times, too, the fervid atmosphere and typical events of those years are in danger of being totally forgotten. I have at night watch'd by the side of a sick man in the hospital, one who could not live many hours. I have seen his eyes flash and burn as he raised himself and recurr'd to the cruelties on his surrender'd brother, and mutilations of the corpse afterward. . . .

Such was the war. It was not a quadrille in a ball-room. Its interior history will not only never be written—its practicality, minutiae of deeds and passions, will never be even suggested. The actual soldier of 1862–'65, North and South, with all his ways, his incredible dauntlessness, habits, practices, tastes, language, his fierce friendship, his appetite, rankness, his superb strength and animality, lawless gait, and a hundred unnamed lights and shades of camp, I say, will never be written—perhaps must not and should not be.

The preceding notes may furnish a few stray glimpses into that life, and into those lurid interiors, never to be fully convey'd to the future. The hospital part of the drama from '61 to '65, deserves indeed to be recorded. Of that many-threaded drama, with its sudden and strange surprises, its confounding of prophecies, its moments of despair, the dread of foreign interference, the interminable campaigns, the bloody battles, the mighty and cumbrous and green armies, the drafts and bounties—the immense money expenditure, like a heavy-pouring constant rain—with, over the whole land, the last three years of the struggle, an unending, universal mourning-wail of women, parents, orphans—the marrow of the tragedy concentrated in those Army Hospitals—(it seem'd sometimes as if the whole interest of the land, North and South, was one vast central hospital, and all the rest of the affair but flanges)—those forming the untold and unwritten history of the war-infinitely greater (like life's) than the few scraps and distortions that are ever told or written. Think how much, and of importance, will be—how much, civic and military, has already been—buried in the grave, in eternal darkness. . . .

CHAPTER 14

A NORTHERN WOMAN WITH THE SANITARY COMMISSION

Mary A. Livermore: "A Trip down the River"

*Before the war, Mary Ashton Rice Livermore (1820–1905) was a minis-
ter's wife and mother who wrote poetry and fiction to supplement her
husband's salary. With the advent of hostilities, she believed it was women's
duty to support the Union war effort. She volunteered her time and later
became a salaried employee of the United States Sanitary Commission, a
quasi-governmental agency that saw to the medical and nutritional needs of
rank and file soldiers. A rival agency called the Christian Commission served
a similar purpose while also proselytizing to the troops. Together these two
organizations attracted thousands of female volunteers. In 1862 Livermore
became co-manager of the Sanitary Commission's Chicago office. Periodi-
cally, she made hospital inspection trips to see that supplies from the Chicago
office reached their intended destination at field hospitals connected with the
Union armies. Her recollections of one such trip in 1863 are notable for the
insights into women's benevolent efforts during the war and also for the discussion of women's interest in the politics of war. After the Civil War ended,
Livermore became a leading proponent of political and legal rights for women.*

The grand passion of the West during the first half of the war was
to re-open the Mississippi. . . .

Gen. [William T.] Sherman's attempt to take the fortifications and
batteries which defended Vicksburg on the north had failed . . . the
whole Western army had been moved down the Mississippi in transports. At that time, the men were living in boats, or were vainly seeking dry land for their encampments, amid the swamps, lagoons,
bayous, and sloughs of the abominable portion of that country,
known as the "river bottoms.". . .

. . . Soon sickness and suffering stalked in among them. The death
which they had escaped on Southern battle-fields sprang upon them

here like a tiger from the jungle. Twelve thousand men lay sick at one time—about thirty-three and one-third per cent of the army at that point—and the wail of agony from the sick and dying was borne to the listening ears of the tender-hearted Northwest. . . .

It was with one of these shipments of sanitary stores, and as one of the relief corps, that I went down the Mississippi in March, 1863. Quartermasters, State Surgeon-Generals, members of the Legislature, representatives of the Chicago Chamber of Commerce, a company of nurses whom I was to locate in hospitals, and some two or three women who had been active in working for our invalid soldiers from the very first, made up the delegation. Two of us only—Mrs. Colt, of Milwaukee, and myself—were connected with the Sanitary Commission. . . . The sanitary supplies, about thrity-five hundred boxes and packages in all, were sent by the Commission and Chicago Board of Trade.

The programme marked out for us was this. We were to visit every hospital from Cairo to Young's Point, opposite Vicksburg; relieve such needs as were pressing; make ourselves useful in any way among the sick and wounded, co-operating harmoniously as far as possible with medical and military authorities. From every point we were to report our movements, the result of our observations,. . . and what we found needing attention, employing the Chicago Press and the bulletins of the Sanitary Commission as our mediums of communication.

Our assortment of stores comprised almost everything necessary in hospital relief; potatoes, onions, sauer-kraut, and vegetables— chiefly for the scorbutic patients, who constituted a majority of the sick—farina, corn starch, lemons, oranges, pearl-barley, tea, sugar, condensed milk, ale, canned fruits, condensed extract of beef, cod- fish, jellies, a small quantity of the best of brandy, with hospital shirts, drawers, sheets, socks, slippers, bandages, lint, rubber rings, and whatever else might be needed for wounded and sick men. We also took down about five hundred "private boxes," forwarded by private parties for particular companies, or squads, or individuals, and com- mitted to our care for safe transmission and delivery. My own per- sonal outfit consisted of a long pair of rubber boots, reaching to the knee, a teapot, a spirit-lamp to boil it, with a large quantity of Japan tea, condensed milk, sugar and crackers.

Through the daily papers, we vounteered to take letters, messages, or small packages, to parties on our route connected with the army, and to deliver them whenever it was possible. For a week before we started, my time was consumed by people who came to the rooms of the Sanitary Commission on these errands. I made memoranda of the verbal messages and inquiries, which were many and mostly from the poor and humble. My memorandum book lies before me. Here are samples of these messages:—

. . . "Lake Providence, Eighteenth Wisconsin, John K——. Father and mother called. Brought four letters for him. Tell him to take care of his health, avoid liquor, *never be tempted to desert.* Brother William in Second Wisconsin, has got well of his wound, and gone back to the Army of the Potomac."

"Try to learn something concerning Herbert B——, of Fifteenth Wisconsin. Has not been heard from since battle of Stone[s] River." (He was never heard from until the lists of the Andersonville dead were published.)

. . . "Try to get discharge for Richard R——, dying in Overton Hospital, Memphis, of consumption, and bring him home to his parents."

• • •

Our headquarters while in Memphis were at the "Gayoso House," which had a great reputation for style, secession proclivities, and discomfort. The last two peculiarities were pre-eminent. . . . We were detained over two weeks in Memphis, so difficult was it to obtain transportation for ourselves and stores down the river. Strict military *surveillance* was kept over the boats bound for the South, and none were allowed to leave Memphis without a pass from the Commander of the Department. Our stores were piled on the levee, waiting reshipment, and a guard was placed over them to keep them from thieves. The Gayoso House was overflowing with *attachés* of the army, waiting a chance to go down the river, like ourselves.

A large company of women were also staying here, who made no secret of their sympathy with the South. . . .

One afternoon, while waiting for a chaplain, who was to drive me to some of the regimental hospitals outside of Memphis, two of these women came into the parlor and sat down. After we had measured each other with our eyes for a moment, one of them commenced a conversation. She was the wife of a member of the Confederate Congress, and her home was in Thibodeauxville, La.

"I am told you are going down below to look after sick Yankee soldiers," was her opening remark.

"I have been sent from Chicago with some thousands of boxes of hospital stores, for the use of United States soldiers," I replied, putting a special emphasis on the words "United States," for I had heard her loudly express her disgust at the name.

"I think it is high time somebody went down to them, for they are dying like sheep, and have just no care at all."

"That is a mistake. They have the best of care, the best of nursing possible under the circumstances, good surgeons, and delegations going down and back all the while in their service."

"Well, anyhow, you're the first woman that has come down here to look after them. This city is full of Yankee women, wives of Yankee officers—cold-blooded, white-faced, lank, lean women, decked out in cotton lace, cheap silks, and bogus jewelry, women who are their own servants at home,—what do *they* care for Yankee soldiers, whether they live or die? We have done wearing silks and jewels in the South until the war is over. I sold my jewels and gave the money to the hospitals; and I'd come down to wearing 'nigger cloth,' and eating corn bread mixed with water, and prepared with my own hands, before the men in our hospitals should want for anything."

"Madam, I honor your devotion to your soldiers, and only regret the badness of your cause. At the North we are equally solicitous for the welfare of our men. But you make the mistake of supposing that we at the North are as poor as you at the South. The war is not impoverishing us as it is you. Our women can afford to wear silks and jewelry, and yet provide everything needful for the soldiers. Whenever it becomes necessary, we shall be ready to make as great sacrifices as you."

"Ah, *we* have soldiers *worth* the sacrifices we make!" she said, with a lofty air. "*Our* men are the flower of our youth; they have the best blood of the world in their veins—*gentlemen*, every one of them. But your Yankee soldiers—ugh!" with a shiver of disgust and a grimace of aversion; "they are the dregs of your cities—gutter-snipes, drunken, ignorant—!"

"Stop!" I interrupted; "stop! I won't hear such calumny. I know just what sort of 'gentlemen' your soldiers are; for we have had seven thousand of them at Camp Douglas in Chicago, taken prisoners at Fort Donelson; and if *they* were the 'flower of your youth,' you are worse off for men in the South than I had supposed."

"And I have seen *your* soldiers, too, to my sorrow and horror. They are barbarians, I tell you. They came to my husband's villa after he had gone to Congress, and I was left alone, with my servants in charge, and they destroyed everything—*everything!* My plate, china, pictures, carpets, even my furniture, were imported; and the wretches! they burned up everything!"

"If your manners were as unbearable as they have been during the two weeks I have seen you in this house, I only wonder you escaped cremation with your villa and furniture. It is astonishing clemency that allows you to be at large in this city, plotting against the government and insulting loyal people."

. . . Afterwards, at the dinner-table, she offered to lay a wager of a dozen pairs of gloves that not one of our party would go below Memphis, but that we would be sent North by the first boat. She would have lost her bet had any one taken it, as we left Memphis for Vicksburg that very night, on the Tigress.

• • •

When we arrived at the [Milliken's] Bend, where some thirty thousand men were encamped, we notified the Medical Director of our arrival with hospital stores. He immediately despatched an "orderly" to every hospital, sending to every surgeon in charge an order on the sanitary boat for whatever he lacked or needed, accompanying it with an order on the quartermaster for teams to remove the packages. In many instances we followed the loads to the hospitals, and witnessed the joy of the poor fellows at this tangible proof that they were not forgotten at home. Here, as in Memphis, most of the patients were sick of miasmatic diseases. There were comparatively few, among the thousands and thousands whom we saw, suffering from wounds. The dejection of sick soldiers we always found greater than that of those wounded. They needed more encouragement and more cheerful talk.

They were homesick, many of them longing for mother, wife, sister, and friend.

Often, as I bent over a sick man with a sympathetic word, he would burst into a passion of weeping, the more violent for long repression. If I found I had not time to go from bed to bed with a few words to each, I would take a central position, and endeavor to cheer the pale, sad, emaciated men, lying with white faces pressed against white pillows, their hearts travelling back to the homes they had left. I would tell them how they were remembered in loving pride by the loyal North; how all the women of the land were planning, and toiling, and sacrificing for them; of the loaded boats at the levee, sent them in care of a special delegation; of the certainty felt by all that our cause would triumph; of the glad welcome that awaited them when they returned conquerors; and of the dear God, who was ever near, in sickness, in camp, on the battle-field, protecting and guiding, and from whose love they could never be separated by any depth of misery, suffering, degradation, or sin.

If any had messages to send home, or letters to write, or friends whom they wished me to visit, I took memoranda of what was desired, in my inseparable notebook. Many a dying message these books contained, from lips hushed a few hours after in death. . . .

From one of the hospitals at the Bend there came no surgeon and no requisition. I ordered the inevitable ambulance, with its pair of mules and colored driver, and rode two and a half miles to visit its surgeon. A sadder sight I never witnessed during the war. It was a regimental hospital—always a comfortless place. It contained about two hundred men, all of them very sick, all lying in their uniforms, on the bare board floor, with their knapsacks for pillows, with no food but army rations, no nurses but convalescent soldiers, themselves too sick to move except on compulsion, the sick men covered with vermin, tormented by flies during the day, and devoured by mosquitoes at night,—and their surgeon dead-drunk in bed.

I went through the four large wards of the hospital, each one as horrible as the other. In all the wards men were dying, and in all they seemed hopeless and despairing. There was no complaint, no lamentation—only now and then some delirious fever patient would clamor for "ice water," or "cold water right from the well." I stooped down and took one man by the hand, who was regarding me with most beseeching looks. "My poor boy," I said, "I am very sad to see you in this dreadful condition." He pressed my hand on his eyes with both his own, and wept aloud.

Weeping is contagious, and in a few moments one half the men in the hospital were sobbing convulsively. I was afraid it would kill them, they were so excessively weak, but it was some time before they could be calmed. I had taken along in the ambulance, tea, sugar, condensed milk, and crackers. After I had made tea and distributed it with the crackers, I went back to medical headquarters to report the disgraceful condition of the hospital. I was fortunate, for I ran across Surgeon-General [E. B.] Wolcott, of Wisconsin, a very noble man. It was a Wisconsin regiment whose sick were left uncared for, to die like dogs—and he rested not until the hospital was broken up, the surgeon sent home in disgrace, and the men removed to the receiving-boat Nashville.

This was a hospital boat, built on a barge, three stories high, fitted up with cooking apparatus, bath-rooms, laundry, cots, and whatever else was necessary. It was towed from landing to landing, receiving the sick temporarily, until they could be taken off by the hospital steamers, and carried farther North. Three weeks later, in passing through the wards of the Nashville, I was hailed from one of the beds in the following jolly fashion: "I say! We are going to live after all, spite of old G——"—the surgeon,—"maggots, flies, mosquitoes, and everything else. We are getting to be pretty *sassy* again." Here they were, sure enough, getting well and already full of fun, and jolly over their discomforts.

The Chicago Mercantile Battery was encamped two miles from the landing, and, as it enrolled over thirty young men from the Sunday-school and society of my own church in Chicago, besides a great many others whom we knew, I determined to visit them, when the hospital work at Milliken's Bend was done. I had already sent them their private packages and letters, and notified them of my intended visit. The ambulance left me a mile from their camp, and in the fragrant twilight of a lovely spring day I walked inside the levee, towards its location. Soon I saw the dear fellows striding along the top of the levee to meet me, their figures standing out clearly against the evening sky. I called to them, and down they rushed. Such a welcome! such a chorus of manly, familiar voices! such a shaking of hands! such hearty embraces from the younger members, sixteen of whom had been members of my own Sunday-school class. As I walked with them into camp, the boys swarmed from tents and "shebangs," bronzed to the color of the Atlantic Monthly covers, all shouting a hearty welcome, noisy, jolly, and excited. What a hubbub! What a jubilee! Here was a guest from home, who had talked a few days before with their fathers and mothers, sisters and wives. The best "shebang" of the encampment was placed at my disposal, for I was to spend the night with them. I was too far from the boat to return, had I desired it, and I had planned to be with them two or three days. There were unvisited hospitals in that neighborhood.

Everything in the way of shelter, in camp parlance, that was not a tent, was a *shebang*. Mine was a rough hut made of boards, with a plank floor, roofed with canvas, with a *bona fide* glass window at one end, and a panelled door at the other. . . .

We had a lively time in the "shebang" that evening. It was packed with the boys, all eager to hear from home, who put me through a course of catechism concerning matters and persons in whom they were interested, that soon exhausted my stock of information, and left me no resource but to draw on imagination. The tide of talk flowed over the night into the morning. The "tattoo" had been beaten for retiring, and still the boys were loath to go. At last I broke up the conference. But before withdrawing, George Throop, one of the young men, drew from his breast pocket a copy of the New Testament. . . .

All heads were instantly uncovered, all hum of voices ceased, and a portion of the fifteenth chapter of Luke's Gospel was read, when Sergeant Dyer, a very noble man belonging to a Baptist church of Chicago, voluntarily offered a brief and appropriate prayer. Alas! I never saw again the young lieutenant who officiated as Bible reader, nor the sergeant who offered prayer. Both are sleeping under the sod on the banks of the Red River, where they fell in battle. One, the young, brave, and handsome lieutenant, was shot from his horse as he was urging his men on to the fight; and the other, the fatherly sergeant, was shot through the heart as he was spiking his gun, before joining in the retreat which was sounded.

I had a wakeful night. It was my first attempt to sleep in camp, and I did better afterwards, when I became used to it. I was in the enemy's country—I heard the steady footfall of the guard past my tent, and the incessant booming of the great guns at Vicksburg, fifteen miles away. I had lived in an atmosphere of suffering ever since I left home; and all the visions of horror I had witnessed now danced about my sleep-less pillow. . . .

CHAPTER 15

A SOUTHERN WOMAN IN SHERMAN'S PATH

Dolly Lunt Burge: "Like Demons They Rush In"

Dolly Burge (1817–1891) was a middle-aged widow with a nine-year-old daughter when the war began. Running a family farm near Atlanta with the help of several slaves, she kept a diary. Widowhood made Burge an independent woman before the war even started, but shortages, inflation, high taxes, refugees, and growing alarm over the Union army's advancement into Georgia made coping increasingly difficult. General William T. Sherman's campaign of destruction in the lower South represented a marked contrast to the war's first two years, when armies fought against each other but not against the civilian population. By 1864 that had changed. "We are not only fighting hostile armies, but a hostile people," Sherman said, convinced that the only way to end the war was to place unyielding pressure on the southern people while at the same time vanquishing their military. Dolly Burge's outrage over the actions of Sherman's army, as groups of "bummers" ransacked homes, food, and crops, is vividly portrayed here. By the end of the war, Burge, like many southern women, had begun to question the cause of southern nationalism and the motives of those who drew the South into war.

January 1st 1864

A new year is ushered in but peace comes not with it. A bloody war is still decimating our nation & thousands of hearts are to day bleeding over the loss of loved ones. Scarcely a family in the land but has given some of its members to their country. Terrible terrible indeed is war. O that its ravages may soon be stopped. Will another year find us amid carnage & bloodshed. Shall we ever be a nation? Or shall we be annihilated? The prices of everything are very high corn 7 dollars a bushel calico 10 dollars a yard salt 60 dollars a hundred cotton from 60 to 80 cents a pound everything in like ratio. . . .

Feb 10th [1864]

. . . By a letter received through "flag of truce" I learn they [her father and stepmother] both died the last day of the old year. Of what disease I know not. Oh this cruel war that has deprived me of being with them & ministering to their wants. I have felt very solemn all day. The generation between me & the grave has passed away. I step into my parents place & will soon follow them to the grave. And my Sadai [her daughter] will stand in my place. Thus one generation cometh & passeth away & another followeth.

[March] 14th [1864]

Finished planting those fields. Have been to town to day & sold three bales of cotton to fund money for my taxes. This year got 75 cents per pound.

[March] 15 [1864]

Sent off cotton & three hundred pounds of meat 5 pounds of wool five bushels of oats for my thithes [*sic*].

April 3d [1864]

I have no plants in the garden. My potatoes have not sprouted & everything looks like January instead of April. We have no corn up though it has been planted a month.

May 5th [1864]

Mr. Ward from Walker County a refugee who has been attending to my business & Miss Rebecca Harwell a second cousin of my husbands also a refugee were married here this evening. Dr. Cheney performing the ceremony. I sent for Saydee to come from School. She was very much surprised & overjoyed to be at a wedding. Nobody present but her cousin Amanda & her sister. All but Saydee dressed in homespun.

[July] 22d [1864]

A never to be forgotten day. We have heard the loud booming of the cannon all day nearly. . . . I walked to the door when such such a stampede I never witnessed before. . . . Judge Floyd stopped saying Mrs. Burge the Yankees are coming they have got my family & here is all I have upon earth. "Hide your mules & carriages & whatever valuables you have. Sadai says Oh Ma what shall we do. Never mind Sadai they won't hurt you & you must help me hide my things. I went to the smoke house & divided out the meat to the servants & bid them hide it. Julia took a jar of lard & buried it. In the meantime Sadai was taking down & picking up our clothes which she was giving to the servants to hide in their cabins. Silk dresses challis muslins & merinos linens & hoseiry [sic] all found their way into the chests of the women & under their beds. China Silver was all laid away under ground & Sadai bid Mary to hide a bit of soap under some bricks that Ma might have a little left. Then she came to me with part of a loaf of bread asking if she had not better put it in her pocket that we might have something to eat that night. And verily we had cause to fear that we might be homeless for on every side we could see smoke arising from burning buildings & bridges. . . . I shall sleep none to night. The woods are full of refugees—

[July] 24 Sunday [1864]

No church. Our preachers horse stolen by the Yankees. Sally & I went up to Mr. Graves to see how they all fared found they had not been molested nor lost neither negroes or mules. Mr. Hinton lost several & fifteen head of horses. . . .

[July] 28th [1864]

I rose early & had the boys to plough the turnip patch their mules were all in there & we were just rising from breakfast when Ben Glass rode up with the cry The Yankees are coming Mrs. Burge "hide your mules." How we were startled. . . . Report says there is forty thousand in Covington & vicinity. Infantry Cavalry & Artillery.

[July] 29 [1864]

. . . The Yankees left Covington for Macon headed by [General George] Stoneman to release prisoners held there. They robbed every house on their road of provisions sometimes taking every peice of meat blankets & wearing apparel silver & arms of every description. They would take silk dresses & put them under their saddles & things for which they had no use. Is this the way to make us love them & their union? Let the poor people answer whom they have deprived of every mouthful of meat & of their stock to make any. Our mills too they have burned destroying an immense amount of property.

[August] 2nd [1864]

Just as I got out of bed this morning Aunt Julia called me to look down the road & see the soldiers. I peeped through the blinds & there they were sure enough the "Yankees" the 'blue coats.' I was not dressed the servant women came running in. Mistress they are coming. They are coming. they are riding into the lot. There are two coming up the steps. I bid Rachel fasten my room door & go to the front door & ask them what they wanted. They did not wait for that but wanted to know "What the door was fastened for." She told them the White folks were not up. Well they said "they wanted breakfast & that quick too." . . . [A]s soon as I could get on my clothing I hastened to the kitchen to hurry up breakfast. Six of them were already in there talking with my women. They asked about our soldiers & passing themselves off as [General Joseph] Wheelers men said "Have you seen any of our men go by." Several of Wheelers men passed last evening. Who are you? Said I. "We are a portion of Wheelers men" said one. "You look like Yankees said I. "Yes" said one stepping up to me "We are Yankees did you ever see one before? Not for a long time & none such as you I replied.

"Well now tell us how many of Wheelers men passed." I told them & asked how many of them I had to get breakfast for; they said "twenty six." They were in a great hurry & were so frightened that I became reassured.

Breakfast was got speedily that morning. A picket was placed before my front gate but one of my servants run to Jo Perrys & told him that they were at my house he informed some of the Calvary [*sic*] that were camped some two miles from here & soon after they left here. Which they did taking off three of my best mules they were captured.

None of my servants went with them for which I feel very thankful. Miss Fanny Perry & Mrs. Ezzard came down this evening. Oh how thankful I feel that they have done me no more injury. They were Ill & Kentucky men but of German origin. To night Capt. Smith of an Alabama regiment with a squad of twenty men are camped opposite in the field. They have all supped with me & I shall breakfast them. We have spent a pleasant evening with music & talk they have a prisoner along. I can't help feeling sorry for him.

[August] 31st [1864]

Atlanta has fallen. We could hear the blowing up of the magizines [*sic*] which shook my house.

[October] 22nd [1864]

. . . Been getting in corn all the week. Shall not make as much as last year. But if I am allowed to keep it I shall have enough for my own family. The servants have a candy pulling to night & are enjoying themselves right merrily dancing & frolicking. How much happier than their mistress—

Nov 8th 1864

To day will probably decide the fate of this confederacy if Lincoln is reelected I think our fate is a hard one, but, we are in the hands of a merciful God & if He sees that we are in the wrong I trust that He will show it unto us. I have never felt that Slavery was altogether right for it is abused by many & I have often heard Mr. Burge say that if he could see that it was sinful for him to own slaves, if he felt that it was wrong, he would take them where he could free them he would not sin for his right hand. The purest & holiest men have own them & I can see nothing in the Scriptures which forbids it. I have never bought nor sold & have tried to make life easy & pleasant to those that have been bequeathed me by the dead. I have never ceased to work, but many a Northern housekeeper has a much easier time than a Southern matron with her hundred negroes.

[November] 11th [1864]

Finished hauling in my corn has made about 1200 bushels have 900 put up but how uncertain whether I keep it. Commenced digging potatoes. Cool & pleasant.

[November] 15 [1864]

Went up to Covington to day to pay Confederate tax. Did not find commissioners. Called at Mrs. Ushers. She is in fine spirits thinks refugees had better all come home. That there is no danger from raiders. That the Federal army is evacuating Atlanta & returning north. . . .

Nov 16th 1864

As I could not obtain in Covington what I went for in the way of dye stuffs & I concluded this morning in accordance with Mrs. Wards wish to go to the "Circle.". . . . On our way home met bro Evans accompanied by John Hinton who inquired if we had heard that the Yankees were coming! Said a large force was at Stockbridge & that a dispatch was received in Covington to that effect & that the Home Guard were all called out. That it was said that they were on their way to Savannah. We rode home chatting about it & finally settled it in our minds that it could not be so probably a foraging party. Some hour or so saw a Mr. Smith returning who had been refugeeing his stock with them all with him. I went out & told him the report, but he did not believe it. . . .

[November] 17th [1864]

Saw men going up from below to town did not believe the report. Have been uneasy all day. At night some of those neighbors called who went to town. Said it was a large force but could not tell what or where they were going. They moved very slow. What shall I do? Where go—

[November] 18th [1864]

Slept very little last night. Went out doors several times. Could see large fires like burning buildings. Am I not in the Hands of a merciful God Who has promised to take care of the widow & the orphan— Sent two of my mules in the night. Mr. Ward & Frank took them away & hid them. In the morning took a barrel of salt which cost me two hundred dollars into one of the black womens gardens put a paper over it & then on the top of that leached ashes fixed it on a board as a leach tub daubing it with ashes. . . . Went to packing my & Sadais clothes fear that we shall be homeless. . . .

[November] 19th [1864]

Slept in my clothes last night as I heard the Yankees went to neighbor Montgomerys thursday night at one o clock & searched his house drank his wine took his money &c &c. As we were not disturbed I after breakfast with Sadai walked up to Mr. Jo Perrys my nearest neighbors where the Yankees were yesterday to learn something of their movements. Saw Mrs. Laura in the road. . . . Accidentally I turned & looked behind me & saw some "blue coats" coming down the hill by old Mrs. Perrys. Said I "I believe there *are some* now." . . . O God the time of trial has come. Give me firmness & remember thy promise to the Widow & Orphan "upon which Thou hast caused thy Servant to hope!" . . .

I walked to the gate, there they came, filing up. I hastened back to my frightened servants & told them they had better hide & then went back to the gate to claim protection & a guard—

But like Demons they rush in. My yards are full. To my smoke house, my Dairy, Pantry, kitchen & cellar like famished wolves they come, breaking locks & whatever is in their way. The thousand pounds of meat in my smoke house is gone in a twinkling my flour my meal, my lard, butter, eggs, pickles of various kinds, both in vinegar & brine. Wine, jars, & jugs, are all gone. My eighteen fat turkeys, my hens, chickens & fowls. My young pigs are shot down in my yard, & hunted as if they were the rebels themselves. Utterly powerless I came to appeal to the guard. I cannot help you Madam it is orders & as I stood there from my lot I saw driven first Old Dutch my dear old Buggyhorse who has carried my dear dead husband so many miles, & who would so quietly wait at the block for him to mount & dismount, & then had carried him to his grave. . . .

But alas little did I think while trying to save my house from plunder & fire—that they were forcing at the point of the bayonet my boys from home. One (Newton) jumped into the bed in his cabin & declared himself sick another crawled under the floor a lame boy he was but they pulled him out & placed him on a horse & drove him off. . . . I had not believed they would force from their homes the poor doomed negroes, but such as been the fact here cursing them & saying that Jeff Davis was going to put them in his army but they should not fight for him but for them. No indeed! No! They are not friends to the slave. We have never made the poor cowardly negro fight & it is strange, passing strange, that the all powerful Yankee Nation with the whole world to back them. Their ports open, their armies filled with soldiers from all nations. Should at last take the poor negro to help them out, against this "little Confederacy" which was to be brought back into the Union in sixty days time. My poor boys my poor boys, what unknown trials are before you. How you have clung to your mistress & assisted her in every way you knew how. You have never known want of any kind. Never have I corrected them. A word was sufficient it was only to tell them what I wanted & they obeyed! Their parents are with me & how sadly they lament the loss of their boys. . . .

A Mr. Webber from Illinois & a Captain came into my house of whom I claimed protection from the vandals that were forcing themselves into my rooms. He said he knew my brother Orrington of Chicago. At that name I could not restrain my feelings but bursting into tears implored him to see my brother & let him know my destitution. I saw nothing before me but starvation. He promised to do this & comforted me with the assurance that my dwelling house would not be burned though my out buildings might. Poor little Sadai went crying to him as a friend & told him that they had her doll Nancy he begged her to come to see him & he would give her a fine waxen one. He felt for me & I given him & several others the character of gentlemen. I don't believe they would have molested women & children had they had their own way. . . . Sherman with a greater portion of his army passed my house all day. All day as its sad moments rolled on were they passing, not only in front of my house, but they came up behind tore down my garden palings, made a road through my back yard & lot field, driving their Stock & riding through, tearing down my fences & desolating my home. Wantonly doing it when there was no necessity for it. Such a day if I live to the age of Methuselah may God spare me from ever seeing again— . . . My Heavenly Father alone saved me from the destructive fire. My carriage house had in it eight bales of cotton with my carriage buggy & harness. On top of the cotton was some corded cotton rolls a hundred pounds or more. These were thrown out of the blanket in which they were taken & a large twist of the rolls set on fire & thrown into the boat of my carriage which was close up to the cotton bales. Thanks to my God the cotton only burned over & then went out! Shall I ever forget the deliverance?

[November] 20 [1864]

. . . I feel so thankful that I have not been burned out that I have tried to spend the remainder of the day as the Sabbath ought to be spent. Eat dinner out of the oven in Julias house some stew, no bread. She is boiling some corn. My poor servants feel so bad at losing what they have worked for. Meat hog meat that they love better than anything else is all gone.

[November] 21st [1864]

We had the table laid this morning but no bread or butter or milk. What a prospect for delicasies!! My house is a perfect fright I had brought in Saturday night some thirty bushels of potatoes & poured down in the hall or passage ten or fifteen bushels of wheat & that poured down on the carpet in the hall. Then the few gallons of syrup saved was daubed all about. A backbone of a hog that I had killed on Friday & which the Yankees did not take when they cleaned out my smoke house I found & hid under my bed & this is all the meat I have. . . . About ten o'clock this morning Mr. Joe Perry called. I was so glad to see him that I could scarcely forbear embracing him. I could not keep from crying for I was so sure that the Yankees had shot him & I felt so much for his poor wife. The soldiers told me repeatedly Saturday that they had hung him & his brother James & George Guise. They had a narrow escape however & only escaped by knowing the country so much better than they did. They laid out until this morning. How rejoiced I am for his family. . . .

[December] 24th [1864]

This has usually been a very busy day with me preparing for Christmas. Not only for my own tables but for gifts for my servants. Now how changed no cakes, pies or confectionary, can I have. We are all Sad. . . . I have nothing to put in Sadais stocking which hangs so invitingly for Santa Claus. How disappointed she will be in the morning though I have explained it all to her why he could not come. Poor children! Why must the innocent suffer with the guilty?

[December] 25th [1864]

Sadai jumped out of bed very early this morning to feel in her stocking. She could not believe but she would find something in it. She crept back into bed pulled the covers over her face & I soon heard her sobbing. The little negroes all came in "Christmas gift mistress Christmas gift mistress." I pulled the cover over my face & was soon mingling my tears with Sadais.

[January] 16th 1865

I have commenced Sadai in her books again & to stimulate her have let come in 5 of the neighbours children, to study & say lessons in the morning. Nothing encouraging from the army. Commenced breaking up land for corn three ploughs. Am trying a mule belonging to Mr. Graham.

April 29 [1865]

Boys ploughing in the old house field corn. We are needing rain. Just finished housecleaning. Sent Eb down to Madison last Monday with letters for Mrs. Cook to take North with her for my brothers & sisters. Everything looks pleasant again. The state of our country is very gloomy. General [Robert E.] Lee has surrendered his army to the victorious Grant. Well if it will only hasten the conclusion of this war I am satisfied. There has been something very strange in this whole affair, to me, & I can, attribute to nothing but the hand of Providence Working out some problem which has not yet been revealed to us poor erring mortals. At the commencement of the struggle the minds of men their wills their self control seemed to be all taken from them in a passionate antagonism to the coming in president (Abraham Lincoln[)]. Our leaders to whom the people looked for wisdom were led by them into this perhaps the greatest error of the age. We will not have this man to rule over us was their cry. For years it has been stirring in the hearts of Southern politicians. The North was enriched & built up by Southern labour & wealth. Mens pockets were always appealed to & appealed to so constantly that an antagonism was excited which had become impossible to allay. They did not believe the North would fight. Said Robert Toombes "I will drink every drop of blood they will shed." Ah blinded men. Rivers deep & strong has been shed & where are we now? A ruined subjugated people & What will be our future? is the question which now rests heavily upon the hearts of all—This has been a month never to be forgotten. Events of a lifetime have transpired within its limits. Two armies have surrendered. The President of the U. States has been assassinated Richmond evacuated & Davis the President of the Confederacy put to grief to flight—The old flag has been raised again upon Sumpter & an armistice accepted.

CHAPTER 16

THE RAVAGES OF WAR

Emma LeConte: Account of the Burning of Columbia, S.C.

Emma LeConte was seventeen years old when the armies of General William Tecumseh Sherman swept through Georgia and the Carolinas. She lived in Columbia, South Carolina, on the campus of South Carolina College where her father taught chemistry. In February 1865 she was a reluctant and horrified witness of Sherman's occupation of Columbia and of the subsequent burning of the town. Sensitive almost beyond her years, Emma described in her diary the ravages of war during the last days of the Confederacy. After four years of fighting, the real meaning of war had been brought home to her and her family. Sherman wrote late in December 1864 that his army was "burning with an insatiable desire to wreak vengeance upon South Carolina." Vengeance it was. Emma's description of the burning of Columbia, the responsibility for which has been a matter of controversy, is unparalleled among contemporary accounts. Intensely patriotic to the Southern cause, she was plunged into a mood of gloom and despair as the nation she had so enthusiastically hailed as a child in 1861 met its demise.

Columbia, South Carolina, December 31st, 1864. The last day of the year—always a gloomy day—doubly so today. Dark leaden clouds cover the sky, and ceaseless pattering rain that has been falling all day. The air is chill and damp, and the morning wind fills one with melancholy. A fit conclusion for such a year—'tis meet, old year, that thou should'st weep for the misfortunes thou hast brought our country! And what hope is there to brighten the new year that is coming up? Alas, I cannot look forward to the new year—'My thoughts still cling to the mouldering past.' Yes, the year that is dying has brought us more trouble than any of the other three long dreary years of this fearful struggle. Georgia has been desolated. The resistless flood has swept through that state, leaving but a desert to mark its track. And now our hateful foes hold Savannah. Noble old Charleston is at last

248

to be given up. They are preparing to hurl destruction upon the State they hate most of all, and Sherman the brute avows his intention of converting South Carolina into a wilderness. Not one house, he says, shall be left standing, and his licentious troops—whites and negroes—shall be turned loose to ravage and violate.

All that is between us and our miserable fate is a handful of raw militia assembled near Branchville. And yet they say there is a Providence who fights for those who are struggling for freedom—who are defending their homes, and all that is held dear! Yet those vandals—those fiends incarnate—are allowed to overrun our land! Oh, my country! Will I live to see thee subjugated and enslaved by those Yankees—surely every man and woman will die first. On every side they threaten—Lee's noble army alone stands firm. Foreign nations look on our sufferings and will not help us. Our men are being killed off—boys of sixteen are conscripted. Speculators and extortioners are starving us. But is this a time to talk of submission? Now when the Yankees have deepened and widened the breach by a thousand new atrocities? A sea rolls between them and us—a sea of blood. Smoking houses, outraged women, murdered fathers, brothers and husbands forbid such a union. Reunion! Great Heavens! How we hate them with the whole strength and depth of our souls!

I wonder if the new year is to bring us new miseries and sufferings. I am afraid so. We used to have bright anticipations of peace and happiness for the new year, but now I dare not look forward. Hope has fled, and in its place remains only a spirit of dogged, sullen resistance. . . .

JANUARY 4TH [1865] . . . I am constantly thinking of the time when Columbia will be given up to the enemy. The horrible picture is constantly before my mind. They have promised to show no mercy in this State. Mother wants to send me off, but of course I would not leave her. I can only hope their conduct in a city will not be so shocking as it has been through the country. Yet no doubt the College buildings will be burned, with other public buildings, and we will at least lose our home. . . .

JANUARY 12TH . . . Troops have been passing through Columbia for some days and I feel a little safer, though if Joe Johnston is put in command, we had as well pack up and prepare to run. He will certainly execute one of his 'masterly retreats' from the coast back to Virginia, and leave us at Sherman's mercy. I hear that Sherman has drawn his troops back from South Carolina to Savannah. Some think this bodes ill for Gen. Hood, who is in Alabama or Mississippi or somewhere else, and may be caught in a trap between Sherman and Thomas. I hope not. Cousin Lula says they had a letter from Julian yesterday. He, who used to be such an ardent Georgian, is down on the State for behaving so shamefully. He says all his company have abjured their State, and made a vow never to live in it, especially in Savannah. As for me, I am a South Carolinian. I have lived here almost since I can remember, and only wish I had been born here instead of in Georgia! That whole State is utterly demoralized, and ready to go back into the Union. Savannah has gone down on her knees, and humbly begged pardon of Father Abraham, gratefully acknowledging Sherman's clemency in burning and laying waste their State! Oh, it is a crying shame, such poltroonery! . . .

JANUARY 23RD . . . We hear so many rumors of the movements of the Yankees and of our own troops, but they are not worth noting. Mother has packed up the clothing and bed-linen that we may save those at least. All the books are packed, too. I have not been in the library since they were taken down. It would make me too sad to look at the empty shelves.

It may be of interest some day to recall the poor style in which we lived during the war, so I shall make a few notes. My underclothing is of coarse unbleached homespun, such as we gave the negroes formerly, only much coarser. My stockings I knit myself, and my shoes are of heavy calfskin. My dresses are two calicoes (the last one bought cost sixteen dollars a yard), a homespun of black and white plaid, and an old delaine of pre-war times that hangs on in a dilapidated condition, a reminiscence of better days. We have a couple of old silks, carefully preserved for great occasions and which do not look shabby for the simple reason that all the other old silks that still survive the war are in the same state of decay. The homespun cost about eight or ten dollars a yard—calico is twenty to thirty dollars a yard now, and going higher from week to week. My shoes are one hundred and fifty dollars a pair. In two or three months these prices will be doubled.

We live tolerably poorly. Two meals a day. Two plates of bread for breakfast, one of wheat flour as five bags of flour were recently made a present to us else we would only have corn bread. Corn itself is forty dollars a bushel. Dinner consists of a very small piece of meat, generally beef, a few potatoes and a dish of hominy and a pone of corn bread. We have no reason to complain, so many families are so much worse off. Many have not tasted meat for months, and we, too, having a cow, are able to have butter. Wood is hard to get at one hundred dollars a load. We keep but one fire in the dining room where we sit. We have been fortunate in having gas thus far (at eighty dollars a thousand), but since the freshet, the supply of rosin has been deficient and now and then it is cut off and we burn tallow candles at two dollars apiece. We never have sweet things now, and even molasses candy is a rarity seldom to be thought of. . . .

FEBRUARY 14TH. TUESDAY. What a panic the whole town is in! I have not been out of the house myself, but Father says the intensest excitement prevails on the streets. The Yankees are reported a few miles off on the other side of the river. How strong no one seems to know. It is decided if this be true that we will remain quietly here, Father alone leaving. It is thought Columbia can hardly be taken by a raid as we have the whole of Butler's cavalry here—and if they do, we have to take the consequences. It is true some think Sherman will burn the town, but we can hardly believe that. Besides these buildings, though they are State property, yet the fact that they are used as a hospital will, it is thought, protect them. I have been hastily making large pockets to wear under my hoopskirt, for they will hardly search our persons. Still, everything of any value is to be packed up to go with Father. I do not feel half so frightened as I thought I would. Perhaps because I cannot realize they are coming. I hope still this is a false report. . . . Our sufferings will probably be of short duration, as they will hardly send more than a raid. They would not have time to occupy the town. But I cannot believe they are coming! . . . Alas, what may we not have gone through with by the end of this week! Ah me, I look forward with terror, and yet with a kind of callousness to their approach. . . .

FEBRUARY 15TH. WEDNESDAY. Oh, how is it possible to write amid this excitement and confusion! We are too far off to hear and see much down here in the Campus, but they tell me the streets in town are lined with panic-stricken crowds, trying to escape. All is confusion and turmoil. The Government is rapidly moving off stores—all day the trains have been running, whistles blowing and wagons rattling through the streets. All day we have been listening to the booming of cannon—receiving conflicting rumors of the fighting. All day wagons and ambulances have been bringing in the wounded over the muddy streets and through the drizzling rain, with the dark, gloomy clouds overhead.

All day in our own household has confusion reigned, too. The back parlor strewed with clothing, etc., open trunks standing about, while a general feeling of misery and tension pervaded the atmosphere. Everything is to go that can be sent—house linen, blankets, clothing, silver, jewelry—even the wine—everything movable of any value. Hospital flags have been erected at the different gates of the Campus—we hope the fact of our living within the walls may be some protection to us, but I fear not. I feel sure these buildings will be destroyed. . . .

FEBRUARY 16TH. THURSDAY. . . . About nine o'clock we were sitting in the dining room, having just returned from the piazza where we had been watching a brigade of cavalry passing to the front. 'Wouldn't it be dreadful if they should shell the city?' someone said. 'They would not do that,' replied Mother, 'for they have not demanded its surrender.' Scarcely had the words passed her lips when Jane, the nurse, rushed in crying out that they were shelling. We ran to the front door just in time to hear a shell go whirring past. It fell and exploded not far off. This was so unexpected. I do not know why, but in all my list of anticipated horrors I somehow had not thought of a bombardment. If I had only looked for it, I wouldn't have been so frightened. As it was, for a few minutes I leaned against the door fairly shivering, partly with cold but chiefly from nervous excitement. After listening to them awhile, this wore off and I became accustomed to the shells. Indeed, we were in no immediate danger, for the shells were thrown principally higher up.

They were shelling the town from the Lexington Heights just over the river, and from the campus gate their troops could be seen drawn up on the hilltops. Up the street this morning the government stores were thrown open to the people and there was a general scramble. Our negroes were up there until frightened home by the shells. The shelling was discontinued for an hour or two and then renewed with so much fury that we unanimously resolved to adjourn to the basement and abandon the upper rooms. Sallie and I went up to our rooms to bring down our things. I was standing at my bureau with my arms full when I heard a loud report. The shell whistled right over my head and exploded. I stood breathless, really expecting to see it fall in the room. When it had passed, I went into the ball and met Sallie, coming from her room, pale and trembling. 'Oh, Emma,' she said, 'this is dreadful!' . . .

FEBRUARY 17TH. FRIDAY. . . . *One o'clock P.M.* Well, they are here. I was sitting in the back parlor when I heard the shouting of the troops. I was at the front door in a moment. Jane came running and crying, 'Oh, Miss Emma, they've come at last!' She said they were then marching down Main Street, before them flying a panic-stricken crowd of women and children who seemed crazy. . . . I ran upstairs to my bedroom windows just in time to see the U.S. flag run up over the State House. Oh, what a horrid sight! What a degradation! After four long bitter years of bloodshed and hatred, now to float there at last! That hateful symbol of despotism! I do not think I could possibly describe my feelings. I know I could not look at it. I left the window and went back downstairs to Mother.

In a little while a guard arrived to protect the hospital. They have already fixed a shelter of boards against the wall near the gate—sentinels are stationed and they are cooking their dinner. The wind is very high today and blows their hats around. This is the first sight we have had of these fiends except as prisoners. The sight does not stir up very pleasant feelings in our hearts. We cannot look at them with anything but horror and hatred, loathing and disgust. The troops now in town are a brigade commanded by Col. Stone. Everything is quiet and orderly. Guards have been placed to protect houses, and Sherman has promised not to disturb private property. How relieved and thankful we feel after all our anxiety and distress!

Later. Gen. Sherman has *assured* the Mayor 'that he and all the citizens may sleep as securely and quietly tonight as if under *Confederate rule.'* Private property shall be carefully respected. Some public buildings have to be destroyed, but he will wait until tomorrow when the wind shall have entirely subsided. . . .

FEBRUARY 18TH. SATURDAY AFTERNOON. What a night of horror, misery and agony! It is useless to try to put on paper any idea of it. The recollection is so fearful, yet any attempt to describe it seems to [be] useless. It even makes one sick to think of writing down such scenes—and yet, as I have written thus far, I ought, while it is still fresh, try even imperfectly to give some account of last night. Every incident is now so vividly before me and yet it does not seem real—rather like a fearful dream, or nightmare that still oppresses.

Until dinner time we saw little of the Yankees, except the guard about the Campus, and the officers and men galloping up and down the street. It is true, as I have since learned, that as soon as the bulk of the army entered, the work of pillage began. But we are so far off and so secluded from the rest of the town that we were happily ignorant of it all. I do not know exactly when Sherman [entered], but I should judge about two or between one and two P.M. We could hear their shouts as they surged down Main Street and through the State House, but were too far off to see much of the tumult, nor did we dream what a scene of pillage and terror was being enacted. I hear they found a picture of President Davis in the Capitol, which was set up as a target and shot at amid the jeers of the soldiery. From three o'clock till seven their army was passing down the street by the Campus, to encamp back of us in the woods. Two corps entered town—Howard's and Logan's—one, the diabolical 15th which Sherman has hitherto never permitted to enter a city on account of their vile and desperate character. Slocum's Corps remained over the river, and I suppose Davis' also. The devils as they marched past, looked strong and well clad in dark, dirty-looking blue. The wagon trains were immense.

Night drew on. Of course we did not expect to sleep, but we looked forward to a tolerably tranquil night. Strange as it may seem, we were actually idiotic enough to believe Sherman would keep his word! A *Yankee*—and *Sherman!* It does seem incredible, such credulity, but I suppose we were so anxious to believe him—the lying fiend! I hope retributive justice will find him out one day.

At about seven o'clock I was standing on the back piazza in the third story. Before me the whole southern horizon was lit up by camp fires which dotted the woods. On one side the sky was illuminated by the burning of Gen. Hampton's residence a few miles off in the country, on the other side by some blazing buildings near the river. I had scarcely gone downstairs again when Henry told me there was a fire on Main Street. Sumter Street was brightly lighted by a burning house so near our piazza that we could feel the heat. By the red glare we could watch the wretches walking—generally staggering—back and forth from the camp to the town—shouting—hurrahing—cursing

South Carolina—swearing—blaspheming—singing ribald songs and using such obscene language that we were forced to go indoors.

The fire on Main Street was now raging, and we anxiously watched its progress from the upper front windows. In a little while, however, the flames broke forth in every direction. The drunken devils roamed about, setting fire to every house the flames seemed likely to spare. They were fully equipped for the noble work they had in hand. Each soldier was furnished with combustibles compactly put up. They would enter houses and in the presence of helpless women and children, pour turpentine on the beds and set them on fire. Guards were rarely of any assistance—most generally they assisted in the pillaging and firing.

The wretched people rushing from their burning homes were not allowed to keep even the few necessaries they gathered up in their flight—even blankets and food were taken from them and destroyed. The firemen attempted to use their engines, but the hose was cut to pieces and their lives threatened. The wind blew a fearful gale, wafting the flames from house to house with frightful rapidity. By midnight the whole town (except the outskirts) was wrapped in one huge blaze. Still the flames had not approached sufficiently near us to threaten our immediate safety, and for some reason not a single Yankee soldier had entered our house. . . .

. . . My God! What a scene! It was about four o'clock and the State House was one grand conflagration. Imagine night turned into noonday, only with a blazing, scorching glare that was horrible—a copper colored sky across which swept columns of black, rolling smoke glittering with sparks and flying embers, while all around us were falling thickly showers of burning flakes. Everywhere the palpitating blaze walling the streets with solid masses of flames as far as the eye could reach, filling the air with its horrible roar. On every side the crackling and devouring fire, while every instant came the crashing of timbers and the thunder of falling buildings.

A quivering molten ocean seemed to fill the air and sky. The library building opposite us seemed framed by the gushing flames and smoke, while through the windows gleamed the liquid fire. . . . The College buildings caught all along that side, and had the incendiary work continued one half hour longer than it did, they must have gone. All the physicians and nurses were on the roof trying to save the buildings, and the poor wounded inmates, left to themselves, such as could crawled out while those who could not move waited to be burned to death.

The Common opposite the gate was crowded with homeless women and children, a few wrapped in blankets and many shivering in the night air. Such a scene as this with the drunken, fiendish soldiery in their dark uniforms, infuriated, cursing, screaming, exulting in their work, came nearer realizing the material ideal of hell than anything I ever expect to see again. They call themselves 'Sherman's Hellhounds.' . . .

Oh, that long twelve hours! Never surely again will I live through such a night of horrors. The memory of it will haunt me as long as I shall live—it seemed as if the day would never come. The sun arose at last, dim and red through the thick, murky atmosphere. It set last night on a beautiful town full of women and children—it shone dully down this morning on smoking ruins and abject misery.

I do not know how the others felt after the strain of the fearful excitement, but I seemed to sink into a dull apathy. We none seemed to have the energy to talk. After a while breakfast came—a sort of mockery, for no one could eat. After taking a cup of coffee and bathing my face, begrimed with smoke, I felt better and the memory of the night seemed like a frightful dream. I have scarcely slept for three nights, yet my eyes are not heavy.

. . . We do not know the extent of the destruction, but we are told that the greater portion of the town is in ashes—perhaps the loveliest town in all our Southern country. This is civilized warfare. This is the way in which the 'cultured' Yankee nation wars upon women and children! Failing with our men in the field, *this* is the way they must conquer! I suppose there was scarcely an able bodied man, except the hospital physicians, in the whole twenty thousand people. It is so easy to burn the homes over the heads of helpless women and children, and turn them with insults and sneers into the streets. One expects these people to lie and steal, but it does seem such an outrage even upon degraded humanity that those who practise such wanton and useless cruelty should call themselves men. It seems to us even a contamination to look at these devils. Think of the degradation of being conquered and ruled by such a people! It seems to me now as if we would choose extermination. . . .

When will these Yankees go that we may breathe freely again! The past three days are more like three weeks. And yet when they are gone we may be worse off with the whole country laid waste and the railroads cut in every direction. Starvation seems to stare us in the face. Our two families have between them a few bushels of corn and a little musty flour. We have no meat, but the negroes give us a little bacon every day. . . .

[About April 20th] . . . The South lies prostrate—their foot is on us—there is no help. During this short time we breathe, but—oh, who could have believed who has watched this four years' struggle that it could have ended like this! They say *right* always triumphs, but what cause could have been more just than ours? Have we suffered all—have our brave men fought so desperately and died so nobly for *this?* For four years there has been throughout this broad land little else than the anguish of anxiety—the misery of sorrow over dear ones sacrificed—for *nothing!* Is all this blood spilled in vain—will it not cry from the ground on the day we yield to these Yankees! We give up to the Yankees! How *can* it be? How can they talk about it? Why does not the President call out the women if there are [not] enough men? We would go and *fight,* too—we would better all die together. Let us suffer still more, give up yet more—anything, anything that will help the cause, anything that will give us freedom and not force us to live with such people—to be ruled by such horrible and contemptible creatures—to submit to them when we hate them so bitterly.

It is cruel—it is *unjust.* I used to dream about peace, to pray for it, but this is worse than war. What is such peace to us? What horrible fate has been pursuing us the last six months? Not much farther back than that we had every reason to hope for success. What is the cause of this sudden crushing collapse? I *cannot* understand it. I never loved my country as I do now. I feel I could sacrifice *everything* to it, and when I think of the future—oh God! It is too horrible. What I most fear is a conciliatory policy from the North, that they will offer to let us come back as before. Oh, no, no! I would rather we were held as a conquered province, rather sullenly submit and bide our time. Let them oppress and tyrannize, but let us take no favors of them. Let them send us away out of the country—anywhere away from them and their hateful presence. . . .

CHAPTER 17

STATES' RIGHTS VERSUS THE CONFEDERACY

Alexander H. Stephens: Speech to the Georgia Legislature, March 16, 1864

A *lexander Hamilton Stephens (1812–1883) represented his native Georgia in the House of Representatives from 1843 to 1859, a staunch defender of Southern interests during the sectional conflict. In 1860 he supported Stephen A. Douglas for the Presidency and opposed the immediate secession of his state following Lincoln's election, although he was elected to Georgia's secession convention. He later justified secession in constitutional terms, and following the war issued the classic statement of the states'-rights argument on the causes of the conflict in* A Constitutional View of the Late War Between the States *(1868–70). When the Confederate States of America was organized, Stephens was elected Vice President of the new nation, a post he held throughout the war. As an officer of the Confederate government, he remained, as he had been in Congress, an exponent of a conservative states'-rights philosophy, and became one of the leading critics of President Davis. Stephens saw in Davis's assumption of emergency war powers a dire threat to the sovereignty of states, and he resisted the efforts to centralize power on the national level during the conflict. By the end of the war Stephens's role as a critic and opposition leader bordered on obstructionism. The action of the Confederate Congress in January, 1864, in enlarging the scope of conscription and continuing the suspension of the writ of* habeas corpus, *measures recommended by Davis as necessary to the war effort, moved Stephens to deliver one of his few addresses against the administration. On March 16, 1864 he appeared before a special session of the Georgia state legislature and, in a three-hour speech, castigated the Davis administration for pursuing an unconstitutional policy. The conservative opposition led by Stephens weakened the Southern independence movement, and at least one historian has held this states'-rights opposition responsible for the defeat of the Confederacy.*

In compliance with your request, or at least with that of a large portion of your respective bodies, I appear before you tonight to speak of the state of public affairs. Never, perhaps, before, have I risen to address a public audience under circumstances of so much responsibility, and never did I feel more deeply impressed with the weight of it. Questions of the most momentous importance are pressing upon you for consideration and action. Upon these I am to address you. Would that my ability, physically, and in all other respects, were commensurate with the magnitude of the occasion. We are in the midst of dangers and perils. Dangers without and dangers within. Scylla on the one side and Charybdis on the other. War is being waged against us by a strong, unscrupulous and vindictive foe; a war for our subjugation, degradation and extermination. From this quarter threaten the perils without. Those within arise from questions of policy as to the best means, the wisest and safest, to repel the enemy, achieve our independence, to maintain and keep secure our rights and liberties. Upon the decision of these questions, looking to the proper development of our limited resources, wisely and patriotically, so that their entire efficiency may be exerted in our deliverance, with at the same time a watchful vigilance to the safety of the citadel itself, as much depends as upon the skill of our commanders and the valor of our citizen soldiers in the field. Every thing dear to us as freemen is at stake. An error in judgment, though springing from the most patriotic motives, whether in councils of war or councils of state, may be fatal. He, therefore, who rises under such circumstances to offer words of advice, not only assumes a position of great responsibility, but stands on dangerous ground. Impressed profoundly with such feelings and convictions, I should shrink from the undertaking you have called me to, but for the strong consciousness that where duty leads no one should ever fear to tread. Great as are the dangers that threaten us, perilous as is our situation—and I do not intend to overstate or understate, neither to awaken undue apprehension, or to excite hopes and expectations never to be realized—perilous, therefore, as our situation is, it is far, far from being desperate or hopeless, and I feel no hesitation in saying to you, in all frankness and candor, that if we are true to ourselves, and true to our cause, all may yet be well.

In the progress of the war thus far, it is true there is much to be seen of suffering, of sacrifice and of desolation; much to sicken the heart and cause a blush for civilization and Christianity. Cities have been taken, towns have been sacked, vast amounts of property have been burned, fields have been laid waste, records have been destroyed, churches have been desecrated, women and children have been driven from their homes, unarmed men have been put to death, States have been overrun and whole populations made to groan under the heel of despotism; all these things are seen and felt, but in them nothing is to be seen to cause dismay, much less despair; these deeds of ruin and savage barbarity have been perpetrated only on the outer borders, on the coast, and on the line of the rivers, where by the aid of their ships of war and gunboats the enemy has had the advantage; the great breadth of the interior—the heart of our country—has never yet been reached by them; they have as yet, after a struggle of nearly three years, with unlimited means, at a cost of not less than four thousand millions of dollars (how much more is unknown) and hundreds of thousands of lives, been able only to break the outer shell of the Confederacy. The only signal advantages they have as yet gained have been on the water, or where their land and naval forces were combined. That they should have gained advantages under such circumstances, is not a matter of much surprise. Nations in war, like individual men or animals, show their real power in combat when they stand upon the advantages that nature has given them, and fight on their own ground and in their own element. The lion, though king of the forest, cannot contend successfully with the shark in the water. In no conflict of arms away from gunboats, during the whole war, since the first battle of Manassas to that of Ocean Pond, have our gallant soldiers failed of victory when the numbers on each side were at all equal. The furthest advance into the interior from the base and protection of their gunboats, either on the coast or the rivers, that the enemy has been able to make for three years was the late movement from Vicksburg to Meridian, and the speedy turn of that movement shows nothing more clearly than the difficulties and disadvantages attending all such; these things should be noted and marked in considering our present situation and the prospects of the future. In all our losses up to this time, no vital blow has yet been given either to our cause or our energies. We still hold Richmond, after repeated efforts to take it, both by force and strategy. We still hold on the Gulf, Mobile, and, on the ocean front, Wilmington, Savannah and Charleston. These places have been, and are still held against the most formidable naval armament ever put afloat.

At Charleston the enemy seem to direct all their power, land and naval, that can be brought to bear in combination—all their energy, rancor, and vengeance. *"Carthago delanda est,"* is their vow as to this devoted city. Every means that money can command and ingenuity suggest, from the hugest engines of war never before known to the fiendish resort of Greek fire, have been and are being applied for its destruction. For nearly nine months the city, under the skill of our consummate commander, his subordinates, and the heroic virtues of our matchless braves in the ranks, still holds out against all the disadvantages of a defence without suitable naval aid. That she may continue to hold out, and her soil never be polluted by the unhallowed footprints of her vengeful besiegers, is, of course, the earnest wish of all. But even if so great a disaster should happen to us as the loss of Charleston, be not dismayed, indulge no sentiment akin to that of despair—Charleston is not a vital part. We may lose that place, Savannah, Mobile, Wilmington, and even Richmond, the seat of government, and still survive. We may lose all our strong places—the enemy may traverse our great interior as they have lately done in Mississippi, and we may still survive. We should, even under such calamities, be no worse off than our ancestors were in their struggle for independence. During the time that "tried men's souls" with them every city on the coast, from Boston to Savannah, was taken by the enemy. Philadelphia was taken, and Congress driven away. South Carolina, North Carolina, portions of Georgia, Virginia, and other States, were overrun and occupied by the enemy as completely as Kentucky, Missouri, Louisiana and Tennessee are now. Take courage from the example of your ancestors—disasters caused with them nothing like dismay or despair—they only aroused a spirit of renewed energy and fortitude. The principles they fought for, suffered and endured so much for, are the same for which we are now struggling—State rights, State sovereignty, the great principle set forth in the declaration of independence—the right of every State to govern itself as it pleases. With the same wisdom, prudence, forecast and patriotism; the same or equal statesmanship on the part of our rulers in directing and wielding our resources, our material of war, that controlled public affairs at that time, in the camp and in the cabinet, and with the same spirit animating the breast of the people, devotion to liberty and right, hatred of tyranny and oppression, affection for the cause for the cause's sake; with the same sentiments and feelings on the part of rulers and people in these days as were in those, we might and may be overrun as they were; our interior may be penetrated by superior hostile armies, and our country laid waste as theirs was, but we can never be conquered, as they never could be. The issues of war depend quite as much upon statesmanship as generalship; quite as much upon what is done at the council board, as upon what is done in the field. Much the greater part of all wars, is business—plain practical every-day-life business; there is in it no art or mystery or special knowledge, except good, strong, common sense—this relates to the finances, the quartermaster's and commissary's departments, the ways and means proper—in a word to the resources of a country and its capacities for war. The number of men that can be spared from production, without weakening the aggregate strength—the prospect of supplies, subsistence, arms and munitions of all kinds. It is as necessary that men called out should be armed, clothed, shod and fed, as that they should be put in the field—subsistence is as essential as men. At present we have subsistence sufficient for the year, if it is taken care of and managed with economy. Upon a moderate estimate, one within reasonable bounds, the tithes of wheat and corn for last year were not less, in the States east of the Mississippi, (to say nothing of the other side,) than eighteen million bushels. Kentucky and Tennessee are not included in this estimate. This would bread an army of five hundred thousand men and one hundred thousand horses for twelve months, and leave a considerable margin for waste or loss. This we have without buying or impressing a bushel or pound. Nor need a bushel of it be lost on account of the want of transportation from points at a distance from railroads. At such places it could be fed to animals, put into beef and pork, and thus lessen the amount of these articles of food to be bought. Upon a like estimate the tithe of meat for the last year, will supply the army for at least six months—rendering the purchase of supplies of this article necessary for only half the year—the surplus in the country, over and above the tithes, is ample to meet the deficiency. All that is wanting is men of business capacity, honesty, integrity, economy and industry in the management and control of that department. There need be no fear of the want of subsistence this year, if our officials do their duty. But how it will be next year, if the policy adopted by Congress, at its late session, is carried out, no one can safely venture to say.

This brings me to the main objects of this address, a review of those acts of Congress to which your attention has been specially called by the governor, and on which your action is invoked—these are . . . the military, and the *habeas corpus* suspension acts. . . .

The military act by which conscription is extended so as to embrace all between the ages of seventeen and fifty, and by which the State is to be deprived of so much of its labor, and stripped of the most efficient portion of her enrolled militia, presents a much graver question. This whole system of conscription I have looked upon from the beginning as wrong, radically wrong in principle and in policy. Contrary opinions, however, prevailed. But whatever differences of opinion may have been entertained as to the constitutionality of the previous conscript acts, it seems clear to my mind that but little difference can exist as to the unconstitutionality of this late act. . . .

For if all the white labor of the country, from seventeen to fifty—except the few exemptions stated—be called out and kept constantly in the field, we must fail, sooner or later, for want of subsistence and other essential supplies. To wage war successfully, men at home are as necessary as men in the field. Those in the field must be provided for, and their families at home must be provided for. In my judgment, no people can successfully carry on a long war, with more than a third of its arms-bearing population kept constantly in the field, especially if, cut off by blockade, they are thrown upon their own internal resources for all necessary supplies, subsistence and munitions of war. This is a question of arithmetic on well settled problems of political economy. But can we succeed against the hosts of the enemy unless all able to bear arms up to fifty years of age are called to and kept in the field? Yes, a thousand times yes, I answer, with proper and skillful management. If we cannot without such a call, we cannot with it, if the war last long. The success of Greece against the invasion by Persia—the success of the Netherlands against Philip—the success of Frederick against the allied powers of Europe—the success of the colonies against Great Britain, all show that it can be done. If our only hope was in matching the enemy with equal numbers, then our cause would be desperate indeed. Superior numbers is one of the chief advantages of the enemy. We must avail ourselves of our advantages. We should not rely for success by playing into his hand. An invaded people have many advantages that may be resorted to, to counterbalance superiority of numbers. These should be studied, sought, and brought into active co-operation. To secure success, brains must do something as well as muskets. . . .

I come, now, to the last of these acts of Congress. The suspension of the writ of *habeas corpus* in certain cases. This is the most exciting as it is by far the most important question before you. Upon this depends the question, whether the courts shall be permitted to decide upon the constitutionality of the late conscript act, should you submit that question to their decision, and upon it also depend other great essential rights enjoyed by us as freemen. This act upon its face, confers upon the President, secretary of war, and the general commanding in the trans-Mississippi department, (the two latter acting under the control and authority of the President,) the power to arrest and imprison any person who may be simply charged with certain acts, not all of them even crimes under any law; and this is to be done without any oath or affirmation alledging probable cause as to the guilt of the party. This is attempted to be done under that clause of the constitution, which authorizes Congress to suspend the privilege of the writ of *habeas corpus,* in certain cases.

In my judgment this act is not only unwise, impolitic and unconstitutional, but exceedingly dangerous to public liberty. Its unconstitutionality does not rest upon the idea that Congress has not got the power to suspend the privilege of this writ, nor upon the idea that the power to suspend it is an implied one, or that clearly implied powers are weaker as a class and subordinate to others, positively and directly delegated.

I do not understand the executive of this State to put his argument against this act upon any such grounds. He simply states a fact, as it most clearly is, that the power to suspend at all is an implied power. There is no positive, direct power delegated to do it. The power, however, is clear, and clear only by implication. The language of the constitution, that "the privilege of the writ of *habeas corpus* shall not be suspended unless, when in cases of rebellion or invasion, the public safety may require it," clearly expresses the intention that the power may be exercised in the cases stated; but it does so by implication only, just as if a mother should say to her daughter, you shall not go unless you ride. Here the permission and authority to go is clearly given, though by inference and implication only. It is not positively and directly given. This, and this only, I understand the governor to mean when he speaks of the power being an implied one. He raises no question as to the existence of the power, or its validity when rightfully exercised, but he maintains, as I do, that its exercise must be controlled by all other restrictions in the constitution bearing upon its exercise. Two of these are to be found in the words accompanying the delegation. It can never be exercised except in rebellion or invasion. Other restrictions are to be found in other parts of the constitution —in the amendments to the constitution adopted after the ratification of the words as above quoted. These amendments were made, as is expressly declared in the preamble to them, to add "further declaratory and restrictive clauses," to prevent "misconstruction or abuse of the powers" previously delegated. To understand all the restrictions, therefore, thrown around the exercise of this power in the constitution, these additional "restrictive clauses" must be read in conjunction with the original grant, whether that was made positively and directly, or by implication only. These restrictions, among other things, declare, that "no person shall be deprived of life, liberty, or property, without due process of law," and that the right of the people to be secure in their persons, houses, papers and effects, against *unreasonable* searches and *seizures, shall not be violated,* and no warrants shall issue but upon probable cause, supported by oath or affirmation, and particularly describing the place to be searched, and the person or thing to be seized.

All admit that under the clause as it stands in the original grant, with the restrictions there set forth, the power can be rightfully exercised only in cases of rebellion or invasion. With these additional clauses, put in as further restrictions to prevent the abuse of powers previously delegated, how is this clause conferring the power to suspend the privilege of the writ of *habeas corpus,* now to be read? In this way, and in this way only: "The privilege of the writ of *habeas corpus* shall not be suspended, unless when in cases of rebellion or invasion the public safety may require it." And no person "shall be deprived of life, liberty, or property, without due process of law." And further. "The right of the people to be secure in their persons, houses, papers and effects against unreasonable searches and seizures, shall not be violated, and no warrants shall issue but upon probable cause, supported by oath or affirmation, and particularly describing the place to be searched, and the persons or things to be seized."

The attempted exercise of the power to suspend the privilege of the writ of *habeas corpus* in this act, is in utter disregard in the very face and teeth of these restrictions, as much so, as a like attempt in time of profound peace would be in disregard of the restrictions to cases of rebellion and invasion, as the constitution was originally adopted. It attempts to provide for depriving persons "of liberty, without due process of law." It attempts to annul and set at naught the great constitutional "right" of the people, to be secure in their persons against "unreasonable seizures." It attempts to destroy and annihilate the bulwark of personal liberty, secured in our great chart to the humblest as well as the highest, that "no warrants shall issue but upon probable cause, supported by oath or affirmation," and "particularly describing the person to be seized." Nay, more, it attempts to change and transform the distribution of powers in our system of government. It attempts to deprive the judiciary department of its appropriate and legitimate functions, and to confer them upon the President, the secretary of war, and the general officer commanding the trans-Mississippi department, or rather to confer them entirely upon the President, for those subordinates named in the act hold their places at his will, and in arrests under this act are to be governed by his orders. This, by the constitution, never can be done. Ours is not only a government of limited powers, but each department, the legislative, executive and judicial, are separate and distinct. The issuing of warrants, which are nothing but orders for arrests, against civilians or persons in civil life, is a judicial function. The President, under the constitution, has not the power to issue any such. As commander-in-chief of the land and naval forces, and the militia when in actual service, he may order arrests for trials before courts—martial, according to the rules and articles of war. But be is clothed with no such power over those not in the military service and not subject to the rules and articles of war. This act attempts to clothe him with judicial functions, and in a judicial character to do what no judge, under the constitution, can do: issue orders or warrants for arrest, by which persons are to be deprived of their liberty, imprisoned, immured in dungeons, it may be without any oath or affirmation, even as to the probable guilt of the party accused or charged with any of the offences or acts stated. This, under the constitution, in my judgment, cannot be done. Congress can confer no such power upon our chief magistrate. There is no such thing known in this country as political warrants, or *"lettres de cachet."* This act attempts to institute this new order of things so odious to our ancestors, and so inconsistent with constitutional liberty.

This act, therefore, is unconstitutional, not because Congress has not power to suspend the privilege of the writ of *habeas corpus*, but because they have no power to do the thing aimed at in this attempted exercise of it. Congress can suspend the privilege of the writ—the power is clear and unquestioned—neither is the power, as it stands, objectionable. Georgia, in the convention, voted against the clause conferring it in the constitution as originally adopted—that, perhaps, was a wise and prudent vote. But, with the restrictions subsequently adopted there can be no well grounded objection to it. It is, under existing restrictions, a wise power. In time of war, in cases of rebellion or invasion, it may often be necessary to exercise it—the public safety may require it. I am not prepared to say that the public safety may not require it now. I am not informed of the reasons which induced the President to ask the suspension of the privilege of the writ at this time, or Congress to undertake its suspension as provided in this act. I, however, know of no reasons that require it and have heard of none. But in the exercise of an undisputed power, they have attempted to do just what cannot be done—to authorize illegal and unconstitutional arrests. There can be no suspension of the writ, under our system of government, against unconstitutional arrests—there can be no suspension allowing, or with a view to permit and authorize, the seizure of persons without warrant issued by a judicial officer upon probable cause, supported by oath or affirmation—the whole constitution must be read together, and so read and construed as that every part and clause shall stand and have its proper effect under the restrictions of other clauses.

If any conflict arises between clauses in the original and the amendments subsequently made, the original must yield to the amendments—as a will previously made always yields to the modifications of a codicil. Such, of course, was the condition of the old constitution with its amendments, when the States of this confederacy adopted it—and it was adopted by these States with the meaning, force and effect it then had. In construing, therefore, those parts of the old constitution which we adopted, we stand just where we should have stood, under like circumstances, under it. With these views it will clearly appear that, under our constitution, courts cannot be deprived of their right or be relieved of their duty to inquire into the legality of all arrests except in cases arising in the land and naval forces or in the militia, when in actual service—for the government of which a different provision is made in the constitution. Under a constitutional suspension of the privilege of the writ, all the courts could do, would be to see that the party was legally arrested and held—upon proper warrant—upon probable cause, supported by oath or affirmation setting forth a crime or some violation of law. Literally and truly, then, the only effect of a constitutional exercise of this power over the writ of *habeas corpus* by Congress is to deprive a person, after being legally confined, of the privilege of a discharge before trial, by giving bail, or on account of insufficiency of proof as to probable cause or other like grounds. This *privilege* can only be *suspended,* and not the writ itself. The words of the constitution are aptly chosen to express the purpose and extent to which a suspension can go in this country. With this view the power is a wise one. It can work no serious injury to the citizen and it sufficiently guards the public safety. The party against whom a grave accusation is brought, supported by oath, or affirmation, founded upon probable cause, must be held for trial, and if found to be guilty is to be punished according to the nature of his offence. The monstrous consequences of any other view of the subject are apparent. The exercise of the power by Congress may be either general or limited to special cases, as in this instance. If it had been general, under any other view, what would have been the condition of every citizen in the land? The weaker would have been completely in the power of the stronger, without remedy or redress. Any one in the community might seize, for any motive or for any purpose, any other, and confine him most wrongfully and shamefully. Combinations of several against a few might be formed for a like purpose, and there would be no remedy or redress against this species of licensed lawlessness. The courts would be closed—all personal security and personal safety would be swept away. Instead of a land of laws, the whole country would be no better than a Whitefriars domain—a perfect Alsatia. This would be the inevitable effect of the exercise of the power, by a general suspension, with any other view of the subject, than this presented. The same effects as to outrages upon personal rights must issue under a limited suspension confined to any specified cases under any other view. No such huge and enormous wrongs can ever spring from our constitution if it be rightly administered. So that the conclusion of the whole matter is well stated by the governor in his late message, in the brief, comprehensive, but exact terms: "The only suspension of the privilege of the writ of *habeas corpus* known to our constitution and compatible with the provisions already quoted, goes to the simple extent of preventing the release, under it, of persons whose arrests have been ordered, under constitutional warrants from judicial authority." . . .

A few thoughts more upon the subject in another view. These relate to the objects and workings of the act, if it be sustained and carried out. You have been told that it affects none but the disloyal, none but traitors, or those who are no better than traitors, spies, bridge-burners, and the like, and you have been appealed to and asked, if any such are entitled to your sympathies? I affirm, and shall maintain before the world that this act affects and may wrongfully oppress as loyal and as good citizens and as true to our cause as ever trod the soil or breathed the air of the South. This I shall make so plain to you that no man will ever venture to gainsay or deny it. This long list of offences, set forth in such array, in the thirteen specifications, are, as I view them, but rubbish and verbiage, which tend to cover and hide what in its workings will be found to be the whole gist of the act. Whether such was the real object and intention of its framers and advocates, I know not. Against their motives or patriotism I have nothing to say. I take the act as I find it. The real gist of the whole of it lies, so far as appears upon its face, covered up in the fifth specification near the middle of the act. It is embraced in these words—"and attempts to avoid military service!"

Here is a plain indisputable attempt to deny every citizen in this broad land the right, if ordered into service, to have the question whether he is liable to military duty under the laws tried and adjudicated by the courts? Whether such was the real object and intention of those who voted for the bill, I know not, but such would be its undeniable effect if sustained and enforced. A man over fifty years of age, with half a dozen sons in the field, who has done every thing in his power for the cause from the beginning of the war, may, under instructions from the secretary of war, be arrested by the sub-enrolling officer and ordered to camp, upon the assumed ground that, in point of fact, he is under fifty. Under this law, if it be law, he would be without remedy or redress. . . .

As I view it, its main effect is to close the doors of justice against thousands of citizens, good and true, who may appeal to the courts for their legal rights. Take the case of those who availed themselves of the law to put in substitutes—some for one motive, and some for another—some, doubtless, for not only good but patriotic motives, believing that they could render the country more service at home than in the field. I know one who has put in two, one when the call was for those up to thirty-five years of age, the other when the call was to forty-five. One of these substitutes was an alien, whose services could not have been commanded by the government, and who is now at Charleston, and has been during the whole siege of that place. This man, who put in these two substitutes, remained at home most usefully employed in producing provisions for the army. All his surplus went that way, while he had two men, abler bodied than he was, fighting for him in the field. Who would say that such a man is disloyal to the cause, if, believing in his heart that he was not liable under his contract, as he supposed, with his government, he should appeal to the courts to decide the question whether he is liable under the law or not? As to the law allowing substitutes in the first instance, and then the law abrogating or annulling it, and calling the principals into the field, I have nothing to say. What I maintain is, that it is the great constitutional right of any and every party affected by the last of these acts on the subject, to have the question of his legal liability judicially determined if he chooses, and then as a good law-abiding citizen act accordingly.

Take another illustration of the practical workings of the act. Congress by law exempted from conscription such State officers as the legislatures of the respective States might designate as proper to be retained for State purposes. At your last session you, by resolution, designated all the civil and militia officers of the State. A late order has been issued by General Cooper, as is seen in the papers, doubtless under order from the secretary of war, to enroll and send to camp a large number of these officers—amongst others, justices of the peace, tax receivers and collectors. This order is clearly against the law of Congress and your solemn resolution. It is in direct antagonism to the decision of the Supreme Court of this State, in the very case in which they sustained the power of Congress to raise troops by conscription, but in which they held that the power was limited, and that the civil officers of the States could not be constitutionally conscripted. I use the word *conscripted* purposely—I know there is no such word in the English language—neither is there any such word as *conscribe*, the one usually in vogue now a days. A new word had to be coined for a process or mode of raising armies, unheard of and undreamed of by our ancestors, and I choose to coin one which best expresses my idea of it. But under this order of General Cooper, is it not the right of these officers, is it not the right of the State, to have the question of their liability to conscription determined by the judiciary? Is it not the high duty of Congress to compel the secretary of war and General Cooper to abide by that decision and to obey their own laws, instead of attempting to close the doors of the courts against the adjudication of all such matters that come within the sphere of their constitutional duties. . . . Tell me not to put confidence in the President. That he will never abuse the power attempted to be lodged in his hands. The abuses may not be by the President. He will not execute the military orders that will be given. This will necessarily devolve upon subordinates, scattered all over the country, from the Potomac to the Rio Grande. He would have to possess two superhuman attributes, to prevent abuses—omniscience and omnipresence.

These things our forefathers knew, and hence they threw around the personal security of the free citizens of this country a firmer, safer, surer protection than confidence in any man, against abuses of power, even when exercised under his own eye and by himself. That protection is the shield of the constitution. See to it that you do not in an evil hour tear this shield off and cast it away, or permit others to do it, lest in a day you wot not of, you sorely repent it.

Enough has been said, without dwelling longer upon this point, to show, without the possibility of a doubt, that the act does affect others, and large classes of others, than spies, traitors, bridge-burners, and disloyal persons—that the very gist of the act, whatever may have been the intent or the motive, will operate most wrongfully and oppressively on as loyal, as patriotic, and as true men as ever inherited a freeman's birthright under a southern sky. You have also seen that there is and can be no necessity for the passage of such an act, even if it were constitutional, in the case of spies, traitors, or conspirators. For, if there be a traitor in the confederacy—if such a monster exists—if any well grounded suspicion is entertained that any such exists, why not have him legally arrested, by judicial warrant, upon oath or affirmation, setting forth *probable* cause, and then he can be held under a constitutional suspension of the privileges of the writ— he can be tried, and if found guilty, punished. What more can the public safety by possibility require? Why dispense with the oath? Why dispense with judicial warrants? Why put it in the power of any man on earth to order the arrest of another on a simple *charge*, to which nobody will *swear*? Who is safe under such a law? Who knows, when he goes forth, when or whether he shall ever return? The President, according to this act, is to have power to arrest and imprison whoever he pleases, upon a bare charge, made, perhaps, by an enemy of disloyalty, the party making the charge not being required to swear to it! Who, I repeat, is safe, or would be, under such a law? What were the real objects of the act, in these clauses, as to treason, disloyalty, and the others, I do not know. To me it seems to be unreasonable to suppose that it was to reach real traitors and persons *guilty* of the offences stated. For that object could have been easily accomplished without any such extraordinary power. I was not at Richmond when the act passed. I heard none of the discussions, and knew none of the reasons assigned, either by the President in asking it, or the members or senators who voted for it. I was at home, prostrate with disease, from which I have not yet recovered, and by reason of which I address you with so much feebleness on this occasion. But I have heard that one object was to control certain elections and expected assemblages in North Carolina, to put a muzzle upon certain presses, and a bit in the mouth of certain speakers in that State. If this be so, I regard it the more dangerous to public liberty. I know nothing of the politics of North Carolina—nothing of the position of her leading public men. If there be traitors there, let them be constitutionally arrested, tried, and punished. No fears need be indulged of bare error there, or anywhere else, if reason is left free to combat it. The idea is incredible, that a majority of the people of that gallant and noble old State, which was foremost in the war of the revolution in her ever memorable Mecklenburg declaration of Independence can, if let alone, ever be induced to prove themselves so recreant to the principles of their fathers as to abandon our cause and espouse the despotism of the North. Her people, ahead of all the colonies, first flaunted in the breeze the flag of Independence and State sovereignty. She cannot be the first to abandon it—no, never! I cannot believe it! If her people were really so inclined, however, we could not prevent it by force—we could not, under the constitution, if we would, and we ought not if we could. Ours is a government founded upon the consent of sovereign States, and will be itself destroyed by the very act whenever it attempts to maintain or perpetuate its existence by force over its respective members. The surest way to check any inclination in North Carolina to quit our sisterhood, if any such really exist even to the most limited extent amongst her people, is to show them that the struggle is continued as it was begun, for the maintenance of constitutional liberty. If, with this great truth ever before them, a majority of her people should prefer despotism to liberty, I would say to her, as to a "wayward sister, depart in peace." I want to see no Maryland this side of the Potomac.

Another serious objection to the measure, showing its impolicy, is the effect it will have upon our cause abroad. I have never looked to foreign intervention, or early recognition, and do not now. European governments have no sympathy with either side in this struggle. They are rejoiced to see professed republicans cutting each other's throats, and the failure, as they think, of the great experiment of self-government on this continent. They saw that the North went into despotism immediately on the separation of the South, and their fondest hopes and expectations are that the same destiny awaits us. This has usually been the fate of republics. This is the sentiment of all the governments in Europe. But we have friends there, as you heard last night, in the eloquent remarks of the gentleman (Hon. L. Q. C. Lamar) who addressed you on our foreign relations, and who has lately returned from those countries. Those friends are anxiously and hopefully watching the issue of the present conflict. In speeches, papers, and reviews they are defending our cause. No argument used by them heretofore has been more effectual than the contrast drawn between the federals and the confederates upon the subject of the writ of *habeas corpus.* Here, notwithstanding our dangers and perils, the military has always been kept subordinate to the civil authorities. Here all the landmarks of English liberty have been preserved and maintained, while at the North scarcely a vestige of them is left. There, instead of courts of justice with open doors, the country is dotted all over with prisons and bastiles. No better argument in behalf of a people struggling for constitutional liberty could have been presented to arouse sympathy in our favor. It showed that we were passing through a fiery furnace for a great cause, and passing through unscathed. It showed that whatever may be the state of things at the North, that at the South at least the great light of the principles of self-government, civil and religious liberty, established on this continent by our ancestors, which was looked to with encouragement and hope by the down-trodden of all nations, was not yet extinguished, but was still burning brightly in the hands of their southern sons, even burning the more brightly from the intensity of the heat of the conflict in which we are engaged. To us, in deed and in truth, is committed the hopes of the world as to the capacity and ability of man for self-government. Let us see to it that these hopes and expectations do not fail. Let us prove ourselves equal to the high mission before us.

One other view only: that relates to the particularly dangerous tendency of this act in the present state of the country, and the policy indicated by Congress. Conscription has been extended to embrace all between seventeen and fifty years of age. It cannot be possible that the intention and object of that measure was really to call and keep in the field all between those ages. The folly and ruinous consequences of such a policy is too apparent. Details are to be made, and must be made, to a large extent. The effect and the object of this measure, therefore, was not to raise armies or procure soldiers, but to put all the population of the country between those ages under military law.

Whatever the object was, the effect is to put much the larger portion of the labor of the country, both white and slave, under the complete control of the President. Under this system almost all the useful and necessary occupations of life will be completely under the control of one man. No one between the ages of seventeen and fifty can tan your leather, make your shoes, grind your grain, shoe your horse, lay your plough, make your wagon, repair your harness, superintend your farm, procure your salt, or perform any other of the necessary vocations of life, (except teachers, preachers, and physicians, and a very few others,) without permission from the President. This is certainly an extraordinary and a dangerous power. In this connection take in view this *habeas corpus* suspension act, by which it has been shown the attempt is made to confer upon him the power to order the arrest and imprisonment of any man, woman or child in the confederacy, on the bare charge, unsupported by oath, of any of the acts for which arrests are allowed to be made. Could the whole country be more completely under the power and control of one man, except as to life or limb? Could dictatorial powers be more complete? In this connection consider, also, the strong appeals that have been made for some time past, by leading journals, openly for a dictator. Coming events often cast their shadows before. Could art or ingenuity have devised a shorter or a surer cut to that end, for all practical purposes, than the whole policy adopted by the last Congress, and now before you for consideration? As to the objects, or motives, or patriotism of those who adopted that policy, that is not the question. The presentation of the case as it stands is what your attention is called to. Nor is the probability of the abuse of the power the question. Some, doubtless, think it for the best interests of the country to have a dictator. Such are not unfrequently to be met with whose intelligence, probity, and general good character in private life are not to be questioned, however much their wisdom, judgment, and principles may be deplored. In such times, when considering the facts as they exist, and looking at the policy indicated in all its bearings, the most ill-timed, delusive, and dangerous words that can be uttered are, can you not trust the President? Have you not confidence in him that he will not abuse the powers thus confided in him? To all such questions my answer is, without any reflection or imputation against our present chief magistrate, that the measure of my confidence in him, and all other public officers, is the constitution. To the question of whether I would not or cannot trust him with these high powers not conferred by the constitution, my answer is the same that I gave to one who submitted a plan for a dictatorship to me some months ago: "I am utterly opposed to every thing looking to, or tending toward a dictatorship in this country. Language would fail to give utterance to my inexpressible repugnance at the bare suggestion of such a lamentable catastrophe. There is no man living, and not one of the illustrious dead, whom, if now living, I would so trust."

In any and every view, therefore, I look upon this *habeas corpus* suspension act as unwise, impolitic, unconstitutional, and dangerous to public liberty.

But you have been asked what can you do? You can do much. If you believe the act to be unconstitutional, you can and ought so to declare your deliberate judgment to be. What can you do? What did Kentucky and Virginia do in 1798–99, under similar circumstances? What did Jefferson do, and what did Madison do, and what did the legislators of those States then do?

Though a war was then threatening with France—though armies were being raised—though Washington was called from his retirement to take command as lieutenant-general—though it was said then as now, that all discussions of even obnoxious measures of Congress would be hurtful to the public cause, they did not hesitate, by solemn resolves by the legislatures, to declare the alien and sedition laws unconstitutional and utterly void. Those acts of Congress, in my judgment, were not more clearly unconstitutional, or more dangerous to liberty, than this act now under review. What can you do? You can invoke its repeal, and ask the government officials and the people in the meantime, to let the question of constitutionality be submitted to the courts, and both sides to abide by the decision.

Some seem to be of the opinion, that those who oppose this act are for a counter-revolution. No such thing; I am for no counter-revolution. The object is to keep the present one, great in its aims and grand in its purposes, upon the right track—the one on which it was started, and that on which alone it can attain noble objects and majestic achievements. The surest way to prevent a counter-revolution, is for the State to speak out and declare her opinions upon this subject. For as certain as day succeeds night, the people of this confederacy will never live long in peace and quiet under any government with the principles of this act settled as its established policy, and held to be in conformity with the provisions of its fundamental law. The action of the Virginia legislature in 1799, saved the old government, beyond question, from a counter and a bloody revolution; kept it on the right track for sixty years afterward, in its unparalleled career of growth, prosperity, development, progress, happiness, and renown. All our present troubles, North and South, sprang from violations of those great constitutional principles therein set forth.

Let no one, therefore, be deterred from performing his duty on this occasion by the cry of counter-revolution, nor by the cry that it is the duty of all, in this hour of peril, to support the government. Our government is composed of executive, legislative and judicial departments, under the constitution. He most truly and faithfully supports the government who supports and defends the constitution. Be not misled by this cry, or that you must not say any thing against the administration, or you will injure the cause. This is the argument of the preacher, who insisted that his derelictions should not be exposed, because if they were, it would injure his usefulness as a minister. Derelict ministers are not the cause. Listen to no such cry. And let no one be influenced by that other cry, of the bad effect such discussions and such action will have upon our gallant citizen soldiers in the field. I know something of the feeling of these men. I have witnessed their hardships, their privations, and their discomforts in camp. I have witnessed and ministered to their wants and sufferings from disease and wounds, in hospitals. I know something of the sentiments that actuated the great majority of them, when they quit home, with all its endearments, and went out to this war—not as mercenaries or human machines, but as intelligent, high-minded, noble-spirited gentlemen, who were proud of their birthright as freemen, and "who knowing their rights," dared maintain them, at any and every cost and sacrifice. The old Barons who extorted *Magna Charta* from their oppressor and wrongdoer by a resort to arms, did not present a grander spectacle for the admiration of the world when they went forth to their work, thoroughly imbued with a sense of the right for the right's sake, than this gallant band of patriots did when they went forth to this war, inspired with no motive but a thorough devotion to and ardent attachment for constitutional liberty. To defend this and maintain it inviolate for themselves and those who should come after them, was their sole object. Their ancient rights, usages, institutions, and liberties were threatened by an insolent foe, who had trampled the constitution of our common ancestors under foot. They and we all had quit the Union, when the rights of all of us were no longer respected under it, but we had rescued the constitution—the ark of the covenant—and this is what they went forth to defend. These were the sentiments with which your armies were raised, as if by magic. These are the sentiments with which re-enlistments for the war have been made. These are the sentiments with which your ranks would have been filled to the last man whose services can be relied upon in action if conscription had never been resorted to.

You cannot, therefore, send these gallant defenders of constitutional liberty, a more cheering message than that, while they are battling for their rights and the common rights of all in the field, you are keeping sacred watch, and guard over the same in the public councils. They will enter the fight with renewed vigor, from the assurance that their toil, and sacrifice and blood will not be in vain, but that when the strife is over and independence is acknowledged, it will not be a bare name, a shadow and a mockery, but that with it they and their children after them shall enjoy that liberty for which they now peril all. Next to this, the most encouraging message you could send them is, that while all feel the brunt of the fight must be borne by them, and the only sure hope of success is in the prowess of their arms, yet every possible and honorable effort will be made by the civil departments of the government to terminate the struggle by negotiation and adjustment upon the principles for which they entered the contest. . . .

But as a parting remembrance, a lasting *memento*, to be engraven on your memories and your hearts, I warn you against that most insidious enemy which approaches with her syren song, "Independence first and liberty afterward." It is a fatal delusion. Liberty is the animating spirit, the soul of our system of government, and like the soul of man, when once lost it is lost forever. There is for it, at least, no redemption, except through blood. Never for a moment permit yourselves to look upon liberty, that constitutional liberty which you inherited as a birthright, as subordinate to independence. The one was resorted to to secure the other. Let them ever be held and cherished as objects coordinate, co-existent, co-equal, co-eval, and forever inseparable. Let them stand together "through weal and through woe," and if such be our fate, let them and us all go down together in a common ruin. Without liberty, I would not turn upon my heel for independence. I scorn all independence which does not secure liberty. I warn you also against another fatal delusion, commonly dressed up in the fascinating language of, "If we are to have a master, who would not prefer to have a southern one to a northern one?" Use no such language. Countenance none such. . . . I would not turn upon my heel to choose between masters. I was not born to acknowledge a master from either the North or South. I shall never choose between candidates for that office. Shall never degrade the right of suffrage in such an election. I have no wish or desire to live after the degradation of my country, and have no intention to survive its liberties, if life be the necessary sacrifice of their maintenance to the utmost of my ability, to the bitter end. As for myself, give me liberty as secured in the constitution with all its guaranties, amongst which is the sovereignty of Georgia, or give me death. This is my motto while living, and I want no better epitaph when I am dead. . . .

CHAPTER 18

AN AFRICAN AMERICAN TEACHES FREED SLAVES

Charlotte Forten: "My Soul Is Glad"

In 1862, twenty-five-year-old Charlotte Forten left her home in Philadel-phia to volunteer as a teacher to freed slaves on Hilton Head Island. A member of a prominent middle class black family, she had worked as a schoolteacher and an abolitionist before the war. Dozens of black and white abolitionists became teachers to the freed slaves during and after the war. Forten (1837–1914) kept a journal during the period she lived in coastal South Carolina, revealing both the tribulations and the joys (mostly the joys) of teaching former slaves. The number of freed slaves who eagerly sought schooling after liberation reveals their understanding of education's importance. Former slaves celebrated Lincoln's signing of the Emancipation Proclamation with jubilant rejoicing, which Forten describes here. Her pride in black soldiers on this occasion is also apparent. After the war Charlotte Forten married Reverend Francis James Grimké, the mixed race nephew of the famous abolitionist sisters, Sarah and Angelina Grimké.

Wednesday, Oct. 29, 1862

A lovely day, but rather cool, I sh'ld think, for the "sunny South.". . . We drove to Oaklands [plantation], our future home. It is very pleasantly situated, but the house is in rather a dilapidated condition, as are most of the houses here, and the . . . yard and garden have a neglected look, when it is cleaned up, and the house made habitable I think it will be quite a pleasant place. There are some lovely roses growing there and quantities of ivy creeping along the ground, even under the house, in wild luxuriance.—The negroes on the place are very kind and polite. I think I shall get on amicably with them. . . .

We went into the school, and heard the children read and spell. The teachers tell us that they have made great improvement in a very short time, and I noticed with pleasure how bright, how eager to learn many of them seem. The singing delighted me most. They sang beautifully in their rich, sweet clear tones, and with that peculiar swaying motion which I had noticed before in the older people, and which seems to make their singing all the more effective. Besides several other tunes they sang "Marching Along" with much spirit, and then one of their own hymns "Down in the Lonesome Valley," which is sweetly solemn and most beautiful. Dear children! Born in slavery, but free at last! May God preserve to you all the blessings of freedom, and may you be in every possible way fitted to enjoy them. My heart goes out to you. I shall be glad to do all that I can to help you.—

Sunday, Nov. 2.

. . . We drove to the Episcopal Church afterwards where the aristocracy of Rebeldom used to worship. The building is much smaller than the others, but there is a fine organ there. . . .

It is all like a dream still, and will be for a long time, I suppose; a strange wild dream. When we get settled in our own house and I have fairly entered into teaching, perhaps I shall begin to realize it all. What we are to do for furniture I know not. Our sole possessions now consist of two bureaus and a bedstead. . . .

Wednesday, Nov. 5.

Had my first regular teaching experience, and to you and you only friend beloved, will I knowledge that it was *not* a very pleasant one. Part of my scholars are very tiny,—babies, I call them—and it is hard to keep them quiet and interested while I am hearing the larger ones. They are too young even for the alphabet, it seems to me. I think I must write home and ask somebody to send me picture-books and toys to amuse them with. . . . Well I *must* not be discouraged. Perhaps things will go on better to-morrow.

Monday, Nov. 10.

We taught—or rather commenced teaching the children "John Brown," which they entered into eagerly. I felt to the full significance of that song being sung here in S[outh] C[arolina] by little negro children, by those whom he—the glorious old man—died to save. . . .

Thursday, Nov. 13.

. . . Talked to the children a little while to-day about the noble Toussaint [L'Ouverture]. They listened very attentively. It is well that they sh'ld know what one of their own color c'ld do for his race. I long to inspire them with courage and ambition (of a noble sort,) and high purpose.

It is noticeable how very few mulattoes there are here. Indeed in our school, with one or two exceptions, the children are all black. A little mulatto child strayed into the school house yesterday—a pretty little thing, with large beautiful black eyes and lovely long lashes. But so dirty! I longed to seize and thoroughly cleanse her. The mother is a good-looking woman, but quite black. "Thereby," I doubt not, "hangs a tale."

This eve. Harry, one of the men on the place, came in for a lesson. He is most eager to learn, and is really a scholar to be proud of. He learns rapidly. I gave him his first lesson in writing to-night, and his progress was wonderful. He held the pen almost perfectly right the first time. He will very soon learn to write, I think. I must inquire if there are not more of the grown people who w'ld like to take lessons at night. Whenever I am well enough it will be a real happiness to me to teach them. . . .

Tuesday, Nov. 18.

After school went to The Corner again. Stopped at old Susy's house to see some sick children. Old Susy is a character. Miss T[owne] asked her if she wanted her old master to come back again. Most emphatically she answered. "No *indeed*, missus, no indeed dey treat we too bad. Dey tuk ebery one of my chilen away from me. When we sick and c'ldnt work dey tuk away all our food from us; gib us nutten to eat. Dey's orful hard Missis." When Miss T told her that some of the people said they wanted their old masters to come back, a look of supreme comtempt came to old Susy's withered face. "Dat's 'cause dey's got no sense den, missus," she said indignantly. Susy has any quantity of children and grandchildren, and she thanks God that she can now have some of them with her in old age. . . .

Thursday, Nov. 20.

. . . Wrote to-night to . . . [author John Greenleaf] Whittier asking him to write a little Christmas hymn for our children to sing. I hope he will do it. . . .

Thursday, Nov. 27. Thanksgiving Day.

. . . This morning a large number—Superintendents, teachers and freed people, assembled in the little Baptist church. It was a sight that I shall not soon forget—that crowd of eager, happy black faces from which the shadow of slavery had forever passed. "Forever free!" "Forever free!" Those magical words were all the time singing themselves in my soul, and never before have I felt so truly grateful to God. The singing was, as usual very beautiful. I thought I had never heard my favorite "Down in the Lonesome Valley" so well sung. . . .

Sunday, Nov. 30.

. . . Am in a writing mood to-night, and think I will give . . . a more minute description of the people around than I've yet given to anyone. . . .

To begin with the older ones. First there is Harriet. She is a very kind, pleasant old soul. Comes from Darien, G[eorgi]a. Her parents were Africans. She speaks a very foreign tongue. Three of her children have been sold from her. Her master's son killed somebody in a duel, and was obliged to "pay money" H[arriet] says. I suppose she means to give bail. And she and her children were sold to this place, to raise the money. Then there is her daughter Tillah. Poor creature, she has a dear little baby, Annie, who for weeks has been dangerously ill with whooping cough. . . . T[illah]'s husband is a gallant looking young soldier—a member of the black regiment. . . .

Cupid our major-domo, is as obliging as possible. A shrewd fellow, who knows well what he is about. His wife Patience, is Tamar's sister, and lives across the creek at Pollywana. Their children—two of them—come to our school. They are good scholars.

I do enjoy hearing Cupid and Harry tell about the time that the Secesh had to flee. The time of the "gun shoot," as they call the taking of Bay Point, which is opposite Hilton Head. It delights them greatly to recal[l] that time. Their master had the audacity to venture back even when the Union Troops were occupying Beaufort. . . . Cupid says the master told the people to get all the furniture together and take it over to Pollywana, and to stay on that side themselves. "So" says Cupid, "dey c'ld jus' swap us all up in a heap and geder us up an' put us in de boat. And he telled me to row Patience and de

chilens down to a certain pint, and den I c'ld come back if I choose."
"Jus' as if I was gwine to be sich a goat" adds Cupid, with a look and
gesture of ineffable contempt. The *finale* of the story is that the people left the premises and hid themselves so that when the master
returned not one of all his "faithful servants" was to be found to go
into slavery with him, and he was obliged to return, a disappointed,
but it is to be hoped, a wiser man.

Monday, Dec. 15.

Had a perfectly *immense* school to-day. 147., of whom I had 58, at
least two thirds of whom were tiny A.B.C. people. Hardly knew what
to do with them at first. But I like a large school. It is inspiriting. . . .
Never heard the children sing so well as they did to-day. There were
so many of them. It was quite grand. . . .

Monday, Dec. 22.

Commenced teaching the children Whittier's hymn. We told
them who had written it; what a great friend he is to them, and that
he had written it *expressly* for them, whereat they seemed greatly
pleased. After school, with some of the larger children we three went
into the woods in search of evergreens to decorate the church. Had a
delightful ramble and got a quantity of greens. . . .

Tuesday, Dec. 23.

We commenced decorating the church and worked hard till dark.
They w'ld insist upon my dressing the pulpit, which I was unwilling
to do, for that is the most conspicuous place. Finished it to-day. Made
a drapery all around it with the lovely hanging moss, and a heading
of casino berries and holly. It looks quite pretty. Came home tired but
sat up till after 11 sewing on the little aprons for Christmas presents.
I *cannot* realize that Christmas is so near.

Christmas Day 1862

A bright and lovely Christmas day. We were waked early by the
people knocking at our window and shouting "Merry Christmas."
After breakfast we went out and distributed the presents;—to each of
the babies a bright red dress, and to little Jessie a white apron
trimmed with crotchet braid, and to each of the other children an
apron and an orange. To each of the workers a pie—an apple pie,
which pleased them much.

Then we went to school. How pretty the evergreens looked in the bright light, after we had thrown open the windows. T'was a long time before the other teachers got there, and I had to keep all the children from getting restless. I kept them out of doors, and had them sing old songs and new. They sang with great spirit. After the others came, we opened school, and at once commenced distributing the presents. . . . Most of the children were much delighted with their gifts, and well they might be, for they were very useful ones,—principally dresses for the girls, and material for shirts and pantaloons for the boys. For the larger ones, also there were little bags, nicely fitted out with sewing utensils. . . . The larger children behaved well, and by great exertions I managed to keep the "babies" quiet. . . .

Friday, Dec. 26.

. . . There was one very sensible man in to-day, whose story interested me much. He had been a carpenter, and had been taken up by his master on the mainland, on "the main" as they call it, to help build houses to which the families of the rebels might retreat when the Yankees sh'ld come. His master sent him back again to this island to bring back a boat and some of the people. He was provided with a pass. On reaching the island, he found that the Union troops had come, so he determined (indeed he had determined before) to remain here with his family, as he knew his master w'ld not dare to come back after them. Some of his fellow servants whom he had left on the "main," hearing that the Union troops had come resolved to try to make their escape. They found a boat of the master's, out of which a piece about six feet square had been cut. In the night, secretly, they went to the boat which had been sunk near the edge of the creek, measured the hole, and went to the woods and, after several nights' work, made a piece large enough to fit in. With this they mended the boat, by another night's work, and then sunk it in the same position in which they had found it. The next night five of them embarked, and after passing through many perils in the shape of the enemy's boats, near which they were obliged to pass, and so making very slow progress, for they c'ld travel only at night, and in the day time, ran their boat close up to the shore, out of sight—they at last passed the enemy's lines and reached one of our gunboats in saf[e]ty. They were taken on board, and their wants attended to, for their provisions had given out and they were much exhausted. After being there some time they were sent to this island, where their families, who had feared they w'ld never see them again welcomed them rejoicingly. . . .

Thursday, New Year's Day, 1863.

The most glorious day this nation has yet seen, *I* think. I rose early—an event here—and early we started, with an old borrowed carriage and a remarkably slow horse. Whither were we going? . . . To the ferry; thence to Camp Saxton, to the Celebration. From the Ferry to the camp the "Flora" took us.

How pleasant it was on board! A crowd of people, whites and blacks, and a band of music—to the great delight of the negroes. . . .

The meeting was held in a beautiful grove, a live-oak grove, ajoining the camp. It is the largest one I have yet seen; but I don't think the moss pendants are quite as beautiful as they are on St. Helena. As I sat on the stand and looked around on the various groups, I thought I had never seen a sight so beautiful. There were the black soldiers, in their blue coats and scarlet pants, and officers of this and other regiments in their handsome uniforms, the crowds of lookers-on, men, women and children, grouped in various attitudes, under the trees. The faces of all wore a happy, eager, expectant look.

The exercises commenced by a prayer from Rev. Mr. Fowler, Chaplain of the reg[iment]. An ode written for the occasion by Prof. Zachos, originally in Greek, now Sup[erintendent] of Paris Island—was read by himself, and then sung by the whites. Col H[igginson] introduced Dr. Brisbane in a few elegant and graceful words. He (Dr. B.) read the President's [Emancipation] Proclamation, which was warmly cheered. . . . Immediately at the conclusion, some of the colored people—of their own accord sang "My Country Tis of Thee." It was a touching and beautiful incident. . . .

The Dress Parade—the first I had ever seen—delighted me. It was a brilliant sight—the long line of men in their brilliant uniform, with bayonets gleaming in the sunlight. The Col. looked splendid. The Dr. said the men went through with the drill remarkably well. It seemed to me nothing c'ld be more perfect. To me it was a grand triumph—the black regiment doing itself honor in the sight of the white officers, many of whom, doubtless "come to scoff." It was typical of what the race, so long downtrodden and degraded will yet achieve on this Continent. . . .

Ah, what a grand, glorious day this has been. The dawn of freedom which it heralds may not break upon us at once; but it will surely come, and sooner, I believe, than we have ever dared hope before. My soul is glad with an exceeding great gladness. . . .

CHAPTER 19

THE LONG WAIT FOR EMANCIPATION

Private Spotswood Rice Wants His Daughters to Be Free

A frican American men showed their support for the war effort by joining the Union army. Early in the war, when reunification of the states was its major goal, the northern army did not recruit black soldiers. In 1863, however, the Lincoln administration formally endorsed emancipation and welcomed black enlistment. By 1865, 189,000 black soldiers and sailors had served their country. Although inequalities in pay were ultimately reversed, few black men were allowed to become officers, and none above the rank of captain. White men commanded black regiments. Black soldiers were often assigned to garrison duty, but they also fought in combat, including heroic performances at Port Hudson and Milliken's Bend during the Vicksburg campaign. African American soldiers felt enormously frustrated by the failure of the war to end slavery quickly. Private Spotswood Rice of Missouri enlisted in the 67th United States Colored Infantry. In a letter written in 1864, Rice told his enslaved daughters he had confidence they would eventually be freed but felt outraged at their continuing bondage. In another letter directed to the owner of one daughter, his anger about slavery is apparent. In the final letter, F. W. Diggs, the owner of another Rice daughter, wrote to a Union officer expressing his ire over Rice's attitude and a sense of self-righteousness about being a loyal slaveholding Unionist, who wanted to protect his investment in human property.

[St. Louis, Mo.,   September 3, 1864]

My Children   I take my pen in hand to rite you A few lines to let you know that I have not forgot you and that I want to see you as bad as ever   now my Dear Children I want you to be contented with whatever may be your lots   be assured that I will have you if it cost me my life   on the 28th of the mounth. 8 hundred White and 8 hundred blacke solders expects to start up the rivore to Glasgow and

288

above there thats to be jeneraled by a jeneral that will give me both of
you   when they Come I expect to be with, them and expect to get
you both in return.   Dont be uneasy my children   I expect to have
you.   If Diggs dont give you up this Government will and I feel confident that I will get you   Your Miss Kaitty said that I tried to steal
you   But I'll let her know that god never intended for man to steal
his own flesh and blood.   If I had no cofidence in God I could have
confidence in her   But as it is If I ever had any Confidence in her I
have none now and never expect to have   And I want her to remember if she meets me with ten thousand soldiers she [will?] meet her
enemy   I once [*thought*] that I had some respect for them but now my
respects is worn out and have no sympathy for Slaveholders. And as
for her cristianantty I expect the Devil has Such in hell   You tell her
from me that She is the frist Christian that I ever hard say that aman
could Steal his own child especially out of human bondage

You can tell her that She can hold to you as long as she can   I never
would expect to ask her again to let you come to me because I know
that the devil has got her hot set againsts that that is write   now my
Dear children I am a going to close my letter to you   Give my love to
all enquiring friends   tell them all that we are well and want to see
them very much and Corra and Mary receive the greater part of it you
sefves   and dont think hard of us not sending you any thing   I you
father have a plenty for you when I see you   Spott & Noah sends their
love to both of you   Oh! My Dear children how I do want to see you
[*Spotswood Rice*]

[*St. Louis, Mo.,   September 3, 1864*]

I received a leteter from Cariline telling me that you say I tried to
steal to plunder my child away from you   now I want you to
understand that mary is my Child and she is a God given rite of my
own and you may hold on to hear as long as you can but I want you
to remembor this one thing that the longor you keep my Child from
me the longor you will have to burn in hell and the qwicer youll get
their   for we are now makeing up a bout one thoughsand blacke
troops to Come up tharough and wont to come through Glasgow and
when we come wo be to Copperhood rabbels and to the Slaveholding
rebbels for we dont expect to leave them there root neor branch   but

we thinke how ever that we that have Children in the hands of you devels we will trie your [vertues?] the day that we enter Glasgow   I want you to understand kittey diggs that where ever you and I meets we are enmays to each orthere   I offered once to pay you forty dollers for my own Child but I am glad now that you did not accept it   Just hold on now as long as you can and the worse it will be for you   you never in you life befor I came down hear did you give Children any thing not eny thing whatever not even a dollers worth of expencs   now you call my children your pro[per]ty   not So with me   my Children is my own and I expect to get them and when I get ready to come after mary I will have bout a powrer and autherity to bring hear away and to exacute vengencens on them that holds my Child   you will then know how to talke to me   I will assure that and you will know how to talk rite too   I want you now to just hold on to hear if you want to   iff your conchosence tells thats the road go that road and what it will brig you to kittey diggs   I have no fears about geting mary out of your hands   this whole Government gives chear to me and you cannot help your self

Spotswood Rice

Glasgow Mo   Sept. 10" 1864

Sir   Enclosed I send you two Letters written one to my Sister the other to two colo girls one beloning to her & the other to myself.   and I write this to ask the favour of you to send the scoundrel that wrote them down to the army   I do not think that he should be allowd to remain in the state   he wrote to my sister to let his child come down to see him and he would send her back   she was hired out   she went to see the person that hired her to let he go but they refused.   The scoundrels wife & ten children were alowed to go to him and the other would have been sent whenevr I could be satisfied that her Mother had goton in situation to support her.   I am and have been [loyal] from the commencement of this wicked rebellion and I may say all I had was in slave property which I connclud at the commencement was defunct never to be resusitated   Six men are in the United States service and I have told the bal[ance] when they wished to go just say so and I would give them a pass   and under all these circumstances my family all being of the same politics of myself and to be thus insulted by such a black scoundrel is more that I can stand   for refference Mr John D Perry   B. W. Lewis   James T Bunch & William Spear of firm of Wm Spear & Co Tobaconists   hopeing You will give this subject the attention it deservs I remain Your obt Servt

F W Diggs

CHAPTER 20

TO ABOLISH SLAVERY FOREVER

Lyman Trumbull: Speech on the Thirteenth Amendment, March 28, 1864

*A*lthough both President Lincoln and Congress had denied early in the war that the conflict was being waged for the purpose of abolishing slavery, it soon became apparent that slavery would have to be one of the casualties of the struggle. To restore the Union with slavery intact would be to return the nation to a condition that both North and South had found intolerable. In spite of this awareness, the government's attitude toward slavery was marked by confusion and uncertainty. Laws were passed by Congress, decrees were issued by military commanders, actions were taken by states, and a proclamation was delivered by the President himself (justified on the ground of military necessity), all providing for degrees of emancipation but without any overall plan or coordination. Congress passed two confiscation acts (August 6, 1861 and July 17, 1862) emancipating slaves engaged in hostile military service and belonging to anyone who committed treason or supported the rebellion. Lincoln's famous Emancipation Proclamation purportedly freed all slaves in areas still in rebellion on January 1, 1863, but its effectiveness was questioned because the authority of the government did not extend to these areas. The limited and ineffective nature of these attempts at emancipation persuaded many Northern leaders that the institution could only be effectively abolished through constitutional amendment. On March 28, 1864, Illinois Senator Lyman Trumbull (1813–1896) reported the proposed Thirteenth Amendment from the Committee on the judiciary. "The first example of the use of the amending process to accomplish a specific reform on a nationwide scale," according to one authority, the amendment aroused immediate opposition. Although it passed in the Senate, it was defeated in the House of Representatives. In January, 1865, the House considered it a second time and passed it. By December of that year, the amendment had been approved by the requisite number of states and was declared in force. Following is Trumbull's speech, delivered on March 28, 1864, which accompanied the amendment when it was reported from the judiciary committee.

M r. President, as the organ of the committee on the judiciary which has reported this resolution to the Senate, I desire to present briefly some of the considerations which induced me, at least, to give it my support. It is a proposition so to amend the Constitution of the United States as forever to prohibit slavery within its jurisdiction, and authorize the Congress of the United States to pass such laws as may be necessary to carry this provision into effect.

Without stopping to inquire into all the causes of our troubles, and of the distress, desolation, and death which have grown out of this atrocious rebellion, I suppose it will be generally admitted that they sprung from slavery. If a large political party in the North attribute these troubles to the impertinent interference of northern philanthropists and fanatics with an institution in the southern States with which they had no right to interfere, I reply, if there had been no such institution there could have been no such alleged impertinent interference; if there had been no slavery in the South, there could have been no abolitionists in the North to interfere with it. If, upon the other hand, it be said that this rebellion grows out of the attempt on the part of those in the interest of slavery to govern this country so as to perpetuate and increase the slaveholding power, and failing in this that they have endeavored to overthrow the Government and set up an empire of their own, founded upon slavery as its chief corner-stone, I reply, if there had been no slavery there could have been no such foundation on which to build. If the freedom of speech and of the press, so dear to freemen everywhere, and especially cherished in this time of war by a large party in the North who are now opposed to interfering with slavery, has been denied us all our lives in one half the States of the Union, it was by reason of slavery.

If these Halls have resounded from our earliest recollections with the strifes and contests of sections, ending sometimes in blood, it was slavery which almost always occasioned them. No superficial observer, even, of our history North or South, or of any party, can doubt that slavery lies at the bottom of our present troubles. Our fathers who made the Constitution regarded it as an evil, and looked forward to its early extinction. They felt the inconsistency of their position, while proclaiming the equal rights of all to life, liberty, and happiness, they denied liberty, happiness, and life itself to a whole race, except in subordination to them. It was impossible, in the nature of things, that a Government based on such antagonistic principles could permanently and peacefully endure, nor did its founders expect it would. They looked forward to the not distant, nor as they supposed uncertain period when slavery should be abolished, and the Government become in fact, what they made it in name, one securing the blessings of liberty to all. The history of the last seventy years has proved that the founders of the Republic were mistaken in their expectations; and slavery, so far from gradually disappearing as they had anticipated, had so strengthened itself that in 1860 its advocates demanded the control of the nation in its interests, failing in which they attempted its overthrow. This attempt brought into hostile collision the slaveholding aristocracy, who made the right to live by the toil of others the chief article of their faith, and the free laboring masses of the North, who believed in the right of every man to eat the bread his own hands had earned.

In the earlier stages of the war there was an indisposition on the part of the executive authority to interfere with slavery at all. For a long time slaves who escaped from their rebel owners and came within our lines were driven back. Congress, however, at an early day took action upon this subject, and at the very first session which met after the rebellion broke out, the special session of July, 1861, a law was passed declaring free all slaves who were permitted by their masters to take any part in the rebellion. Under the provisions of that act, had it been efficiently executed, a great many slaves must necessarily have obtained their freedom. The constitutionality of the act would seem to be clear. I do not suppose that even my honorable friend from Kentucky (Mr. Davis) would deny the proposition that if we captured a slave engaged, by consent of his master, in constructing rebel works and fortifications, we might set him free.

That act, however, has not been executed. So far as I am advised not a single slave has been set at liberty under it. Subsequently, at the regular session of Congress which convened in December, 1861, an act of a more comprehensive character was passed—a law providing for the freedom of all slaves who should come within the lines of our armies, who should be deserted by their masters, or who should be found in regions of country which had been occupied by rebel troops and afterwards came within our possession, and who belonged to rebel masters. It is under the provisions of this law that most of the slaves made free have been emancipated. This act also authorized the President of the United States to organize and employ as many persons of African descent as he should think proper to aid in the suppression of the rebellion. But it was a long time before this law was put in operation. Although it was an act called for by the public sentiment of the country, and although it was the duty of those charged with the execution of the laws to see that it was faithfully executed, it was more than a year after its enactment before any considerable number of persons of African descent were organized and armed; and even at this day a much smaller number are in the service than would have been by an efficient execution of the law. It was not until after the passage of this act that our officers, especially in the West, ceased to expel slaves who came within the lines of our Army; and so persistently was this practice persevered in that Congress had to interfere by positive enactment, and declare that any officer of the Army or Navy who aided in restoring a slave to his master should be dismissed from the public service, before it could be stopped.

But, sir, had these laws, all of them, been efficiently executed they would not wholly have extirpated slavery. They were only aimed at the slaves of rebels. Congress never undertook to free the slaves of loyal men; no act has ever passed for that purpose. At a later period, the President by proclamation undertook to free the slaves in certain localities. Notice of this proclamation was given in September, 1862, and it was to become effective in January, 1863. Unlike the acts of Congress, which undertook to free the slaves of rebels only, and of such as came under our control, the President's proclamation excepted from its provisions the regions of country subject to our authority, and declared free the slaves only who were in regions of country from which the authority of the United States was expelled, enjoining upon the persons proposed to be made free to abstain from all violence unless in necessary self-defense, and recommending them in all cases, when allowed, to labor faithfully for reasonable wages.

The force and effect of this proclamation are understood very differently by its advocates and opponents. The former insist that it is and was within the constitutional power of the President, as Commander-in-Chief, to issue such a proclamation; that it is the noblest act of his life or the age; and that by virtue of its provisions all slaves within the localities designated become *ipso facto* free; while others declare that it was issued without competent authority, and has not and cannot effect the emancipation of a single slave. These latter insist that the most the President could do, as commander of the armies of the United States, would be, in the absence of legislation, to seize and free the slaves which came within the control of the Army; that the power exercised by a commander-in-chief, as such, must be a power exercised in fact, and that beyond his lines where his armies cannot go his orders are mere *brutum fulmen,* and can neither work a forfeiture of property nor freedom of slaves; that the power of Fremont and Hunter, commanders-in-chief for a certain time in their departments, who assumed to free the slaves within their respective commands, was just as effective within the boundaries of their commands as that of the Commander-in-Chief of all the departments, who as commander could not draw to himself any of his presidential powers; and that neither had or could have any force except within the lines and where the Army actually had the power to execute the order; that to that extent, the previous acts of Congress would free the slaves of rebels, and if the President's proclamation had any effect it would only be to free the slaves of loyal men, for which the laws of the land did not provide. I will not undertake to say which of these opinions is correct, nor is it necessary for my purposes to decide. It is enough for me to show that any and all these laws and proclamations, giving to each the largest effect claimed by its friends, are ineffectual to the destruction of slavery. The laws of Congress if faithfully executed would leave remaining the slaves belonging to loyal masters, which, considering how many are held by children and females not engaged in the rebellion, would be no inconsiderable number, and the President's proclamation excepts from its provisions all of Delaware, Maryland, Kentucky, Tennessee, Missouri, and a good portion of Louisiana and Virginia—almost half the slave States.

If then we are to get rid of the institution, we must have some more efficient way of doing it than by the proclamations that have been issued or the acts of Congress which have been passed.

Some, however, say that we may pass an act of Congress to abolish slavery altogether, and petitions are sent to Congress asking it to pass such a law. I am as anxious to get rid of slavery as any person; but has Congress authority to pass a law abolishing slavery everywhere, freeing the slaves of the loyal, the slaves of the friends of the Government as well as the slaves of the disloyal and of the enemies of the Government? Why, sir, it has been an admitted axiom from the foundation of this Government, among all parties, that Congress had no authority to interfere with slavery in the States where it existed. But it is said this was in a time of peace, and we are now at war, and Congress has authority to carry on war, and in carrying on war we may free the slaves. Why so? Because it is necessary; for no other reason. If we can do it by act of Congress it must be because it is a necessity to the prosecution of the war. We have authority to put down the enemies of the country; we have the right to slay them in battle; we have authority to confiscate their property; but, mark you, does that give any authority to slay the friends of the country, to confiscate the property of the friends of the country, or to free the slaves of the friends of the country?

But it is said that freeing slaves would aid us in raising troops; that slaves are unwilling to volunteer and enter the public service unless other slaves are made free, and that we could raise troops better, sooner, and have a more efficient army if slavery were declared abolished. Suppose that were so, is it a necessity? Can we not raise an army without doing this? Has not the Congress of the United States unlimited authority to provide for the raising of armies by draft, by force to put any and every man capable of bearing arms into its service? Have we not already passed a law compelling men to enter the service of the Government in its defense and for the putting down this rebellion? Then there is no necessity to free the slaves in order to raise an army.

But it is a convenience, perhaps some will say. Sir, it is not because a measure would be convenient that Congress has authority to adopt it. The measure must be appropriate and needful to carry into effect some granted power, or we have no authority to adopt it. I can imagine a thousand things that would aid us to raise troops which no one would contend Congress had authority to do. We now find that it is costing us a large sum of money to carry on this war. There are apprehensions in some quarters that the finances of the country will not be sufficient to prosecute it to the end. A measure that would enable us to carry on the war cheaper would certainly be one in aid of this war power. In consequence of the prosperity which prevails in the coun-

try, wages at this time are very high. Men are unwilling to enlist without large bounties and large pay, because they get high wages at
home. Suppose we introduce a bill that no man shall be paid in any
manufacturing establishment, at any mechanic art, or for his daily
labor, more than ten cents a day, and we visit with penalties and punishment any man who shall give to his employé more than that sum;
do you not think that would hold out an additional inducement to
volunteer? But who would contend that Congress had any such
authority? Manifestly it has not. Nor can I find the constitutional
authority to abolish slavery everywhere by act of Congress as a
necessity to prosecuting the war.

Then, sir, in my judgment, the only effectual way of ridding the
country of slavery, and so that it cannot be resuscitated, is by an
amendment of the Constitution forever prohibiting it within the
jurisdiction of the United States. This amendment adopted, not only
does slavery cease, but it can never be reëstablished by State authority, or in any other way than by again amending the Constitution.
Whereas, if slavery should now be abolished by act of Congress or
proclamation of the President, assuming that either has the power to
do it, there is nothing in the Constitution to prevent any State from
reëstablishing it. This change of the Constitution will also relieve us
of all difficulty in the restoration to the Union of the rebel States when
our brave soldiers shall have reduced them to obedience to the laws.

To secure its passage requires, in the first instance, a vote of two
thirds in its favor in each branch of Congress, and its ratification subsequently by three fourths of the States of the Union. Can these
majorities be obtained? It is very generally conceded, I believe, by
men of all political parties, that slavery is gone; that the value of slavery is destroyed by the rebellion. What objection, then, can there be
on the part of any one, in the present state of public feeling in the
country, to giving the people an opportunity to pass upon this question? I would appeal to Senators upon the opposite side of the Chamber, and ask them—for I expect some of them to support this
measure, and I trust all of them will—what objection they have to
submitting this question to the people and letting them pass upon it?
Do any of you deny that slavery lies at the bottom of this rebellion?
Do you believe that we should have had this terrible war upon us
had there been no slavery in the land? I repeat, then, why not afford

an opportunity to the people to pass upon this amendment? I trust I do not assume too much when I assume that it will receive the requisite vote of two thirds of each branch of Congress.

Having obtained that, the question then arises, is it probable that it can have the ratification of three fourths of the States? We have now thirty-five States, and bills have passed both branches of Congress and been approved by the President for the creation of two more, Colorado and Nevada, which will make thirty-seven. When these States are admitted it will require the concurring vote of twenty-eight States in order to adopt this amendment.

If Nebraska should be admitted, for the admission of which a bill is now pending, that would make the number of States thirty-eight, and the votes of twenty-nine States would then be requisite to adopt the amendment. But the admission of Nebraska would not probably affect the result, as, if admitted, she would most probably vote for the amendment.

Of the thirty-seven States, twenty-one are free States, including Colorado and Nevada, and I assume that all those States would vote for this constitutional amendment. There are, then, the States of Maryland, West Virginia, Missouri, Arkansas, Tennessee, and Louisiana, all of which have taken initiatory steps for the abolition of slavery within their borders; and I think we might confidently count that they would unite with the free States to pass this amendment. Those six added to the twenty-one free States would make twenty-seven. Then there is the State of Delaware, with hardly slaves enough in it to count, which would be left standing alone with free States all around her. Although she has not yet, so far as I am aware, taken any legislative steps for the abolition of slavery, though the question is agitated among her people, I cannot think she would stand alone in such a locality, resisting a constitutional amendment which would forever give us peace on this question.

I have assumed that all the free States will adopt the amendment. It is now very generally conceded that slavery is not a divine institution. The few in the northern or free States who attempt to uphold it do so on constitutional grounds, denying the authority of the Government to interfere with it; but none of these persons deny or can deny the power of the people to amend the Constitution in the mode prescribed by the instrument itself. If, then, they shall oppose an

amendment for the abolition of slavery, it will not be because to abolish it in that form is unconstitutional, but because it is not right, or, if
right, not expedient.

I think, then, it is reasonable to suppose that if this proposed
amendment passes Congress, it will within a year receive the ratification of the requisite number of States to make it a part of the Constitution. That accomplished, and we are forever freed of this
troublesome question. We accomplish then what the statesmen of this
country have been struggling to accomplish for years. We take this
question entirely away from the politics of the country. We relieve
Congress of sectional strifes, and, what is better than all, we restore
to a whole race that freedom which is theirs by the gift of God, but
which we for generations have wickedly denied them.

I know that the passage of this measure will not end this rebellion.
I do not claim that for it. There is but one way to do that; and that is
by the power of our brave soldiers. We can never have the Union
restored, the authority of the Constitution recognized, and its laws
obeyed and respected, until our armies shall overcome and vanquish
the rebel armies. We must look to our soldiers, to our patriotic Army,
to put down the rebellion. But, Sir, when they shall have accomplished that, this measure will secure to us future peace. That is what
I claim for it. I trust that within a year, in less time than it will take to
make this constitutional amendment effective, our armies will have
put to flight the rebel armies. I think it ought long ago to have been
done; and I think but for the indecision, the irresolution, the want of
plan, and the scattering of our forces, it would have been done long
ago. Hundreds of millions of treasure and a hundred thousand lives
would have been saved had the power of this Republic been concentrated under one mind and hurled in masses upon the main rebel
armies. This is what our patriotic soldiers have wanted, and what I
trust is now soon to be done.

But instead of looking back and mourning over the errors of the
past, let us remember them only for the lessons they teach for the
future. Forgetting the things which are past, let us press forward to
the accomplishment of what is before. We have at last placed at the
head of our armies a man in whom the country has confidence, a man
who has won victories wherever he has been, and I trust that his
mind is to be permitted uninterfered with to unite our forces, never

before so formidable as to-day, in one or two grand armies and hurl them upon the rebel force. Let him put to flight the main rebel army which has threatened the capital for the last three years, and the small rebel armies will quickly succumb. I look for that result during the coming campaign, and with that result, if we civilians do our duty, we shall have the authority of the Constitution vindicated, constitutional liberty reëstablished, the Union restored, and freedom everywhere proclaimed.

CHAPTER 21

COPING IN THE
AFTERMATH OF FREEDOM

Family Letters from Roseland Plantation

*A*frican Americans faced a variety of challenges in the aftermath of war, as they pondered their economic choices and established new and often uneasy relationships with former masters. Early in 1865 Congress created the Freedmen's Bureau, a governmental agency designed to help former slaves make the transition to life after emancipation. With mixed success, the Bureau founded schools, helped freed people set up bank accounts and buy land. Sometimes bureau agents attempted to adjudicate labor disputes between land owners and freedmen and women. The families of black soldiers faced an uncertain transition period in the aftermath of war, for African American soldiers often remained in the army for many months following its conclusion. Although the Union army quickly began mustering out regiments, this task was accomplished in the order in which these units had been mobilized. Because black regiments were not recruited in earnest until 1863, they were not immediately dismissed after the war. With men still in uniform, women had to cope with postwar conditions alone, including the resentment of their former owners, resentment that was often especially virulent toward soldiers' families. Two of these letters, from the soldier's wife and sister, reveal their difficulties attempting to subsist in postwar Louisiana. The third letter is from a white officer who reports the "innumerable threats and at least one attempt to put out the family" to the Louisiana headquarters of the Freedmen's Bureau. Although all three letters are signed, the identity of the soldier is not known.

Roseland Plantation [*La*.] July 16th 1865

*M*y Dear Husband   I received a letter from you week before last and was glad to hear that you were well and happy.

This is the fifth letter I have written you and I have received only one—   Please write as often as you can as I am always anxious to hear from you.   I and the children are all well—but I am in a great deal of trouble as Master John Humphries has come home from the Rebel army and taken charge of the place and says he is going to turn us all out on the Levee unless we pay him (8.00) Eight Dollars a month for house rent— Now I have no money of any account and I am not able to get enough to pay so much rent, and I want you to get a furlough as soon as you can and come home and find a place for us to live in.   and besides Amelia is very sick and wants you to come home and see her if possible   she has been sick with the fever now over two weeks and is getting very low— Your mother and all the rest of your folks are well and all send their regards & want to see you as soon as you can manage to come— My mother sends her compliments & hopes to see you soon

My children are going to school, but I find it very hard to feed them all, and if you can not come I hope you will send me something to help me get along

I get all the work I can and am doing the best I can to get along, but if they turn me out I dont know what I shall do— However I will try & keep the children along until you come or send me some assistance

Thank God we are all well, and I hope we may always be so   Give my regards to all the boys.   Come home as soon as you can, and cherish me as ever   Your Aff wife

Emily Waters

Roseland Plantation [La.] July 30th 1865

My Dear Brother   I learn by Hannibal that you are well and happy— Mother and all the rest of us are well but we are in deep trouble— Your wife has left Trepagnia and gone to the city and we dont know where or how she is, we have not heard a word from her for four weeks

Master John has come home and is going to turn us all out of doors unless we pay him $3.00 per month rent, and we have no way to earn the money and it is coming mighty hard on us   David has left and gone some where— He has been gone over two weeks and we dont know what has become of him—

My little boy has been very sick, but is getting quite well now— Moses is well and sends his regards,   Aunt Rosalie and Aunt Liddie both send their love & best wishes

Moses wants you to send him a pair of soldiers pants if you can—
Hopeing to hear from you soon   I am Your Aff Sister

Alsie Thomas

Fort St. Philip.   La.   Aug. 1st, 1865.

Sir.   I am an officer in a co. of 140 men.—have been with them
continually Since their organization as a Co., and most of the time
the Sole officer with them.   Feeling an interest in the advancement
and prosperity of the colored race and always sympathizing with
them in their trials and Sufferings, which are now very great, owing
to the peculiar condition of the country, and their people, those under
my immediate charge have learned to look to me for consolation in
regard to many matters not Strictly military.   I always do what I can
but frequently that is nothing at all.   One of the most frequent complaints brought to me is the mistreatment of Soldiers wives, and in
Some cases their ejectment for non-payment of rent by *returned rebels*
who seem to be resuming their old positions all over the country.   This of course is inhuman as well as contrary to Genl. Orders.
No. 99. Hd Qrs. Dept. of the Gulf. June 30th, 1865, which declares that
the families of Soldiers in the Service of the Gov't. either on land or
water, Shall not be ejected for rent past due, and no collections of rent
forced until further orders. This is a very humane provision but
owing to the ignorance of many colored persons it is *very* often violated.   Those who know of the provision do not know how to go to
work to receive their rights under it, frequently, and when they do
attempt it they are often snubbed by those who they feel a right to
expect as their friends.   Truly, the colored race are passing through an
ordeal that will test every virtue they possess, and it will not be astonishing if, in many cases they fail to meet the expectation of an uncharitable world.

My object in writing you this letter is to call your attention to a Mr.
John Humphrey, who I am told is a returned rebel officer, now living
on Roseland Plantation, St. Charles Parish, who is Said to have made
innumerable threats and at least one attempt to put out the family of
one of my Soldiers.—*for non-payment of rent.*—   I gave the man a furlough and he got home Just in time to find a *Provost Guard* at his
house for the purpose of ousting his wife and children.   These look

like Strange proceedings viewed at this distance with my under-standing of the law. The fact is, persecution is the order of the day amongst these returned rebels, against the colored race in general, and Soldiers families *in particular*. And I am grieved to Say that many wearing the U. S. uniform are too easily bought body and Soul over to the evil designs and purposes of these same individuals. It seems to me that your Bureau and its agents are the "forlorn hope" of the colored people.— These rebels Strongly object to these agents, and declare that they will only keep up a confusion and dis-turbance, continually. That means that they do not intend to mani-fest the "good faith" for which Genl. [O. O.] Howard hopes, but intend to take Such a course with the colored people as will *oblige* the interference of the agents of your Bureau.

These are my views, although I owe you an apology for express-ing them at Such length. If it pleases you I shall be glad to lay the frequent cases which arise in my Co. before you, as I know your voice is very potent With great respect I am Your Most Obt. Servt.

Hugh P. Beach.

CHAPTER 22

AFRICAN AMERICAN
COMMUNITY BUILDING

Reverend L. S. Burkhead:
The Fight for Control of the Front Street Methodist
Church of Wilmington, North Carolina, 1865

African American community building is an important theme during Reconstruction. Nowhere is this more readily apparent than in religious institutions. After emancipation, blacks built new churches and rejected the influence of white men in existing churches. Faced with the prospect of receiving black members as equals, some white members of biracial congregations deeded their churches to black members, but in other instances power struggles resulted. Such was the case with the Front Street Methodist Church in Wilmington, North Carolina, a congregation of 1,400, about one-third white and two-thirds black. Although the version of events presented here comes from the pen of Front Street's white minister, Reverend L. S. Burkhead, the African American perspective is also apparent as Burkhead recounts the actions of Reverend W. Hunter, a black chaplain in the Union army, along with others Burkhead called "secessionists." Both sides appealed to General John Schofield, revealing the military's delicate position as an army of occupation. The struggle continued through the end of 1865, when the white minority recaptured jurisdiction over church property and African Americans left to form a new church, free of white control.

At the North Carolina Annual Conference held in Mocksville, Davie County, December, 1864, I was appointed the Pastor of the Front Street M.E. Church, South, Wilmington, North Carolina. I reached Wilmington December 24, 1864. On the 25th—the birthday of Jesus Christ, the Saviour of the world—which was the holy Sabbath, I preached to a small congregation. Early in the day an attack was made on Fort Fisher at the mouth of Cape Fear, by the United States fleet, and a furious shelling kept up throughout the whole day which was heard in the city. . . .

I did not find the church in a prosperous state. Many of the members were absent in different parts of the State, and those who remained were so much troubled at the dangers of the situation, and seemed so anxious about their property and the clash of hostile armies in their midst, that they were nearly all sad and in "heaviness through manifold temptations."

The evil could not be deferred. Again on January 13, shot and shell commenced to rain upon the Fort, and after a most heroic resistance the little garrison, under the command of General [William Whiting] and Colonel [William] Lamb, was compelled to surrender to a vastly superior force, and the "Stars and Stripes" waved in triumph over the captured Fort. A few days and nights of anxious solitude and the 22d of February dawned upon us—a day to be noted in the history of this City, for on this day the Confederates retired and the Army of the United States took possession. . . .

Having taken charge of Front Street Methodist Church—a church composed of both white and colored members—I commenced my labors with the single desire to glorify God and to be instrumental in building up the church and leading sinners to the cross of Christ. I had already seen enough to satisfy me that I had been called to the pastorate of this church at a most critical period and that the position would be exceedingly difficult to fill. Just after the fall of Fort Fisher I called my colored Class Leaders together for the purpose of laying before them the line of policy which I intended to pursue. In that meeting I stated to them substantially: That I had never taken an active part in political affairs, and that, the Grace of God assisting me, I should continue to labor for the salvation and happiness of my whole charge. That I believed the City of Wilmington would soon be given up by the Confederate and occupied by the Union troops; that therefore in a few days they would be practically free from their masters, but in no sense free from their solemn vows and binding obligations to the Church of God. . . . That Yankee chaplains—even colored chaplains—might labor to win their hearts and by professing *special* friendship persuade them to leave their own church and pastor and *vote* them in as their preachers, and thus break up the church in a row. That I desired them to remember that *I was their pastor,* and that no military power or appointment could properly and legally interfere with these church questions. . . .

When I had concluded my talk the colored leaders *unanimously* endorsed all that I had said and assured me of their fixed determination to stand by me *as their pastor* in every trying hour. . . .

On Saturday evening after the fall of Wilmington I was told by Col. Jordan, Provost Marshal, a member of the M.E. Church, that I "could hold service as usual in the church provided I would not pray for Jeff. Davis and the so-called Southern Confederacy!" I told him I was not in the habit of using a form of prayer, and I usually prayed for all in lawful authority and for all men. . . .

On Sunday morning, accompanied by Mr. John C. Codner, I attended the "sunrise prayer-meeting" of the colored friends—an institution of long standing in this church. I was anxious to hear their exercises and to witness the spirit which they might manifest in the first Sabbath of their political freedom. The large basement was crowded to its utmost capacity. I took my seat just outside of the altar, where I could see and hear everything that should transpire.

Charles R., one of the colored class leaders, conducted the services. He read as only Charles could read, "de ninf psawms." The whole congregation was wild with excitement, and extravagant beyond all precedent with shouts, groans, amens. . . .

About the middle of the services a colored chaplain, Rev. W. H[unter], with all the grandeur of the "the gentleman from Africa," with the "finishing touches of Boston," hitched unto the "Southern slave," marched up the aisle and took the seat usually vacated for the pastor, but which he had on that occasion left unoccupied. After another song and prayer, Charles rose and stated that there was a strange brother present who would like to make some remarks. Whereupon the chaplain arose, stretching himself to his full size and displaying to the best advantage for a profound impression his fine uniform, spoke in substance as follows:

My brethren and friends (Amen), I rise to address you, but I scarcely know what line of thought to pursue (hallelujah, Amen, etc.). When a thousand thoughts crowd upon my mind it is difficult to select that which will be more appropriate than the rest. (Oh, yes! Amen). A few short years ago I left North Carolina a slave (hallelujah, oh, yes); I now return a man. (Amen). I have the honor to be a regular minister of the Gospel in the Methodist Episcopal Church of the United States (glory to God, Amen) and also a regularly commissioned chaplain in the American Army. (Amen). I am proud to inform you that just three weeks ago today, as black a man as you ever saw, preached in the city of Washington to the Congress of the United States; and that a short time ago another colored man was admitted to the bar of the Supreme Court of the United States as a lawyer. (Long, loud and continued applause, beating on benches, etc.). One week ago you were all slaves; now you are all free. (Uproarious screamings). Thank God the armies of the Lord and of Gideon has triumphed and the Rebels have been driven back in confusion and scattered like chaff before the wind. (Amen! Hallelujah!) I listened to your prayers, but I did not hear a single prayer offered for the President of the United States or for the success of the American Army (Amen! O, yes, I prayed all last night, etc.). But I know what you meant. You were not quite sure that you were free, therefore a little afraid to say boldly what you felt. I knew how it is. I remember how we used to have to employ our dark symbols and obscure figures to cover up our real meaning. The profoundest philosopher could not understand us. (Amen! Hallelujah! That's so). I honor the President of the United States; I honor all men who are in authority under him, but I honor more highly the private in the ranks who goes forward to the front to meet the whizzing minnie, etc., etc.

After the tumultuous uproar began to abate, I arose and soon silence was restored. Then in a low tone of voice I announced the appointments for the day, requested the leaders to meet me in my office soon after the benediction should be pronounced, and dismissed them. . . .

At 10:30 o'clock I was in the pulpit. Small congregation. Several of these officers who came, I have no doubt, to try to entangle me in my talk. It was a trying time. I lifted up my heart to God for divine help. . . .

In the afternoon I preached for the colored people from John 5:40, a deliberate discourse designed to suit the temper of their minds. An impassioned appeal would have almost thrown them into convulsions; at least they would have raised an uproar. To these colored people this was their great jubilee. . . .

On Monday night after the arrival of the Union Army I met the colored leaders again. After the regular business meeting was over, I took occasion to point out to them their duties, as leaders, reading from the Discipline and explaining their obligations. I was now satisfied that they were arranging plans, under the leadership of a colored chaplain, to try to get possession of the church. . . .

They then stated to me that they "had never heard an educated man of their own race and color preach; that they now had an opportunity of doing so, as Brother Hunter was in the City and was anxious to preach for them; and they expressed a desire that I should invite him to preach in the church." I now began to dimly see the breakers. I stated to them that I was anxious to gratify their desires whenever I could consistently do so, but they were aware that my position was a delicate one (being the pastor of both white and colored congregations), and as there was no pastor at the Fifth Street Church, I would suggest that they invite their colored brother to preach down there. But this did not satisfy them. They insisted with some vehemence that Hunter should preach in "Front Street Church" and that *I should invite him*. I reminded them that *I had control* of the pulpit as their pastor, and that I was responsible for the preaching done there by my consent. I did not recognize their right to dictate to me whom I should invite into my pulpit. . . . I would give my consent for Hunter to preach for them one, two, three or more Sabbaths in the afternoon. They affirmed this to be their only desire and design; that they did not wish to get me out of the church or interfere with my pastoral authority in any way; they had no objection to me, and affirmed that I had given universal satisfaction, etc. I now was about to conclude I had passed the breakers and was almost ready to congratulate myself upon my wisdom in compromising, but imagine my surprise when these colored leaders gravely demanded that I should invite Hunter into the pulpit and *occupy it with him* when he should preach! I now told them emphatically that I could not comply with their demand. They seemed much surprised at my positive refusal, and I think were disposed to conclude that I must be a very great sinner because I would not exchange pulpit courtesies with the Rev. African Gentleman! . . .

During the next few days I discovered that these Leaders were very active and seemed to be often in secret council with this Rev. Hunter. On Friday, March 3d, Maj. Wm. M. Wherry, one of Gen. [John M.] Schofield's aides called on me at the parsonage to gain what information he could in reference to the ownership of the Front Street Church. He stated that the colored Leaders had presented a document to Gen. Scofield in regard to the Church; that they claimed it was theirs, etc. I told the Major I had some curiosity to hear the paper read. He then read to me the following letter.

"Wilmington, N. C., March 1, 1865.

General:

We, the undersigned, members of the M. E. Church of Wilmington, N. C., having been under the jurisdiction of the M. E. Church, South, whose teachings are in opposition to the interests of the Government of the United States, desire to transfer our relations to the A. M. E. Church of the U. S. We also desire to dispense with the services of the Rev. Mr. Burkhead, appointed by the North Carolina Methodist Episcopal Conference, South, which he claims still has jurisdiction in this place; and according to the appointment his term of service will not end until next November. . . .

Resolved, That we, in our official capacity, as representatives of a majority of the members of the above named Church, do this day dissolve all connection with the M. E. Church, South, and also that we from this date dispense with the services of the present pastor, Rev. Mr. Burkhead, . . .

Resolved, That we hereby appoint Chaplain W. Hunter, 4th U. S. C. T., as our agent to secure to us the services of a minister of the said A. M. E. Church.

[Signed] JAMES GALLEY,
THOMAS NICHOLS,
ELISHA BOON,
JOHN BROWN,
DAVID NICHOLS,
JOS. MILLER,
HENRY TUCKER,

BERRY HOWARD,
ELIAS HALSEY,
AND TWELVE OTHERS.

. . . After hearing this remarkable "spread-eagle" document, which scarcely contains a single truth, I made a statement to Maj. Wherry setting forth the facts in the case. I assured him that the Church was in no sense an "African Church," but that it was the property of the Methodist Episcopal Church, South. . . . Stated to him that if they desired to withdraw, or "secede" from the M. E. Church, South, they could do so, but I could not conceive upon what ground they could base their claim to the property. . . ."

"By Command of Maj. General Scofield. . . .
HEADQUARTERS DEPT. OF NORTH CAROLINA,
ARMY OF THE OHIO,
WILMINGTON, N. C., MARCH 5, 1865.
Special Orders
     No. 22.
The Church building in Wilmington known as the African Methodist Episcopal Church, will be subject to the use of the colored members of the congregation during one-half each day (morning or evening) when the pulpit will be occupied by such minister, white or colored, as the colored members may select.

This is not to exclude white persons from attendance upon the preaching of colored ministers, nor of colored people upon that of white ministers."

Now is not this a remarkable order? Is it not enough to try a second cousin of Job? I think so. . . . The order made a deeper impression than this, for it struck a blow at the very foundation of religious liberty—that liberty which is guaranteed to all Americans by the Constitution. . . . I showed these "Special Orders" to a chaplain in the Union Army—a man who bore himself while at my house as a gentleman and a Christian—and asked what course he would pursue should a similar order be issued in reference to his church in his native State of Kentucky. He replied, "With my loyalty undoubted, I would fight it to the death. But you can't do that. Your loyalty is doubted." I acknowledged the force of his remarks. . . .

. . . I called on Gen Scofield at his Headquarters. . . . the following dialogue, substantially, took place:

Burkhead.   General, I have called to see you in reference to your "Special Orders." . . . You speak in these orders of a church building as an "African Methodist Church." I assure you that to the best of my knowledge and belief there is no such church in this City. I am not the pastor of any such church. I am the pastor of the Front Street M. E. Church, South. I suppose, General, you have been incorrectly informed as to the *name* and *ownership* of the church.

Gen. S[cofield].   I intended no offense. It was so represented to me. But if it is not an African Church who does own the property?

B.   The property belongs to the M. E. Church, South, held by a Board of Trustees, who are all white men, "for the uses and purposes of said Church."

Gen. S.   Well, I do not wish to interfere in church matters. As to the legal title to the property, that must be settled by the civil courts after the war.

B.   But I see, General, from this order, that you do interfere directly with the legitimate work of the pastorate. You give these negroes the right and defend them in its exercise, of electing a new pastor in contravention of the laws and usages of the Church to which they belong. . . .

Gen. S.   I cannot help that. In my position, I must recognize the great American principle that the people have a right to select their rulers, and if the colored people violate their church obligations, these matters are with themselves.

B.   But, General, I suppose you are aware that if the colored members of my charge select another pastor under your encouragement and order, that they would *by that act sever their connection* with the M. E. Church, South, and therefore be merely outsiders, or *seceders;* and could never *after that act* lay any claim to property belonging to the M. E. Church, South.

Gen. S.   I *am aware* of all that, and I do not propose to interfere with your pastoral duties *in any way.* Perhaps the order may give you trouble, but you must manage it the best you can.

B.   But, General, if you will allow me, I desire to know whether during the half-day I am permitted to hold service I can control the *seating* of my *congregation?*

Gen. S.   I so understand it. You will be permitted to conduct your services in your own way, or in any way you may think proper.

The interview was pleasant but not so *full* as I desired. The General was crowded with business, and as I was regarded as a "rebel" I deemed it best to have only a short conversation. . . .

On Sunday morning, March 12th [1865], I preached to a large congregation. A number of negroes attempted to take seats among the whites in the body of the church. They manifested a disposition to ignore the military orders for Divine worship in my church. I asked them to please take seats in the gallery and not disturb the worship. That I should obey the military orders and hoped the colored friends would do likewise. Though they crowded to hear me preach, they refused to take up collections in the gallery, and though they had promised to stand by me in every trying hour, they now deliberately set at naught my pastoral authority and disregarded all the regulations of the church. . . .

. . . About this time the *seceded* colored Leaders, in a body, called on Gen. Hawley and represented me as a most *inveterate rebel.* . . .

. . . I was never a *secessionist per se*; but after the proclamation of Abraham Lincoln calling for troops to coerce the Southern States, I was of [the] opinion that as we must of necessity fight, we should fight the radical abolition party which had goaded the Southern States to desperation. I did not see how we could do otherwise. I deeply regretted the necessity which forced the States to take up arms, and yet I could see no way to avoid the *necessity.* I loved the Union. . . .

. . . I must, therefore, take the oath [of allegiance]. . . . It is only a matter of time and expediency. . . .

I have been visited by two other colored preachers of the "A. M. E. Zion Church"—Hood and Williams. They seem to be very different men from Rev. Hunter. They talk with more practical sense and manifest a far better spirit. They desired to occupy the "Fifth Street Church." I recommended the trustees of that Church loan them the church building until Rev. Mr. Peeler, the pastor, should return to his post. They consented to do so and these colored preachers obligated themselves to give up the church as soon as Rev. S. D. Peeler should return. I was told by Hood that he went to the meeting of the colored leaders of the "Front Street" and desired to make a talk, that the colored leaders might understand something of the operations of his church; but Hunter refused to grant him the privilege! Thus it appears that his "Reverence" manifests the same contemptible bigotry to his own color that he does to white men. . . .

. . . One of the first things their "African preachers" did, in order to promote the *secession* of the members, was to appoint as many officers as possible. . . . you will not be surprised to learn that some of their sermons and exhortations are *very curious* and original, if not as orthodox and chaste as could be desired. These young, newly-fledged, sable, public speakers possess, however, some of the elements of great *orators*. They have the volume of voice, strength of muscle, and the "gift of continuance" to a remarkable degree. Any one living within half a mile of Front St. Church during the year 1865 will bear testimony to these facts. If the seats of my church could tell their sufferings, and describe the awful beatings they have received, methinks the hard-hearted brick wall would cry out in sympathy with them. And could some of their most eloquent strains of oratory and powerful logical deductions, clothed in their own language and imagery, be set before Horace Greeley, Chief Justice [Salmon P.] Chase, [Senator Charles] Sumner, [Wendell] Phillips and others, I am inclined to think they could plead more potently for the elective franchise to be conferred upon the multitudes who listen enraptured to the thrilling discourses of these rising public men of the nation. There can no longer be a doubt about their intellectual proportions. Whether you would "expect" it or not, they can "speak in public on the stage.". . .

ACTION OF THE NORTH CAROLINA CONFERENCE, 1865

. . . WHEREAS, by the decision of the Supreme Court of the United States the M. E. Church, South, has been declared to be the legitimate Methodist Episcopal Church in the Southern States, and all the church property within the limits of her jurisdiction has been justly and legally awarded to her; and

WHEREAS, Certain colored persons, formerly members of Front Street M. E. Church, South, under the lead of a colored chaplain, soon after the occupation of Wilmington by the U. S. Troops, *seceded* from the M. E. Church, South, to another denomination and falsely represented to the Military authorities that the Front Street Church was an "African Church," . . .

Resolved: 1. That we, the members of the N. C. A. Conf. in Conference assembled, having taken the oath prescribed by His Excellency, Andrew Johnson, President of the United States, May 29, 1865, and avowing ourselves true and loyal citizens of the Government of the U. S., do most respectfully and earnestly protest against the continuance of the unjust and illegal Military Rule, in matters purely ecclesiastical and spiritual, by which our people of the Front Street Church in the City of Wilmington, N. C., are deprived of their legal rights and religious privileges. . . .

CHAPTER 23

SOCIAL AND POLITICAL CONDITIONS IN THE POSTWAR SOUTH

Sidney Andrews: The South Since the War

Sidney Andrews (1835–1880) was a New England born journalist who spent most of his early years in Illinois. From 1864 to 1869, he was a special correspondent in Washington, D.C., for the Chicago Tribune *and the* Boston Advertiser. *After the Civil War, in the fall of 1865, Andrews traveled through the Carolinas and Georgia and recorded his observations and impressions in a series of letters to the Chicago and Boston newspapers. In the following year, the letters were collected and published as a book,* The South Since the War. *Although frequently tinged with an anti-Southern viewpoint, Andrews' letters nevertheless revealed much valuable information on social and political conditions in the South during this very critical period.*

CHARLESTON, SEPTEMBER 4, 1865.

A city of ruins, of desolation, of vacant houses, of widowed women, of rotting wharves, of deserted warehouses, of weed-wild gardens, of miles of grass-grown streets, of acres of pitiful and voiceful barrenness,—that is Charleston, wherein Rebellion loftily reared its head five years ago, on whose beautiful promenade the fairest of cultured women gathered with passionate hearts to applaud the assault of ten thousand upon the little garrison of Fort Sumter!

"The mills of the gods grind slow, but they grind exceedingly small." Be sure Charleston knows what these words mean. Be sure the pride of the eyes of these men and women has been laid low. Be sure they have eaten wormwood, and their souls have worn sackcloth. "God's ways seem dark, but soon or late they touch the shining hills of day." Henceforth let us rest content in this faith; for here is enough of woe and want and ruin and ravage to satisfy the most insatiate heart, enough of sore humiliation and bitter overthrow to appease the desire of the most vengeful spirit.

Who kindled the greedy fire of December, 1861, whereby a third of the city was destroyed? No one yet knows. "It was de good Jesus hisself," said an old negro to me when I asked him the question,—"it was de Almighty Hand workin' fru de man's hand." Certain it is that the people were never able to discover the agency of the fire; though, so far as I can learn, no one doubts that it was the work of an incendiary,—"some man," say the ex-Rebels, "who wanted to do you Federals a good turn."

Recall last winter's daily bulletin about the bombardment—so many shells and no damage done,—so many shells and no damage done, day after day the same old story, till one almost believed it true. Yet ex-Rebel officers will tell you now that our aim was so perfect that we killed their sentinels with our Parrott guns; and go where you will, up and down the streets in almost any portion of the city, and you find the dumb walls eloquent with praises of our skill.

We never again can have the Charleston of the decade previous to the war. The beauty and pride of the city are as dead as the glories of Athens. Five millions of dollars could not restore the ruin of these four past years; and that sum is so far beyond the command of the city as to seem the boundless measure of immeasurable wealth. Yet, after all, Charleston was Charleston because of the hearts of its people. St. Michael's Church, they held, was the centre of the universe; and the aristocracy of the city were the very elect of God's children on earth. One marks now how few young men there are, how generally the young women are dressed in black. The flower of their proud aristocracy is buried on scores of battle-fields. If it were possible to restore the broad acres of crumbling ruins to their foretime style and uses, there would even then be but the dead body of Charleston.

The Charleston of 1875 will doubtless be proud in wealth and intellect and rich in grace and culture. Let favoring years bring forward such fruitage! Yet the place has not in itself recuperative power for such a result. The material on which to build that fair structure does not here exist, and, as I am told by dozens, cannot be found in the State. If Northern capital and Northern energy do not come here, the ruin, they say, must remain a ruin; and if this time five years finds here a handsome and thriving city, it will be the creation of New England,—not necessarily the pattern of New England, for the influences from thence will be moulded by and interfused with those now existing here; but yet, in the essential fact, the creation of New England.

It was noted on the steamship by which I came from New York that, leaving out the foreign element, our passengers were from Charleston and from Massachusetts. We had nearly as many Boston men as Charleston men. One of the Charleston merchants said to me that when he went North the passengers were also almost equally divided between Massachusetts and South Carolina; and he added, that, in Eastern Massachusetts, where he spent some days, he found many men who were coming to Charleston.

Of Massachusetts men, some are already in business here, and others came on to "see the lay of the land," as one of them said. "That's all right," observed an ex-Rebel captain in one of our after-dinner chats,—"that's all right; let's have Massachusetts and South Carolina brought together, for they are the only two States that amount to anything."

"I hate all you Yankees most heartily in a general sort of way," remarked another of these Southerners; "but I find you clever enough personally, and I expect it'll be a good thing for us to have you come down here with your money, though it'll go against the grain with us pretty badly."

There are many Northern men here already, though one cannot say that there is much Northern society, for the men are either without families or have left them at home. Walking out yesterday with a former Charlestonian,—a man who left here in the first year of the war and returned soon after our occupation of the city,—he pointed out to me the various "Northern houses"; and I shall not exaggerate if I say that this classification appeared to include at least half the stores on each of the principal streets. "The presence of these men," said he, "was at first very distasteful to our people, and they are not liked any too well now; but we know they are doing a good work for the city."

I fell into some talk with him concerning the political situation, and found him of bitter spirit toward what he was pleased to denominate "the infernal radicals." When I asked him what should be done, he answered: "You Northern people are making a great mistake in your treatment of the South. We are thoroughly whipped; we give up slavery forever; and now we want you to quit reproaching us. Let us back into the Union, and then come down here and help us build up the country."

Every little variation from the old order of things excites the comment "Yankee notion," in which there is sometimes good-natured querulousness and sometimes a sharp spice of contempt. Stopping a moment this afternoon in a store where were three or four intelligent men, one of them asked me the use of the "thing" I had in my hand. It was one of the handle-and-straps so common in the North for carrying shawls, cloaks, overcoats, &c. Seeing that none of them had any idea what it was, I explained its use. "Well, now, what a Yankee notion!" "Yes," answered another, "but how handy it is."

To bring here the conveniences and comforts of our Northern civilization, no less than the Northern idea of right and wrong, justice and injustice, humanity and inhumanity, is the work ready for the hand of every New England man and woman who stands waiting. There is much prejudice to overcome, and some of it is bitter and aggravating; but the measure of success won by Northern men already in the field is an earnest of the reward for others. Self-interest is a masterful agent in modern civilization.

Business is reviving slowly, though perhaps the more surely. The resident merchants are mostly at the bottom of the ladder of prosperity. They have idled away the summer in vain regrets for vanished hopes, and most of them are only just now beginning to wake to the new life. Some have already been North for goods, but more are preparing to go; not heeding that, while they vacillate with laggard time, Northern men are springing in with hands swift to catch opportunity. It pains me to see the apathy and indifference that so generally prevails; but the worst feature of the situation is, that so many young men are not only idle, but give no promise of being otherwise in the immediate future.

Many of the stores were more or less injured by the shelling. A few of these have been already repaired, and are now occupied,—very likely by Northern men. A couple of dozen, great and small, are now in process of repair; and scores stand with closed shutters or gaping doors and windows. The doubt as to the title of property, and the wise caution of the President in granting pardons, unquestionably has something to do with the stagnation so painfully apparent; but very much of it is due to the hesitating shiftlessness of even the Southern merchant, who forever lets *I dare not* wait upon *I would.* Rents of eligible storerooms are at least from one fourth to one third higher than before the war, and resident business men say only Northern men who intend staying but a short time can afford to pay present prices. I'm sure I can't see how any one can afford to pay them, but I know the demand is greater than the supply.

I queried of the returning merchants on the steamship how they were received in the North. An Augusta man complained that he could get no credit, and that there was a disposition to be grinding and exacting. One Charleston man said he asked for sixty days, and got it without a word of objection. Another told me that he asked for four months, was given three, and treated like a gentleman everywhere. Another showed me the receipt for a debt of about fifteen hundred dollars contracted before the war, which he had paid in full; and when he asked for four months on a bill of eight thousand dollars, it was readily given. Still another settled his old indebtedness with one third cash and eight and twelve months notes for the balance, while he got ninety days on three fourths of his new bill. One man said he had many friends in the North, and they all knew him for a thorough Rebel; he expected some taunts, but tried to carry himself like a gentleman, and was courteously received, "even in Boston."

I judge that such of the merchants as first went North and settled with their creditors made more favorable terms than those who went later. If it be said that those were men who had loved the Union, while these are men who had not; that those were men of keen sense of commercial honor and integrity, while these are men who cared less for an adjustment; that those are men who deserved favors, while these are men who have forfeited all claim to special consideration,—if this be said, the pith of the matter will probably be hit so far as regards most of those who now complain of their reception.

Yet there are men who deserved better than they have received. These are they who, whatever their views on the questions at issue in the war, meant to pay all their debts. Most of them are men who loved the Union and hated secession. That there were such men in all parts of the State is beyond question. When the negroes say any one was a Union man during the war, the fact is established; from their judgment and testimony there is no appeal. These men, having no faith in the Confederacy, put everything they could into cotton or rosin or turpentine,—hoping to save something from the general wreck they saw impending,—only to find in the end that they are scarcely richer than those who invested everything in Confederate bonds.

It would seem that it is not clearly understood how thoroughly Sherman's army destroyed everything in its line of march, destroyed it without questioning who suffered by the action. That this whole-sale destruction was often without orders, and often against most positive orders, does not change the fact of destruction. The Rebel leaders were, too, in their way, even more wanton, and just as thorough as our army in destroying property. They did not burn houses and barns and fences as we did; but, during the last three months of the war, they burned immense quantities of cotton and rosin.

The action of the two armies put it out of the power of men to pay their debts. The values and the bases of value were nearly all destroyed. Money lost about everything it had saved. Thousands of men who were honest in purpose have lost everything but honor. The cotton with which they meant to pay their debts has been burned, and they are without other means. What is the part of wisdom in respect to such men? It certainly cannot be to strip them of the last remnant. Many of them will pay in whole or in part, if proper consideration be shown them. It is no question of favor to any one as a favor, but a pure question of business,—how shall the commercial relations of the two sections be re-established? In determining it, the actual and exceptional condition of the State with respect to property should be constantly borne in mind.

Yet when all this is said in favor of one class of merchants, it must, in good conscience, be added, that by far a larger class is showing itself unworthy of anything but stringent measures. "How do you find the feeling?" said I to a gentleman of national reputation, who is now here settling the affairs of a very large New York house. "Well, there are a good many merchants who don't mean to pay anything more than they are obliged to," said he in reply. I asked of one of the leading merchants this morning, "Are your people generally disposed to settle their accounts?" His answer was, "Those who expect to continue business must of course do so." "How about the others?"

I queried. "I'm afraid there isn't so much commercial honor as there should be," he replied. I am told of one firm which represented itself entirely ruined, when subsequent investigation showed that it had five thousand pounds sterling to its credit in Liverpool; and of another which offered only thirty cents on the dollar, when its property in New York alone will cover over seventy cents on the dollar of its entire indebtedness.

That Rebellion sapped the foundations of commercial integrity in the State is beyond question. That much of the Northern indebtedness will never be paid is also beyond question. What is desirable is, that creditors should become cognizant of all the facts in the case before fixing terms. For the rascal there is but one set of terms; for the honest man there should be every possible consideration.

The city is under thorough military rule; but the iron hand rests very lightly. Soldiers do police duty, and there is some nine-o'clock regulation; but, so far as I can learn, anybody goes anywhere at all hours of the night without molestation. "There never was such good order here before," said an old colored man to me. The main street is swept twice a week, and all garbage is removed at sunrise. "If the Yankees was to stay here always and keep the city so clean, I don't reckon we'd have 'yellow jack' here any more," was a remark I overheard on the street. "Now is de fust time sence I can 'mem'er when brack men was safe in de street afer nightfall," stated the negro tailor in whose shop I sat an hour yesterday.

On the surface, Charleston is quiet and well behaved; and I do not doubt that the more intelligent citizens are wholly sincere in their expressions of a desire for peace and reunion. The city has been humbled as no other city has been; and I can't see how any man, after spending a few days here, can desire that it shall be further humiliated merely for revenge. Whether it has been humiliated enough for health is another thing. Said one of the Charlestonians on the boat, "You won't see the real sentiment of our people, for we are under military rule; we are whipped, and we are going to make the best of things; but we hate Massachusetts as much as we ever did." This idea of making the best of things is one I have heard from scores of persons. I find very few who hesitate to frankly own that the South has been beaten. "We made the best fight we could, but you were too strong for us, and now we are only anxious to get back into the old

Union and live as happily as we can," said a large cotton factor. I find very few who make any special profession of Unionism; but they are almost unanimous in declaring that they have no desire but to live as good and quiet citizens under the laws.

For the first two months of our occupancy of the city scarcely a white woman but those of the poorer classes was seen on the street, and very few were even seen at the windows and doors of the residences. That order of things is now, happily, changed. There doesn't yet appear to be as much freedom of appearance as would be natural; but very many of what are called the "first ladies" are to be seen shopping in the morning and promenading in the evening. They, much more than the men, have contemptuous motions for the negro soldiers; and scorn for Northern men is frequently apparent in the swing of their skirts when passing on the sidewalk.

One doesn't observe so much pleasantness and cheerfulness as would be agreeable; but the general demeanor is quite consonant with the general mourning costume. A stroller at sunset sees not a few pale and pensive-faced young women of exquisite beauty; and a rambler during the evening not unfrequently hears a strain of touching melody from the darkened parlor of some roomy old mansion, with now and then one of the ringing, passionate airs with which the Southern heart has been fired during the war.

Mothers yet teach their children hate of the North, I judge; for when I asked a bright-eyed girl of half a dozen years, with whom I walked on a back street for a block or two, whose girl she was, she promptly answered, "A Rebel mother's girl." Patience, good people who love liberty, patience; this petty woman's spite will bite itself to death in time.

Down in the churchyard of St. Philip's, one of the richest and most aristocratic of churches in this proud city, is a grave which every stranger is curious to see. There are only the four plain panelled brick walls about three feet high, and on them a mottled white marble slab, some nine feet by four in size. At the head of the grave is a single sickly ten-foot-high magnolia tree. At each corner of the foot is a sprawling and tangled damask rose-bush, and about midway on the right there is also a small white rose-bush. All around the little plat is a border of myrtle, sweet in its rich greenness, but untrimmed and broken and goat-eaten. It is the grave of the father of the Rebellion, and on the marble slab there is cut the one word,—

"CALHOUN"

This churchyard symbolizes the city of Charleston. Children and goats crawl through a convenient hole in the front wall, and play at will among the sunken graves and broken tombstones. There is everywhere a wealth of offal and garbage and beef-bones. A mangy cur was slinking among the stones, and I found a hole three feet deep which he had dug at the foot of one of the graves. Children were quarrelling for flowers over one of the more recent mounds. The whole yard is grown up to weeds and brush, and the place is desolate and dreary as it well can be; more desolate because cruel hands have broken away the corners of the great marble slab of Calhoun,— for mementos, I suppose. Time was when South Carolina guarded this grave as a holy spot. Now it lies in ruin with her chief city. When Northern life shall rebuild and revivify that city, let us pray it may also set chaste and simple beauty around this grave; for there is no need to wish the brave but bad spirit of Calhoun greater punishment than it must have in seeing the woe and waste and mourning which the war has brought the region he loved so well. . . .

ORANGEBURG C[OURT] H[OUSE], SEPTEMBER 9, 1865.

Recalling how persistently the whites of this State have claimed, for twenty-five years, to be the negro's special friends, and seeing, as the traveller does, how these whites treat this poor black, one cannot help praying that he may be saved from his friends in future. Yet this cannot be. Talk never so plausibly and eloquently as any one may of colonization or deportation, the inexorable fact remains, that the negro is in South Carolina, and must remain here till God pleases to call him away. The problem involved in his future must be met on the soil of which he is native; and any attempt to solve it elsewhere than in the house of these his so-called special friends will be futile.

The work of the North, in respect to South Carolina, is two-fold: the white man must be taught what the negro's rights are, and the negro must be taught to wait patiently and wisely for the full recognition of those rights in his own old home. He waited so long in the house of bondage for the birthright of freedom, that waiting is weary work for him now; yet there is nothing else for him and us,—nothing but faith, and labor, and waiting, and, finally, rest in victory.

The city negro, and the country negro are as much unlike as two races. So, too, the city white man and the country white man differ much from each other. The latter, however, is just what he chooses to be, while the country negro is just what slavery and his late owners have made him. Tell me what you will derogatory of the country negro, and very likely I shall assent to most of the language you use. He is very often, and perhaps generally, idle, vicious, improvident, negligent, and unfit to care well for his interests. In himself, he is a hard, coarse, unlovely fact, and no amount of idealizing can make him otherwise. Yet, for all that, he is worth quite as much as the average country white.

The negro, one may say, is made by his master. I even doubt if he is, in many cases, morally responsible for his acts. With him there is no theft when be takes small property from the white; there is, of course, crime in the eye of the law, but there is none in the design or consciousness of the negro. Has not every day of his existence taught him that robbery is no crime? So, too, if this uncouth freedman, just from the plantation, falls into a passion and half kills somebody, you will utterly fail in your effort to make him understand that he has committed a grave crime. Has not his whole life been witness of just such right and lawful outrage on humanity? This language may indicate a bad state of affairs; but it points out certain conditions with respect to the negro that must be taken into account by any one undertaking to deal with him as a freedman.

Everybody talks about the negro, at all hours of the day, and under all circumstances. One might in truth say—using the elegant language of opposition orators in Congress—that "the people have got nigger on the brain." Let conversation begin where it will, it ends with Sambo.

I scarcely talk with any white man who fails to tell me how anxious many of the negroes are to return to their old homes. In coming up from Charleston I heard of not less than eleven in this condition, and mention has been made to me here in Orangeburg of at least a score. The first curious circumstance is, that none of them are allowed to return; and the second is, that I can't find any of those desirous of returning. I presume I have asked over a hundred negroes here and in Charleston if they wanted to go back and live with their old masters as slaves, or if they knew any negro who did desire to return to that condition, and I have yet to find the first one who hesitates an instant in answering "No."

I spoke of this difficulty I have in finding a single negro who loved slavery better than he does freedom to an intelligent gentleman whom I met here last evening,—a member of the Rhett family. "I am surprised to hear that," said he; "but I suppose it's because you are from the North, and the negro don't dare to tell you his real feeling." I asked if the blacks don't generally consider Northern men their friends. "O yes," he answered, "and that's the very reason why you can't find out what they think."

They deserve better treatment than they get at our hands in Orangeburg, at least; and I am told that what I see here is a forecast of what I shall see in all parts of the State. Theoretically, and in the intent of Congress, the Freedmen's Bureau stands as the next friend of the blacks; practically, and in the custom of the country, it appears to stand too often as their next enemy. That General Saxton is their good friend does not need to be asserted. Very likely the district commissioners under him are wise and humane men, and unquestionably the general regulations for the State are meant to secure justice to the freedmen.

The trouble arises from the fact that it is impossible for the State Commissioner or his chief deputies to personally know all, or even half, their various local agents. Take the case right in hand. Headquarters for this district are thirty miles below here; and the ranking officer of the bureau has, probably, agents in at least forty different towns, the majority of whom are doubtless lieutenants from the volunteer forces of the army. They are detailed for this duty by the military commander of the post or the district,—sometimes after consultation with the district commissioner, but quite generally without. As the post garrisons are constantly changing, there may be a new agent of the bureau once a month in each town of the district; and I need not add, that the probabilities are that half the aggregate number on duty at any given time are wholly unfit for the work intrusted to them.

Again, take the case right in hand. The acting agent here at present is a lieutenant from a New York regiment. He is detailed by the colonel commanding, and has been on duty several weeks. Yet he never has seen the district commissioner of the bureau. His duties are to examine, and approve or disapprove, all contracts between the planters and the negroes, and to hear and determine all cases of complaint or grievance arising between the negroes themselves, or between the whites and the negroes. He treats me courteously, but he has no sympathy with the poor and lowly; and his ideas of justice are of the bar-room order,—might makes right. He doesn't really intend to outrage the rights of the negroes, but he has very little idea that they have any rights except such as the planters choose to give them. His position, of course, is a difficult one; and he brings to it a head more or less muddled with liquor, a rough and coarse manner, a dictatorial and impatient temper, a most remarkable ability for cursing, and a hearty contempt for "the whole d—n pack o' niggers." I speak from the observation of a good deal of time spent in and around his office.

I found Charleston full of country negroes. Whites of all classes concur in saying that there is a general impression throughout the back districts that lands are to be given the freed people on the seacoast; and this, I am told, renders them uneasy and unreliable as plantation hands. Whites of all classes also concur in saying that they will not work.

"I lost sixteen niggers," said a Charleston gentleman; "but I don't mind it, for they were always a nuisance, and you'll find them so in less than a year." I asked, as usual, what they are now doing. Two or three of the men went into the army, one of the women had gone North as a cook, another is chambermaid on a steamer, and he found three of the men at work on one wharf the other day. "But," said I, laughing, "I thought the free negro wouldn't work." "O well, this is only a temporary state of affairs, and they'll all be idle before winter; and I don't look for nothing else when cold weather comes but to have them all asking me to take them back; but I sha'n't do it. I wouldn't give ten cents apiece for them."

Many of the private soldiers on duty here tell me that the planters generally overreach the negroes on every possible occasion; and my observation among such as I have seen in town tends to confirm this assertion to a considerable extent.

Coming up in the cars from Charleston I had for seat-mate part of the way one of the delegates to the Convention which meets at

Columbia next week. He was a very courteous and agreeable gentleman, past middle age, and late the owner of twenty-two negroes. He was good enough to instruct me at some length in respect to the character of the negro. "You Northern people are utterly mistaken in supposing anything can be done with these negroes in a free condition. They can't be governed except with the whip. Now on my plantation there wasn't much whipping, say once a fortnight; but the negroes knew they would be whipped if they didn't behave themselves, and the fear of the lash kept them in good order." He went on to explain what a good home they always had; laying stress on the fact that they never were obliged to think for themselves, but were always tenderly cared for, both in health and sickness; "and yet these niggers all left me the day after the Federals got into Charleston!" I asked where they now are; and he replied that he hadn't seen anybody but his old cook since they ran away; but he believed they were all at work except two, who had died. Yet I am told constantly that these ungrateful wretches, the negroes, cannot possibly live as free people.

Yesterday morning while I sat in the office of the agent of the Freedmen's Bureau there came in, with a score of other men, a planter living in this district, but some sixteen miles from town. He had a woful tale of an assault upon himself by one of his "niggers,"—"a boy who I broughten up, and who's allers had a good home down ter my place." While the boy was coming in from the street the man turned to me and explained, "It never don't do no good to show favor to a nigger, for they's the most ongratefullest creeturs in the world." The dreadful assault consisted in throwing a hatchet at the white man by one of a crowd of negroes who were having a dispute among themselves, and suddenly discovered, in the early evening, somebody sneaking along by the fence. The boy said it wasn't a hatchet, but a bit of brick; and added, that the man was so far away that no one could tell whether he was white or black, and that he didn't throw the brick till after he called out and told the man to go away. I followed the negro out after he had received his lecture from the officer, and had some talk with him. "D—n him," said he, referring to his employer, "he never done nufin all his d—n life but beat me and kick me and knock me down; an' I hopes I git eben with him some day."

Riding with an ex-Confederate major, we stopped at a house for water. The owner of the property, which was a very handsome one, was absent; and it was in charge of a dozen negroes, former slaves of the proprietor.

"Now here," said the late officer, "here is a place where the negroes always had the pleasantest sort of a home,— everything to eat and drink and wear, and a most kind master and mistress."

Pompey, aged about twelve, came to bring us the water.

"Pompey," said the Major, "Pompey, how do you like your freedom?"

He hung his head, and answered, "Dun know, mawssa."

"O, well, speak right out; don't be afraid; tell us just how it is now," said he again.

Whereupon Pompey: "Likes to be free man, sah; but we's all workin' on yer like we did afore."

"That's right, Pompey," said I; "keep on working; don't be a lazy boy."

"It won't do," said the Major; "he'll grow up idle and impudent and worthless, like all the rest."

"No, sah," answered Pompey, "I's free nigger now, and I's goin' to work."

There is much talk among the country people about a rising of the blacks. A planter who stopped here last night, and who lives twelve miles to the west, told me that it was believed in his neighborhood that they had guns and pistols hid in the timber, and were organizing to use them. His ideas were not very clear about the matter; but he appeared to think they would make serious trouble after the crops are gathered. Another man, living in Union district, told the company, with evident pleasure, that they'd been able to keep control of the niggers up to his section till 'bout three weeks ago; he 'lowed thar'd bin some lickin', but no more'n was good fur the fellows. Now the Federals had come in, and the negroes were in a state of glad excitement, and everybody feared there would be bloody business right away.

A thing that much shocks me is the prevalent indifference to the negro's fate and life. It is a sad, but solemn fact, that three-fourths of the native whites consider him a nuisance, and would gladly be rid of his presence, even at the expense of his existence. And this in face of the fact that all the planters are complaining about the insufficiency of labor. Thus, in Charleston, a merchant told me, with relishing detail, a story to the effect that, soon after the promulgation of the order against wearing Confederate buttons, a negro soldier doing duty in the city halted a young man, informed him of the regulations, and told him that if he was seen on the street again wearing the obnoxious buttons, he would probably be arrested; whereupon the hopeful scion of the Charleston aristocracy whipped out a large knife, seized the negro by the beard, and cut his throat. The soldier died in about a week; but nothing had been done with the man who killed him. So, too, a man who seems to be acting as stage-agent here says "a d—d big black buck nigger" was shot near Lewisville about three weeks ago; and the citizens all shield the man who shot him, and sanction his course. All the talk of men about the hotel indicates that it is held to be an evidence of smartness, rather than otherwise, to kill a freedman; and I have not found a man here who seems to believe that it is a sin against Divine law.

CHAPTER 24

A RADICAL REPUBLICAN SPEAKS OUT

Thaddeus Stevens: Speech on Reconstruction, December 18, 1865

Thaddeus Stevens (1792–1868) emerged as the unquestioned leader of the Radical Republicans during the years following the end of the Civil War. A member of the House of Representatives from Pennsylvania since 1859, Stevens had been a bitter critic of President Lincoln and a determined opponent of the President's plan for reconstructing the Union. With the cessation of hostilities, Stevens became an outspoken advocate of a vindictive policy against the former Confederacy. One historian has described Stevens as a "strange mixture of disinterested philanthropy and partisan vindictiveness." Genuinely interested in the lot of the newly freed Negro, Stevens was at the same time determined to humiliate the South and to guarantee the perpetuation of Northern and Republican leadership in national politics. Until his death in 1868, Stevens led the opposition to President Andrew Johnson's plans for a reconstruction of the South, not only demanding a harsher program but declaring that reconstruction policy was the exclusive concern of the legislative branch of the government.

A candid examination of the power and proper principles of reconstruction can be offensive to no one, and may possibly be profitable by exciting inquiry. One of the suggestions of the message which we are now considering has special reference to this. Perhaps it is the principle most interesting to the people at this time. The President assumes, what no one doubts, that the late rebel States have lost their constitutional relations to the Union, and are incapable of representation in Congress, except by permission of the Government. It matters but little, with this admission, whether you call them States out of the Union, and now conquered territories, or assert that because the Constitution forbids them to do what they did do, that they are therefore only dead as to all national and political action, and will remain so until the Government shall breathe into them the

332

breath of life anew and permit them to occupy their former position. In other words, that they are not out of the Union, but are only dead carcasses lying within the Union. In either case, it is very plain that it requires the action of Congress to enable them to form a State government and send representatives to Congress. Nobody, I believe, pretends that with their old constitutions and frames of government they can be permitted to claim their old rights under the Constitution. They have torn their constitutional States into atoms, and built on their foundations fabrics of a totally different character. Dead men cannot raise themselves. Dead States cannot restore their own existence "as it was." Whose especial duty is it to do it? In whom does the Constitution place the power? Not in the judicial branch of Government, for it only adjudicates and does not prescribe laws. Not in the Executive, for he only executes and cannot make laws. Not in the Commander-in-Chief of the armies, for he can only hold them under military rule until the sovereign legislative power of the conqueror shall give them law.

There is fortunately no difficulty in solving the question. There are two provisions in the Constitution, under one of which the case must fall. The fourth article says:

"New States may be admitted by the Congress into this Union."

In my judgment this is the controlling provision in this case. Unless the law of nations is a dead letter, the late war between two acknowledged belligerents severed their original compacts, and broke all the ties that bound them together. The future condition of the conquered power depends on the will of the conqueror. They must come in as new States or remain as conquered provinces. Congress—the Senate and House of Representatives with the concurrence of the President—is the only power that can act in the matter. But suppose, as some dreaming theorists imagine, that these States have never been out of the Union, but have only destroyed their State governments so as to be incapable of political action; then the fourth section of the fourth article applies, which says:

"The United States shall guaranty to every State in this Union a republican form of government."

Who is the United States? Not the judiciary; not the President; but the sovereign power of the people, exercised through their representatives in Congress, with the concurrence of the Executive. It means the political Government—the concurrent action of both branches of Congress and the Executive. The separate action of each amounts to nothing either in admitting new States or guarantying republican governments to lapsed or outlawed States. Whence springs the preposterous idea that either the President, or the Senate, or the House of Representatives, acting separately, can determine the right of States to send members or Senators to the Congress of the Union?

To prove that they are and for four years have been out of the Union for all legal purposes, and being now conquered, subject to the absolute disposal of Congress, I will suggest a few ideas and adduce a few authorities. If the so-called "confederate States of America" were an independent belligerent, and were so acknowledged by the United States and by Europe, or had assumed and maintained an attitude which entitled them to be considered and treated as a belligerent, then, during such time, they were precisely in the condition of a foreign nation with whom we were at war; nor need their independence as a nation be acknowledged by us to produce that effect. In the able opinion delivered by that accomplished and loyal jurist, Mr. Justice Grier, in the prize cases, all the law on these points is collected and clearly stated. (2 Black, page 66.) Speaking of civil wars, and following Vattel, he says:

> "When the party in rebellion occupy and hold in a hostile manner a certain portion of territory; have declared their independence; have cast off their allegiance; have organized armies; have commenced hostilities against their former sovereign, the world acknowledges them as belligerents, and the contest a war."

And

> "The parties belligerent in a public war are independent nations. But it is not necessary, to constitute war, that both parties should be acknowledged as independent nations or foreign States. A war may exist where one of the belligerents claims sovereign rights as against the other."

The idea that the States could not and did not make war because the Constitution forbids it, and that this must be treated as a war of individuals, is a very injurious and groundless fallacy. Individuals cannot make war. They may commit murder, but that is no war. Communities, societies, States, make war. . . .

But why appeal to reason to prove that the seceded States made war as States, when the conclusive opinion of the Supreme Court is at hand? In the prize cases already cited, the Supreme Court say:

"Hence, in organizing this rebellion, they have acted as States claiming to be sovereign over all persons and property within their respective limits, and asserting a right to absolve their citizens from their allegiance to the Federal Government. Several of these States have combined to form a new confederacy, claiming to be acknowledged by the world as a sovereign State. Their right to do so is now being decided by wager of battle. The ports and territory of each of these States are held in hostility to the General Government. It is no loose, unorganized insurrection, having no defined boundary or possession. It has a boundary marked by lines of bayonets, and which can be crossed only by force. South of this line is enemies' territory, because it is claimed and held in possession by an organized hostile and belligerent power."

Again, the court say, what I have been astonished that any one should doubt:

"The proclamation of blockade is itself official and conclusive evidence to the court that a state of war existed."

Now, what was the legal result of such war?

"The conventions, the treaties, made with a nation are broken or annulled by a war arising between the contracting parties."—*Vattel*, 372; *Halleck*, 371, section 23.

If gentlemen suppose that this doctrine applies only to national and not to civil wars, I beg leave to refer them to Vattel, page 423. He says:

"A civil war breaks the bands of society and government, or at least suspends their force and effect; it produces in the nation two independent parties, who consider each other as enemies, and acknowledge no common judge. These two parties must therefore be considered as thenceforward constituting, at least for a time, two separate bodies; two distinct societies. They stand, therefore, in precisely the same predicament as two nations who engage in a contest, and being unable to come to an agreement, have recourse to arms."

At page 427:

"And when a nation becomes divided into two parties absolutely independent, and no longer acknowledge a common superior, the State is dissolved, and the war between the two parties stands on the same ground, in every respect, as a public war between two different nations."

But must the belligerent be acknowledged as an independent nation, as some contend? That is answered in the case referred to in 2 Black, as follows:

"It is not the less a civil war, with belligerent parties in hostile array, because it may be called an 'insurrection' by one side, and the insurgents be considered as rebels or traitors. It is not necessary that the independence of the revolted province or State be acknowledged in order to constitute it a party belligerent in a war, according to the law of nations."

This doctrine, so clearly established by publicists, and so distinctly stated by Mr. Justice Grier, has been frequently reiterated since by the Supreme Court of the United States. In Mr. Alexander's case (2 Wallace, 419) the present able Chief Justice, delivering the opinion of the court, says:

"We must be governed by the principle of public law so often announced from this bench as applicable to civil and international wars, that all the people of each State or district in insurrection against the United States must be regarded as enemies until by the action of the Legislature and Executive, or otherwise, that relation is thoroughly and permanently changed."

After such clear and repeated decisions it is something worse than ridiculous to hear men of respectable standing attempting to nullify the law of nations, and declare the Supreme Court of the United States in error, because, as the Constitution forbids it, the States could not go out of the Union in fact. A respectable gentleman was lately reciting this argument, when he suddenly stopped and said, "Did you hear of that atrocious murder committed in our town? A rebel deliberately murdered a Government official." The person addressed said, "I think you are mistaken." "How so? I saw it myself." "You are wrong, no murder was or could be committed, for the law forbids it."

The theory that the rebel States, for four years a separate power and without representation in Congress, were all the time here in the Union, is a good deal less ingenious and respectable than the metaphysics of Berkeley, which proved that neither the world nor any human being was in existence. If this theory were simply ridiculous it could be forgiven; but its effect is deeply injurious to the stability of the nation. I cannot doubt that the late confederate States are out of the Union to all intents and purposes for which the conqueror may choose so to consider them.

But on the ground of estoppel, the United States have the clear right to elect to adjudge them out of the Union. They are estopped both by matter of record and matter *in pais.* One of the first resolutions passed by seceded South Carolina in January, 1861, is as follows.

> "*Resolved, unanimously,* That the separation of South Carolina from the Federal Union is final, and she has no further interest in the Constitution of the United States; and that the only appropriate negotiations between her and the Federal Government are as to their mutual relations as foreign States."

Similar resolutions appear upon all their State and confederate government records. The speeches of their members of congress, their generals and executive officers, and the answers of their government to our shameful sueings for peace, went upon the defiant ground that no terms would be offered or received except upon the prior acknowledgment of the entire and permanent independence of the confederate States. After this, to deny that we have a right to treat them as a conquered belligerent, severed from the Union in fact, is not argument but mockery. Whether it be our interest to do so is the only question hereafter and more deliberately to be considered.

But suppose these powerful but now subdued belligerents, instead of being out of the Union, are merely destroyed, and are now lying about, a dead corpse, or with animation so suspended as to be incapable of action, and wholly unable to heal themselves by any unaided movements of their own. Then they may fall under the provision of the Constitution which says "the United States shall guaranty to every State in the Union a republican form of government." Under that power can the judiciary, or the President, or the Commander-in-Chief of the Army, or the Senate or House of Representatives, acting separately, restore them to life and readmit them into the Union? I insist that if each acted separately, though the action of each was identical with all the others, it would amount to nothing. Nothing but the joint action of the two Houses of Congress and the concurrence of the President could do it. If the Senate admitted their Senators, and the House their members, it would have no effect on the future action of Congress. The Fortieth Congress might reject both. Such is the ragged record of Congress for the last four years.

In Luther *vs.* Borden (7 Howard, 1–42) the Supreme Court say:

> "Under this article of the Constitution [the one above cited] it rests with Congress to decide what government is the established one in a State. For as the United States guaranty to each State a republican government, Congress must necessarily decide what government is established in the State before it can determine whether it is republican or not."

Congress alone can do it. But Congress does not mean the Senate, or the House of Representatives, and President, all acting severally. Their joint action constitutes Congress. Hence a law of Congress must be passed before any new State can be admitted; or any dead ones revived. Until then no member can be lawfully admitted into either House. Hence it appears with how little knowledge of constitutional law each branch is urged to admit members separately from these destroyed States. The provision that "each House shall be the judge of the elections, returns, and qualifications of its own members," has not the most distant bearing on this question. Congress must create States and declare when they are entitled to be represented. Then each House must judge whether the members presenting themselves from a recognized State possess the requisite qualifications of age, residence, and citizenship; and whether the election and returns are according to law. The Houses, separately, can judge of nothing else. It seems amazing that any man of legal education could give it any larger meaning.

It is obvious from all this that the first duty of Congress is to pass a law declaring the condition of these outside or defunct States, and providing proper civil governments for them. Since the conquest they have been governed by martial law. Military rule is necessarily despotic, and ought not to exist longer than is absolutely necessary. As there are no symptoms that the people of these provinces will be prepared to participate in constitutional government for some years, I know of no arrangement so proper for them as territorial governments. There they can learn the principles of freedom and eat the fruit of foul rebellion. Under such governments, while electing members to the Territorial Legislatures, they will necessarily mingle with those to whom Congress shall extend the right of suffrage. In Territories Congress fixes the qualifications of electors; and I know of no better place nor better occasion for the conquered rebels and the conqueror to practice justice to all men, and accustom themselves to make and to obey equal laws.

As these fallen rebels cannot at their option reënter the heaven which they have disturbed, the garden of Eden which they have deserted, and flaming swords are set at the gates to secure their exclusion, it becomes important to the welfare of the nation to inquire when the doors shall be reopened for their admission.

According to my judgment they ought never to be recognized as capable of acting in the Union, or of being counted as valid States, until the Constitution shall have been so amended as to make it what its framers intended; and so as to secure perpetual ascendency to the party of the Union; and so as to render our republican Government firm and stable forever. The first of those amendments is to change the basis of representation among the States from Federal numbers to actual voters. Now all the colored freemen in the slave States, and three fifths of the slaves, are represented, though none of them have votes. The States have nineteen representatives of colored slaves. If the slaves are now free then they can add, for the other two fifths, thirteen more, making the slave representation thirty-two. I suppose the free blacks in those States will give at least five more, making the representation of non-voting people of color about thirty-seven. The whole number of representatives now from the slave States is seventy. Add the other two fifths and it will be eighty-three.

If the amendment prevails, and those States withhold the right of suffrage from persons of color, it will deduct about thirty-seven, leaving them but forty-six. With the basis unchanged, the eighty-three southern members, with the Democrats that will in the best times be elected from the North, will always give them a majority in Congress and in the Electoral College. They will at the very first election take possession of the White House and the halls of Congress. I need not depict the ruin that would follow. Assumption of the rebel debt or repudiation of the Federal debt would be sure to follow. The oppression of the freedmen; the reamendment of their State constitutions, and the reëstablishment of slavery would be the inevitable result. That they would scorn and disregard their present constitutions, forced upon them in the midst of martial law, would be both natural and just. No one who has any regard for freedom of elections can look upon those governments, forced upon them in duress, with any favor. If they should grant the right of suffrage to persons of color, I think there would always be Union white men enough in the South, aided by the blacks, to divide the representation, and thus continue the Republican ascendency. If they should refuse to thus alter their election laws it would reduce the representatives of the late slave States to about forty-five and render them powerless for evil.

It is plain that this amendment must be consummated before the defunct States are admitted to be capable of State action, or it never can be.

The proposed amendment to allow Congress to lay a duty on exports is precisely in the same situation. Its importance cannot well be overstated. It is very obvious that for many years the South will not pay much under our internal revenue laws. The only article on which we can raise any considerable amount is cotton. It will be grown largely at once. With ten cents a pound export duty it would be furnished cheaper to foreign markets than they could obtain it from any other part of the world. The late war has shown that. Two million bales exported, at five hundred pounds to the bale, would yield $100,000,000. This seems to be the chief revenue we shall ever derive from the South. Besides, it would be a protection to that amount to our domestic manufacturers. Other proposed amendments—to make all laws uniform; to prohibit the assumption of the rebel debt—are of vital importance, and the only thing that can prevent the combined forces of copperheads and secessionists from legislating against the interests of the Union whenever they may obtain an accidental majority.

But this is not all that we ought to do before these inveterate rebels are invited to participate in our legislation. We have turned, or are about to turn, loose four million slaves without a hut to shelter them or a cent in their pockets. The infernal laws of slavery have prevented them from acquiring an education, understanding the commonest laws of contract, or of managing the ordinary business of life. This Congress is bound to provide for them until they can take care of themselves. If we do not furnish them with homesteads, and hedge them around with protective laws; if we leave them to the legislation of their late masters, we had better have left them in bondage. Their condition would be worse than that of our prisoners at Andersonville. If we fail in this great duty now, when we have the power, we shall deserve and receive the execration of history and of all future ages.

Two things are of vital importance.

1. So to establish a principle that none of the rebel States shall be counted in any of the amendments of the Constitution until they are duly admitted into the family of States by the lawmaking power of their conqueror. For more than six months the amendment of the Constitution abolishing slavery has been ratified by the Legislatures of three fourths of the States that acted on its passage by Congress, and which had Legislatures, or which were States capable of acting, or required to act, on the question.

I take no account of the aggregation of whitewashed rebels, who without any legal authority have assembled in the capitals of the late rebel States and simulated legislative bodies. Nor do I regard with any respect the cunning by-play into which they deluded the Secretary of State by frequent telegraphic announcements that "South Carolina had adopted the amendment;" "Alabama has adopted the amendment, being the twenty-seventh State," &c. This was intended to delude the people, and accustom Congress to hear repeated the names of these extinct States as if they were alive; when, in truth, they have now no more existence than the revolted cities of Latium, two

thirds of whose people were colonized and their property confis-
cated, and their right of citizenship withdrawn by conquering and
avenging Rome.

2. It is equally important to the stability of this Republic that it
should now be solemnly decided what power can revive, recreate,
and reinstate these provinces into the family of States, and invest
them with the rights of American citizens. It is time that Congress
should assert its sovereignty, and assume something of the dignity of
a Roman senate. It is fortunate that the President invites Congress to
take this manly attitude. After stating with great frankness in his able
message his theory, which, however, is found to be impracticable,
and which I believe very few now consider tenable, he refers the
whole matter to the judgment of Congress. If Congress should fail
firmly and wisely to discharge that high duty it is not the fault of the
President.

This Congress owes it to its own character to set the seal of repro-
bation upon a doctrine which is becoming too fashionable, and
unless rebuked will be the recognized principle of our Government.
Governor Perry and other provisional governors and orators proclaim that "this is the white man's Government." The whole copperhead party, pandering to the lowest prejudices of the ignorant, repeat
the cuckoo cry, "This is the white man's Government." Demagogues
of all parties, even some high in authority, gravely shout, "This is the
white man's Government." What is implied by this? That one race of
men are to have the exclusive right forever to rule this nation, and to
exercise all acts of sovereignty, while all other races and nations and
colors are to be their subjects, and have no voice in making the laws
and choosing the rulers by whom they are to be governed. Wherein
does this differ from slavery except in degree? Does not this contradict all the distinctive principles of the Declaration of Independence?
When the great and good men promulgated that instrument, and
pledged their lives and sacred honors to defend it, it was supposed
to form an epoch in civil government. Before that time it was held
that the right to rule was vested in families, dynasties, or races, not
because of superior intelligence or virtue, but because of a divine
right to enjoy exclusive privileges.

Our fathers repudiated the whole doctrine of the legal superiority
of families or races, and proclaimed the equality of men before the

law. Upon that they created a revolution and built the Republic. They were prevented by slavery from perfecting the superstructure whose foundation they had thus broadly laid. For the sake of the Union they consented to wait, but never relinquished the idea of its final completion. The time to which they looked forward with anxiety has come. It is our duty to complete their work. If this Republic is not now made to stand on their great principles, it has no honest foundation, and the Father of all men will still shake it to its center. If we have not yet been sufficiently scourged for our national sin to teach us to do justice to all God's creatures, without distinction of race or color, we must expect the still more heavy vengeance of an offended Father, still increasing his inflictions as he increased the severity of the plagues of Egypt until the tyrant consented to do justice.

And when that tyrant repented of his reluctant consent, and attempted to reënslave the people, as our southern tyrants are attempting to do now, he filled the Red sea with broken chariots and drowned horses, and strewed the shores with dead carcasses.

Mr. Chairman, I trust the Republican party will not be alarmed at what I am saying. I do not profess to speak their sentiments, nor must they be held responsible for them. I speak for myself, and take the responsibility, and will settle with my intelligent constituents.

This is not a "white man's Government," in the exclusive sense in which it is used. To say so is political blasphemy, for it violates the fundamental principles of our gospel of liberty. This is man's Government; the Government of all men alike; not that all men will have equal power and sway within it. Accidental circumstances, natural and acquired endowment and ability, will vary their fortunes. But equal rights to all the privileges of the Government is innate in every immortal being, no matter what the shape or color of the tabernacle which it inhabits.

If equal privileges were granted to all, I should not expect any but white men to be elected to office for long ages to come. The prejudice engendered by slavery would not soon permit merit to be preferred to color. But it would still be beneficial to the weaker races. In a country where political divisions will always exist, their power, joined with just white men, would greatly modify, if it did not entirely prevent, the injustice of majorities. Without the right of suffrage in the late slave States, (I do not speak of the free States,) I believe the slaves had far better been left in bondage. I see it stated that very distinguished advocates of the right of suffrage lately declared in this city that they do not expect to obtain it by congressional legislation, but only by administrative action, because, as one gallant gentleman said, the States had not been out of the Union. Then they will never get it. The President is far sounder than they. He sees that administrative action has nothing to do with it. If it ever is to come, it must be constitutional amendments or congressional action in the Territories, and in enabling acts.

How shameful that men of influence should mislead and miseducate the public mind! They proclaim, "This is the white man's Government," and the whole coil of copperheads echo the same sentiment, and upstart, jealous Republicans join the cry. Is it any wonder ignorant foreigners and illiterate natives should learn this doctrine, and be led to despise and maltreat a whole race of their fellow-men?

Sir, this doctrine of a white man's Government is as atrocious as the infamous sentiment that damned the late Chief Justice to everlasting fame; and, I fear, to everlasting fire.

CHAPTER 25

OPPOSITION TO THE
RECONSTRUCTION ACT

Andrew Johnson: Veto Message, March 2, 1867

*A*ndrew Johnson (1808–1875), a Southerner and a War Democrat, was elected to the vice presidency in 1864 on Lincoln's coalition Union ticket. On Lincoln's death, Johnson had to assume the difficult task of leading the nation through the intricate paths of Reconstruction. Convinced that reconstruction policy was the responsibility of the executive and that it should be formulated with the end of restoring normal relations between North and South as soon as possible, Johnson found himself at odds with the Congressional Radicals almost from the beginning of his Presidency. His weapon against Congress was the Presidential veto power, but it proved to be an ineffective weapon as the Radicals were able to muster enough support to override Johnson's objections. Early in 1867 Congress passed a comprehensive Reconstruction Act, embodying the Radical program and purportedly outlining the steps by which the Southern states might be readmitted to the Union. The bill divided the ten unreconstructed states (excluding Tennessee) into five military districts, each to be commanded by a Federal officer. The existing state governments were to be reorganized under the supervision of the military officer, who was granted sweeping, arbitrary powers, on the basis of Negro suffrage and the disfranchisement of ex-Confederates. On March 2, 1867 President Johnson vetoed the bill and, in the message that follows, discussed his objections to it. The bill was promptly passed over his veto.

WASHINGTON, *March 2, 1867.*

To the house of representatives:

I have examined the bill "to provide for the more efficient government of the rebel States" with the care and anxiety which its transcendent importance is calculated to awaken. I am unable to give it my assent, for reasons so grave that I hope a statement of them may have some influence on the minds of the patriotic and enlightened men with whom the decision must ultimately rest.

The bill places all the people of the ten States therein named under the absolute domination of military rulers; and the preamble undertakes to give the reason upon which the measure is based and the ground upon which it is justified. It declares that there exists in those States no legal governments and no adequate protection for life or property, and asserts the necessity of enforcing peace and good order within their limits. Is this true as matter of fact?

It is not denied that the States in question have each of them an actual government, with all the powers—executive, judicial, and legislative—which properly belong to a free state. They are organized like the other States of the Union, and, like them, they make, administer, and execute the laws which concern their domestic affairs. An existing *de facto* government, exercising such functions as these, is itself the law of the state upon all matters within its jurisdiction. To pronounce the supreme law-making power of an established state illegal is to say that law itself is unlawful.

The provisions which these governments have made for the preservation of order, the suppression of crime, and the redress of private injuries are in substance and principle the same as those which prevail in the Northern States and in other civilized countries. They certainly have not succeeded in preventing the commission of all crime, nor has this been accomplished anywhere in the world. There, as well as elsewhere, offenders sometimes escape for want of vigorous prosecution, and occasionally, perhaps, by the inefficiency of courts or the prejudice of jurors. It is undoubtedly true that these evils have been much increased and aggravated, North and South, by the demoralizing influences of civil war and by the rancorous passions which the contest has engendered. But that these people are maintaining local governments for themselves which habitually defeat the object of all government and render their own lives and property insecure is in itself utterly improbable, and the averment of the bill to that effect is not supported by any evidence which has come to my knowledge. All the information I have on the subject convinces me that the masses of the Southern people and those who control their public acts, while they entertain diverse opinions on questions of Federal policy, are completely united in the effort to reorganize their society on the basis of peace and to restore their mutual prosperity as rapidly and as completely as their circumstances will permit.

The bill, however, would seem to show upon its face that the establishment of peace and good order is not its real object. The fifth section declares that the preceding sections shall cease to operate in any State where certain events shall have happened. These events are, first, the selection of delegates to a State convention by an election at which negroes shall be allowed to vote; second, the formation of a State constitution by the convention so chosen; third, the insertion into the State constitution of a provision which will secure the right of voting at all elections to negroes and to such white men as may not be disfranchised for rebellion or felony; fourth, the submission of the constitution for ratification to negroes and white men not disfranchised, and its actual ratification by their vote; fifth, the submission of the State constitution to Congress for examination and approval, and the actual approval of it by that body; sixth, the adoption of a certain amendment to the Federal Constitution by a vote of the legislature elected under the new constitution; seventh, the adoption of said amendment by a sufficient number of other States to make it a part of the Constitution of the United States. All these conditions must be fulfilled before the people of any of these States can be relieved from the bondage of military domination; but when they are fulfilled, then immediately the pains and penalties of the bill are to cease, no matter whether there be peace and order or not, and without any reference to the security of life or property. The excuse given for the bill in the preamble is admitted by the bill itself not to be real. The military rule which it establishes is plainly to be used, not for any purpose of order or for the prevention of crime, but solely as a means of coercing the people into the adoption of principles and measures to which it is known that they are opposed, and upon which they have an undeniable right to exercise their own judgment.

I submit to Congress whether this measure is not in its whole character, scope, and object without precedent and without authority, in palpable conflict with the plainest provisions of the Constitution, and utterly destructive to those great principles of liberty and humanity for which our ancestors on both sides of the Atlantic have shed so much blood and expended so much treasure.

The ten States named in the bill are divided into five districts. For each district an officer of the Army, not below the rank of a brigadier-general, is to be appointed to rule over the people; and he is to be supported with an efficient military force to enable him to perform his duties and enforce his authority. Those duties and that authority, as defined by the third section of the bill, are "to protect all persons in their rights of person and property, to suppress insurrection, disorder, and violence, and to punish or cause to be punished all disturbers of the public peace or criminals." The power thus given to the commanding officer over all the people of each district is that of an absolute monarch. His mere will is to take the place of all law. The law of the States is now the only rule applicable to the subjects placed under his control, and that is completely displaced by the clause which declares all interference of State authority to be null and void. He alone is permitted to determine what are rights of person or property, and he may protect them in such way as in his discretion may seem proper. It places at his free disposal all the lands and goods in his district, and he may distribute them without let or hindrance to whom he pleases. Being bound by no State law, and there being no other law to regulate the subject, he may make a criminal code of his own; and he can make it as bloody as any recorded in history, or he can reserve the privilege of acting upon the impulse of his private passions in each case that arises. He is bound by no rules of evidence; there is, indeed, no provision by which he is authorized or required to take any evidence at all. Everything is a crime which he chooses to call so, and all persons are condemned whom he pronounces to be guilty. He is not bound to keep any record or make any report of his proceedings. He may arrest his victims wherever he finds them, without warrant, accusation, or proof of probable cause. If he gives them a trial before he inflicts the punishment, he gives it of his grace and mercy, not because he is commanded so to do.

To a casual reader of the bill it might seem that some kind of trial was secured by it to persons accused of crime, but such is not the case. The officer "may allow local civil tribunals to try offenders," but of course this does not require that he shall do so. If any State or Federal court presumes to exercise its legal jurisdiction by the trial of a malefactor without his special permission, he can break it up and punish the judges and jurors as being themselves malefactors. He can save his friends from justice, and despoil his enemies contrary to justice.

It is also provided that "he shall have power to organize military commissions or tribunals;" but this power he is not commanded to exercise. It is merely permissive, and is to be used only "when in his judgment it may be necessary for the trial of offenders." Even if the sentence of a commission were made a prerequisite to the punishment of a party, it would be scarcely the slightest check upon the officer, who has authority to organize it as he pleases, prescribe its mode of proceeding, appoint its members from his own subordinates, and revise all its decisions. Instead of mitigating the harshness of his single rule, such a tribunal would be used much more probably to divide the responsibility of making it more cruel and unjust.

Several provisions dictated by the humanity of Congress have been inserted in the bill, apparently to restrain the power of the commanding officer; but it seems to me that they are of no avail for that purpose. The fourth section provides: First. That trials shall not be unnecessarily delayed; but I think I have shown that the power is given to punish without trial; and if so, this provision is practically inoperative. Second. Cruel or unusual punishment is not to be inflicted; but who is to decide what is cruel and what is unusual? The words have acquired a legal meaning by long use in the courts. Can it be expected that military officers will understand or follow a rule expressed in language so purely technical and not pertaining in the least degree to their profession? If not, then each officer may define cruelty according to his own temper, and if it is not usual he will make it usual. Corporal punishment, imprisonment, the gag, the ball and chain, and all the almost insupportable forms of torture invented for military punishment lie within the range of choice. Third. The sentence of a commission is not to be executed without being approved by the commander, if it affects life or liberty, and a sentence of death must be approved by the President. This applies to cases in which there has been a trial and sentence. I take it to be clear, under this bill, that the military commander may condemn to death without even the form of a trial by a military commission, so that the life of the condemned may depend upon the will of two men instead of one.

It is plain that the authority here given to the military officer amounts to absolute despotism. But to make it still more unendurable, the bill provides that it may be delegated to as many subordinates as he chooses to appoint, for it declares that he shall "punish

or cause to be punished." Such a power has not been wielded by any
monarch in England for more than five hundred years. In all that
time no people who speak the English language have borne such
servitude. It reduces the whole population of the ten States—all persons, of every color, sex, and condition, and every stranger within
their limits—to the most abject and degrading slavery. No master
ever had a control so absolute over the slaves as this bill gives to the
military officers over both white and colored persons. . . .

I come now to a question which is, if possible, still more important. Have we the power to establish and carry into execution a measure like this? I answer, Certainly not, if we derive our authority from
the Constitution and if we are bound by the limitations which it
imposes.

This proposition is perfectly clear, that no branch of the Federal
Government—executive, legislative, or judicial—can have any just
powers except those which it derives through and exercises under
the organic law of the Union. Outside of the Constitution we have no
legal authority more than private citizens, and within it we have only
so much as that instrument gives us. This broad principle limits all
our functions and applies to all subjects. It protects not only the citizens of States which are within the Union, but it shields every human
being who comes or is brought under our jurisdiction. We have no
right to do in one place more than in another that which the Constitution says we shall not do at all. If, therefore, the Southern States
were in truth out of the Union, we could not treat their people in a
way which the fundamental law forbids.

Some persons assume that the success of our arms in crushing the
opposition which was made in some of the States to the execution of
the Federal laws reduced those States and all their people—the innocent as well as the guilty—to the condition of vassalage and gave us a
power over them which the Constitution does not bestow or define or
limit. No fallacy can be more transparent than this. Our victories subjected the insurgents to legal obedience, not to the yoke of an arbitrary
despotism. When an absolute sovereign reduces his rebellious subjects,
he may deal with them according to his pleasure, because he had that
power before. But when a limited monarch puts down an insurrection,
he must still govern according to law. If an insurrection should take
place in one of our States against the authority of the State government

and end in the overthrow of those who planned it, would that take away the rights of all the people of the counties where it was favored by a part or a majority of the population? Could they for such a reason be wholly outlawed and deprived of their representation in the legislature? I have always contended that the Government of the United States was sovereign within its constitutional sphere; that it executed its laws, like the States themselves, by applying its coercive power directly to individuals, and that it could put down insurrection with the same effect as a State and no other. The opposite doctrine is the worst heresy of those who advocated secession, and can not be agreed to without admitting that heresy to be right.

Invasion, insurrection, rebellion, and domestic violence were anticipated when the Government was framed, and the means of repelling and suppressing them were wisely provided for in the Constitution; but it was not thought necessary to declare that the States in which they might occur should be expelled from the Union. Rebellions, which were invariably suppressed, occurred prior to that out of which these questions grow; but the States continued to exist and the Union remained unbroken. In Massachusetts, in Pennsylvania, in Rhode Island, and in New York, at different periods in our history, violent and armed opposition to the United States was carried on; but the relations of those States with the Federal Government were not supposed to be interrupted or changed thereby after the rebellious portions of their population were defeated and put down. It is true that in these earlier cases there was no formal expression of a determination to withdraw from the Union, but it is also true that in the Southern States the ordinances of secession were treated by all the friends of the Union as mere nullities and are now acknowledged to be so by the States themselves. If we admit that they had any force or validity or that they did in fact take the States in which they were passed out of the Union, we sweep from under our feet all the grounds upon which we stand in justifying the use of Federal force to maintain the integrity of the Government.

This is a bill passed by Congress in time of peace. There is not in any one of the States brought under its operation either war or insurrection. The laws of the States and of the Federal Government are all in undisturbed and harmonious operation. The courts, State and Federal, are open and in the full exercise of their proper authority. Over every State comprised in these five military districts, life, liberty, and property are secured by State laws and Federal laws, and the National Constitution is everywhere in force and everywhere obeyed. What, then, is the ground on which this bill proceeds? The title of the bill announces that it is intended "for the more efficient government" of these ten States. It is recited by way of preamble that no legal State governments "nor adequate protection for life or property" exist in those States, and that peace and good order should be thus enforced. The first thing which arrests attention upon these recitals, which prepare the way for martial law, is this, that the only foundation upon which martial law can exist under our form of government is not stated or so much as pretended. Actual war, foreign invasion, domestic insurrection—none of these appear; and none of these, in fact, exist. It is not even recited that any sort of war or insurrection is threatened. Let us pause here to consider, upon this question of constitutional law and the power of Congress, a recent decision of the Supreme Court of the United States in *ex parte* Milligan.

I will first quote from the opinion of the majority of the court:

> Martial law can not arise from a threatened invasion. The necessity must be actual and present, the invasion real, such as effectually closes the courts and deposes the civil administration.

We see that martial law comes in only when actual war closes the courts and deposes the civil authority; but this bill, in time of peace, makes martial law operate as though we were in actual war, and becomes the *cause* instead of the *consequence* of the abrogation of civil authority. One more quotation:

> It follows from what has been said on this subject that there are occasions when martial law can be properly applied. If in foreign invasion or civil war the courts are actually closed, and it is impossible to administer criminal justice according to law, *then*, on the theater of active military operations, where war really prevails, there is a necessity to furnish a substitute for the civil authority thus overthrown, to preserve the safety of the army and society; and as no power is left but the military, it is allowed to govern by martial rule until the laws can have their free course.

I now quote from the opinion of the minority of the court, delivered by Chief Justice Chase:

We by no means assert that Congress can establish and apply the laws of war where no war has been declared or exists. Where peace exists, the laws of peace must prevail.

This is sufficiently explicit. Peace exists in all the territory to which this bill applies. It asserts a power in Congress, in time of peace, to set aside the laws of peace and to substitute the laws of war. The minority, concurring with the majority, declares that Congress does not possess that power. Again, and, if possible, more emphatically, the Chief Justice, with remarkable clearness and condensation, sums up the whole matter as follows:

> There are under the Constitution three kinds of military jurisdiction—one to be exercised both in peace and war; another to be exercised in time of foreign war without the boundaries of the United States, or in time of rebellion and civil war within States or districts occupied by rebels treated as belligerents; and a third to be exercised in time of invasion or insurrection within the limits of the United States, or during rebellion within the limits of the States maintaining adhesion to the National Government, when the public danger requires its exercise. The first of these may be called jurisdiction under military law, and is found in acts of Congress prescribing rules and articles of war or otherwise providing for the government of the national forces; the second may be distinguished as military government, superseding as far as may be deemed expedient the local law, and exercised by the military commander under the direction of the President, with the express or implied sanction of Congress; while the third may be denominated martial law proper, and is called into action by Congress, or temporarily, when the action of Congress can not be invited, and in the case of justifying or excusing peril, by the President, in times of insurrection or invasion or of civil or foreign war, within districts or localities where ordinary law no longer adequately secures public safety and private rights.

It will be observed that of the three kinds of military jurisdiction which can be exercised or created under our Constitution there is but one that can prevail in time of peace, and that is the code of laws enacted by Congress for the government of the national forces. That body of military law has no application to the citizen, nor even to the citizen soldier enrolled in the militia in time of peace. But this bill is not a part of that sort of military law, for that applies only to the soldier and not to the citizen, whilst, contrariwise, the military law provided by this bill applies only to the citizen and not to the soldier.

I need not say to the representatives of the American people that their Constitution forbids the exercise of judicial power in any way but one—that is, by the ordained and established courts. It is equally well known that in all criminal cases a trial by jury is made indispensable by the express words of that instrument. I will not enlarge on the inestimable value of the right thus secured to every freeman or speak of the danger to public liberty in all parts of the country which must ensue from a denial of it anywhere or upon any pretense. A very recent decision of the Supreme Court has traced the history, vindicated the dignity, and made known the value of this great privilege so clearly that nothing more is needed. To what extent a violation of it might be excused in time of war or public danger may admit of discussion, but we are providing now for a time of profound peace, when there is not an armed soldier within our borders except those who are in the service of the Government. It is in such a condition of things that an act of Congress is proposed which, if carried out, would deny a trial by the lawful courts and juries to 9,000,000 American citizens and to their posterity for an indefinite period. It seems to be scarcely possible that anyone should seriously believe this consistent with a Constitution which declares in simple, plain, and unambiguous language that all persons shall have that right and that no person shall ever in any case be deprived of it. The Constitution also forbids the arrest of the citizen without judicial warrant, founded on probable cause. This bill authorizes an arrest without warrant, at the pleasure of a military commander. The Constitution declares that "no person shall be held to answer for a capital or otherwise infamous crime unless on presentment by a grand jury." This bill holds every person not a soldier answerable for all crimes and all charges without any presentment. The Constitution declares that "no person shall be deprived of life, liberty, or property without due process of law." This bill sets aside all process of law, and makes the citizen answerable in his person and property to the will of one man, and as to his life to the will of two. Finally, the Constitution declares that "the privilege of the writ of *habeas corpus* shall not be suspended unless when, in case of rebellion or invasion, the public safety may require it;" whereas this bill declares martial law (which of itself suspends this great writ) in time of peace, and authorizes the military to make the arrest, and gives to the prisoner only one privilege, and that is a trial "without unnecessary delay." He has no hope of release from custody, except the hope, such as it is, of release by acquittal before a military commission.

The United States are bound to guarantee to each State a republican form of government. Can it be pretended that this obligation is not palpably broken if we carry out a measure like this, which wipes away every vestige of republican government in ten States and puts the life, property, liberty, and honor of all the people in each of them under the domination of a single person clothed with unlimited authority?

The Parliament of England, exercising the omnipotent power which it claimed, was accustomed to pass bills of attainder; that is to say, it would convict men of treason and other crimes by legislative enactment. The person accused had a hearing, sometimes a patient and fair one, but generally party prejudice prevailed instead of justice. It often became necessary for Parliament to acknowledge its error and reverse its own action. The fathers of our country determined that no such thing should occur here. They withheld the power from Congress, and thus forbade its exercise by that body, and they provided in the Constitution that no State should pass any bill of attainder. It is therefore impossible for any person in this country to be constitutionally convicted or punished for any crime by a legislative proceeding of any sort. Nevertheless, here is a bill of attainder against 9,000,000 people at once. It is based upon an accusation so vague as to be scarcely intelligible and found to be true upon no credible evidence. Not one of the 9,000,000 was heard in his own defense. The representatives of the doomed parties were excluded from all participation in the trial. The conviction is to be followed by the most ignominious punishment ever inflicted on large masses of men. It disfranchises them by hundreds of thousands and degrades them all, even those who are admitted to be guiltless, from the rank of freemen to the condition of slaves.

The purpose and object of the bill—the general intent which pervades it from beginning to end—is to change the entire structure and character of the State governments and to compel them by force to the adoption of organic laws and regulations which they are unwilling to accept if left to themselves. The negroes have not asked for the privilege of voting; the vast majority of them have no idea what it means. This bill not only thrusts it into their hands, but compels them, as well as the whites, to use it in a particular way. If they do not form a constitution with prescribed articles in it and afterwards elect a legislature which will act upon certain measures in a prescribed way, neither blacks nor whites can be relieved from the slavery which the bill imposes upon them. Without pausing here to consider the policy or impolicy of Africanizing the southern part of our territory, I would simply ask the attention of Congress to that manifest, well-known, and universally acknowledged rule of constitutional law which declares that the Federal Government has no Jurisdiction, authority, or power to regulate such subjects for any State. To force the right of suffrage out of the hands of the white people and into the hands of the negroes is an arbitrary violation of this principle.

This bill imposes martial law at once, and its operations will begin so soon as the general and his troops can be put in place. The dread alternative between its harsh rule and compliance with the terms of this measure is not suspended, nor are the people afforded any time for free deliberation. The bill says to them, take martial law first, then deliberate. And when they have done all that this measure requires them to do other conditions and contingencies over which they have no control yet remain to be fulfilled before they can be relieved from martial law. Another Congress must first approve the Constitution made in conformity with the will of this Congress and must declare these States entitled to representation in both Houses. The whole question thus remains open and unsettled and must again occupy the attention of Congress; and in the meantime the agitation which now prevails will continue to disturb all portions of the people.

The bill also denies the legality of the governments of ten of the States which participated in the ratification of the amendment to the Federal Constitution abolishing slavery forever within the jurisdiction of the United States and practically excludes them from the Union. If this assumption of the bill be correct, their concurrence can not be considered as having been legally given, and the important fact is made to appear that the consent of three-fourths of the States—the requisite number—has not been constitutionally obtained to the ratification of that amendment, thus leaving the question of slavery where it stood before the amendment was officially declared to have become a part of the Constitution.

That the measure proposed by this bill does violate the Constitution in the particulars mentioned and in many other ways which I forbear to enumerate is too clear to admit of the least doubt. It only remains to consider whether the injunctions of that instrument ought to be obeyed or not. I think they ought to be obeyed, for reasons which I will proceed to give as briefly as possible.

In the first place, it is the only system of free government which we can hope to have as a nation. When it ceases to be the rule of our conduct, we may perhaps take our choice between complete anarchy, a consolidated despotism, and a total dissolution of the Union; but national liberty regulated by law will have passed beyond our reach.

It is the best frame of government the world ever saw. No other is or can be so well adapted to the genius, habits, or wants of the American people. Combining the strength of a great empire with unspeakable blessings of local self- government, having a central power to defend the general interests, and recognizing the authority of the States as the guardians of industrial rights, it is "the sheet anchor of our safety abroad and our peace at home." It was ordained "to form a more perfect union, establish justice, insure domestic tranquillity, promote the general welfare, provide for the common defense, and secure the blessings of liberty to ourselves and to our posterity." These great ends have been attained heretofore, and will be again by faithful obedience to it; but they are certain to be lost if we treat with disregard its sacred obligations.

It was to punish the gross crime of defying the Constitution and to vindicate its supreme authority that we carried on a bloody war of four years' duration. Shall we now acknowledge that we sacrificed a million of lives and expended billions of treasure to enforce a Constitution which is not worthy of respect and preservation?

Those who advocated the right of secession alleged in their own justification that we had no regard for law and that their rights of property, life, and liberty would not be safe under the Constitution as administered by us. If we now verify their assertion, we prove that they were in truth and in fact fighting for their liberty, and instead of branding their leaders with the dishonoring name of traitors against a righteous and legal government we elevate them in history to the rank of self-sacrificing patriots, consecrate them to the admiration of the world, and place them by the side of Washington, Hampden, and Sidney. No; let us leave them to the infamy they deserve, punish them as they should be punished, according to law, and take upon ourselves no share of the odium which they should bear alone.

It is a part of our public history which can never be forgotten that both Houses of Congress, in July, 1861, declared in the form of a solemn resolution that the war was and should be carried on for no purpose of subjugation, but solely to enforce the Constitution and laws, and that when this was yielded by the parties in rebellion the contest should cease, with the constitutional rights of the States and of individuals unimpaired. This resolution was adopted and sent forth to the world unanimously by the Senate and with only two dissenting voices in the House. It was accepted by the friends of the Union in the South as well as in the North as expressing honestly and truly the object of the war. On the faith of it many thousands of persons in both sections gave their lives and their fortunes to the cause. To repudiate it now by refusing to the States and to the individuals within them the rights which the Constitution and laws of the Union would secure to them is a breach of our plighted honor for which I can imagine no excuse and to which I can not voluntarily become a party.

The evils which spring from the unsettled state of our Government will be acknowledged by all. Commercial intercourse is impeded, capital is in constant peril, public securities fluctuate in value, peace itself is not secure, and the sense of moral and political duty is impaired. To avert these calamities from our country it is imperatively required that we should immediately decide upon some course of administration which can be steadfastly adhered to. I am thoroughly convinced that any settlement or compromise or plan of action which is inconsistent with the principles of the Constitution will not only be unavailing, but mischievous; that it will but multiply the present evils, instead of removing them. The Constitution, in its whole integrity and vigor, throughout the length and breadth of the land, is the best of all compromises. Besides, our duty does not, in my judgment, leave us a choice between that and any other. I believe that it contains the remedy that is so much needed, and that if the coordinate branches of the Government would unite upon its provisions they would be found broad enough and strong enough to sustain in time of peace the nation which they bore safely through the ordeal of a protracted civil war. Among the most sacred guaranties of that instrument are those which declare that "each State shall have at least one Representative," and that "no State, without its consent, shall be deprived of its equal suffrage in the Senate." Each House is made the "judge of the elections, returns, and qualifications of its own members," and may, "with the concurrence of two-thirds, expel a member." Thus, as heretofore urged, "in the admission of Senators and Representatives from any and all of the States there can be no just ground of apprehension that persons who are disloyal will be clothed with the powers of legislation, for this could not happen when the Constitution and the laws are enforced by a vigilant and faithful Congress." "When a Senator or Representative presents his certificate of election, he may at once be admitted or rejected; or, should there be any question as to his eligibility, his credentials may be referred for investigation to the appropriate committee. If admitted to a seat, it must be upon evidence Satisfactory to the House of which he thus becomes a member that he possesses the requisite constitutional and legal qualifications. If refused admission as a member for want of due allegiance to the Government, and returned to his constituents, they are admonished that none but persons loyal to the United States will be allowed a voice in the legislative councils of the nation, and the political power and moral influence of Congress are thus effectively exerted in the interests of loyalty to the Government and fidelity to the Union." And is it not far better that the work of restoration should be accomplished by simple compliance with the plain requirements of the Constitution than by a recourse to measures which in effect destroy the States and threaten the subversion of the General Government? All that is necessary to settle this simple but important question without further agitation or delay is a willingness on the part of all to sustain the Constitution and carry its provisions into practical operation. If to-morrow either branch of Congress would declare that upon the presentation of their credentials members constitutionally elected and loyal to the General Government would be admitted to seats in Congress, while all others would be excluded and their places remain vacant until the selection by the people of loyal and qualified persons, and if at the same time assurance were given that this policy would be continued until all the States were represented in Congress, it would send a thrill of joy throughout the entire land, as indicating the inauguration of a system which must speedily bring tranquillity to the public mind.

While we are legislating upon subjects which are of great importance to the whole people, and which must affect all parts of the country, not only during the life of the present generation, but for ages to come, we should remember that all men are entitled at least to a hearing in the councils which decide upon the destiny of themselves and their children. At present ten States are denied representation, and when the Fortieth Congress assembles on the 4th day of the present month sixteen States will be without a voice in the House of Representatives. This grave fact, with the important questions before us, should induce us to pause in a course of legislation which, looking solely to the attainment of political ends, fails to consider the rights it transgresses, the law which it violates, or the institutions which it imperils.

CHAPTER 26

The Impeachment Crisis

Congressman George Julian Supports Impeachment, December 11, 1867

The antagonistic relationship between Radical Republicans and President Andrew Johnson was fueled by differing visions of Reconstruction and antagonism over whether the legislative or executive branch should control the South's postwar destiny. Johnson's opposition to Congressionally sponsored Reconstruction, including the Freedmen's Bureau, the civil rights bill, and the Fourteenth Amendment, enraged the Radicals. Over time, they grew to hate him personally, which fueled an effort to remove Johnson through impeachment in 1868. Congressman George W. Julian of Indiana (1817–1899) was among the President's most outspoken opponents and one of the most articulate and vociferous in calling for his impeachment. Speaking on behalf of six members of the Indiana Congressional delegation on December 11, 1867, Julian expressed the view that impeachment was a "solemn duty" in order to safeguard the public welfare. The following year, the House of Representatives charged Johnson with committing "high crimes or misdemeanors." Most of their specific charges involved the President's removal of Secretary of War Edwin M. Stanton, a violation of a law that mandated Senate approval before a President could fire an appointee confirmed by the Senate and replace him with another. Article X charged the President with attempting to "excite the odium and resentment of all the good people of the United States against Congress and the laws by it duly and constitutionally enacted." The votes at Johnson's Senate trial fell one short of conviction.

After the Journal was read, Mr. Julian asked and obtained leave to make a personal explanation, and preliminary thereto had read at the Clerk's desk the following paragraph from the Washington correspondence of the "New York Tribune": —

> Of the fifty-seven members who voted for the resolution it must not be thought that all sincerely desired the impeachment of the

President. The Indiana delegation which voted almost solidly in the affirmative, did so in the belief that some future deed of the President would justify their course. Others voted for impeachment, well knowing that it could not be carried, on the principle that their action would seem bold, and might be quoted with effect in future canvasses. Had the passage of the resolution depended on the votes of these gentlemen they would have been found against it; but there were probably forty men who were convinced that the testimony justified the House in bringing the President to a trial, though they did not undertake to usurp the functions of the Senate in judging of his innocence or guilt.

Mr. Julian then proceeded: —

This is certainly a remarkable display of the freedom of the press, and I must claim the right to refer to that portion of the extract which relates to the Indiana delegation. The writer says we voted for impeachment because we believed "that some future deed of the President would justify" our course. Sir, I do not speculate about the future deeds of the President. I know the past, and in the light of the past the Indiana delegation judged of their duty, and acted. That the President will pause in his career of maladministration and crime I do not for a moment believe. His capacity for evil stands out in frightful disproportion to his other gifts. He is a genius in depravity, and not merely "an obstinate man who means honestly to deal with" the problem of reconstruction. His hoarded malignity and passion have neither been fathomed nor exhausted, and will not be during his term of office. If I may judge of the effect of the President's late message of defiance, acting on the inflammable temper of Southern rebels, and followed swiftly by the strong vote of this House renouncing its jurisdiction over his crimes, I can have no hesitation in believing that a new dispensation of rapine and misrule will be the result. This will be morally and logically inevitable; and while I respectfully commend it to the consideration of gentlemen who voted *against* impeachment, I desire to say in behalf of myself and the five of my colleagues who voted with me that in the vote we gave we assumed no jurisdiction whatever over acts of the President which have not yet transpired. We had neither the right nor the disposition to do this, but were governed by the following among other good and sufficient reasons: —

We voted to impeach the President because he usurped the power to call conventions, set up governments, and decide the qualifications of voters, in seven of the States lately in rebellion.

Because he recognized these governments thus unconstitutionally established by himself as valid civil governments, and condemned and denounced Congress for lawfully exercising the powers and performing the acts which he exercised and performed in violation of law and of the Constitution.

Because he created the office of provisional governor, as a civil office, which is unknown to the Constitution, and appointed to such office in the rebel States notorious traitors, well knowing them to be such, and that they could not enter upon the duties of the office without the crime of perjury.

Because he deliberately trampled under his feet a law of Congress enacted in 1862 prescribing an oath of office, and which law he was sworn to execute, and appointed to offices under the laws of the United States men who were well known to him as traitors, who could not take the oath required.

Because he refused to execute the confiscation laws, and the laws against treason, and by the most monstrous abuse of the pardoning power in innumerable instances has made himself the powerful ally and best friend of the conquered traitors of the South, whose unmatched crimes have thus utterly defied even the ordinary administration of criminal justice.

Because the power of impeachment as defined in the Constitution clearly comprehends *political* offenses, like those of which the President has been proved guilty in the case recently before the House, and would otherwise be an empty and unmeaning mockery, leaving Congress wholly powerless to protect the nation against the most wanton acts of Executive maladministration and lawlessness.

And because, finally, in the language of the majority of the Judiciary Committee, he has "retarded the public prosperity, lessened the public revenues, disordered the business and finances of the country, encouraged insubordination in the people of the States recently in rebellion, fostered sentiments of hostility between different classes of citizens, revived and kept alive the spirit of the rebellion, humiliated the nation, dishonored republican institutions, obstructed the restoration of said

States to the Union, and delayed and postponed the peaceful and fraternal reorganization of the Government of the United States.

Sir, these are some of the reasons which compelled six of the Indiana delegation to vote "solidly in the affirmative." We had no occasion to carry our researches into the future in order to find a justification for our votes. And I desire to say, sir, as emphatically as I can, that under our view of the evidence and the law there was but one alternative left us. We could not allow our sense of duty, under the oaths we have taken, to be swayed by any calculations as to the effect of impeachment upon the finances of the country, or upon our own party relations, or upon the success of the Republican party next year. Neither could we pause to consider whether the impeachment would be sustained in the Senate, or whether it would provoke the President to renewed acts of violence and render him more devil-bent than before. We had nothing whatever to do with considerations of this character. Sir, impeachment is not a policy, but a solemn duty under the Constitution, which expressly provides for its performance. The "New York Tribune" itself says that "impeachment is the constitutional safeguard between the people and a dictatorship. To regard the Presidency as an intact, independent office, responsible only to the moral influence called 'the people,' and to a political mob called 'a convention,' is to make our ruler as absolute as the Emperor of China."

Sir, not to impeach in a case fairly requiring it is itself an act revolutionary and rebellious in its character. So the Indiana delegation believed, and so they acted under their sworn duty of fidelity to the Constitution of the United States. And having so believed and acted they have no apologies to make, no man's pardon to beg, and no favors to ask in any quarter. In common with the fifty-seven members who voted in the affirmative, and the one hundred and eight who voted in the negative, we shall be judged by the people. None of us can "escape history," and for one I am willing to accept its final verdict. I only beg leave to say, in conclusion, that if the leading newspapers of the country had allowed the people to see the report in full of the majority of the Judiciary Committee, the correspondent of the "Tribune" would probably have felt less inclined to volunteer an apology for the Indiana delegation which is as dishonorable to himself as to them.

CHAPTER 27

A WAR HERO BECOMES PRESIDENT

Ulysses S. Grant:
First Inaugural Address, March 4, 1869

*U*lysses S. Grant (1822–1885) served as president for eight years during Reconstruction. A West Point graduate with a lackluster prewar military career, Grant rose to become the nation's most illustrious soldier in wartime, and the architect of a successful strategy to defeat the Confederacy. Grant became president in 1869 at a time when the South was embroiled in violence, and much of the nation was rocked by political divisions including the impeachment of Grant's predecessor. His first inaugural address, March 4, 1869, reveals Grant's good intentions, and his sincere desire to bring peace to the South and voting rights to African American men. His lack of an identifiable political philosophy is also apparent in the speech. Although Grant succeeded in bringing a certain degree of peace to the South and kept the Ku Klux Klan in check, his two terms in office were marked by a series of bribery and kickback scandals, which did not implicate him personally but did reach high levels of his administration.

CITIZENS OF THE UNITED STATES:

Your suffrage having elivated me to the office of President of the United States I have, in conformity with the Constitution of our country, taken the oath of office prescribed therein. I have taken this oath without mental reservation, with the determination to do, to the best of my ability, all that it requires of me. The responsibilities of the position I feel, but accept them without fear. The office come[s] to me unsought, I commence its duties untramelled. I bring to it a conscientious desire, and determination, to fill it, to the best of my ability, to the satisfaction of the people. On all leading questions agitating the public mind I will always express my views to Congress, and urge them according to my judgement, and when I think it advisable, will exercise the constitutional privilege of interposing a veto to defeat measures which I oppose. But all laws will be faithfully executed whether they meet my approval or not. I shall, on all subjects, have a policy to recommend, but none to enforce against the will of the people. Laws are to govern all alike, those opposed to as well as those who favor them. I know no method to secure the repeal of bad or obnoxious laws so effective as their stringent execution.

The country having just emerged from a great rebellion many questions will come before it for settlement, in the next four years, which preceding Administrations have never had to deal with. In meeting these it is desirable that they should be approached calmly, without prejudice, hate or sectional pride; remembering that the greatest good to the greatest number is the object to be attained. This requires security of person, property, and for religious and political opinions in every part of our common country, without regard to local prejudice. All laws to secure these ends will receive my best efforts for their enforcement.

A great debt has been contracted in securing to us, and our posterity, the Union. The payment of this *principle* and *interest*, as well as the return to a specie basis, as soon as it can be accomplished without material detriment to the debtor class, or to the country at large, must be provided for. To protect the national honor every dollar of Government indebtedness should be paid in gold unless otherwise expressly stipulated in the contract. Let it be understood that no repudiator of one farthing of our public debt will be trusted in public place and it will go far towards strengthening a credit which ought to be the best in the world, and will ultimately enable us to replace the debt with bonds bearing less interest than we now pay. To this should be added a faithful collection of [the] revenue, a strict accountability to the Treasury for every dollar collected, and the greatest practicable retrenchment in expenditure, in every department of the government.

When we compare the paying capacity of the country now, with ten states still in poverty from the effects of war, but soon to emerge, I trust, into greater prosperity than ever before, with its paying capacity twenty-five years ago, and calculate what it probably will be twenty-five years hence, who can doubt the feasibility of paying every dollar then with more ease than we now pay for useless luxuries. Why; it looks as if providence had bestowed upon us a strong box,—the precious metals locked up in the sterile mountains of the far West,—which we are now forging the key to unlock, to meet the very contingency that is now upon us.

Ultimately it may be necessary to increase the facilities to reach these riches; and it may be necessary also that the general government should give its aid to secure this access. But that should only be when a dollar of obligation to pay secures precisely the same sort of dollar to use now and not before. Whilst the question of specie payments is in abeyance the prudent business man is careful about contracting debts payable in the distant future. The nation should follow the same rule. A prostrate commerce is to be rebuilt and all industries encouraged.

The young men of the country, those who from their age must be its rulers twenty-five years hence, have a peculiar interest in maintaining the national honor. A moments reflection as to what will be our commanding influence among the nations of the earth, in their day, if they are only true to themselves, should inspire them with national pride. All divisions, geographical, political and religious can join in this common sentiment.

How the public debt is to be paid, or specie payments resumed, is not so important as that a plan should be adopted, and acquiesced in. A united determination to do is worth more than divided counsils upon the method of doing. Legislation on this subject may not be necessary now, nor even advisable, but it will be when the civil law is more fully restored in all parts of the country, and trade resumes its wanted channel.

It will be my endeavor to execute all laws in good faith, to collect all revenues assessed, and to have them properly accounted for, and economically disbursed. I will, to the best of my ability, appoint to office those only who will carry out this design.

In regard to foreign policy I would, deal with nations as equitable law requires individuals to deal with each other, and I would protect the law abiding citizen, whether native or of foreign birth, where ever his rights are jeopardised or the flag of our country floats. I would respect the rights of all nations demanding equal respect for our own; but if others depart from this rule, in their dealings with us, we may be compelled to follow their precede[n]t.

The proper treatment of the original occupants of the land, the Indian, is one deserving of careful study. I will favor any course towards them which tends to their civilization, christianization and ultimate citizenship.

The question of suffrage is one which is likely to agitate the public so long as a portion of the citizens of the nation are excluded from its privileges in any state. It seems to me very desirable that the question should be settled now, and I entertain the hope and express the desire that it may be by the ratification of the fifteenth article of amendment to the Constitution.

In conclusion I ask patient forbearance one towards another throughout the land, and a determined effort on the part of every citizen to do his share towards cementing a happy union, and I ask the prayers of the nation to Almighty God in behalf of this consummation.

CHAPTER 28

REFORMERS CHALLENGE GRANT

Horace Greeley: "They Can't Buy the People"

*After four years in the White House, Ulysses S. Grant had alienated lib-
erals and reformers in his own Republican party because of sensational
bribery scandals in his administration. Many northerners also grew weary of
Reconstruction. Critics of the president and his policies met in convention at
Cincinnati during May 1872 and nominated Horace Greeley for president.
As editor of the* New York Tribune *for thirty years, Greeley (1811–1872)
had championed a variety of reforms including antislavery; thus when the
Democratic party also gave Greeley the nod, white Southern Democrats
found it difficult to support him. It was a low point for the party, which had
never recovered its loss of power and influence in the war period. Nevertheless, Greeley ran a surprisingly strong campaign, delivering speeches in
Ohio, Indiana, and Pennsylvania during an era in which it was considered
unseemly for presidential candidates to campaign personally. Greeley
endorsed a withdrawal of federal troops from the South and civil service
reform. In this speech delivered at Scranton, Pennsylvania, during September 1872, Greeley speaks of "Reconciliation and Reform" and castigates the
Grant administration for patronage abuses. With his formidable strength
among veterans, African Americans, and business interests, President
Grant defeated Greeley by 700,000 votes to win a second term. Greeley died
three weeks later, a bitterly disappointed man.*

Men of Pennsylvania: You will not expect me to address you in
many words, for I have been traveling and speaking for days
past. What seemed best worth saying and most pertinent to the occasion has been said and reported, so that, if you choose to listen to me,
to defer to my words, you will have had an opportunity to do so
already. Let me put, then, as briefly as I may, some few points which
seem to me to demand your attention. You know I have made prominent during my several utterances the question of National Reconciliation and real, genuine peace between section and section, between

class and class, between all portions of the American people. Now, if you choose to say to me that this is not the most important topic of the time, I answer that other topics defer to and stand behind it, are crowded back by it, so that this must be discussed before those can be considered. Questions of labor, questions of taxation, questions of finance, questions of education—all are important, doubtless, and above all are questions of Civil Service Reform. But, when one of these is presented, a side issue is made upon us which overrides and dwarfs it. We say that certain candidates have dishonestly used the public moneys; and we are answered that they were very gallant soldiers, fought well in our late civil war, and that their adversaries did not fight, or fought as they should not have fought. So, then, begin to talk about corrupt legislation or Crédit Mobiliers, whereby the public money is diverted into private pockets, and a debt piled upon the people of the nation and the State, the answer comes at once that the Rebels are all on our side, and that the soldiers must vote as they fought, and so fight down us who are friends of the Rebels. I tell you, friends, that until we have completed this work of National Reconciliation, until we are willing to allow all Americans a fair and equal voice in everything that concerns the well-being and destinies of our country, we cannot have other questions fairly considered at all: wherefore I am for disposing of this, putting out of sight all controversy concerning rebellion, or slaves, or negroes, or the equal rights of man, or anything like this, and, having finished this, we will take up other questions in their order and dispose of them likewise. [Applause.] But this stands in the way.

I will give you, then, a few practical hints on Civil Service Reform, and close. Our adversaries tell us, "Why, we are for Civil Service Reform. Don't you see our platform?" Yes, I say; I see it. What is there is all right, but what you do is quite opposed to it. There is now a great election pending in Pennsylvania; and what do we see? The Secretary of the Treasury is lecturing the people; the Secretary of the Interior, the Postmaster-General, and the Attorney-General, are all out on the stump. All are trying to dragoon the people into an indorsement of their policy and their conduct. I protest that this is in direct defiance of every rational conception of Civil Service Reform. I insist that these great officers, who are drawing their salary from your pockets and mine, and who are paid for faithful attention to the business of the people—I insist that they shall attend to that business, and not be traversing State after State, and trying to twist the people into subserviency to their policy and their retention in office. [Applause.] This is not Civil Service Reform. Well, then, take the next subordinate officers. We cannot expect them to do better than the example set them by their superiors. Hence, there are revenue officers, postmasters, secret service officers, deputies and assistants to these great Secretaries, racing from State to State, from city to city, from county to county, telling their story and trying to make you believe that those of us who differ from them are absolutely Rebels or the friends of Rebels, and therefore to be fought down. I protest that this does violence to all just conceptions of Civil Service Reform. Take now, for instance, my friend Gen. Harriman, who is now harrying your State as he has harried others. He is a Naval Officer of this Government, whose duties should confine him at the port of Boston, where his salary goes on regularly and he goes off just as regularly. In February, if not in January also, he was stumping the State of New-Hampshire. In March, I met him in Connecticut. Then he had a little respite; and very soon after we hear of him, in July, stumping North Carolina; in August stumping the State of Maine, and in September he is traversing the State of Pennsylvania, trying to convince you that everything is lovely, and that his boss and himself ought to be retained in office. If they should be, they should do the duties of office, and earn the salaries of office. But the fact that they are in Pennsylvania and other States proves that they are not—that they cannot be faithfully earning the money they are receiving from the Treasury. [Applause.] Now, then, I demand a real Civil Service Reform. I demand it just as the people in the mighty uprising of 1840 insisted that there should be no reëlection of President, and that office-holders should confine themselves to their duties and let the people take care of elections. These were the watchwords that carried the country in 1840. "Go away with your office-holders, and let the people regulate elections, while you attend to your duties," was the cry that swept over New-York, Pennsylvania, and three-fourths of the States, like a whirlwind. It was a righteous cry, and the people have not yet forgotten its echoes.

THE SIGNS OF VICTORY IN OCTOBER.

Well, now, one word more with regard to what I have seen and felt of popular uprising within the last eight or ten days. It was reported, I do not say how truly, but it was joyfully telegraphed back that I left New-York desponding and sad. I say if that were a fact, I had scarcely crossed the Delaware into Pennsylvania when I met such a joyous, confident, hearty people, that all apprehensions were dispelled. As I went from place to place, at Lancaster, Harrisburg and Altoona, and at that mighty uprising of the people in Pittsburgh, I was not merely restored to confidence and cheerfulness, but I was gloriously upheld and strengthened. Then down through the great State of Ohio. [Cheering.] People of Pennsylvania, some of you have distrusted Ohio. I bid you distrust her no longer. I have looked into the faces of her intelligent, manly people. They are not dismayed by the charges made upon them by Custom-house officers and the head of the Treasury. No matter how many post-office agents ride the State back and forth; no matter how many Inspectors and Supervisors of Revenue there may be hurrying through from end to end, I tell you that the people have resolved that their voices shall be heard and their votes recorded on the side of Reconciliation and Reform. [Applause.] From that State, I passed into Indiana. But why talk of Indiana? Her prairies and her plains are alive with confidence. With cheerful, hearty faith, they say, "Send on your Vice-President, send on your Secretaries, send on your orators, gentlemen of the Renomination party; we can stand them here. Bring them on, no matter how many." They have made up their minds; they have heard, considered, and decided, and I shall be sadly disappointed if the majority for Hendricks as Governor of that State, and the whole Reform ticket, which he heads, is not told by figures nearer 10,000 than 5,000. [Applause.]

Well, fellow-citizens, they have one resource yet left; they have a great deal more money than we have, and they get money a great deal easier than we can. [Laughter.] They can afford to pay for votes; but the people cannot afford to sell them. Their immense Rings, their offices, all the easy ways of making money in the country, are lavishly taxed to fill their party treasury, and money flows over the land in immense streams of corruption. They don't expect to carry this State unless they can buy it; and they cannot carry one of these great States unless they can corrupt and influence voters by money. [Cries of "They can't do it," and cheers.] I tell you, my friends, that is your danger; and I call upon you for a most vigorous organization. Let every man's elbow touch his nearest neighbor's. Let word go from voice to ear throughout the whole State, so that no man is bought. They can buy Legislatures; and they know how they can bribe measures through Congress, for they understand it. They can't buy the people, if there be such organization, such unity of effort, that every man is marked and known, so that when their money goes you can watch it and see what it has done. I charge you not to do what other men are telling you to do. Men say, "Take their money and then vote right against them." No, no; do n't disgrace yourselves in that way. Do n't touch their money. It will poison you if you take it. "Get thee behind me, Satan," must be your reply to every man who offers to buy your vote or purchase your absence from the polls. Stand up to your manhood! Every dollar they put into your pocket for votes they will take out again in taxes and in other ways. [Applause.]

So, friends of Reform in Pennsylvania! I beg you to believe that your brethren in other States, who are to hold elections simultaneously with you, are trying to make their verdict on the side of right as emphatic as your own. [Applause.] They have resolved that whatever joyful news you shall send them on the 8th of October shall be amply duplicated and repaid by the news they shall send you in return. So be earnest, be vigilant. Take hold with resolute purpose to deserve victory and win it, and the shouts of an emancipated country shall drown yours in the cheers of 40,000,000 of free, magnanimous, and honest people.

CHAPTER 29
DEBATE OVER THE
FIFTEENTH AMENDMENT

Meeting of the American Equal Rights Association

For several decades before the Civil War, the antislavery and woman's rights movements were linked by overlapping memberships, similar tactics, and the shared goal of human equality. In 1865, abolitionists and feminists united to found the American Equal Rights Association, an organization dedicated to furthering rights for blacks and women. The organization divided over whether to support civil rights and voting rights for black men as defined in the Fourteenth and Fifteenth Amendments, both of which excluded women. African American activists and some white feminists, believing the needs of blacks in the South to be more urgent than the needs of women, supported these amendments, arguing that women could "wait their turn." Other white feminists contended the proposed amendments were fatally flawed. Their disagreements were aired at a contentious meeting of the organization May 12–14, 1869 in Brooklyn. Ultimately the organization disbanded and two rival suffrage groups took its place.

*M*r. [Frederick] Douglass— . . . I must say that I do not see how any one can pretend that there is the same urgency in giving the ballot to woman as to the negro. With us, the matter is a question of life and death, at least, in fifteen States and the Union. When women, because they are women, are hunted down through the cities of New York and New Orleans; when they are dragged from their houses and hung upon lamp-posts; when their children are torn from their arms, and their brains dashed out upon the pavement; when they are objects of insult and outrage at every turn; when they are in danger of having their homes burnt down over their heads; when their children are not allowed to enter schools; then they will have an urgency to obtain the ballot equal to our own. (Great applause.)

A Voice:—Is that not all true about black women?

374

Mr. Douglass:—Yes, yes, yes; it is true of the black woman, but not because she is a woman, but because she is black. (Applause.) Julia Ward Howe at the conclusion of her great speech delivered at the convention in Boston last year, said: "I am willing that the negro shall get the ballot before me." (Applause) Woman! why, she has 10,000 modes of grappling with her difficulties. I believe that all the virtue of the world can take care of all the evil. I believe that all the intelligence can take care of all the ignorance. (Applause.) I am in favor of woman's suffrage in order that we shall have all the virtue and vice confronted. Let me tell you that when there were few houses in which the black man could have put his head, this wooly head of mine found a refuge in the house of Mrs. Elizabeth Cady Stanton, and if I had been blacker than sixteen midnights, without a single star, it would have been the same. (Applause)

Miss [Susan B.] Anthony:—The old anti-slavery school say women must stand back and wait until the negro shall be recognized. But we say, if you will not give the whole loaf of suffrage to the entire people, give it to the most intelligent first. (Applause.) If intelligence, justice, and morality are to have precedence in the Government, let the question of woman be brought up first and that of the negro last. (Applause.) While I was canvassing the State with petitions and had them filled with names for our cause to the Legislature, a man dared to say to me that the freedom of women are all a theory and not a practical thing. (Applause.) When Mr. Douglass mentioned the black man first and the woman last, if he had noticed he would have seen that it was the men that clapped and not the women. There is not the woman born who desires to eat the bread of dependence, no matter whether it be from the hand of father, husband, or brother; for any one who does so eat her bread places herself in the power of the person from whom she takes it. (Applause.) Mr. Douglass talks about the wrongs of the negro; but with all the outrages that he to-day suffers, he would not exchange his sex and take the place of Elizabeth Cady Stanton. (Laughter and applause.)

Mr. Douglass:—I want to know if granting you the right of suffrage will change the nature of our sexes? (Great laughter.)

Miss Anthony:—It will change the pecuniary position of woman; it will place her where she can earn her own bread. (Loud applause.)

She will not then be driven to such employments only as man chooses for her. . . .

Mrs. Lucy Stone:—Mrs. Stanton will, of course, advocate the precedence for her sex, and Mr. Douglass will strive for the first position for his, and both are perhaps right. If it be true that the government derives its authority from the consent of the governed, we are safe in trusting that principle to the uttermost. If one has a right to say that you can not read and therefore can not vote, then it may be said that you are a woman and therefore can not vote. We are lost if we turn away from the middle principle and argue for one class. I was once a teacher among fugitive slaves. There was one old man, and every tooth was gone, his hair was white, and his face was full of wrinkles, yet, day after day and hour after hour, he came up to the school-house and tried with patience to learn to read, and by-and-by, when he had spelled out the first few verses of the first chapter of the Gospel of St. John, he said to me, "Now, I want to learn to write." I tried to make him satisfied with what he had acquired, but the old man said, "Mrs. Stone, somewhere in the wide world I have a son; I have not heard from him in twenty years; if I should hear from him, I want to write to him, so take hold of my hand and teach me." I did, but before he had proceeded in many lessons, the angels came and gathered him up and bore him to his Father. Let no man speak of an educated suffrage. The gentleman who addressed you claimed that the negroes had the first right to the suffrage, and drew a picture which only his great word-power can do. He again in Massachusetts, when it had cast a majority in favor of [presidential candidate Ulysses S.] Grant and negro suffrage, stood upon the platform and said that woman had better wait for the negro; that is, that both could not be carried, and that the negro had better be the one. But I freely forgave him because he felt as he spoke. But woman suffrage is more imperative than his own; and I want to remind the audience that when he says what the Ku-Kluxes did all over the South, the Ku-Kluxes here in the North in the shape of men, take away the children from the mother, and separate them as completely as if done on the block of the auctioneer. Over in New Jersey they have a law which says that *any* father—he might be the most brutal man that ever existed—*any* father, it says, whether he be under age or not, may by his last will and testament dispose of the custody of his child, born or to be born, and that such disposition shall be good against all persons, and that the mother may not recover her child; and that law modified in form exists over every State in the union except in Kansas. Woman has an ocean of wrongs too deep for any to plummet, and the negro, too has an ocean of wrongs that can not be fathomed. There are two great oceans; in the one is the black man, and in the other is the woman. But I thank God for the XV. Amendment, and hope that it will be adopted in every State. I will be thankful in my soul if *any* body can get out of the terrible pit. But I believe that the safety of the government would be more promoted by the admission of woman as an element of restoration and harmony than the negro. I believe that the influence of woman will save the country before every other power. (Applause.) I see signs of the times pointing to this consummation, and I believe that in some parts of the country women will vote for the President of these United States in 1872. (Applause.)

At the opening of the evening session Henry B. Blackwell presented a series of resolutions.

Resolved, That the extension of suffrage to woman is essential to the public safety and to the establishment and permanence of free institutions; that the admission of woman to political recognition in our national reconstruction is as imperative as the admission of any particular class of men.

Resolved, That as woman, in private life, in the partnership of marriage, is now the conservator of private morals, so woman in public life, in the partnership of a republican State, based upon Universal suffrage, will become the conservator of public morals.

Resolved, That the petitions of more than 200,000 women to Congress and to their State Legislature during the past winter, are expressions of popular sympathy and approval, everywhere throughout the land, and ought to silence the cavil of our opponents that "women do not want to vote."

Resolved, That while we heartily approve of the Fifteenth Amendment, extending suffrage to men, without distinction of race, we nevertheless feel profound regret that Congress has not submitted a parallel amendment for the enfranchisement of women.

Resolved, That any party professing to be democratic in spirit or republican in principle, which opposes or ignores the political rights of woman, is false to its professions, short-sighted in its policy, and unworthy of the confidence of the friends of impartial liberty. . . .

The President, Mrs. *[Elizabeth Cady]* Stanton, argued that not another man should be enfranchised until enough women are admitted to the polls to outweigh those already there. [Applause.] She did not believe in allowing ignorant negroes and foreigners to make laws for her to obey. [Applause.]

Mrs. [Frances Ellen Watkins] Harper (colored) asked Mr. [Henry] Blackwell to read the fifth resolution of the series he submitted, and contended that that covered the whole ground of the resolutions of Mr. Douglass. When it was a question of race, she let the lesser question of sex go. But the white women all go for sex, letting race occupy a minor position. She liked the idea of working women, but she would like to know if it was broad enough to take colored women?

Miss Anthony and several others: Yes, yes.

Mrs. Harper said that when she was at Boston there were sixty women who left work because one colored woman went to gain a livelihood in their midst. [Applause.] If the nation could only handle one question, she would not have the black women put a single straw in the way, if only the men of the race could obtain what they wanted. [Great applause.]

CHAPTER 30

VIOLENCE IN THE
RECONSTRUCTION SOUTH

The Ku Klux Klan Hearings

*W*hite southern opposition to Reconstruction led to the formation of terrorist organizations designed to prevent African Americans from
exercising political rights and rising economically. The Ku Klux Klan
became the most notorious of these organizations. Operating in secret and
lacking headquarters, membership lists, or other means to identify them, the
KKK proved difficult to stop. Local whites often provided accused Klan
members with alibis, or in the case of uncooperative witnesses, succumbed
to threats when asked to testify against them. In 1871 Congress held hearings about Klan violence in the South. This excerpt focuses on the testimony
of Samuel T. Poinier, formerly a soldier in the Union army, who moved to
South Carolina in 1866. Poinier held a patronage position, making him a
"Carpetbagger." While their numbers were small in the South, their presence was often deeply resented by the white population. Poinier's testimony
shows the Klan's methods as well as the difficulty in apprehending them.
Congress took action to stop the Klan by passing the Ku Klux Act in April
1871. This bill gave the president authority to use military force against the
Klan and suspend habeas corpus in locations where terrorists held sway.

Washington, D. C., *June 7*, 1871.

SAMUEL T. POINIER sworn and examined.

By the CHAIRMAN:

Question. Please state in what part of South Carolina you reside.

Answer. In Spartanburg County, the most northern county in the
State.

Question. How long have you resided there?

Answer. Since February, 1866; a little over five years.

Question. From what part of the United States did you go to South
Carolina?

379

Answer. I went there from Louisville, Kentucky.

Question. Please go on and state the public positions which you have occupied in the State, the manner in which you came to hold them, and your knowledge of State affairs, so obtained, down to the present time.

Answer. I went there in 1866 with no intention whatever of remaining, I went entirely from social reasons—to marry—and I was persuaded to remain there. My wife was a native of Charleston, and I found her up in Spartanburg after the war, where a large number of the Charleston people went during the bombardment of the city. She was an invalid, and I remained there. After I had been there probably eight or ten months, the Post Office Department was about to close the post office at Spartanburg. Several appointments had been made, but none of the appointees could take the required test oath. . . . [I] received the appointment.

• • •

After the election was over, and we saw the result, the legislature being filled with colored men, I saw Colonel Farrow and other prominent men there and told them that the only possible way for the people to recover possession of the State was to take right hold of the colored people, and treat them in every respect as the republican party did there. But they would not do anything of that kind. They seemed to be perfectly blind. After that I was United States commissioner. I lost the position of postmaster and deputy collector in the changes which were made. But I held the position of United States commissioner, and had a good deal to do in connection with the revenue troubles which occurred in our county. There has been a good deal of illicit distilling going on there in the mountains bordering on North and South Carolina; and a year ago last spring we were obliged to call in the aid of the military to suppress the illicit distilling. We made one or two expeditions through the mountains and collected a good many stills. The people all seemed to uphold this illicit traffic; there seemed to be an opposition to the enforcement of the law by the United States troops. I was at that time editing a democratic paper there. I was forced to uphold the action of the Government and its officers. I did everything I could in that direction. As a Union man—a man who was born at the North, and who had been in the Army—I found that the only party in the State which recognized the Government or recognized the results of the war in any way was the republican party.

• • •

Just before our last campaign—it was May, a year ago—I went with Governor [James] Orr and a number of the other citizens there and identified myself publicly with the republican party. I made my paper a republican paper. I did everything I could in the last State election for the reëlection of Governor [Robert] Scott and our other State officers. From that time I have been in very deep water.

Question. During the time you were acting as United States commissioner, and in aid of the officers in upholding the revenue laws, were you at any time ordered away?

Answer. Not at that time.

Question. At any time?

Answer. Well, I was ordered away last fall, immediately after our last election, in November. It was soon after the first appearance of this Ku-Klux organization, or whatever it is. Soon after these outrages occurred in our county I received a note ordering me away from there, stating that I must leave the county; that all the soldiers of the United States Army could not enable me to live in Spartanburg. It arose, I presume, from the direct prejudice toward me—the ill-feeling—the feeling of hostility. About sixteen miles from Spartanburg, in Limestone Springs Township, two days prior to our election, a party of disguised men went, at night, and took out two white men and three negroes, one of them a colored woman, and whipped them most brutally. Two of them were managers of the box at that election; and the men told them that if they dared to hold an election at that box they would return and kill them. That was the first appearance of any trouble in the State. I went out there in connection with the magistrate and State constable, and we arrested five parties. I took these two negro men and the colored woman into town. They were afraid to remain where they were. The day after the election I took these colored people to Columbia and showed them to Governor Scott, Senator Robertson, and others. It was just at that time that the Laurens difficulties occurred. It was from that action of mine that the people became so incensed toward me.

Question. Were those persons of whom you spoke in disguise?

Answer. They were all in disguise. One of the colored men who were whipped swore positively as to the identity of some of them, and the parties were arrested, but nothing could ever be done with them; they prov[id]ed an *alibi,* and some of them have since gone to Texas. That was the first outrage that occurred in the State. It was just prior to the last election.

Question. In what month was the election held?

Answer. In October.

Question. Go on and state any similar occurrences in that county since that time, of which you have derived knowledge in your capacity as United States commissioner, and as a citizen of that county.

Answer. Since that time outrages of that nature have occurred every week. Parties of disguised men have ridden through the county almost nightly. They go to a colored man's house, take him out and whip him. They tell him that he must not give any information that he has been whipped. They tell him, moreover, that he must make a public renunciation of his republican principles or they will return and kill him. Just prior to my leaving home an old man came to town on sales day; he was a white man, sixty-eight years of age, who has had no connection whatever with the State government. Coming to town on sales day, he called a few of us together and showed us his back, stating that the Saturday night previous a party of disguised men came to his house, took him out and whipped him, and ordered him to come to town on sales day, and, in the presence of the crowd, publicly renounce his republican principles, and ask for pardon of the people for ever having identified himself with the republican party. He asked us what he should do. There was a lieutenant there in charge of twenty-four men, a little detachment of infantry sent up there on account of the disturbances. This lieutenant told the old man that he would send a squad of men down to his house, if he feared any trouble that night. The men who had whipped him had told him that unless he did this thing they would return and kill him, and that if he gave any information of what had occurred to him, they would kill him. The result was that the old man was obliged to get up there on the court-house steps in the presence of the people of the county and tell them that he was very sorry he had ever acted with the republican party, and hoped they would forgive him for it.

Question. What do you mean by "sales day;" is that the day of your judicial sales?

Answer. Yes, sir; all the sheriff's sales and all the sales by order of the court occur on the first Monday of every month.

Question. Is there a general attendance of the people of the county on those days?

Answer. Yes, sir; a very general attendance; and it was, perhaps, larger on that day. It seemed to be understood among the people, and among the leading citizens of the town, that this old man was to make this public renunciation; for old Mr. Bobo, a prominent lawyer—the oldest lawyer at the bar there—went to the sheriff and asked him to suspend the sales in order that this old man could make his speech before the crowd dispersed. They were all there assembled to hear him; and after he had got through they went up and congratulated him, shook hands with him, welcomed him, and so on.

Question. State the name of this man.

Answer. His name is John Genobles.

Question. Was he a leader among the colored people?

Answer. Not at all; he was a man of no special influence.

Question. He was a white man?

Answer. Yes, sir. Then again it has come to my knowledge officially that a number of negroes are employed in building the air-line railroad which is being constructed between Atlanta, Georgia, and Charlotte, North Carolina; and these disguised men go there to the road, take these negroes out and whip them, and force them from the road back to the farms to labor. They receive higher wages for working on the railroad; and these men go there and force them back to the farms. In one instance an old negro man came to town from Broad River and stated that parties had taken his portion of the crop away and had forced him back to labor with his old master, stating that he was just as much a slave as ever. These parties have complete control of the county. The colored people are all intimidated—subdued. The few prominent white men who are republicans cannot say a word because the people are unprotected. They cannot state these things publicly. I could not do so because I knew that if I did these parties were liable to further ill-treatment—I could not say anything about it.

Question. How many cases of actual violence within the county of Spartanburg have come to your knowledge since the first case of which you spoke? I mean violence inflicted by persons in disguise upon either negroes or white men.

Answer. Well, I suppose there have been fifty or sixty. They are occurring constantly. Little squads of men—I do not believe they are the regular Ku-Klux organization—get together to the number of eight or ten, disguise themselves, go to some negro's house, and whip him. It seems to be an amusement with them. Every Saturday night they go to somebody's house, take him out, and whip him.

Question. Has complaint been made to you in your capacity as United States commissioner?

Answer. No, sir; not in my capacity as United States commissioner. At that time the Ku-Klux bill had not passed, and I had no authority in any way to take cognizance of those matters. But they were all told to me privately; and people consulted me as to what they could do.

Question. As publisher of a newspaper in that town, you did not feel at liberty to give publicity to these cases?

Answer. No, sir; I did not.

Question. For what reason?

Answer. Because the people had no protection. Every one who was whipped was told that if he gave any information of it, the party would return and kill him, or treat him more severely. As there was no protection for these people in any way—the State afforded them none—I would not make known through the press any of these troubles.

Question. What was the result of any proceedings that were instituted in the State courts against parties charged with these offenses?

Answer. There never has been but one case. That was the first case that occurred—the whipping of some colored man. He was examined before a magistrate. On that preliminary examination the party was bound over to appear before the court; I think it was last November. He appeared there; and a number of young men came into court with pistols slung around them. The grand jury found no bill; and they cheered in the court-house when the grand jury made their return. This is the only case that has ever been brought before the courts.

Question. Who cheered?

Answer. These young men broke right out into a hurrah.

Question. Who was the judge of that court?

Answer. At that time Judge Vernon was the judge; he has since resigned.

Question. Did he take any action in regard to a contempt of that kind in his court?

Answer. No, sir.

Question. Were those armed persons who were in the court at that time implicated in the charge?

Answer. No, sir; not directly.

Question. Were they from the neighborhood in which the occurrence took place?

Answer. Yes, sir; they were all from the same neighborhood as the young men who, we have every reason to believe, are connected with these things.

Question. In your statement, a moment ago, did you mean to imply that many of these offenses are committed by persons who are not members of the regular Ku-Klux organization?

Answer. I think so.

Question. What do you know of the existence or extent of that organization in that county or in that part of the State?

Answer. Well, I know nothing directly, except that at the time of the jail delivery in Union, a neighboring county, there were five hundred men raised within two days; and I am confident a great many of them went from our town and from our county. I think that was done by the general organization, whatever it is. But as to these minor outrages I doubt very much whether they are.

Question. Do the facts that have transpired and the manner in which they have occurred satisfy you of the existence of the organization in that portion of South Carolina?

Answer. Yes, sir; I have no doubt of it in the world. I have received anonymous communications signed by the order of "K. K. K.," directing me to leave the county, stating that I could not live there; that I was a carpet-bagger. But personally I have never met with any trouble.

Question. Were any threats used against the magistrate by whom these men were committed for trial?

Answer. He has since been obliged to remove to town for protection—he and his whole family. I don't know whether it was on that account or not. It was near his house that this outrage occurred, just prior to the last election. The election was to be held at his house. His son was one of the managers. He was a magistrate, and bound this man over to appear before the court. But he and his whole family were obliged to come to town, and are there now. They cannot go to their farm to remain. We have a number of persons in town—I suppose there are twenty-five altogether, black and white—who cannot go to their farms and live on them.

Question. To what extent and in what manner are these offenses connected with political parties there?

Answer. Well, I think it is altogether a political matter there, because the county is a democratic county. They have their representatives in the legislature; they have possession of all the county offices—sheriff, clerk, probate judge, county commissioners, &c., and they require almost all those upon whom they commit these outrages to renounce publicly, through the press or in some other way, their republican principles. They state plainly that they intend to keep down the negro and get the control of the State. There is no occasion for anything of the kind there. There may be occasion in some counties for something of this kind; but in ours there is not the slightest occasion for it, because the whole political machinery is in their hands; they have control of it. Yet there are more outrages occurring right there than in any other portion of the State, and they are kept up more continuously.

Question. You spoke of a gentleman who gave notice to the sheriff of this renunciation which was to be made at the court-house. Was he a member of the democratic party, and of prominence in it?

Answer. Yes, sir; he has always been a prominent man there. His name is Simpson Bobo. He is a very prominent lawyer.

Question. What is the name of the sheriff?

Answer. John Dewberry. He is a very good man and a very fair man. A party of fifty men came in there one night and went to the jail in order to release a white man who was condemned to be hung for the murder of a colored man. They demanded entrance, but the sheriff refused to admit them, and they finally went away without accomplishing their object.

Question. When was that?

Answer. That was some time last spring; I cannot remember the date.

Question. Were they in disguise?

Answer. Yes, sir.

CHAPTER 31

A WHITE SOUTHERNER WELCOMES "REDEMPTION"

Henry William Ravenel on "Radical Misrule"

Even those moderate Southern whites who accepted military defeat and the end of slavery came to resent the military occupation of the South during Reconstruction. Henry William Ravenel (1814–1887) was one such individual. A member of the planter elite in South Carolina, he kept a diary from 1859 until his death in 1887. A graduate of South Carolina College, Ravenel hoped to become a medical doctor but was discouraged by his father and became a planter instead. An amateur botanist, he won widespread recognition in this field. After the Civil War he earned a small income writing journal articles and selling plant specimens but struggled to support his large family. Although he owned a plantation called Hampton Hill, Ravenel eventually moved permanently to the town of Aiken. His diary entries during the postwar period reveal changing attitudes about race. A thoughtful and religious man, Ravenel acknowledged Southern defeat and the end of slavery. However, his growing resentment toward radical Republican rule in the South led him to welcome "Redemption" of his state by white Democrats, including the election of former Confederate cavalry general Wade Hampton as governor in 1876. The enthusiasm of white Southerners for Redemption was matched by the weariness of Northerners toward radical Reconstruction, which they associated with political turmoil, violence, and corruption. These dynamics helped set the stage for federal military withdrawal from the South in 1877.

Monday, May 22, 1865

We begin now to realize the ruin to property which the war has entailed upon us. All classes & conditions of men will suffer who had property, except the small farmers who owned no negroes. Confederate securities, I consider a total loss. Bank stock, confederation & private bonds, are all more or less dependent for their availability upon Confed securities, & upon the value of negro property; both of which are lost. The Rail road companies are nearly all ruined by the destruction of their roads & the heavy debt they must incur to rebuild. The only money now in possession of our people is coin in small quantities which had been hoarded through the war, & some bills of the local banks. There will be but little means of increasing this amount for some time to come, as provisions are scarce, & the cotton has been mostly burnt, captured or sold. . . .

Monday, May 29, 1865

. . . Chief Justice [Salmon P.] Chase's opinion announces the freedom of the negroes[;] there is no further room to doubt that it is the settled policy of the country. I have today formally announced to my negroes the fact, & made such arrangements with each as the new relation rendered necessary. Those whose whole time we need, get at present clothes & food, house rent & medical attendance. The others work for themselves giving me a portion of their time on the farm in lieu of house rent. Old Amelia & her two grandchildren, I will spare the mockery of offering freedom to. I must support them as long as I have any thing to give.

Tuesday, May 30, 1865

My negroes all express a desire to remain with me. I am gratified at the proof of their attachment. I believe it to be real & unfeigned. For the present they will remain, but in course of time we must part, as I cannot afford to keep so many, & they cannot afford to hire for what I could give them. As they have always been faithful & attached to us, & have been raised as family servants, & have all of them been in our family for several generations, there is a feeling towards them somewhat like that of a father who is about to send out his children on the world to make their way through life. Those who have brought the present change of relation upon us are ignorant of these ties. They have charged us with cruelty. They call us, man stealers, robbers, tyrants. The indignant denial of these changes & the ill feelings engendered during 30 years of angry controversy, have culminated at length in the four years war which has now ended. It has pleased God that we should fail in our efforts for independence—& with the loss of independence, we return to the Union under the dominion of the abolition sentiment. The experiment is now to be tried. The negro is not only to be emancipated, but is to become a citizen with all the rights & privileges! It produces a financial, political & social revolution at the South, fearful to contemplate in its ultimate effects. Whatever the result may be, let it be known & remembered that neither the negro slave nor his master is responsible. It has been done by those who having political power, are determined to carry into practice the sentimental philanthropy they have so long & angrily advocated. Now that is fixed. I pray God for the great issues at stake, that he may bless the effort & make it successful—make it a blessing & not a curse to the poor negro. . . .

Whitsunday, June 4, 1865

. . . In the last few weeks since the utter loss of our property has been realized, my thoughts have frequently reverted to various periods during the war & at its commencement, when if I could have forseen the present state of things, I might have saved my property & have "laid up treasures" against this time of want. I might have sold my negroes & converted the proceeds into specie or land. I might have invested in some safer securities than Confederate bonds which would now be available—But I did not. I permitted the opportunities to slip by—I even aggravated the evil by avariciously selling articles because they brought me a large profit (as I supposed) & which I might now have owned, had I not disposed of them. And now what is it all worth? May I not learn a lesson of wisdom from this experience? Does it not teach me that I must not lay up my treasures here. . . .

Monday, June 5, 1865

In consideration of the result of the war, & the emancipation policy now determined upon, I cannot avoid the conclusion, based upon all my opinions of a superintending Providence, that God has seen fit to terminate the institution of African slavery in this country. Were it otherwise, He would have so directed affairs that His will should have prevailed. Believing as we did that it had received the divine sanction, we were bound in conscience to strive according to our convictions of right. That we are *mistaken* does not prove that we have sinned in maintaining it or that the base charge of cruelty urged against us by Northern fanatics was true. That we erred & sinned grievously in the sight of God in our management of the negroes, & fell short of our duty towards them, I believe but this may be said of all human institutions. The parent rarely (perhaps never) acts sinlessly in his management of his children, the husband toward the wife, or the master toward his apprentice & yet we are not prepared to condemn & destroy these relations, because of their abuses. . . .

Monday, July 10, 1865

Walked into Aiken & called at the hotel to see Capt. Jackson the Provost Marshall about the necessity of making contracts with my negroes. Capt Jackson had gone to Augusta, but I saw the Lieutenant Comdg. He says it is not "necessary" to make a contract but only advisable, as in case of disagreement they might have the right of claiming wages according to the "labour regulations", since the 1st of May. I will probably draw out a form of contract & have it executed, so as to avoid all risk, though I do not apprehend any trouble with my negroes. . . . B. F. Perry of GreenVille has been appointed Provisional Governor of the State, a very good appointment, & one which will be acceptable to the people. . . .

Tuesday, April 10, 1866

The Couriers Washington correspondent speaks of the radical party in Congress & the North as flushed with power & the victories in the late elections, & indifferent to the Presidents [Andrew Johnson] proclamation of Peace. They have their purposes to accomplish & care for nothing else. There is danger yet of a more terrible revolution than the four years [of] civil war. Anarchy & repudiation may bring down a just retribution upon those who are thus trifling with the rights & most vital interests of their fellow countrymen,—giving themselves loose to the vindictive passions & trying to crush out every emotion of good feelings & of returning harmony. Verily Man is more unforgiving than his Maker.

Tuesday, July 10, 1866

Yesterdays paper gives an account of another riot in Charleston by the African savages dressed in U. S. uniform. Some 30 or 40 shots were fired by them in Meeting St. near the market at the police, because the latter attempted to obey their instructions of keeping the passage way through the market unobstructed. These disgraceful atrocities are committed now so frequently that walking at night out in the streets is unsafe, & yet it continues. Why is not the commanding officer cashiered by [for] neglect of his duty in restraining these riots? Or why are these savages quartered in the city at all? If it is necessary for them to be there, why are they allowed to parade the streets at all hours with pistols & bayonets to the peril of the lives of peaceable citizens?

Sunday, February 24, 1867

The political sky is becoming more & more overcast. Bills have passed both Houses of Congress which repudiate & destroy the present civil government of the lately seceded States, & substitute in their place a military government. Most of the whites are disfranchised & ineligible to office, whilst the negroes are invested with the right of voting. The political power is therefore thrown into the hands of an ignorant mass of human beings who having just emerged from a state of servitude, are ignorant of the very forms of Govt., & totally unfit to exercise this the highest priviledge of freedmen. The president it is expected, will veto the Bill, but the Radicals have their ⅔ majority ready to pass it over the veto. President Johnson is powerless to arrest these evils, though if not impeached, he may mitigate somewhat their rigor in its execution. We are entirely passive from necessity. We can only submit, until the storm of passion has passed away & Reason, Justice, Common Sense & Prudence will return to the minds of the dominant party. . . .

Tuesday, March 5, 1867

The President has sent his veto of the *Military Reconstruction Bill,* & it has been passed over his veto by a ⅔ vote & is now the law of the land. Our civil governments are abrogated or declared Provisional only, & such portions to be valid as Congress may permit. Negroes are enfranchised & now can vote, sit on juries &c. All whites who ever having taken the oath to support the Constitution of the U. S. A., afterwards participated in the "rebellion," are disfranchised. We can only regain our position as states by favoring a Constitution which will give universal suffrage & then accept the "[Fourteenth] Constitutional Amendment." If we reject the mode they offer, we remain under military rule.

Saturday, March 23, 1867

. . . There have been large meetings of the Freedmen held lately in Charleston & Columbia. At the Columbia meeting the disposition evinced was quite friendly to the whites—& all antagonism & hostility was deprecated. They invited several of the leading gentlemen of

Columbia to address them. Beverly Nash & a Revd Picket were the chief speakers. In Charleston, they have been instigated by the Radical & "Loyal Unionists" so called to adopt a platform which is defiant & hostile to the whites of the States. Much of the future destiny of our State will depend upon issues made, & the position of the Colored vote. My own opinion is very decided on the subject. Justice, Right, Humanity, as well as good policy require us "to meet them half way"—to accord to them fully the priviledges with which by law they are now invested—to be kind & considerate, & thus to win their confidence & prove to them what we have always been claiming, that we are their best friends. We can thus direct this power in their hands to good purposes, & frustrate the inimical projects of those who have given them the power of voting that they may control & regulate the policy & policies of the South. I hope our people will act wisely & justly. . . .

Tuesday, August 25, 1868

. . . In yesterdays Courier is an appeal to the people of Charleston signed by the most respectable & older citizens on the fearful condition of affairs. Since the Military authority has been withdrawn, & before the Courts were organized under the new Government, there is no administration of law, no restraints upon the disorderly & lawless, & no means of checking or preventing riotous acts or disturbance of the peace. Of late the negroes have become very over bearing & violent in their behaviour, breaking up meetings of the Colored Democrats & threatening towards the white population. So riotous have they become that at the late Democratic meeting in Charleston called to ratify the Presidential nominations the whites found it prudent to go armed; & a threatened violent interruption of the meeting was only averted by the appeal & interference of the more prudent colored Radicals. The few white Radicals in the city seem desirous of bringing on a collision in the hopes of making political capital. This address to the people counsels prudence & forbearance as long as it is possible, but at the same time, announces to the citizens that the danger is imminent & they must be prepared to protect themselves & their property, as there is no civil or military power at hand to aid them. It was decided at a meeting to send on Hon J B Campbell to have an interview with the President & inform him of the state of affairs. I see by the papers, that one Regiment of troops have been ordered to

Charleston, but as yet they have not arrived. The negroes boast that they are fully organized on the Sea board, & trust "every plantation has its captain." This is the state to which we have been reduced by Radical misrule. . . .

Tuesday, August 2, 1870

The "Union Reform Party" lately organized in this State, to unite all parties, colours & condition, in opposition to the horde of thieves & plunderers now in possession of the government, is making great progress in the upper country. Judge [R. B.] Carpenter [a Northerner and Republican lawyer who moved to the state during Reconstruction] the nominee for Govn. & Gen. [M. C.] Butler for Lieut Gov. are canvassing the State with much success apparently. Large & enthusiastic meetings have been held in Edgefield, Charleston, Pendleton, Pickens, Oconee, Anderson & GreenVille, at which there were crowds of whites & coloured to hear the speakers. The negroes are so governed & controled [sic] by the Union League & so ignorant of the first principles of civil government, that they are shy of attending the meetings, & fear they may be again reduced to slavery, as they are told by the Radicals who control them. If this movement is successful . . . we may hope for a return of peace & prosperous times in our State.

Tuesday, November 25, 1870

Today the ballots which were cast on Wednesday last, are to be counted. It will not probably be known who are elected for several days yet. It is generally believed that with a fair ballot & no intimidation at the polls, the Reform ticket would easily have been elected in the State. As it is, the Radical party have all the Commissioners & managers of elections (most of whom are candidates for office), & they have the keeping of the boxes, the counting of votes & declaring the election. Even to honest men, this temptation to fraud is too great, but with such a party, as it has proved itself in the past two years in this state, there is but little hope of the election of Carpenter & Butler. . . .

Sunday, October 22, 1871

Many of the upper Districts of our State are now under Martial law, by Proclamation of the President [Ulysses S. Grant]. The alleged cause is outlawism & resistance to the law by armed & disguised citizens (Ku Klux). The real reason, as every man of common sense knows, is political necessity—an effort to intensify & concentrate the party, & embitter the minds of the ignorant Northern masses against our State, & ultimately against the Democratic party with which the white voters here sympathize. That there is no real necessity is obvious from the fact that Gov. [Robert K.] Scott & most of the prominent Republicans of the State are opposed to it as unnecessary & uncalled for. The civil courts are quite competent to deal with all cases of crime (they say) —& it is certain that these outrages are unknown to the people of those counties where martial law is declared. But these counties have Democratic majorities, & they must be punished. There is much alarm & many are leaving the country to escape arrest on suspicion, & incarceration.

Tuesday, October 6, 1874

I have made no allusions to politics or the political condition of our State of late, because it was a sickening subject, & one which I would gladly avoid for peace of mind. There has been so much of fraud & corruption in high places, such heavy taxation & such fraudulent squandering of the public money, that the whole country North & South has been thoroughly disgusted with South Carolina politics. The Republicans at the North have demanded Reform in the party here, and at length we see some hopeful signs of its accomplishment. . . . A large minority of the [Republican] Convention who seem in earnest for reform, have since organized an *Independent Republican Party.* At their convention held last week in Charleston, they nominated Judge [John T.] Green a [southern-born] Republican for Governor, & Major [Martin] Delaney [an African American Democrat] for Lieut. Gov. & ask the aid of the Conservatives to assist them in putting these men in office. The Conservative Convention will be held this week in Columbia, & it is probable no other nomination will be made, but a recommendation that the Conservatives unite with the Independent Republicans in electing honest Republicans to office. I am in favour of this movement, & believe it will result in good—dividing the Republican party, & breaking down the ascendancy of the corrupt Rings that have had control of their party in this State. . . .

Tuesday, November 3, 1874

This is Election day throughout the State for Gov.—Lieut Gov.—& County officers. I have voted the Green & Delany ticket for Gov. & Lieut Gov.—& the County Conservative ticket for County officers. . . .

Friday, November 27, 1874

The Legislature assembled on Tuesday. [Robert] Elliott elected Speaker of the House, & Lieut Gov. [Richard] Gleaves is Presidt. of the Senate. The Legislature of South Carolina is presided over in both branches by negroes! . . .

Friday, November 3, 1876

I open a new journal of record today—in the midst of great political excitement, attendant on the effort of our people to throw off the incubus of corrupt negro government which has been weighing upon our unfortunate State for the past eight years. In a few days we will know if our Democratic ticket with Wade Hampton for Governor will be elected, or if for two years more we are to be trodden under by the odious "carpet bag" government of [Governor Daniel H.] Chamberlain & his followers. . . .

CHAPTER 32

A BLACK POLITICIAN PROTESTS
ELECTION FRAUD

Senator Blanche Kelso Bruce:
"The Late Election in Mississippi"

*B*lanche Kelso Bruce (1841–1898) was the first black man to serve a full *term in the Senate, 1875–1881. Born a slave in Virginia, he learned to read and write with the help of his owner's son. When the Civil War began, Bruce, then living in Missouri, escaped from bondage and ultimately began a school for freedmen in Hannibal. After the war ended, he moved to Mississippi, where he purchased land, rose rapidly in local politics, and caught the attention of the state's white Republicans. In 1874 they elected him to the Senate. During his six years there, he called for desegregation of the army and land grants for African American settlers in the West. He led an investigation of fraud in the Freedman's Savings and Trust Company, issuing a report assigning blame, and helping 61,000 depositors receive some restitution for their losses. In the speech presented here, Bruce spoke with great conviction about efforts to prevent blacks from voting during Mississippi's 1875 elections. After Redemption, when Bruce lost his Senate seat, he held a series of patronage appointments until his death in 1898.*

M r. BRUCE   Mr. President, I had hoped that no occasion would arise to make it necessary for me again to claim the attention of the Senate until at least I had acquired a larger acquaintance with its methods of business and a fuller experience in public affairs; but silence at this time would be infidelity to my senatorial trust and unjust to both the people and the State I have the honor in part to represent.

The conduct of the late election in Mississippi affected not merely the fortunes of partisans—as the same were neccessarily involved in the defeat or success of the respective parties to the contest—but put in question and jeopardy the rights of the citizen; and the investigation contemplated in the pending resolution has for its object not the determination of the question whether the offices shall be held and the public affairs of that State be administered by democrats or republicans, but the higher and more important end, the protection in all their purity and significance of the political rights of the people and the free institutions of the country. I believe the action sought is within the legitimate province of the Senate; but I shall waive a discussion of that phase of the question, and address myself to the consideration of the importance of the proposed investigation.

The demand of the substitute of the Senator from Michigan proceeds upon the allegation that fraud and intimidation were practiced by the opposition in the late State election, so as not only to deprive many citizens of their political rights, but so far as practically to have defeated a fair expression of the will of a majority of the legal voters of the State of Mississippi, resulting in placing in power many men who do not represent the popular will.

The truth of the allegations relative to fraud and violence is strongly suggested by the very success claimed by the democracy. In 1873 the republicans carried the State by 20,000 majority; in November last the opposition claimed to have carried it by 30,000; thus a democratic gain of more than 50,000. Now, by what miraculous or extraordinary interposition was this brought about? I can conceive that a large State like New York, where free speech and free press operate upon intelligent masses—a State full of railroads, telegraphs, and newspapers—on the occasion of a great national contest, might furnish an illustration of such a thorough and general change in the political views of the people; but such a change of front is unnatural and highly improbable in a State like my own, with few railroads, and a widely scattered and sparse population. Under the most active and friendly canvass the voting masses could not have been so rapidly and thoroughly reached as to have rendered this result probable.

There was nothing in the character of the issues nor in the method of the canvass that would produce such an overwhelming revolution in the sentiments of the colored voters of the State as is implied in this pretended democratic success. The republicans—nineteen-twentieths of whom are colored—were not brought, through the press or public discussions, in contact with democratic influences to such an extent as would operate a change in their political convictions, and there was nothing in democratic sentiments nor in the proscriptive and violent temper of their leaders to justify such a change of political relations.

The evil practices so naturally suggested by this view of the question as probable will be found in many instances by the proposed investigation to have been actual. Not desiring to anticipate the work of the committee nor to weary Senators with details, I instance the single county of Yazoo as illustrative of the effects of the outrages of which we complain. This county gave in 1873 a republican majority of nearly two thousand. It was cursed with riot and bloodshed prior to the late election, and gave but seven votes for the republican ticket, and some of these, I am credibly informed, were cast in derision by the democrats, who declared that republicans must have some votes in the county.

To illustrate the spirit that prevailed in that section, I read from the Yazoo Democrat, an influential paper published at its county seat:

> Let unanimity of sentiment pervade the minds of men. Let invincible determination be depicted on every countenance. Send forth from our deliberative assembly of the eighteenth the soul stirring anouncement that Mississippians shall rule Mississippi though the heavens fall. Then will woe, irretrievable woe, betide the radical tatterdemalions. Hit them hip and thigh, everywhere and at all times.

> Carry the election peaceably if we can, forcibly if we must.

> Again:

> There is no radical ticket in the field, and it is more than likely there will be none; for the leaders are not in this city, and dare not press their claims in this county.

Speaking of the troubles in Madison County, the Yazoo City Democrat for the 26th of October says:

> Try the rope on such characters. It acts finely on such characters here.

The evidence in hand and accessible will show beyond peradventure that in many parts of the State corrupt and violent influences were brought to bear upon the registrars of voters, thus materially affecting the character of voting or poll lists; upon the inspectors of election, prejudicially and unfairly thereby changing the number of votes cast; and, finally, threats and violence were practiced directly upon the masses of voters in such measure and strength as to produce grave apprehensions for their personal safety, and as to deter them from the exercise of their political franchises.

Lawless outbreaks have not been confined to any particular section of the country, but have prevailed in nearly every State at some period in its history. But the violence complained of and exhibited in Mississippi and other Southern States, pending a political canvass, is exceptional and peculiar. It is not the blow that the beggared miner strikes that he may give bread to his children, nor the stroke of the bondsman that he may win liberty for himself, nor the mad turbulence of the ignorant masses when their passions have been stirred by the appeals of the demagogue; but it is an attack by an aggressive, intelligent, white political organization upon inoffensive, law-abiding fellow-citizens; a violent method for political supremacy, that seeks not the protection of the rights of the aggressors, but the destruction of the rights of the party assailed. Violence so unprovoked, inspired by such motives, and looking to such ends, is a spectacle not only discreditable to the country, but dangerous to the integrity of our free institutions.

I beg Senators to believe that I refer to this painful and reproachful condition of affairs in my own State not in resentment, but with sentiments of profound regret and humiliation.

If honorable Senators ask why such flagrant wrongs were allowed to go unpunished by a republican State government, and unresented by a race claiming 20,000 majority of the voters, the answer is at hand. The civil officers of the State were unequal to meet and suppress the muderous violence that frequently broke out in different parts of the State, and the State executive found himself thrown for support upon a militia partially organized and poorly armed. When he attempted to perfect and call out this force and to use the very small appropriation that had been made for their equipment, he was met by the courts with an injunction against the use of the money, and by the proscriptive element of the opposition with such fierce outcry and show of counter-force, that he became convinced a civil strife, a war of races, would be precipitated unless he staid his hand.

As a last resort, the protection provided in the national Constitution for a State threatened with domestic violence was sought; but the national Executive—from perhaps a scrupulous desire to avoid the appearance of interference by the Federal authority with the internal affairs of that State—declined to accede to the request made for Federal troops.

It will not accord with the laws of nature or history to brand the colored people as a race of cowards. On more than one historic field, beginning in 1776 and coming down to this centennial year of the Republic, they have attested in blood their courage as well as love of liberty. I ask Senators to believe that no consideration of fear or personal danger has kept us quiet and forbearing under the provocations and wrongs that have so sorely tried our souls. But feeling kindly toward our white fellow-citizens, appreciating the good purposes and offices of the better classes, and, above all, abhorring a war of races, we determined to wait until such time as an appeal to the good sense and justice of the American people could be made.

A notable feature of the outrages alleged is that they have referred almost exclusively to the colored citizens of the State. Why is the colored voter to be proscribed? Why direct the attack upon him? While the methods of violence, resorted to for political purposes in the South, are foreign to the genius of our institutions as applied to citizens generally—and so much is conceded by even the opposition— yet they seem to think we are an exceptional class and citizens, rather by sufferance than right; and when pressed to account for their bitterness and proscription toward us they, with more or less boldness, allege incompetent and bad government as their justification before the public opinion of the country. Now, I declare that neither political incapacity nor venality are qualities of the masses of colored citizens. The emancipation of the colored race during the late civil strife was an expression alike of the magnanimity and needs of the nation; and the subsequent and early subtraction of millions of industrial values from the resources of the insurrectionary States and the presence of many thousand additional brave hearts and strong hands around the flag of the country vindicated the justice and wisdom of the measure.

The close of the war found four millions of freedmen, without homes or property, charged with the duty of self-support and with the oversight of their personal freedom, yet without civil and political rights! The problem presented by this condition of things was one of the gravest that has ever been submitted to the American people. Shall these liberated millions of a separate race, while retaining personal liberty, be deprived of political rights? The practical sense of the American people definitely settled this delicate and difficult question, and the demand for a more pronounced loyal element in the work of reconstruction in the lately rebellious States furnished an opportunity for the recognition of the political rights of the race, both in the interest of justice and good government.

The history of my race since enfranchisement, considered in connection with the difficulties that have environed us, will exhibit hopeful progress and attest that we have been neither ungrateful for the civil and political privileges received nor wanting in appreciation of the correspondingly weighty obligations imposed upon us.

• • •

. . . [W]e began our political career under the disadvantages of the inexperience in public affairs that generations of enforced bondage had entailed upon our race. We suffered also from the vicious leadership of some of the men whom our necessities forced us temporarily to accept. Consider further that the States of the South, where we were supposed to control by our majorities, were in an impoverished and semi-revolutionary condition—society demoralized, the industries of the country prostrated, the people sore, morbid, and sometimes turbulent, and no healthy controlling public opinion either existent or possible—consider all these conditions, and it will be seen that we began our political novitiate and formed the organic and statutory laws under great embarrassments.

Despite the difficulties and drawbacks suggested, the constitutions formed under colored majorities, whatever their defects may be, were improvements on the instruments they were designed to supersede; and the statutes framed, though necessarily defective because of the crude and varying social and industrial conditions upon which they were based, were more in harmony with the spirit of the age and the genius of our free institutions than the obsolete laws that they supplanted. Nor is there just or any sufficient grounds upon which to charge an oppressive administration of the laws.

• • •

Mr. President, do not misunderstand me; I do not hold that all the white people in the State of Mississippi aided and abetted the white-league organizations. There is in Mississippi a large and respectable element among the opposition who are not only honest in their recognition of the political rights of the colored citizen and deprecate the fraud and violence through which those rights have been assailed, but who would be glad to see the color line in politics abandoned and good-will obtain and govern among all classes of her people. But the fact is to be regretted that this better class of citizens in many parts of the State is dominated by a turbulent and violent element of the opposition, known as the White League—a ferocious minority—and has thus far proved powerless to prevent the recurrence of the outrages it deprecates and deplores.

The uses of this investigation are various. It will be important in suggesting such action as may be found necessary not only to correct and repair the wrongs perpetrated, but to prevent their recurrence. But I will venture to assert that the investigation will be most beneficial in this, that it will largely contribute to the formation of a public sentiment that, while it restrains the vicious in their attacks upon the rights of the loyal, law-abiding voters of the South, will so energize the laws as to secure condign punishment to wrong-doers, and give a security to all classes, which will effectively and abundantly produce the mutual good-will and confidence that constitute the foundations of the public prosperity.

We want peace and good order at the South; but it can only come by the fullest recognition of the rights of all classes. The opposition must concede the necessity of change, not only in the temper but in the philosophy of their party organization and management. The sober American judgment must obtain in the South as elsewhere in the Republic, that the only distinctions upon which parties can be safely organized and in harmony with our institutions are differences of opinions relative to principles and policy of government, and that differences of religion, nationality, or race can neither with safety nor propriety be permitted for a moment to enter into the party contests of the day. The unanimity with which the colored voters act with a party is not referable to any race prejudice on their part. On the contrary, they invite the political co-operation of their white brethren, and vote as a unit because proscribed as such. They deprecate the establishment of the color line by the opposition, not only because the act is unwise and wrong in principle, but because it isolates them from the white men of the South, and forces them, in sheer self-protection and against their inclination, to act seemingly upon the basis of a race prejudice that they neither respect nor entertain. As a class they are free from prejudices, and have no uncharitable suspicions against their white fellow-citizens, whether native born or settlers from the Northern States. . . .

CHAPTER 33

THE PRESIDENTIAL ELECTION OF 1876 AND THE END OF RECONSTRUCTION

Samuel J. Tilden on His Loss to Rutherford B. Hayes

The presidential election of 1876 occurred in the nation's centennial year, but revealed a politically divided country. In that bitterly fought and closely watched election, Samuel J. Tilden (1814–1886), a former governor of New York, lost to Ohio governor Rutherford B. Hayes, after a Republican-dominated special commission appointed by Congress determined that contested votes in three Southern states belonged to Hayes. Following his inauguration, Hayes, as promised, withdrew federal troops from the South, thereby ending Reconstruction. In declining to be considered for the Democratic nomination in 1880, Tilden ruminated about his loss four years earlier. His strong showing in the election marked the revival of the Democratic party, and his dignity in accepting his defeat at the hands of a Congressional commission was applauded by many. Nonetheless, his bitterness about the contest is apparent in this statement.

. . . In the canvass that ensued, the Democratic party represented reform in the administration of the Federal Government and a restoration of our complex political system to the pure ideals of its founders. Upon these issues the people of the United States, by a majority of more than a quarter of a million, chose a majority of the electors to cast their votes for the Democratic candidates for President and Vice-President. It is my right and privilege here to say that I was nominated and elected to the Presidency absolutely free from any engagement in respect to the exercise of its powers or the disposal of its patronage. Through the whole period of my relation to the Presidency I did everything in my power to elevate and nothing to lower moral standards in the competition of parties.

By what nefarious means the basis of a false count was laid in several of the States, I need not recite. These are now matters of history, about which whatever diversity of opinion may have existed in either of the great parties of the country at the time of their consummation has since practically disappeared.

I refused to ransom from the returning boards of Southern States the documentary evidence by the suppression of which, and by the substitution of fraudulent and forged papers, a pretext was made for the perpetration of a false count.

The constitutional duty of the two Houses of Congress to count the electoral votes as cast, and give effect to the will of the people as expressed by their suffrages, was never fulfilled. An Electoral Commission, for the existence of which I have no responsibility, was formed, and to it the two Houses of Congress abdicated their duty to make the count, by a law enacting that the count of the Commission should stand as lawful unless overruled by the concurrent action of the two Houses. Its false count was not overruled, owing to the complicity of a Republican Senate with the Republican majority of the Commission.

Controlled by its Republican majority of eight to seven, the Electoral Commission counted out the men elected by the people, and counted in the men not elected by the people. That subversion of the election created a new issue for the decision of the people of the United States, transcending in importance all questions of administration; it involved the vital principle of self-government through elections by the people.

The immense growth of the means of corrupt influence over the ballot-box, which is at the disposal of the party having possession of the executive administration, had already become a present evil and a great danger, tending to make elections irresponsive to public opinion, hampering the power of the people to change their rulers, and enabling the men holding the machinery of government to continue and perpetuate their power. It was my opinion in 1876 that the opposition attempting to change the administration needed to include at least two thirds of the voters at the opening of the canvas in order to retain a majority at the election.

If after such obstacles had been overcome, and a majority of the people had voted to change the administration of their government, the men in office could still procure a false count founded upon frauds, perjuries, and forgeries furnishing a pretext of documentary evidence on which to base that false count,—and if such a transaction were not only successful, but, after allotment of its benefits were made to its contrivers, abetters, and apologists by the chief beneficiary of the transaction, it were also condoned by the people,—a practical destruction of elections by the people would have been accomplished.

The failure to instal the candidates chosen by the people—a contingency consequent upon no act or omission of mine, and beyond my control—has left me for the last three years and until now, when the Democratic party by its delegates in National Convention assembled shall choose a new leader, the involuntary but necessary representative of this momentous issue.

As such, denied the immunities of private life, without the powers conferred by public station, subject to unceasing falsehoods and calumnies from the partisans of an Administration laboring in vain to justify its existence, I have nevertheless steadfastly endeavored to preserve to the Democratic party of the United States the supreme issue before the people for their decision next November, whether this shall be a government by the sovereign people through elections, or a government by discarded servants holding over by force and fraud; and I have withheld no sacrifice and neglected no opportunity to uphold, organize, and consolidate against the enemies of representative institutions the great party which alone, under God, can effectually resist their overthrow.

Having now borne faithfully my full share of labor and care in the public service, and wearing the marks of its burdens, I desire nothing so much as an honorable discharge. I wish to lay down the honors and toils of even *quasi* party leadership, and to seek the repose of private life. . . .